This series of three guides to Norfolk churches is dedicated to those who have assisted me in compiling and checking my text:
Elizabeth Arkieson, Ann Johnson & Bryan Samain.

part three of the parishfinder series

Published by ASPYE.
aspye@talktalk.net

Front cover: Buckenham Ferry, St Nicholas, Norfolk
Back cover: The Royal Arms of Elizabeth I at Tivetshall St Margaret, Norfolk.

A photographic and historical guide to the

Parish Churches

of

East Norfolk

as defined by the 1914 Deaneries of :

Blofield, Brooke, Flegg, Lothingland (Norfolk), City of
Norwich and surrounding hamlets & Waxham.
Parts of Depwade, Ingworth, Redenhall, Repps & Taverham.

Including a supplement for identifying
Royal Arms and Achievements
Glossary of Terms Architectural & Ecclesiastical

Compiled and with all colour
photographs by
Adrian S. Pye

Preface

Since the completion of my first book, Parish Churches of East Suffolk, the response I received, even before completing the West Suffolk companion, was extremely encouraging. These Norfolk guides meanwhile have been eagerly awaited.

It was decided to cover Norfolk in three volumes due to the quantity of churches in the county. The parishes in the east of the county are, however, considerably smaller than those in the west. The division for each guide is along a very rough north to south line in an effort to achieve an equal number of churches in each volume. In the case of West Norfolk, the division is almost central to the county, running from Stiffkey to Thetford. The corresponding division for the East Norfolk guide is from Runton near Cromer in the north to Thorpe Abbots near Diss in the south.

Readers will notice that although Lothingland is in the Norfolk Diocese, not all of that particular deanery have been included. I have adhered to the County boundaries as they are at the time of going to press. The Suffolk portion of the Lothingland Deanery can be found in the East Suffolk edition.

In compiling the information contained in the guides, I have found that postcodes in certain instances were, some distance away from the church, especially in scattered communities. Therefore, although the postcode given is that of the nearest inhabited dwelling it may be some distance away, although the church will usually be in sight. I have endeavoured to give the best directions possible in the limited space available.

I would like to make it quite clear that the impressions I give in the text on visiting a church, and the people I meet in so doing, are those experienced at the time, and do not necessarily reflect those of other people associated with the church. The sentiments expressed regarding the contents and conditions I find when entering a church are mine and mine alone, and I accept that sometimes they may differ from the opinions of others.

I have endeavoured to give a truthful impression of what is to be discovered when visiting a church but interests differ and opinions vary on all matters aesthetic and ecclesiastical.

Except where there is no ancient church in the parish, 20th century churches have not been included in the guides as this is a historical guide and the churches concerned have no great historical interest.
Only Anglican churches are featured in the guides. Cathedrals, Roman Catholic, Baptist, Methodist, and Reformist churches or chapels etc. do not come under the designation or description of a Parish church and are therefore not included.
I hope that as a result of my campaigning activities to campaign for churches to be kept open for all, at least during daylight hours, anyone visiting a church will find the door open. Whist I have every sympathy with the dilemma of some Parochial Church Councils in protecting a church and its contents, I feel a better effort could be made, and an answer found, if they were willing to consider the visitors instead of themselves. It is no good leaving a sign on the door proclaiming 'Welcome to St Mary's church' if the door is locked. "There is no salvation outside a church". A locked door is not a very Christian welcome to the traveller. In my travels, I have found not only some churches locked, but also the porch containing information about the keyholders barred. Yet others have a wonderful open door policy, and at some there is a kettle, fresh water, tea, coffee, milk and even biscuits waiting for the visitors to avail themselves of refreshment.
The reader will notice some churches have been awarded four or five stars (i.e.*). These are churches which in my opinion have something extra special to offer, and should interest any visitor.
Out of necessity, I have adhered rigidly to one church, one page. throughout the guides, whether the church is large or small. It is not a reflection on the church or the wealth of the interior, simply a matter of convenient format and ease of reading.
Almost every parish is listed alphabetically under the name on the Ordnance Survey maps; South under S; North under N; Great under G and Little under L, etc.
I hope the reader will get as much enjoyment from reading these guides and visiting the churches as I did in compiling them.

Adrian S. Pye. Lowestoft 2010

The author gratefully acknowledges the information gleaned from the following sources, not all of which has been verified as being completely up to date.

White's Directory for Norfolk 1864.	William White
Norfolk Churches	H. Munro Cautley
The King's England, Norfolk	Arthur Mee
Boutell's Manual of Heraldry	V. Wheeler-Holohan

College of Arms, London
Scores of guide booklets supplied in the individual churches
Ordnance Survey for the grid references.
Norwich Diocese for the post codes and modern deaneries.

Printed by Micropress Printers Halesworth

ISBN 978-0-9558797-2-2

ACLE St Edmund

No of Bells: 5
19th c. Deanery: Blofield
Hundred: Walsham
Union house: Acle
21st c. Deanery: Blofield
Benefice: Acle

11 miles east of Norwich. Turn north off the A47 and proceed to the centre of Acle on the old Norwich Road.
O.S. grid ref: TG 401103
Post Code: NR13 3JS

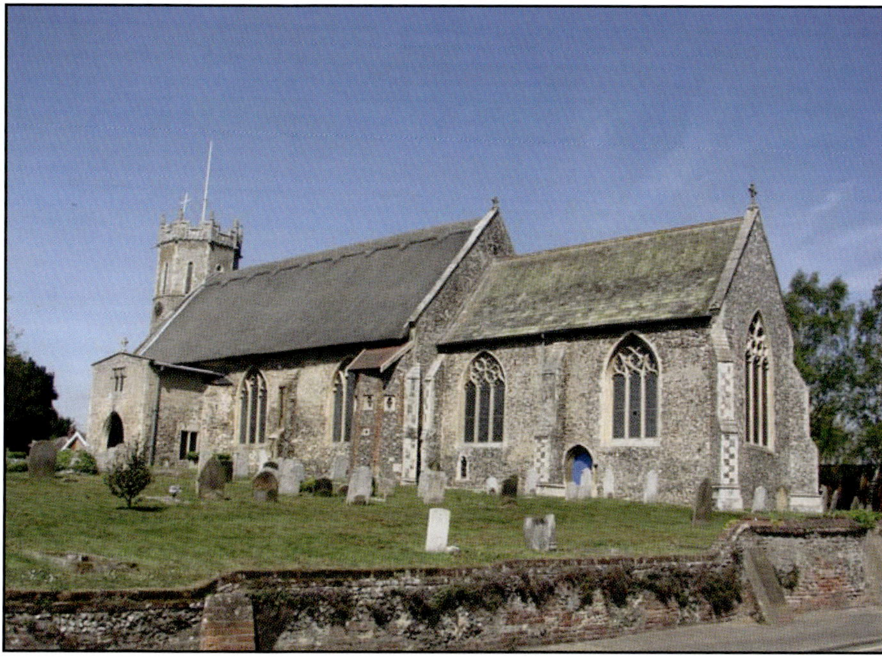

Standing proudly in the centre of the town, this thatched church was probably originally constructed by the Normans. The lower section of the round tower is almost certainly Norman, the upper octagonal stage is much later. Erect figures stand looking outwards on each point of the octagon. Inside the church the early 15th c. font is of typical East Anglian type and still has paint in the eight panels. The screen is still quite intact, although heavily restored, displaying the Apostles in the lower panels. The piscina is a nice example with a dropped-sill sedilia adjacent to it. On the north wall behind glass is a very early example of graffiti, discovered last century during restoration. It consists of six lines of verse about the pestilence that had descended upon the town, probably written in the 15th c. when the plague was still upon them.

ALBURGH All Saints

No of Bells: 8

19th c. Deanery: Redenhall

Hundred: Earsham

Union house: Pulham St Mary

21st c. Deanery: Pulham St Mary

Benefice: Ditchingham

3 m NE of Harleston in Denton Road, Alburgh, slightly set back off the road at the end of a gravel driveway and car park.

O.S. grid ref: TM 270873

Post Code: IP20 0DA

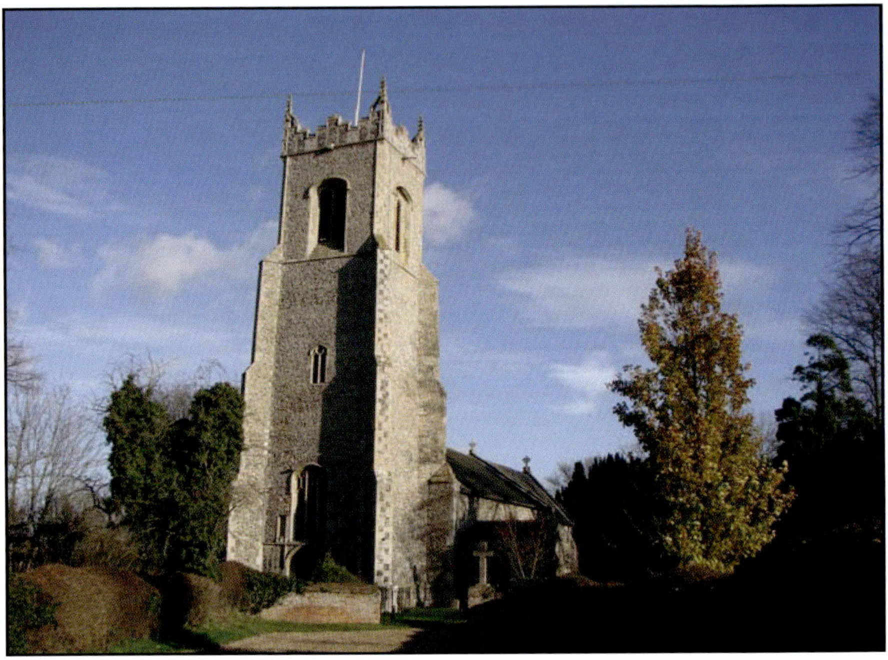

This tower is tall, with flying buttresses on the parapet giving it a light and elegant crown. Inside is a 19th c. sketch when the church had a different parapet. In the base of the tower is a doorway to the belfry, the door itself is studded with hundreds of hand-made nails. The octagonal font is a strange bulbous relatively modern design. The timber roof of the nave is arch-braced, whereas the chancel has a barrel roof. The single piscina has a trefoil arch and is adjacent to the dropped-sill sedilia. Behind the altar is a relatively modern retable depicting saints. What remains of the rood screen are the lower 12 panels which have been somewhat over-restored and repainted and look totally out of place. There are two WWI wall plaques to two brothers, 2nd Lieutenant (1916) and Captain Springfield (1914).

ALDEBY St Mary
No of Bells: 4
19th c. Deanery: Brooke
Hundred: Clavering
Union house: Heckingham
21st c. Deanery: Loddon
Benefice: Raveningham

3 miles NE of Beccles. Turn south as you enter the village and follow the road to the right. Ample parking beside the road.
O.S. grid ref: TM 450933
Post Code: NR34 0BH

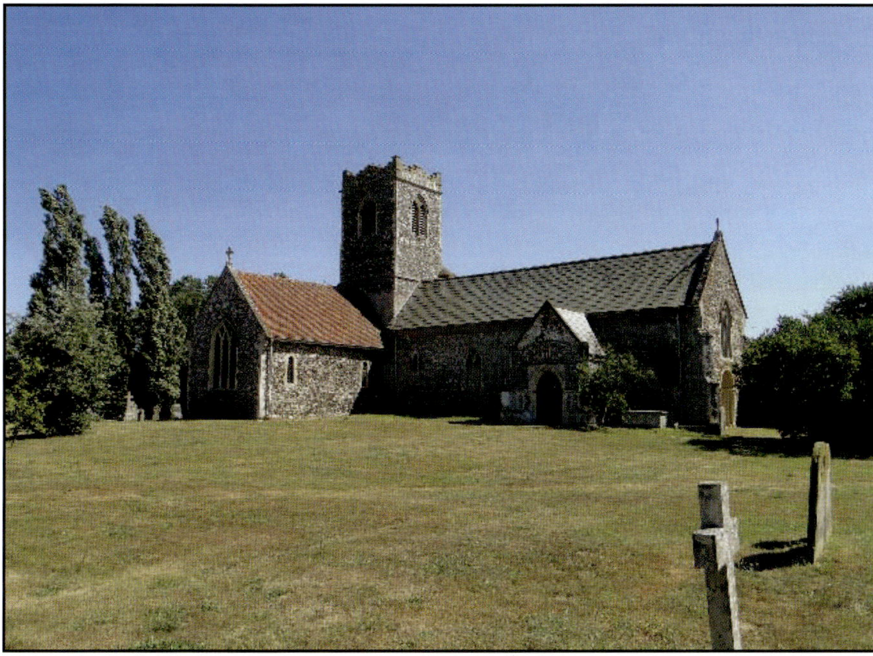

As you approach the church you cannot help noticing the great Norman doorway with its three engaged columns and moulded arch. On the wall below the central tower a sign proclaims 'THIS STEPLE WAS BILT 1633' although it is constructed on a Norman foundation. The transept is 13th c. and contains a few 17th c. burials. Some recent modernisation has taken place but has been carried out with great care not to destroy any of the fabric. In the chancel is the late 13th c. piscina and a double sedile on two levels. Shields decorate the 14th c. octagonal font with eight engaged columns around the shaft. Behind it, against the wall, is the largest bier I have seen with wheels three feet in diameter. 19th c. monuments in the chancel are all to members of the Carpenter family. An interesting history but no church guide.

ANTINGHAM St Margaret

No of Bells: -
19th c. Deanery: Repps
Hundred: North Erpingham
Union house: West Beckham
21st c. Deanery: -
Benefice: -

2 miles NW of North Walsham. Turn left 1 mile south of the Hotel complex, into Southrepps Road then into Church Lane.
O.S. grid ref: TG 253329
Post Code: NR28 0NL

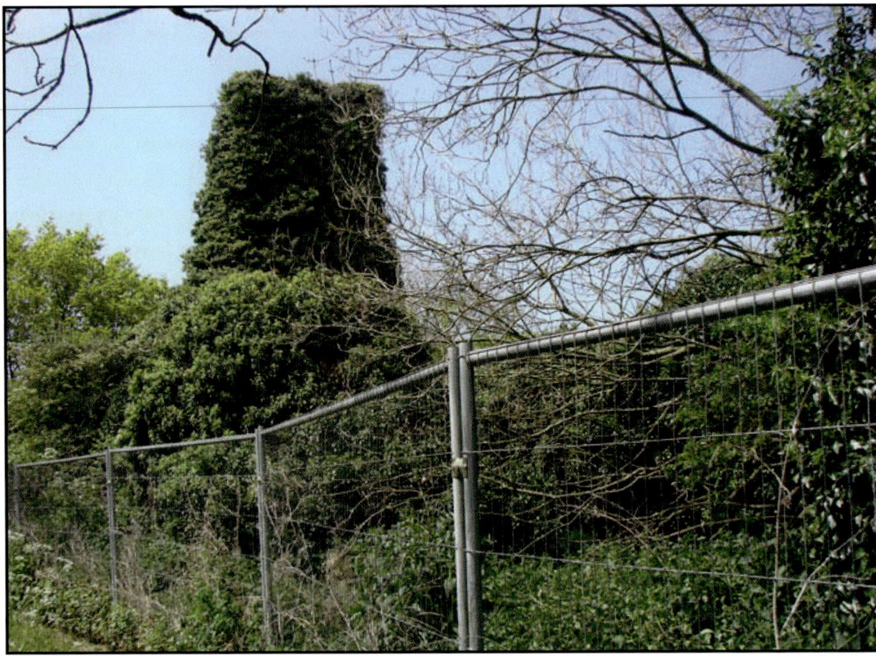

St Margaret's church has been a ruin since the early 18th c. The church existed because there were two manors in Antingham, each having its own church. After the Reformation everything changed and the church fell into disuse in favour of St Mary's (see opposite). At the start of the 19th c. St Mary's was in need of repair, and stone from St Margaret's was used for the task. The tower still stands although it has a large crack; hence the fencing. Parts of the walls still stand and are shrouded in elder and ivy, which go some way to protect them from the worst of the weather. However, overgrowth like this also demolishes walls and towers and if it were removed I feel there wouldn't be much left standing. Meanwhile it is a home for all kinds of wildlife and is therefore serving a useful purpose.

ANTINGHAM St Mary the Virgin
No of Bells: 1
19th c. Deanery: Repps
Hundred: North Erpingham
Union house: West Beckham
21st c. Deanery: Repps
Benefice: Trunch Team Ministry

2 miles NW of North Walsham, in Church Lane, Antingham. Both churches share the same churchyard. See previous page.
O.S. grid ref: TG 253329
Post Code: NR28 0NL

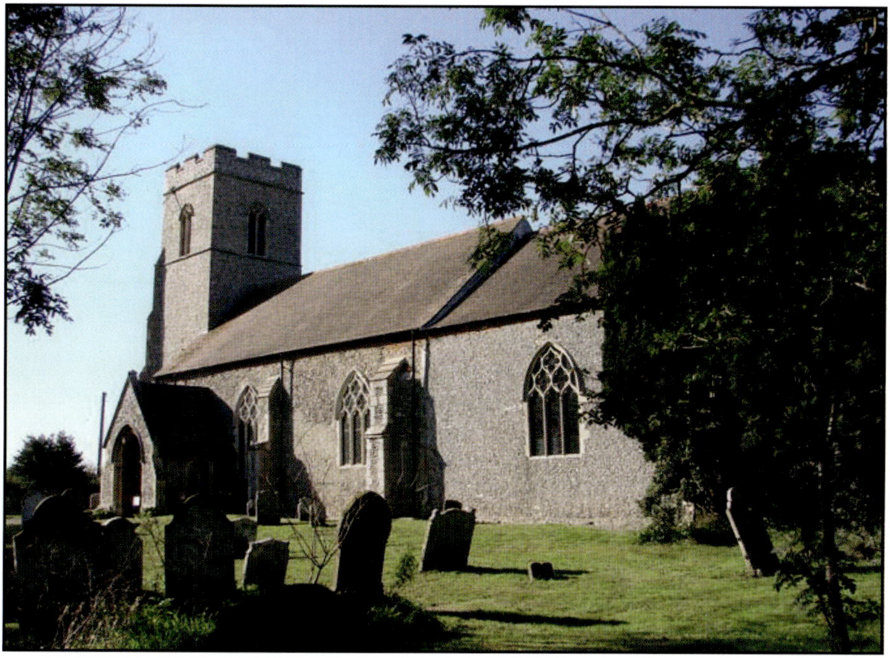

The church was built around the early 14th c. and has been modified by Victorian restorers. The font is a typical very plain 13th c. example standing on eight columns around a central shaft on a tall plinth. The chancel piscina bowl has been deliberately removed flush to the wall. I believe there was a second angle piscina in the side of the sedilia at one time, and yet another close to the rood loft stairs. Above this is a lovely window of the two St. Marys and St. Martha. There is a simple arch-braced roof over the nave and a complete arch-brace over the chancel roof. The lower part of the rood stairs remain open. A partly iron-bound 17th c. parish chest is on view. Most of the furnishings are Victorian but are in keeping with the age of the building. Some nice poppyheads are carved on the bench-ends of the choir stalls.

ARMINGHALL St Mary the Virgin

No of Bells: 1
19th c. Deanery: Brooke
Hundred: Henstead
Union house: Swainsthorpe
21st c. Deanery: Loddon
Benefice: Venta

3 miles SSE of Norwich, in Main Road, Arminghall. East side of the church is best for parking, in Church close.

O.S. grid ref: TG 252043
Post Code: NR14 8SE

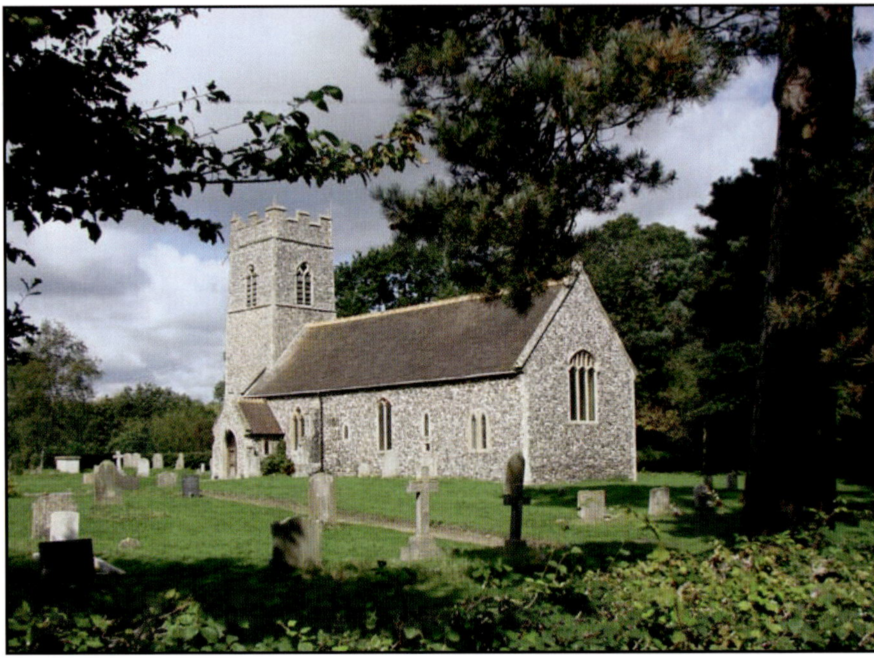

This pleasant church was obviously well built; it has only two buttresses, one each side of the nave. An old drawing inside the church shows it was once thatched and without a porch but very little has changed. The church was built in the 13th c. as can be seen from the chancel windows and Early English slit windows in the nave. In comparison, the font is quite modern. The Victorian chancel arch is of wood and has tracery in the spandrels. Most of the fittings are Victorian. Some of the old bench ends have been incorporated in the construction of new benches, which I found very pleasing. On the south wall of the chancel is a memorial to Mary Herne (1697). She was the daughter of a local man, George Pit, and wife of Sir John Herne (1679). His ledger slab is on the north east of the chancel.

ASHBY St Mary

No of Bells:	3
19th c. Deanery:	Brooke
Hundred:	Loddon
Union house:	Heckingham
21st c. Deanery:	Loddon
Benefice:	Thurton

7 miles SE of Norwich quite near Ashby Hall. Probably best accessed from Thurton. Turn east at the bottom of the hill.

O.S. grid ref: TG 329023
Post Code: NR14 7BJ

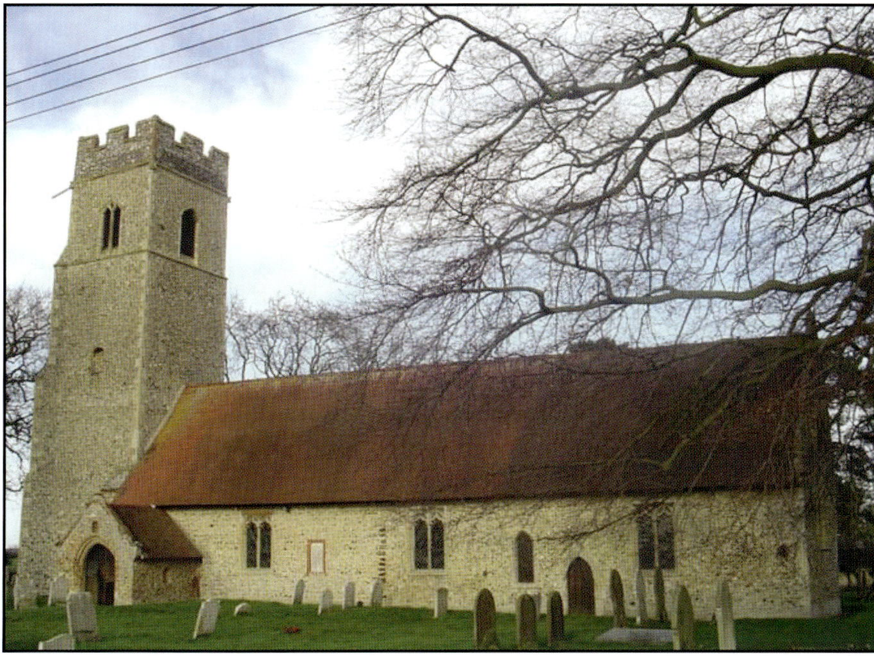

If you want to see one of the finest Norman doorways in a small country church, Ashby is a must. Most of the decoration is of chevrons with two engaged columns either side. The roof is of uniform height for its complete length and terminates at the west end with a well-proportioned square-embattled 15th c. tower. Just inside the church is a 'poor-mans' box and a battered old plain chest. An unusual 17th c. font is quite plain with some minor decoration. The nave roof is plastered and the chancel has a barrel roof. The altar rails are the original 17th c. Laudian style. The black pulpit is, I think, a Victorian copy of a Jacobean design. There is an attractive roundel in the east window, which is French in origin and dated 1604. There is no piscina or sedilia; probably removed during Victorian restoration.

ASHMANHAUGH St Swithin

No of Bells:	1
19th c. Deanery:	Waxham
Hundred:	Tunstead
Union house:	Smallburgh
21st c. Deanery:	Waxham & Tunstead
Benefice:	Ashmanhaugh

7 miles S of North Walsham and 3 miles N of Hoveton, about a mile west of the A1151 situated in Church Road.

O.S. grid ref: TG 314212

Post Code: NR12 8YL

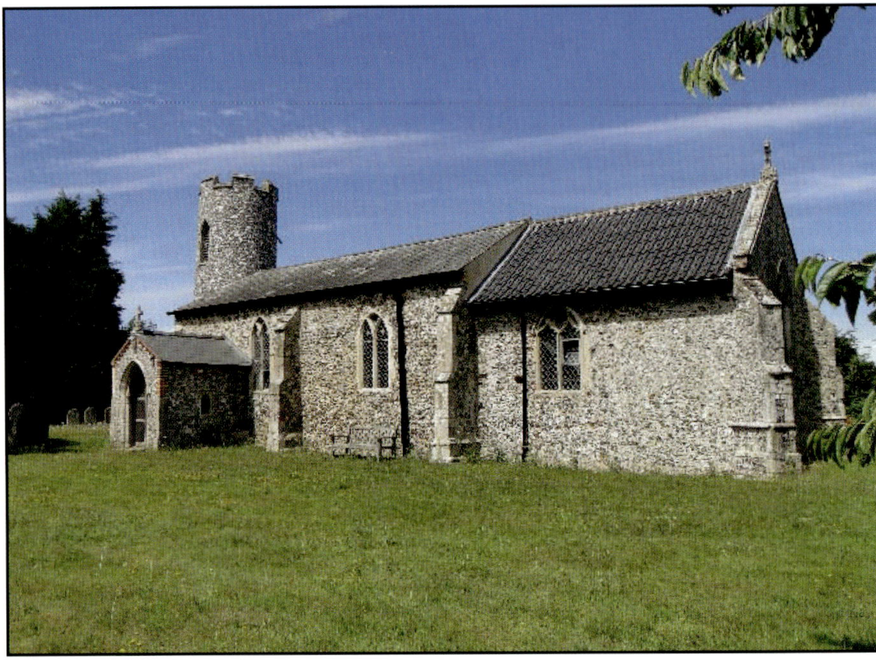

In comparison to the wide nave of the church, the tower is diminutive, and only has a six-feet internal diameter. Just inside the door is a bench, the back of which is carved with shields and the wounds of Christ, and dated MVCXXXI, which Cautley interpreted as 1531. (Assuming the carver thought the Roman numerals for 500 were VC). The nave roof is plastered, as is the chancel, the latter still revealing the rafters. The font is a frightful, plain round bowl standing on an octagonal shaft. In the chancel is probably the most interesting item in the church: a tomb to Honor Bacon, half concealed by a screen behind and to the side of the altar. It bears the date 25th December 1591. The large holes which at one time supported the weight of the rood loft are still visible in the nave walls.

BACTON	St Andrew
No of Bells:	5
19th c. Deanery:	Waxham
Hundred:	Tunstead
Union house:	Smallburgh
21st c. Deanery:	Waxham & Tunstead
Benefice:	Coastal

5 miles NE of North Walsham. The church is south of the North Sea Gas Terminal up a narrow unmade track.

O.S. grid ref: TG 335337

Post Code: NR12 0JP

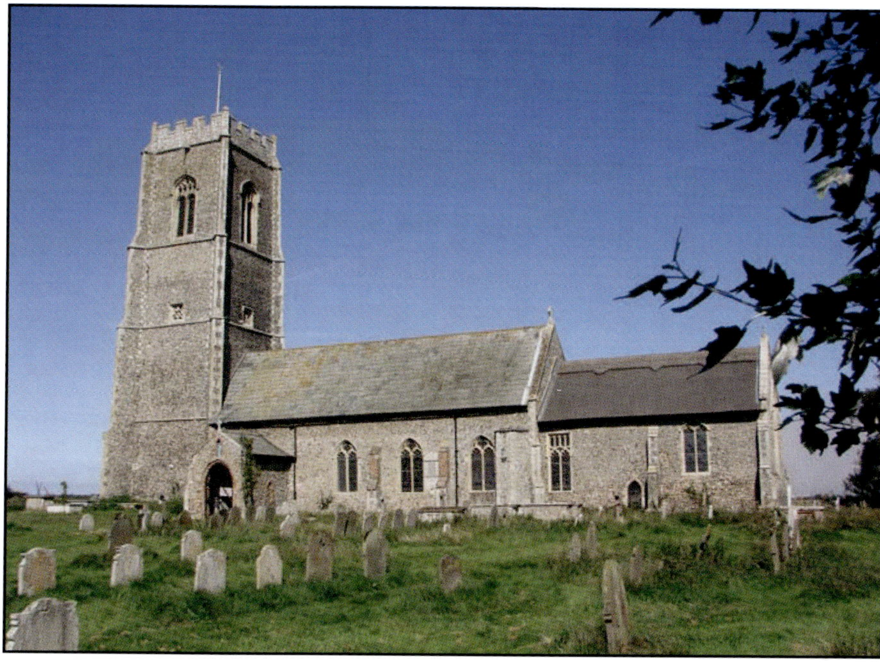

A fine church standing a little remotely, as many of these coastal churches seem to be. The buttresses of the tower have niches with stools which are canopied, but the statuettes have long gone. The nave benches are a mass of colour with brightly decorated kneelers. Just inside the south door is a niche for a bowl of Holy water. The font is beautifully carved and is quite unusually decorated including armorial shields, religious emblems and angelic heads; the steps upon which it stands have quatrefoil decoration. Although part of the chancel is panelled the piscina has been incorporated in a panel: the adjoining graduated sedilia is very plain and without embellishment. The Victorian pulpit is oak with tracery in the panels. This is obviously a vibrant and much loved church.

BARTON TURF St Michael & All Angels

No of Bells: 3
19th c. Deanery: Waxham
Hundred: Tunstead
Union house: Smallburgh
21st c. Deanery: Waxham & Tunstead
Benefice: Ashmanhaugh

11 miles NE of Norwich. Turn east at Beeston St Lawrence church and follow road for 1 mile.
O.S. grid ref: TG 343219
Post Code: NR12 8YU

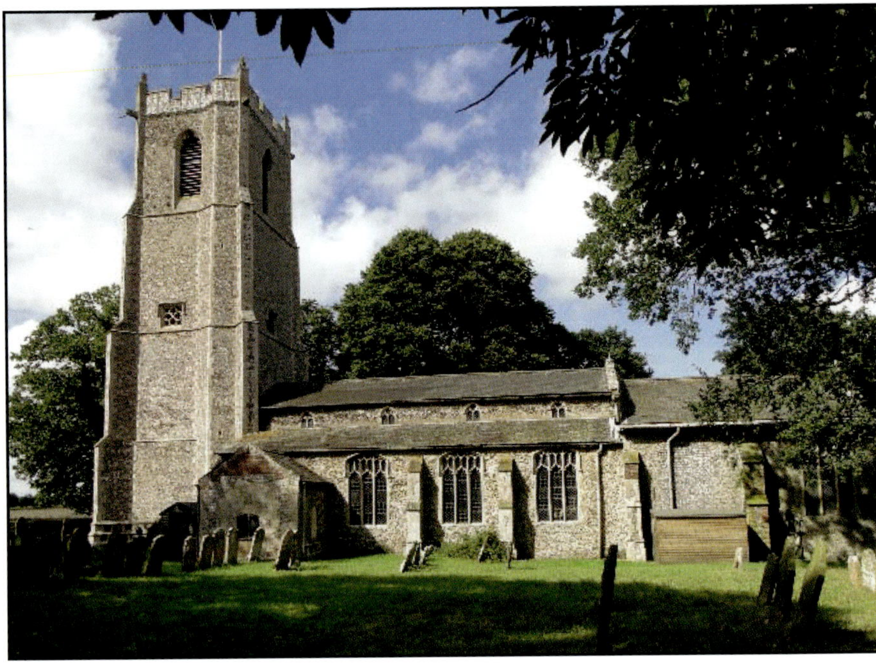

The church was built in the 13th c. but not many of the features are coeval with this date. At close examination, the pinnacles on the tower are figures. The porch has three stooled niches above the doorway and a groined roof with a parvise above, which is used as a storeroom. The arcades date back to the origin of the church but most other features are 15th c. including the traceried octagonal font. Beyond the screen, in the chancel, is a pillar piscina which is quite uncommon. The coved chancel screen itself is the treasure of this church, containing twelve painted panels depicting saints and other important religious figures. The screen in the south aisle alludes to St Thomas' chapel and depicts the Kingly saints of Edmund, Henry VI, Edward the Confessor, and Olaf. Worth a visit for the screens.

BASTWICK (with Repps) St Peter

No of Bells: -
19th c. Deanery: Flegg
Hundred: West Flegg
Union house: Rollesby
21st c. Deanery: -
Benefice: -

10 miles NW by N of Great Yarmouth. Turn east into Tower Road just off the A149 in the grounds of a private house on a bend.
O.S. grid ref: TG 426181
Post Code: NR29 5JW

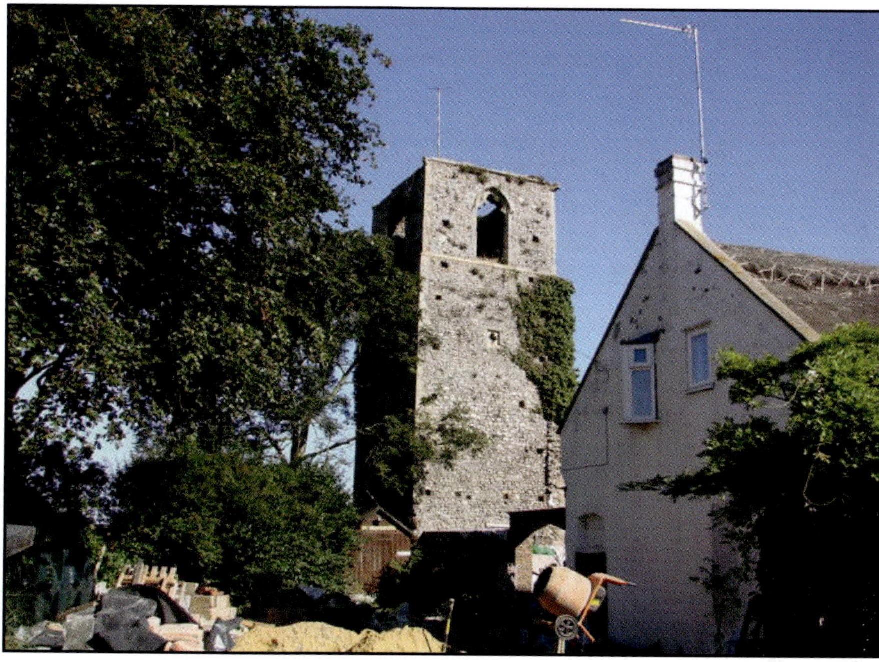

Nothing of the church remains here at Bastwick except the 14th c. tower, which now stands as a monument to the past in the garden of a private house. The church fell into disuse about the time of the 16th c. Reformation and about a hundred years ago was repaired and converted into offices. The cottage must have been built on the graveyard, something that wouldn't be allowed today, or would it? If you ask permission, the owner I am sure will be happy to allow you to have a look round and show you, in the front garden of his cottage, the old 14th c. (*I think*) octagonal font and the base of an ancient cross. Very little is known of the history of the church that was here but I believe the future of the tower is secure. It is well looked after and in good hands.

BEDINGHAM	St Andrew
No of Bells:	5 unusable
19th c. Deanery:	Brooke
Hundred:	Loddon
Union house:	Heckingham
21st c. Deanery:	Depwade
Benefice:	Hempnall

4 miles NW of Bungay; from the B1332 turn west, head for Priory Farm. The church can be seen in the distance.

O.S. grid ref: TM 285933

Post Code: NR35 2DA

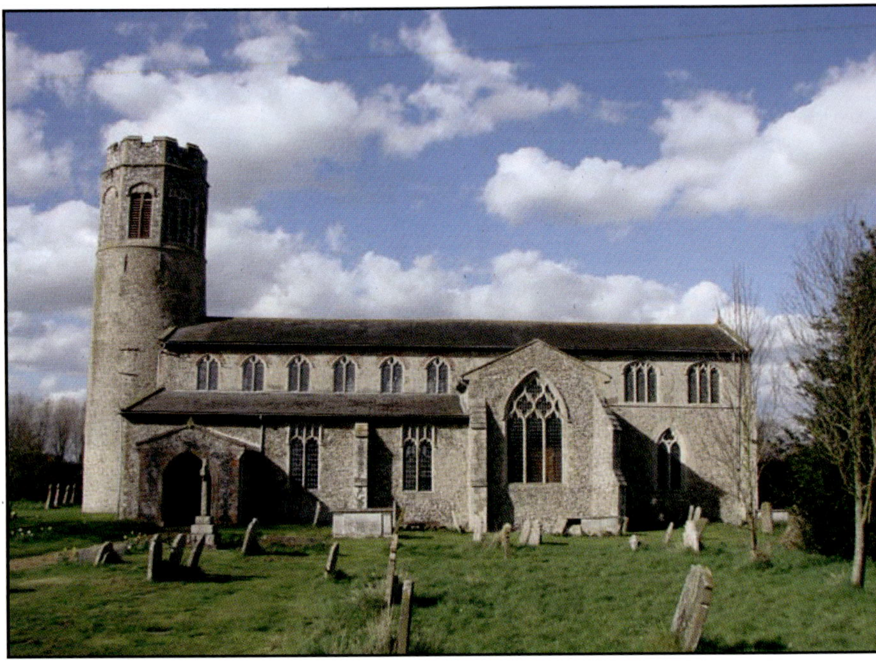

This is quite a large church and has a good clerestory, part of which is obscured by the south chancel. Interesting old ironwork on the south door is worth noting. There are two chancel aisles; both are set apart from the nave by fine 14th c. arcades. The north doorway is late 12th c. with two engaged columns either side of a moulded arch. Three engaged shafts adorn either side of the chancel door. The Tudor font rests on a typical East Anglian shaft. Tracery on the screen dates from the 15th c. and has, perhaps, some of the original paintwork. In the chancel there are what appear to be two piscinæ: one however, is a credence shelf. Between them is a dropped-sill sedilia. Laudian-style altar rails are unusual with a twist and are close together as stipulated by Archbishop William Laud in the 17th c. Quite different!

BEESTON ST LAWRENCE

No of Bells:	0
19th c. Deanery:	Waxham
Hundred:	Tunstead
Union house:	Smallburgh
21st c. Deanery:	Waxham & Tunstead
Benefice:	Ashmanhaugh

10 miles NE of Norwich on the A1151, 2½ miles north of Hoveton on the right hand side heading north. Park in adjoining lay-by.
O.S. grid ref: TG 328220
Post Code: *NR12 8YS

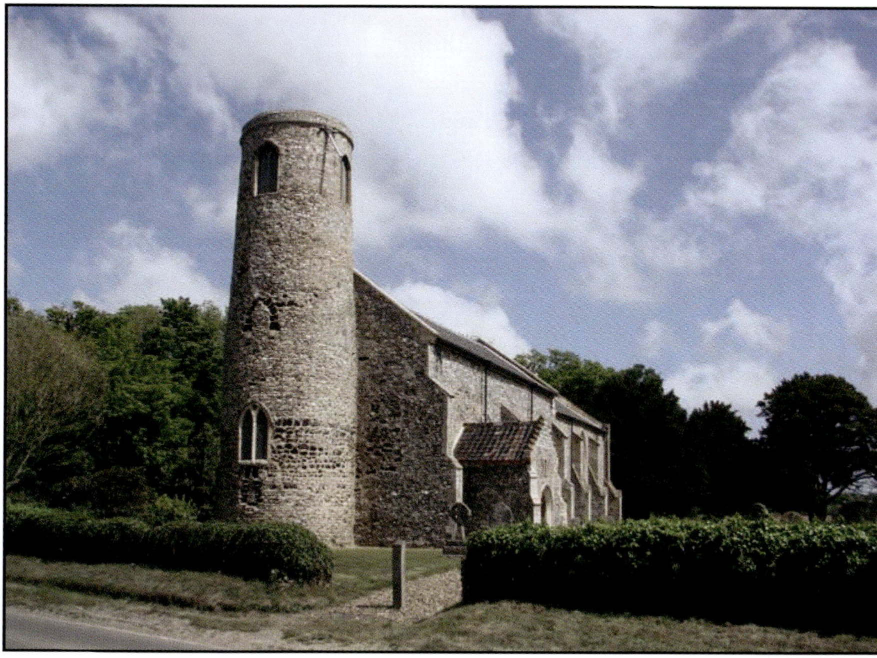

*North of the postcode above. This recently renovated church has little to offer the visitor, except a passing interest. The round tower, however, is probably pre-Conquest and has been rather poorly re-pointed of late. The buttresses to the chancel hold interest for the architectural student, as they have gablettes at their mid-point. Flushwork panelling on the east wall is uncommon. In the nave is the font, with quatrefoil and trefoil decoration. The roof of both nave and chancel is plastered and divided into panels. The pine pulpit is very run of the mill, as are the benches. There are many and various monuments to the Preston family, the earliest I found was 1673. Unfortunately, the once beautiful piscina on the south wall of the chancel has been viciously mutilated by more recent monuments.

BEIGHTON	All Saints	2½ miles SW of Acle and 4 miles north of Cantley, just off the B1140 north of the village at three-way junction near farm buildings.
No of Bells:	1	
19th c. Deanery:	Blofield	
Hundred:	Walsham	
Union house:	Acle	
21st c. Deanery:	Blofield	O.S. grid ref: TG 386083
Benefice:	Acle	Post Code: NR13 3JZ

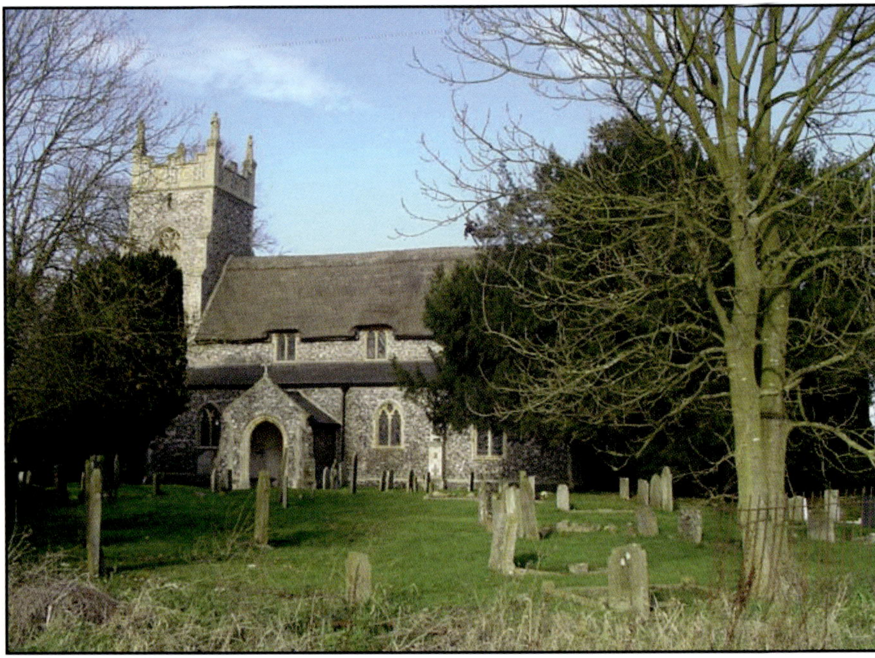

The evangelists that look out from each corner of the low heavily buttressed tower are unusually large. The nave roof is thatched and the chancel tiled. Access to the bell tower is by an external octagonal turret. Just inside the south door is a niche for a stoup. The octagonal arcaded font is 13th c. but I am sure the columns and shaft upon which it stands are probably 15th or even later. The nave roof is of scissor beam construction. The piscina and sedilia group are beautifully carved trefoil arches but I think Victorian, installed when the other restorations took place here, including the reconstruction of the rood screen. There are some nicely carved bench ends and although of no great age they are worth seeking out, especially the sow and suckling piglets.

BELAUGH	St Peter
No of Bells:	2
19th c. Deanery:	Ingworth
Hundred:	South Erpingham
Union house:	Aylsham
21st c. Deanery:	Waxham & Tunstead
Benefice:	Wroxham

8½ miles NNE of Norwich in Church Lane, Belaugh. Turn south off the B1354 and continue ¾ of a mile down narrow roads.

O.S. grid ref: TG 289185
Post Code: NR12 8XA

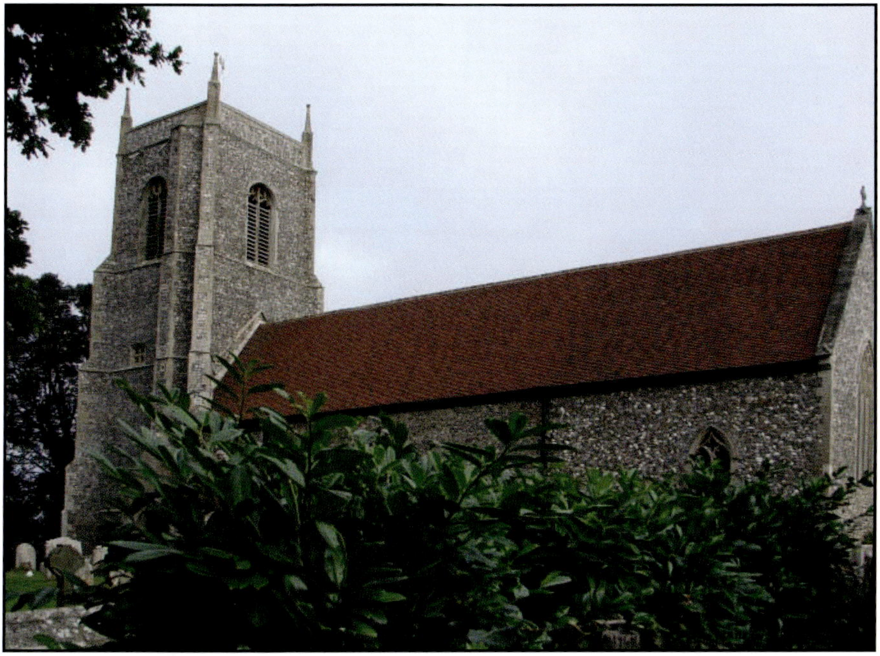

Belaugh is pronounced 'Beeler'. The 15th c. tower with its fine pinnacles and sound holes is a landmark. The nave and chancel roof are as one with no distinction in the red-tiled roof. Inside the church, there is no chancel arch; it is divided only by the vaulted screen which depicts the twelve apostles and, although defaced, are still discernible by their emblems. The ancient font is Norman with a circular bowl decorated with arches and is supported on four columns and a central shaft. In the chancel is a simple corner piscina with a smaller additional arch into the dropped-sill sedilia. There is a small north transept. All the fittings and furnishings except those mentioned above are Victorian. The arch-braced roof is modern with wall posts on corbels, those in the nave differing from those in the chancel.

BELTON All Saints

No of Bells: 1

19th c. Deanery: Lothingland

Hundred: Mutford & Lothingland

Union house: Oulton

21st c. Deanery: Great Yarmouth

Benefice: Belton

3 miles W of Gorleston in Church Lane, Belton, which is a narrow roadway with a few passing places. There is parking at the church.

O.S. grid ref: TG 485029

Post Code: NR31 9JJ

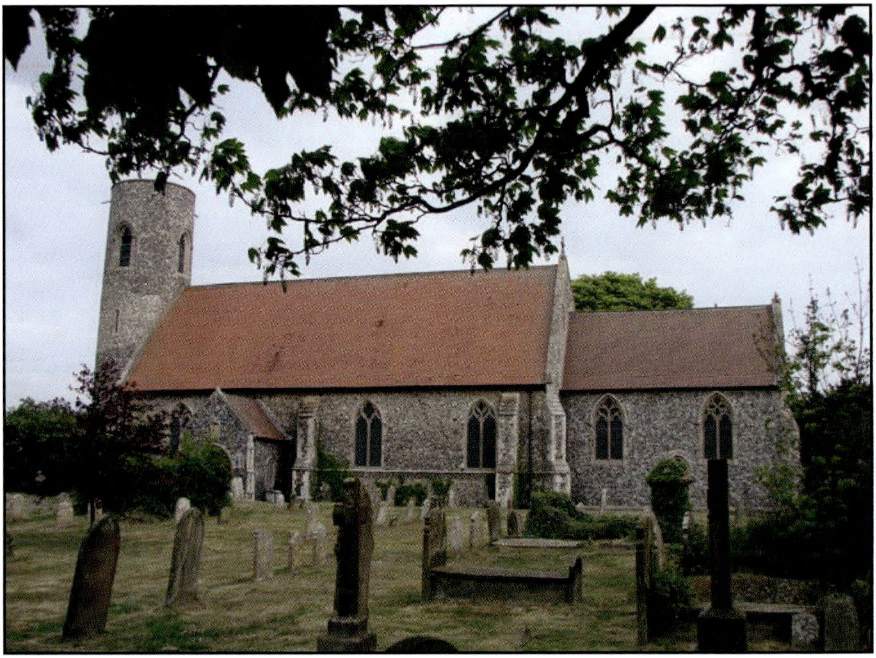

The tower, although very early, is refaced and none of the original work can be seen from the outside. The body of the church is 14th c. The most easterly pair of buttresses are set diagonally to the wall, as if the chancel was an afterthought and is therefore probably later. A scratch-dial can be found on a nave buttress. There is a broken font of the early 12th c. but a later 14th c. font is the one in use. In the sanctuary there is a 14th c. recessed tomb with a cusped ogee arch. The wall paintings are noteworthy but are now badly faded. They are of St James the Great and St Christopher (who appears in almost every church that has wall paintings on display) and 'The three quick and the three dead'. It is a neat church and worth finding a key. John Ives, who wrote the history of Great Yarmouth, is buried here.

BERGH APTON St Peter & St Paul

No of Bells: 6
19th c. Deanery: Brooke
Hundred: Clavering
Union house: Heckingham
21st c. Deanery: Loddon
Benefice: Thurton

3 miles NW of Loddon, the church is over a mile south of the village centre in Wellbeck Road, as marked on the O.S. map.
O.S. grid ref: TM 310999
Post Code: NR15 1AU

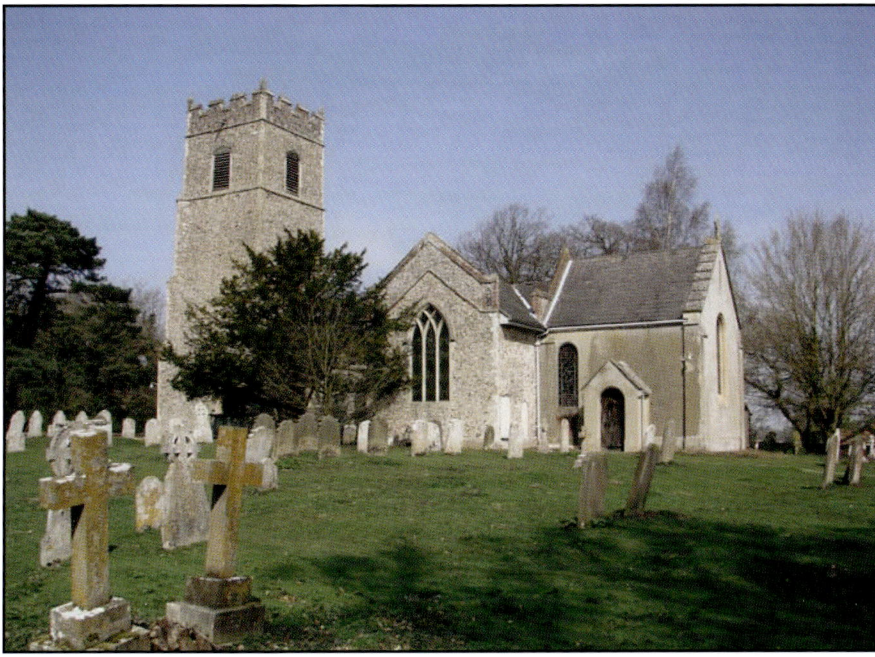

An earlier church of St Martin stood in the parish but was demolished and the site cleared in 1834. This replacement church has a large clock-face on the tower and is a cruciform type with a transept both north and south. The roofline has changed as can be seen on the east face of the tower. There was originally a sanctus window in the apex of the roof. The south doorway has three faces on the hood-mould. The whole church has been much restored and there is little left to see inside the church that is earlier than 19th c. One exception is the typical 15th c. East Anglian font. There is a good mass dial complete with remains of the gnomon on the south transept. The roofs have been either panelled or plastered and the general character of the church has unfortunately been lost.

BILLOCKBY	All Saints	8½ miles NW of Great Yarmouth, in the centre of a triangle of the A1064, B1152 & a country lane, standing remote in a field.
No of Bells:	0	
19th c. Deanery:	Flegg	
Hundred:	West Flegg	
Union house:	Rollesby	
21st c. Deanery:	Great Yarmouth	O.S. grid ref: TG 429135
Benefice:	Flegg South Trinity	Post Code: NR29 3BQ

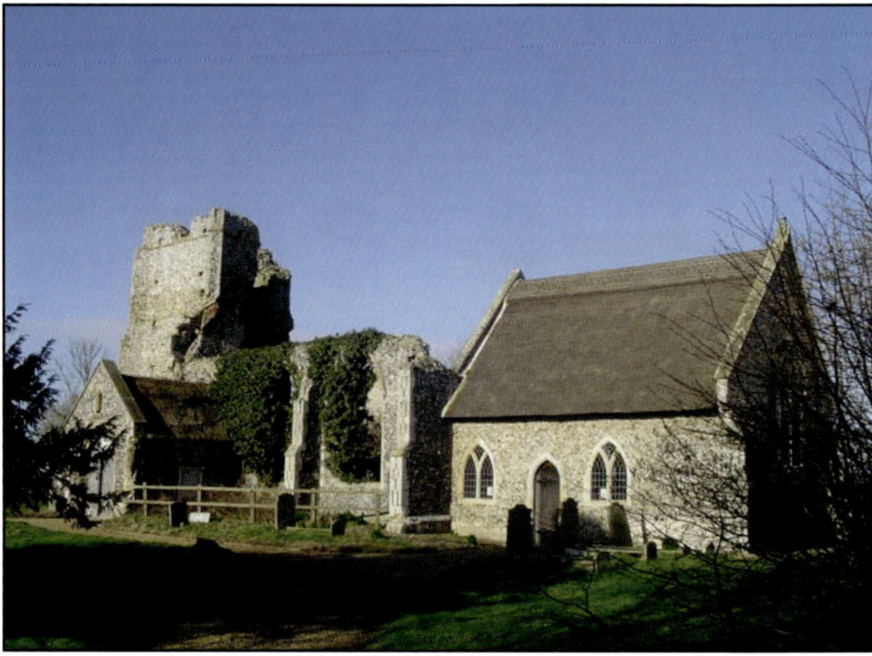

In 1762 the tower was struck by lightning and fell on the nave, and was never rebuilt. In 1872 the chancel was restored and converted into a church. The ruins remain although much material has been cleared away and used elsewhere. The crack down the length of the tower renders it unrepairable. I would imagine that this church will one day be left to nature to take its inevitable course. The font is Victorian and undecorated. A few of the poppy-head benches seem to have survived the damage, unless they came from elsewhere. There is really nothing of interest inside the church, either historically or architecturally. The interest here lies in the ruin and evidence of construction and building technique which we are usually unable to see in a standing church. I cannot, however, recommend that you disregard the safety fence.

BIXLEY	St Wandregesilus
No of Bells:	1
19th c. Deanery:	Brooke
Hundred:	Henstead
Union house:	Swainsthorpe
21st c. Deanery:	Loddon
Benefice:	Poringland

2½ miles SSW of Norwich and almost invisible from the B1332. Turn left up a grassy driveway to a copse. Very easily missed.
O.S. grid ref: TG 258049
Post Code: NR14 8RY

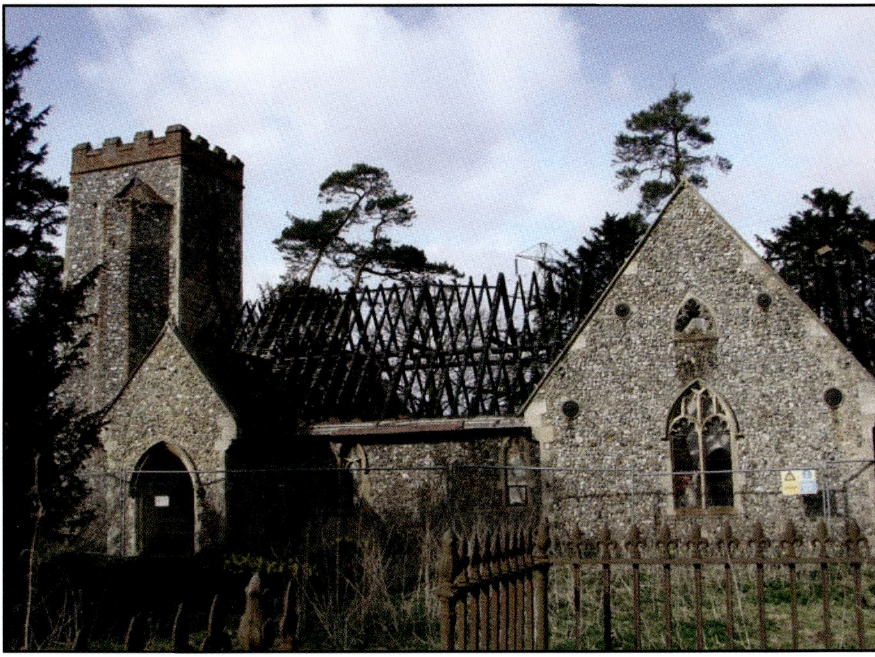

Bixley, until it burned down on May 13th 2004, was an interesting church. Its dedication is unique in England. St Wandregesilus was a monk who founded a monastery at Fontonelles near Rouen. In the Middle Ages pilgrimages were made here to honour him. Built by William de Dunwich in 1272, it was an ancient structure, which has since been almost completely rebuilt over the centuries. In the 15th c. new windows were inserted and the latest changes were made in 1863. The later 14th c. tower has an external octagonal stair turret attached, giving access to the belfry. Inside it had (or maybe still has) monuments to many members of the Ward family and one particularly nice one to Susan, Countess of Rosebery (1771). Although the church in some ways is unique, I cannot see it ever being rebuilt.

BLOFIELD St Andrew & St Peter

No of Bells:	8
19th c. Deanery:	Blofield
Hundred:	Blofield
Union house:	Lingwood
21st c. Deanery:	Blofield
Benefice:	Blofield

7 miles E of Norwich in Church Road, Blofield, south of the A47. The tall tower can be seen from some distance away.
O.S. grid ref: TG 335092
Post Code: NR13 4NA

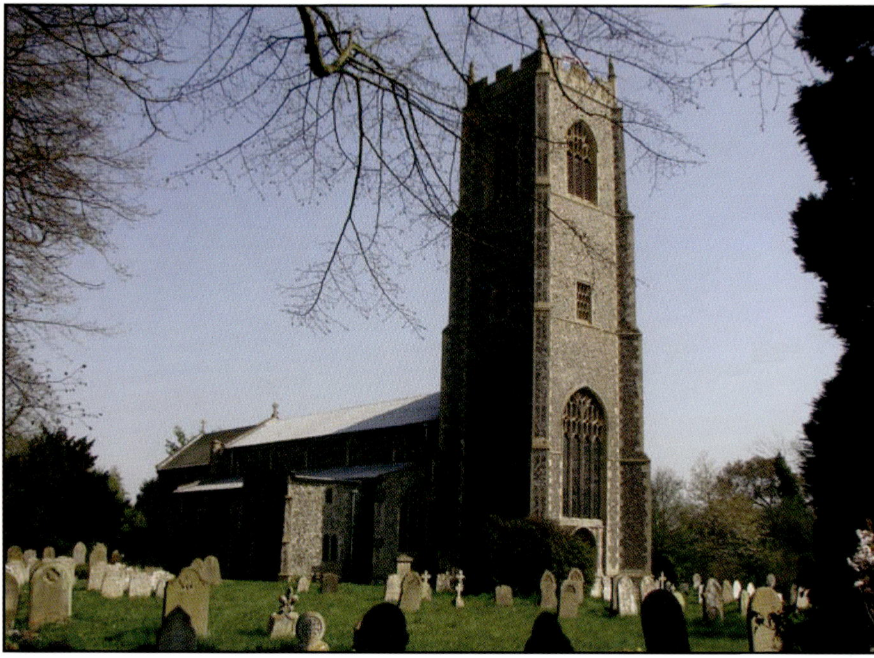

The tower is a lofty edifice and can be easily recognised from a distance with its tall pinnacles. The western doorway has good flushwork and a large window above. Over the north porch is a parvise. Inside the church splendid arcades separate the north and south aisles. In the nave is the unique 15/16th c. font, decorated around the octagonal bowl with eight scenes from the life of Jesus. The bowl is corbelled with angels which have been defaced. The screen is noteworthy, decorated with the twelve apostles and although repainted in 1850 is still outstanding. Both piscina and dropped-sill sedilia are 15th c. Monuments include many of the Paston family, particularly Sir Edward who served Henry VIII. Other memorials are to Ann Catelyn (1681), Peter Deneaw (1678), and Lydia Reve (1687).

BRADFIELD St Giles
No of Bells: 1
19th c. Deanery: Waxham
Hundred: Tunstead
Union house: Smallburgh
21st c. Deanery: Repps
Benefice: Trunch Team Ministry

2 miles N by W of North Walsham, the church is at the southern-most end of the village in Church Road. Easily found.
O.S. grid ref: TG 267333
Post Code: NR28 0NX

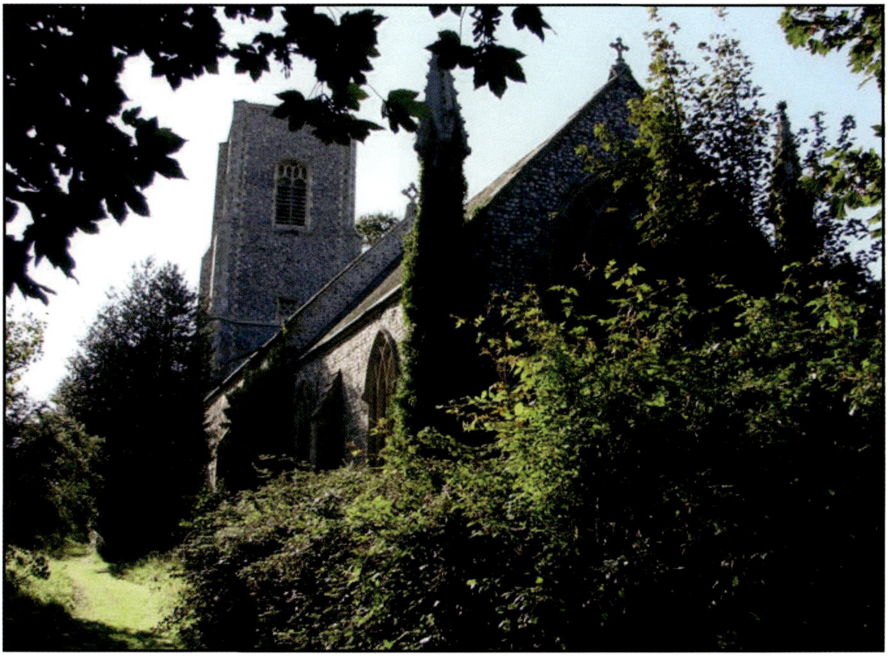

The 15th c. tower looks quite strange at first glance; it has no parapet and no battlements. Unadorned, it somehow appears unfinished. The buttresses at the east end are pentagonal and have crocketted pinnacles. It is however a fine and grand church. Inside the nave, the font is of the 14th c. and is decorated with tracery, and is supported on eight engaged columns around a central shaft. Above the chancel arch is a wall painting of an unrecognisable subject. The Victorian pulpit is rather ordinary and unattractive. The observant eye will notice arches of the arcade, blocked when the aisles were removed, are still visible in the make-up of the walls, both inside and out. The Victorian altar rails amused me, as their original purpose was to keep dogs out of the sanctuary. These look almost inviting to a dog.

BRADWELL St Nicholas
No of Bells: 3
19th c. Deanery: Lothingland
Hundred: Mutford & Lothingland
Union house: Oulton
21st c. Deanery: Great Yarmouth
Benefice: Bradwell

1 mile W of Gorleston between Gorleston & Burgh Castle. Off Green Lane in Church Walk and surrounded by trees.
O.S. grid ref: TG 502038
Post Code: NR31 8QW

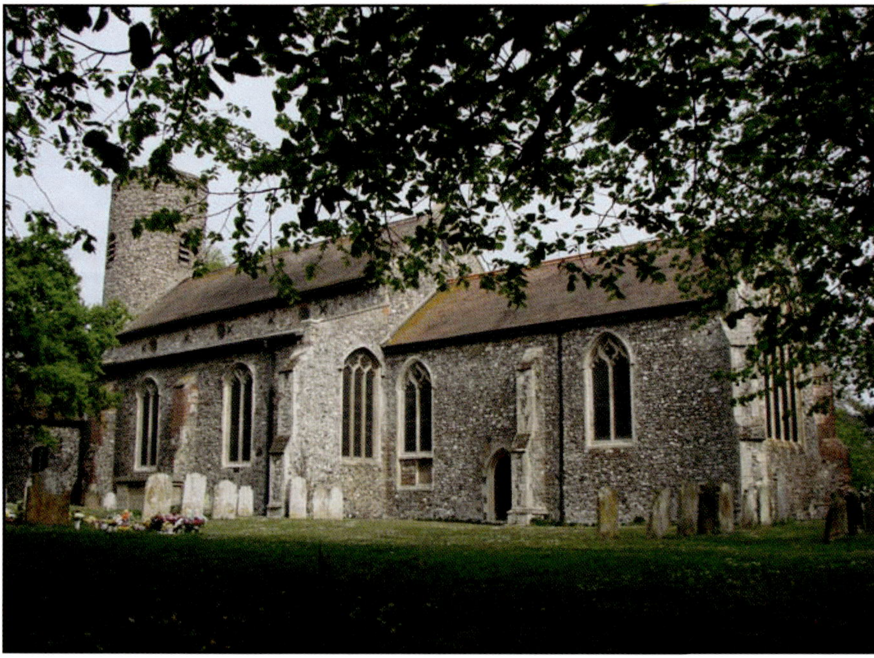

Bradwell is one of the many heavily restored churches that offer little to the historian. However, there are a few items of interest for the visitor to see. The structure of the church is 14th c. as is the traditional East Anglian font which is in remarkably good condition. Around the octagonal bowl are carvings of winged angels and other creatures with lions guarding the base. There is a monument to William Vesey who is flanked by his two wives; behind each is a child. On a frieze below is a reclining man flanked by what appear to be four more children. Although the woodwork in the church is of good quality, it is comparatively modern. The rood loft stairs are still open. There are two piscinas, one 14th c. and the other a cusped Victorian reproduction with matching sedilia.

BRAMERTON St Peter

No of Bells:	3
19th c. Deanery:	Brooke
Hundred:	Henstead
Union house:	Swainsthorpe
21st c Deanery:	Loddon
Benefice:	Bramerton

4½ miles SE of Norwich. In the main street as you pass through the village. Wet weather prevents use of the grass car park.

O.S. grid ref: TG 295046

Post Code: NR14 7DW

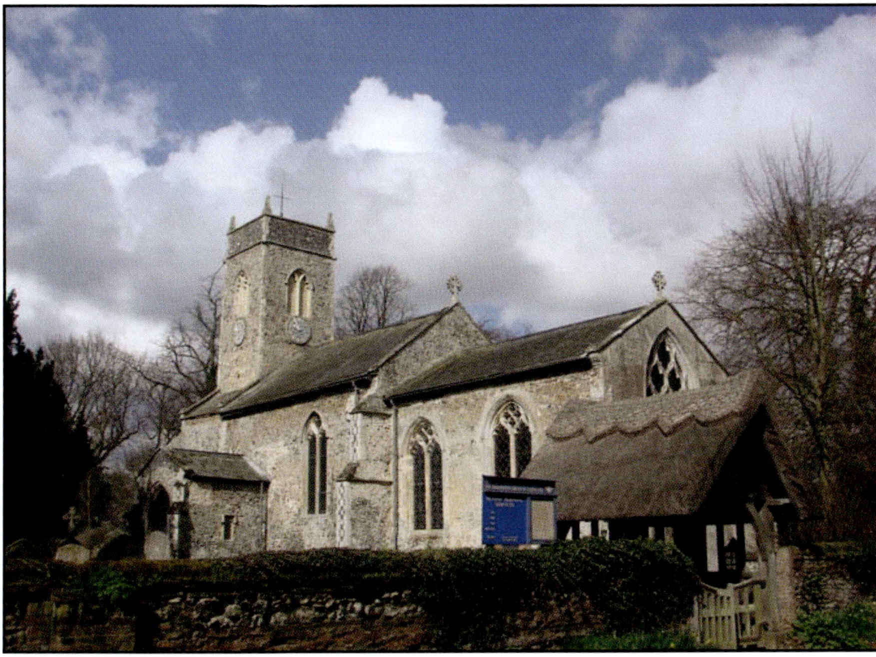

This pleasantly situated church has a lovely weathercock and a chiming clock. The unusual wrap-around nave envelopes the tower on three sides, forming extensions to the nave. Each part of the west walls has a squint, although one is blocked. Most of the church is Victorian restructuring which removed most of the fabric of an earlier church built in 1462, replacing an even earlier building. A Tudor brick priest's door is quite decorative. The octagonal font is 14th c. and quite plain except for the carvings around the bottom of the bowl. The roofs have been plastered, concealing most of the timberwork, except in the north transept, which was added in 1858 as a tribute to John Blake, a local resident. The octagonal traceried wooden pulpit stands on a stone base. The Royal Arms are those of George III.

BRAYDESTON St Michael

No of Bells:	1 (3 before 1762)
19th c. Deanery:	Blofield
Hundred:	Blofield
Union house:	Lingwood
21st c. Deanery:	Blofield
Benefice:	Brundell

7 miles E of Norwich, just south of Blofield near Braydeston Hall at the end of a cul-de-sac. Or ½ m. walk from Braydeston village.
O.S. grid ref: TG 337087
Post Code: NR13 5AP

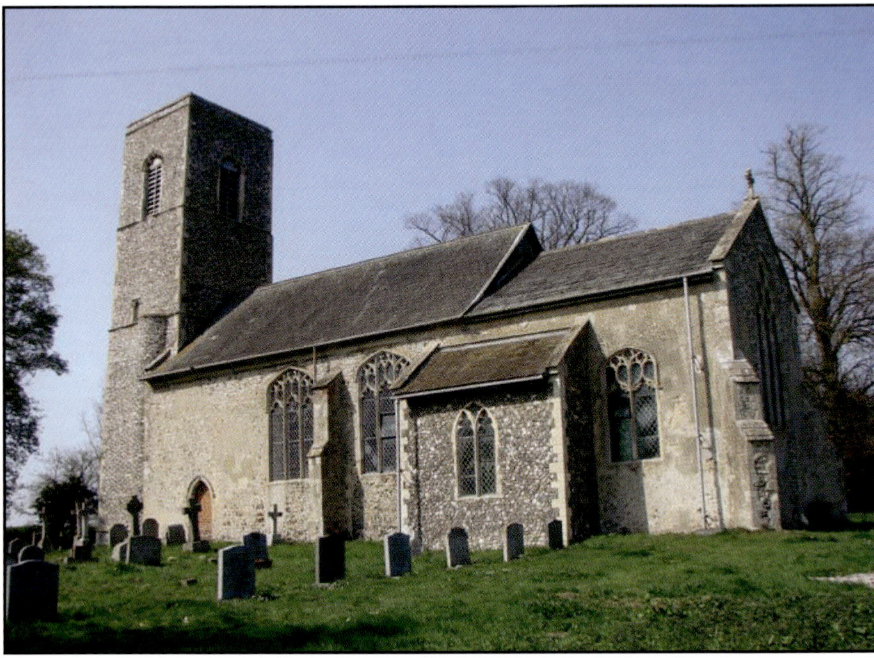

Also spelt Bradestone or Bradiston. The church is a long way from the present centre of civilisation, but can be easily reached by road. This is another of Norfolk's Saxon churches, which was virtually rebuilt by the Normans. Remains of a former south aisle can still be seen by the blocked arcade. The hexagonal font is 14th c. and has shallow decoration around the bowl. A drawing in the church shows little change in the external appearance in the last 100 years or so. Considerable Victorian restoration took place here in 1874 when new seating was installed. Poppyheads adorn the bench ends, every one different. The pulpit and reading desk are both from the same period. The roof gives the appearance of being in a barrel. The original piscina with cusped arch and the dropped-sill sedilia have survived.

BROCKDISH	St Peter & St Paul
No of Bells:	6
19th c. Deanery:	Redenhall
Hundred:	Earsham
Union house:	Pulham St Mary
21st c Deanery:	Redenhall
Benefice:	Scole

3 miles SW of Harleston turn off the A143 into Brockdish, along the old A143 which runs through the village. Then into Church Road.
O.S. grid ref: TM 204796
Post Code: IP21 4JJ

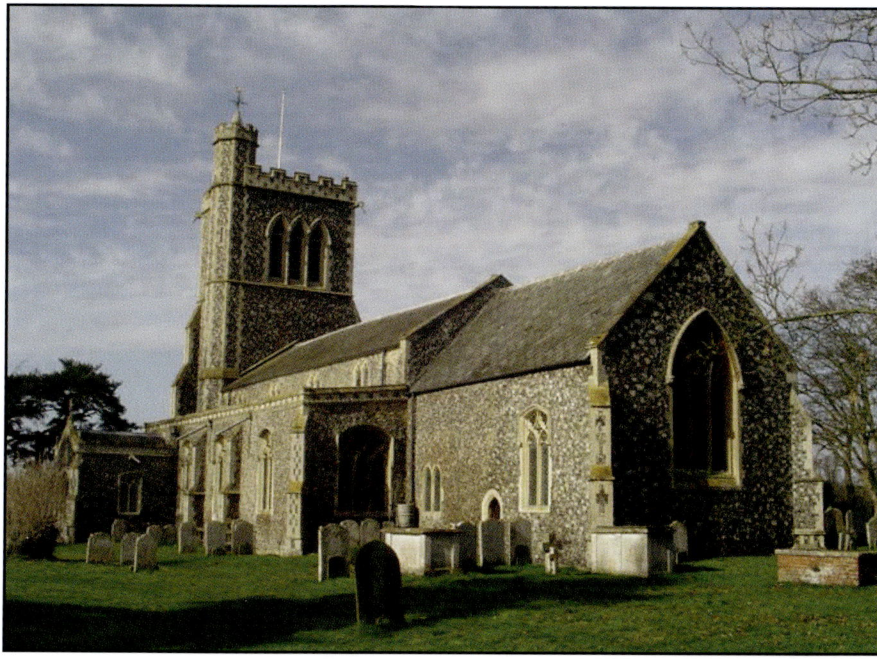

This was once a lovely little church with a Norman tower, as can be seen from the drawing hanging in the nave. The new tower, built in 1864, is a fine example of over-indulgence. Inside the nave there is a 14th c. arcade, the easternmost column has a canopy beneath the cap. A hexagonal font is quite uncommon but it is of no great age. The 13th c. piscina in the south aisle has a beautifully decorated arch and engaged columns. The chancel font is also attractive and the sedile is a stone bench, large enough for three. Both are Victorian. In the nave, you may notice a small and ancient slit window that is covered by a buttress, so constructed as to still allow light to enter. An old bier is used as a table for leaflets. Why, oh why, are these so often neglected as items of interest to visitors and covered in such a way?

BROOKE	St Peter	****
No of Bells:	1	
19th c. Deanery:	Brooke	
Hundred:	Clavering	
Union house:	Heckingham	
21st c Deanery:	Depwade	
Benefice:	Brooke	

7 miles SSE of Norwich at the eastern end of the village right on a bend with no parking facilities except for one car in the entrance.
O.S. grid ref: TM 293995
Post Code: NR15 1JU

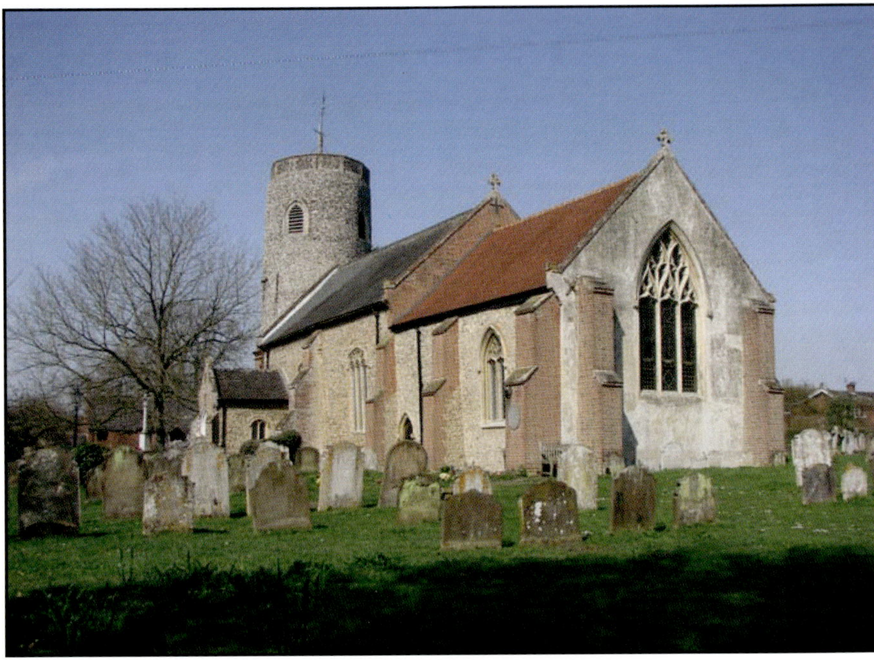

This church is Norman in its origins, and the base of the tower early 13th c. Slit windows, although modified, can be clearly seen. Notice too how the flints are set in rows as the tower was raised by the builders. Inside the porch, the south doorway is a mixture of Norman and 15th c., the door having a coeval tracery design. Passing into the nave, the lovely 15th c. Seven Sacraments font is a treat for the eye; it is one of only forty in the county. A glance upwards will reveal the Royal Hanoverian Arms of Victoria. The roof of the nave and chancel are arch-braced, and the angels holding shields, I believe, bear the names of past churchwardens. The piscina is late 13th c. There is an aumbry, the door of which is carved with the deposition. The choir stalls are elaborately carved but are relatively modern.

BROOME	St Michael	2 miles NNE of Norwich.
No of Bells:	5, unusable	Situated north of the village
19th c. Deanery:	Brooke	past Broome Place, at the
Hundred:	Loddon	north end of Church Lane.
Union house:	Heckingham	(NR35 2EJ)
21st c Deanery:	Redenhall	O.S. grid ref: TM 346931
Benefice:	Ditchingham (Earsham)	Post Code: NR35 2HT

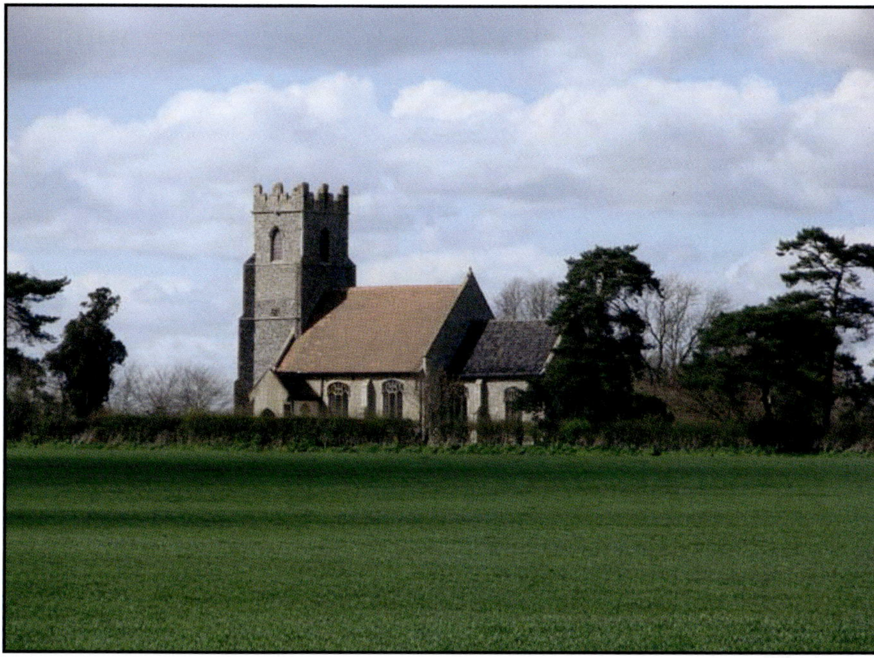

Set well back off the road up a trackway this church is usually left securely locked. The lovely 15th c. tower has a niche above the west window, decoration above the door, and a decorative band around the base. The font is a hotch-potch of 19th c. bowl and 15th c. East Anglian style shaft standing on a possibly even older base. The 19th c. pulpit stands on a stone pedestal. The piscina has been concealed behind panelling but the tri-level sedilia proves that the chancel floor has been raised as the third sedile is only three inches high. A blocked doorway near the chancel can be seen on the north wall half-concealed by a buttress. A black ledger slab remembers Dame Mary Cooke (1686) while another bears an hourglass, four skulls and bones. None of the churches in the area have Royal Arms. I wonder why?

BRUMSTEAD St Peter
No of Bells: 1
19th c. Deanery: Waxham
Hundred: Happing
Union house: Smallburgh
21st c Deanery: Waxham & Tunstead
Benefice: Stalham

7 miles ESE of North Walsham. From Stalham go north on the B1159 until the village sign for Brunstead, then follow the lane.
O.S. grid ref: TG 369268
Post Code: NR12 9EZ

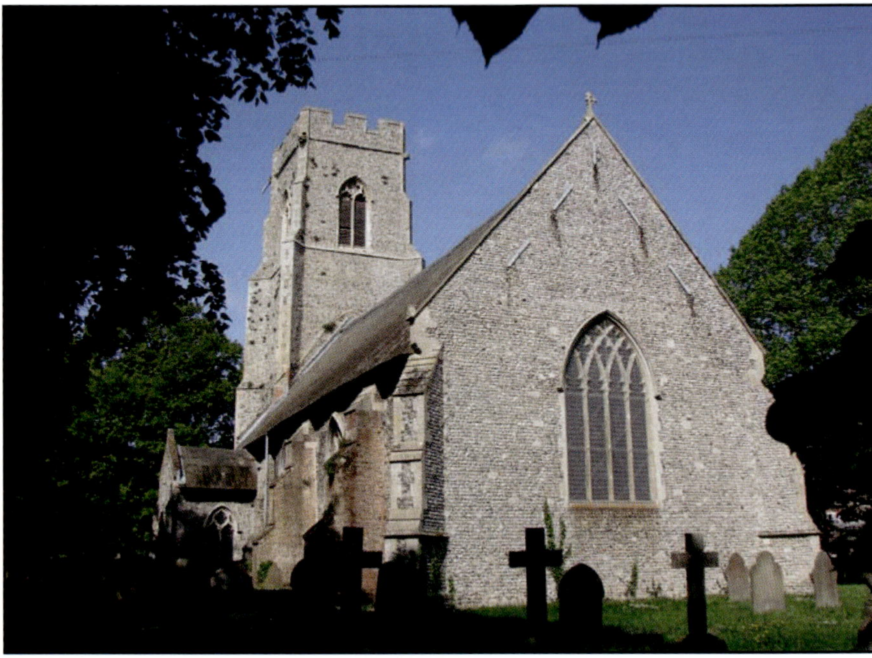

Anciently called Brunstead but since a cartographer's error has been called Brumstead. The wholly thatched church is built close to the hall and dates from around the 14th c. A south doorway that has engaged columns is testament to the fact. The embattled tower is 15th c. and has traceried sound holes midway. Quatrefoil decoration on the 14th c. octagonal font saved it from mutilation by the Puritans. A cusped piscina in the chancel is devoid of an accompanying sedilia. The roofs are modern as are the poppy-head benches. Black ledger slab memorials are to Elizabeth Harcourt (1667), beside her is her husband, Boys Harcourt (1697) and his mother, also Elizabeth (1685). A stone coffin lid set into the floor near the font is much earlier. Left very basic by the Victorians but a nevertheless interesting church.

BRUNDALL St Laurence

No of Bells:	1
19th c. Deanery:	Blofield
Hundred:	Blofield
Union house:	Lingwood
21st c Deanery:	Blofield
Benefice:	Brundell

5½ miles E of Norwich. Turn off the A47 at the service station roundabout and follow into The Street. The church is in a short lane.
O.S. grid ref: TG 329085
Post Code: NR13 5NA

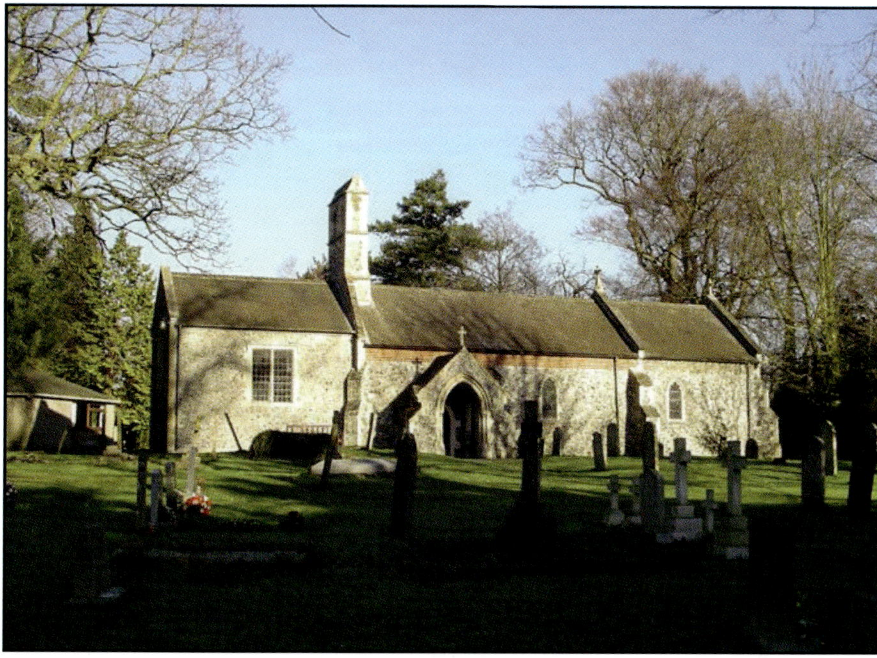

The churchyard is entered by a lychgate erected in 1909 in memory of a parishioner. Brundall church has never had a tower and the twin bell turret has only one bell. Originally the church was Norman but so many changes have taken place there is nothing left of the period. The 13th c. font is the only one of its type in Norfolk and one of only twenty-six in the country, being lead covered and depicting the crucifixion on all of the eight facets. The west extension was built in the 1960s at about the same time the rood screen was installed. Most of the fittings and fixtures are from around the late Victorian period and the church seems to retain very little of historical interest. Despite this it is an interesting little church and seems to be thriving. An old clock hangs on the wall with no hands; time does not matter here.

BUCKENHAM St Nicholas

No of Bells: 1
19th c. Deanery: Blofield
Hundred: Blofield
Union house: Lingwood
21st c Deanery: -
The Churches Conservation Trust

9 miles E by S of Norwich. Best approached from Cantley, turn west at the x-roads on the B1140, and through Hassingham.
O.S. grid ref: TG 356058
Post Code: NR13 4HW

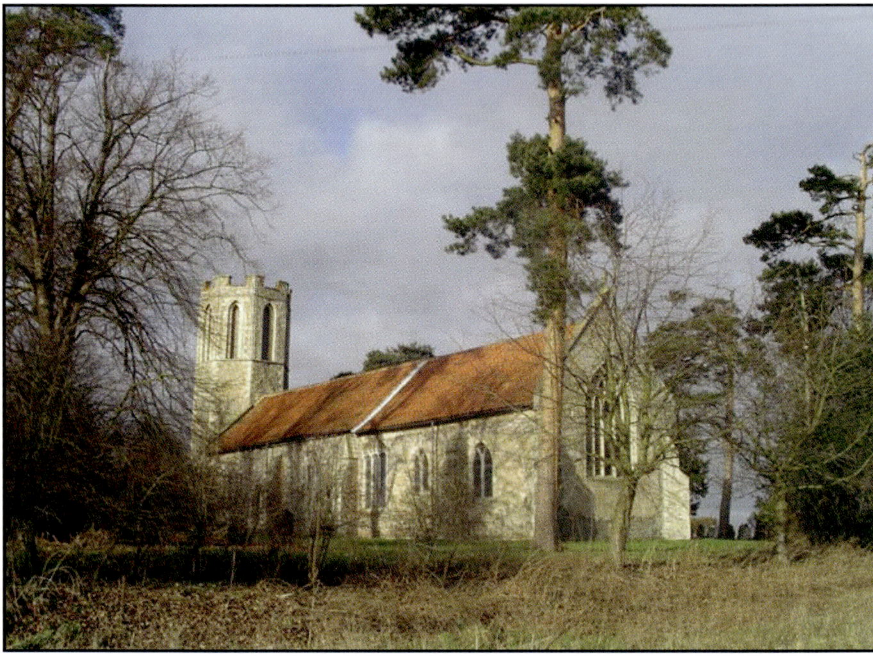

The church is maintained by the Churches Conservation Trust and always open to the visitor. The 13th c. wholly octagonal, arcaded tower is what makes this beautiful church outstanding. The red tiled roof is a perfect foil for the pine trees that surround it. The south doorway has the typical Norman chevron carving to the arch, whereas the north doorway, now inside the small vestry, has small crosses with a later pointed arch. The tower doorway is unusual in that it is traceried. Just above it is the date 1841, referring to the restorations which were carried out. The font dates from the late 14th c. The piscina has a broad trefoil arch and is adjacent to a dropped-sill two-seat sedilia with a central armrest in stone. There is a wall memorial to Anne, wife of William Newbury, who died in 1707.

BURGH CASTLE St Peter & St Paul
No of Bells: 3
19th c. Deanery: Lothingland
Hundred: Mutford & Lothingland
Union house: Oulton
21st c Deanery: Great Yarmouth
Benefice: Belton

3 miles W of Gt. Yarmouth between Great Yarmouth & Belton. From the A143 turn north then to Church Road. Near the Roman Fort.
O.S. grid ref: TG 476049
Post Code: NR31 9QG

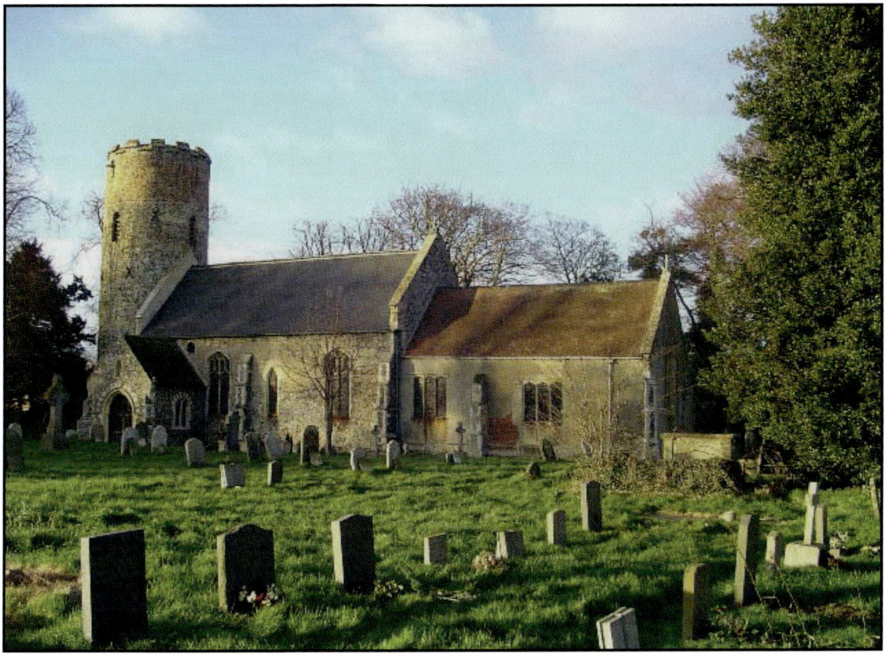

Rough and ready would be the way to describe this little church, which is often ignored by visitors to the nearby Roman fort of Burgh Castle after which the parish is named. The tower notably is built from Roman building materials, bricks, tiles and flint. The castle has been robbed of materials for all kinds of uses including roads, driveways and cottages. Inside the church the windows are modern but worth further investigation. One is to Herbert Laws, killed on Martinique when a volcano erupted. Another is to St Fursey, an obscure saint and evangelist to the castle. King Alfred and Queen Victoria are also represented in glass. The font is the typical octagonal variety with figures around. Some of the wood carving is well executed but there is nothing of exceptional note.

BURGH ST MARGARET St Margaret

No of Bells: 3
19th c. Deanery: Flegg
Hundred: West Flegg
Union house: Rollesby
21st c Deanery: Great Yarmouth
Benefice: Flegg (South Trinity Broads)

7½ miles NW of Great Yarmouth. The church is beside the A1164 virtually in the centre of the village.
O.S. grid ref: TG 444140
Post Code: NR29 3AB

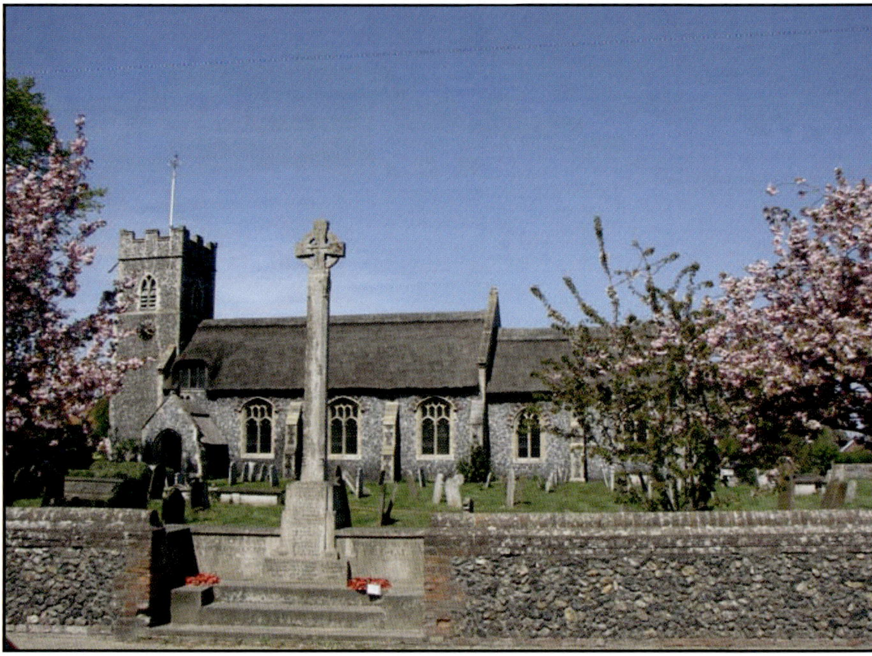

The area is now known as Fleggburgh although no parish bears that name. The church is entirely thatched and picturesque, Above the south porch is a dormer window to the gallery. Inside the south porch is a Norman doorway with two columns both sides and three orders of decoration. The quite modern font is octagonal and in the 15th c. style, decorated with Tudor roses and some ecclesiastical symbols. In fact, most of the furnishings and fittings are late Victorian as the whole building was virtually restructured by Herbert Green, Diocesan architect. It is plain and uninteresting with very little character remaining, which is such a pity. The stone reredos is well carved, but the piscina has gone and the sedilia unusable, thanks to an ill-placed book-rest. The glass in the east window is the only thing to admire.

BURGH ST MARY St Mary

No of Bells: -
19th c. Deanery: Flegg
Hundred: West Flegg
Union house: Rollesby
21st c Deanery: -
Benefice: -

½ mile E of Burgh St Margaret in Tower Road just off the A1164. Access is by a footpath across a field.

O.S. grid ref: TG 454141
Post Code: NR29 3DW

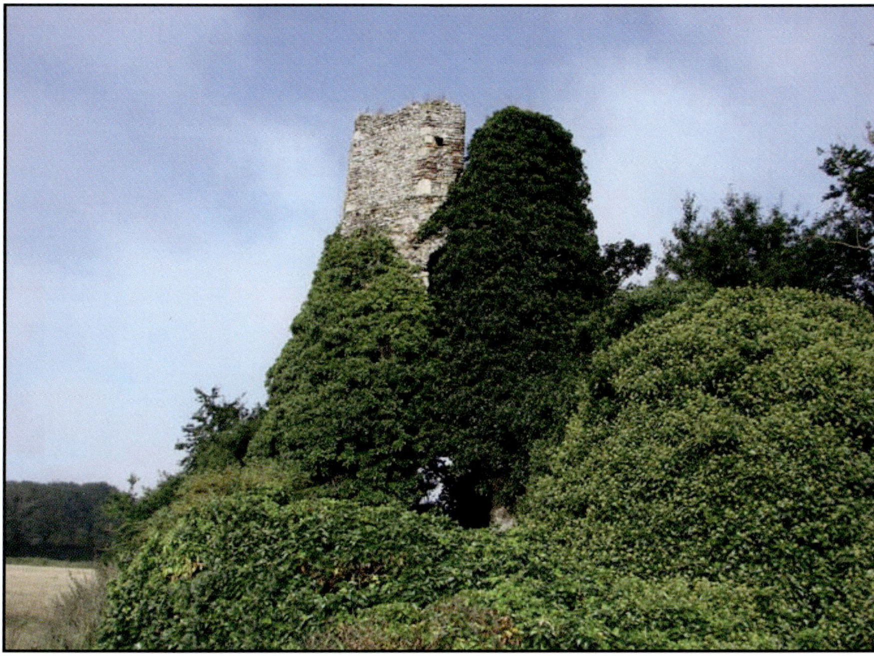

Burgh St Mary ceased to exist when the parish was united with Burgh St Margaret; the conjoined parishes are now part of Fleggburgh. This is a lovely ruin to visit and there are no Health and Safety notices to tell you to keep out. You can explore the ruins to your heart's content. It was built by the Normans and fell into disrepair centuries ago. Little is written or known about the history of the church and why it was abandoned but it was probably due to the remoteness and general decline of the populace. Some of the walls are still standing and the tower still stands almost as tall as it ever was. The bell stage was added about a century after the church was built and probably contained only one bell. This splendid ruin is home to many of our native birds and other wildlife which should not be disturbed.

BURGH ST PETER St Mary

No of Bells:	1
19th c. Deanery:	Brooke
Hundred:	Clavering
Union house:	Heckingham
21st c Deanery:	Loddon
Benefice:	Raveningham

9 miles SE of Loddon. Head in the general direction of Burgh Staithe; the church is close by, at the end of a lane.

O.S. grid ref: TM 493937
Post Code: NR34 0BT

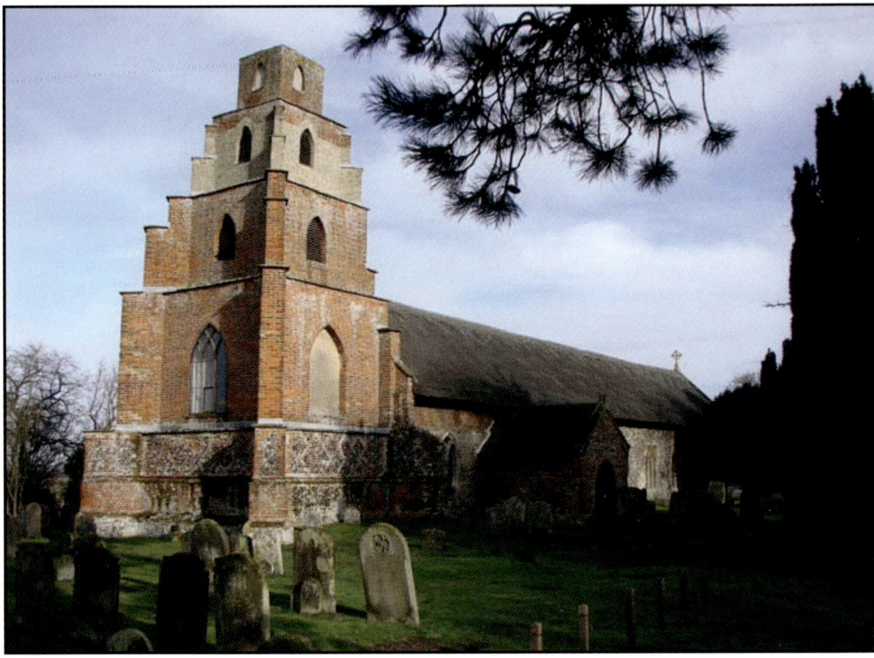

The strange tower the dedication to St Mary while the parish is known as St Peter are two anomalies. An earlier church dedicated to St Peter was here long before St Mary's was built, but the name of St Peter has perpetuated. The tower was constructed by Samuel Boycott whose descendants are entombed in the 16th c. base. Charles Cunningham Boycott, great grandson of the above, gave his name to the term 'to boycott' after trouble in Ireland. The late 14th c. octagonal font is quite uninteresting; the rood screen is 20th c. and a memorial to a past incumbent. The piscina and corresponding sedilia are 600 years earlier. They are in such good condition that they are obviously much restored. There is a good mass or scratch dial adjacent to the priest's door.

BURLINGHAM St Peter
No of Bells: 3
19th c. Deanery: Blofield
Hundred: Blofield
Union house: Lingwood
21st c Deanery: -
In private ownership

8 miles E of Norwich on the old A47 situated in a cottage garden. About 200yds or so east of St Andrew's, Burlingham.
O.S. grid ref: TG 371100
Post Code: NR13 4TA

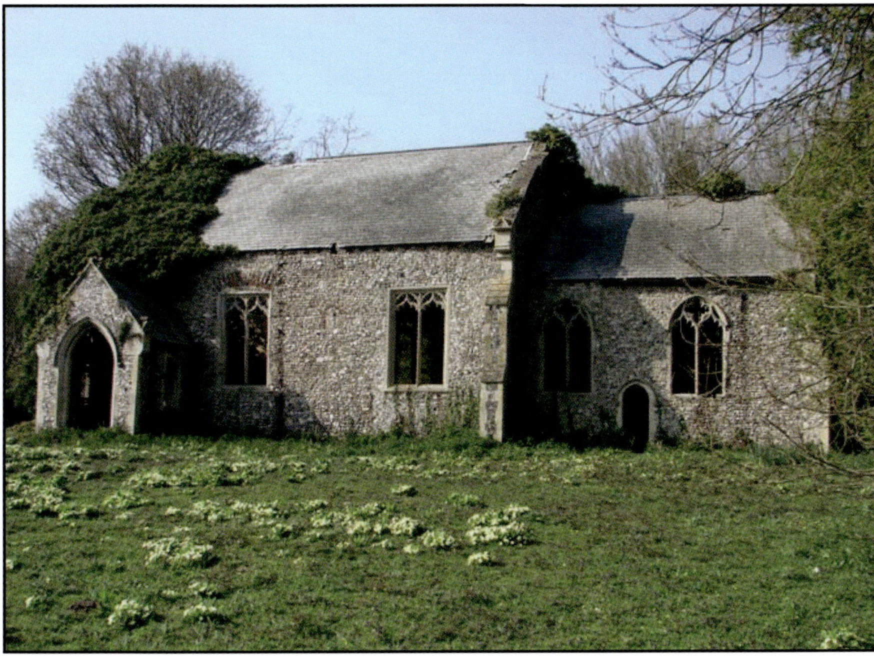

This tiny church has been neglected for many decades; it was once an attractive building with a lovely round tower. The collapse of the round tower in 1906, however, effectively brought about the final closure of the church 30 years later. The chancel arch is offset to the left of the nave but is central to the chancel, the nave being built a foot further to the south. It was probably done intentionally to create a place for the pulpit in a remarkably narrow church. It was refurbished by the Victorians, who removed most of its Norman origins. The font that once occupied the west of the nave was 14th c. Some of the fittings have been removed to St. Andrew's church about 200 yards west of here. The mediaeval benches went to Blofield.
Note: Please seek the owner's permission before viewing.

CAISTER	Holy Trinity
No of Bells:	1
19th c. Deanery:	Flegg
Hundred:	Flegg
Union house:	Rollesby
21st c Deanery:	Great Yarmouth
Benefice:	Caister

2½ miles N of Great Yarmouth, turn off the A1164 at the roundabout to Caister and follow road to the church at traffic lights.
O.S. grid ref: TG 519122
Post Code: NR 30 5JZ

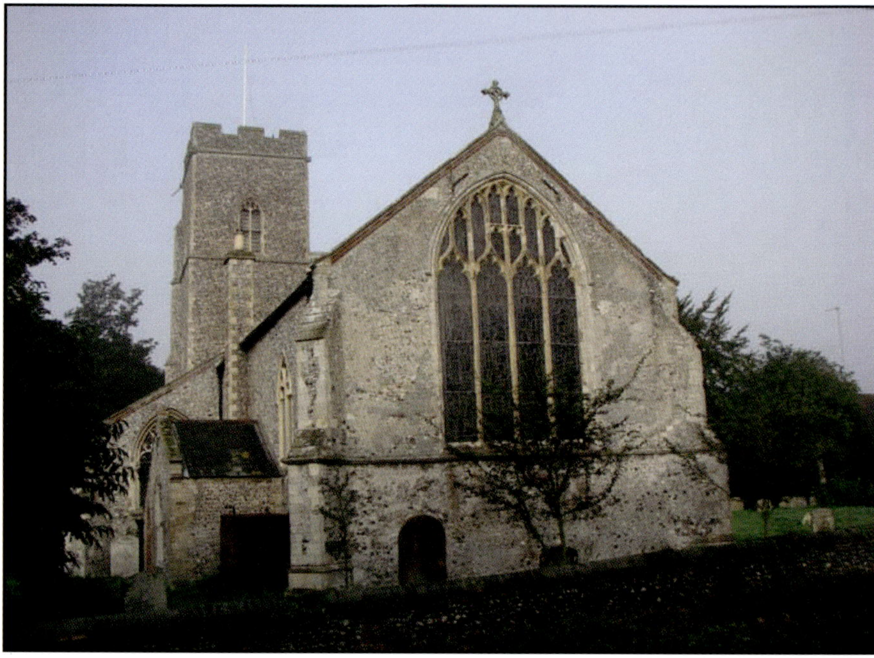

A very standard type of church with the south porch as an entrance into the nave. An impressively enormous octagonal font has a double battlemented rim. The bowl, which has traceried designs, stands on a central shaft surrounded by eight engaged columns. A rood screen in the south aisle leads into the chapel. The arcade forming the south aisle is 14th c. Both the Blennerhassett and Clowes families had a great local influence and were benefactors to the church and parish. Half hidden behind the organ is a wall plaque to Mrs Eliza Blennerhassett and I am told that another memorial is completely hidden. The 15th c. piscina and sedilia have freestanding columns and are quite attractive. Much of what is seen today is the result of Victorian restoration. [*See also West Caister*]

CAISTOR ST EDMUND St Edmund

No of Bells: 3
19th c. Deanery: Brooke
Hundred: Henstead
Union house: Swainsthorpe
21st c Deanery: Loddon
Benefice: Venta

3 miles S of Norwich in the boundaries and overlooking the Roman fort of Venta Icenorum on the road to Stoke Holy Cross.
O.S. grid ref: TG 233034
Post Code: NR14 8QN

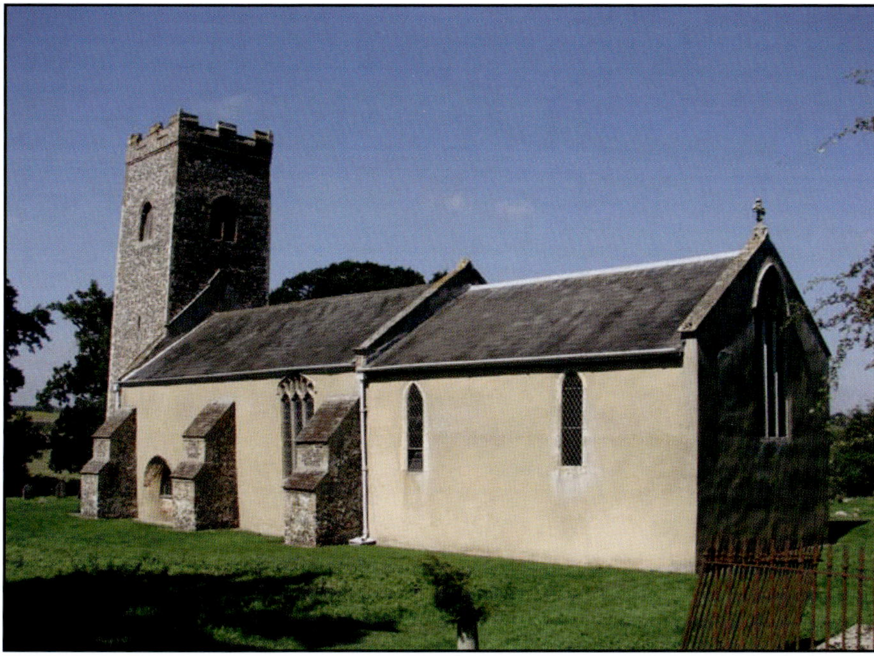

Sitting on a rise overlooking the Roman town of Venta Icenorum this church has been much altered since it was reconstructed in the 13th c. from what was a Saxon church. Initially thatched, the pitch of the roofline has been lowered much to the detriment of its appearance. Most of the building today is 15th c. but the tower is a century earlier. Although I am not a lover of cement-rendering, this is well maintained and quite acceptable. Entry into the nave is by the north porch and through the 13th c. doorway which has large hood-mould stops in the form of the heads of a bishop and king. A traditional East Anglian 15th c. font has four lions around the base of the shaft. A wall painting is so faded that it is almost unrecognisable as St Christopher. From the chancel the buttering of the walls is very noticeable.

CANTLEY	St Margaret
No of Bells:	1
19th c. Deanery:	Blofield
Hundred:	Blofield
Union house:	Lingwood
21st c Deanery:	Blofield
Benefice:	Freethorpe

10 miles SE by E of Norwich. Between Norwich and Acle (A47) turn south onto B1140 at Nth Burlingham to Cantley and follow signs to the church.
O.S. grid ref: TG 382042
Post Code: NR13 3SN

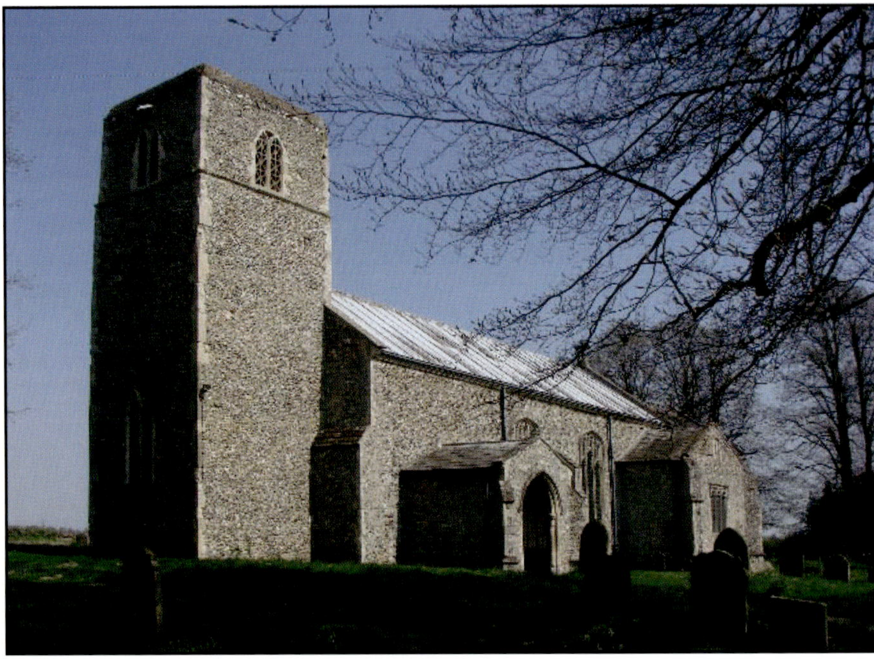

The tower looks strange and unfinished without a parapet, the nave and chancel roofline are as one. Basically the church is 15th c. in the Perpendicular style although traces of an earlier church are here. In the nave stands the font which has the design of the early Norman period but is the wrong shape and not genuine. Once a Lady chapel, the south transept contains a plain piscina. The chancel piscina is almost as plain and is adjacent to the dropped-sill sedilia. The roof is a simple arch-braced type and relatively modern, as is the pulpit with traceried arches around the octagonal design. Most of the bench ends are of the same period and it is difficult to find anything of historical interest here. A few monuments adorn the walls, one to Mrs Rose Wells (1729); another to two brothers, Jonathan and Charles Layton.

CARLETON ST PETER

No of Bells:	4 unusable
19th c. Deanery:	Brooke
Hundred:	Loddon
Union house:	Heckingham
21st c Deanery:	Loddon
Benefice:	Bramerton

8 miles SE of Norwich. Most easily found by going north at the top of the hill on the Loddon side of the A146 at Thurton village.
O.S. grid ref: TG 339022
Post Code: NR14 7BD

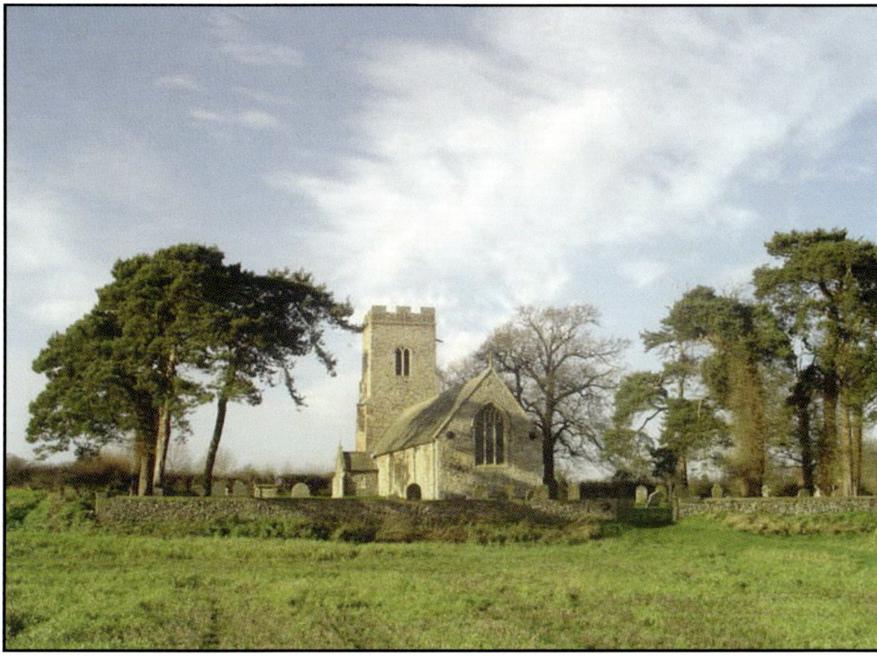

Standing on a rise in the middle of a field this attractive little church is well worth a visit for its tranquillity alone. It is always open, for there is nothing left to steal. This building started its life in the Norman period and has a lovely 13th c. piscina with detached columns. The roof is a continuous and unbroken apex, with no distinction between the nave and chancel. Entry is gained through a mediaeval door with its original ironwork. On the west wall of the tower hang the Hanoverian Arms, now heavily whitewashed. Within the 14th c. screen is most of the original tracery design. The small octagonal font is comparatively recent and of little interest. In the chancel you will find an Easter sepulchre dating from the Elizabethan period with well faded writing in the recess above the slab.

CATFIELD	All Saints
No of Bells:	5
19th c. Deanery:	Waxham
Hundred:	Happing
Union house:	Smallburgh
21st c Deanery:	Waxham & Tunstead
Benefice:	Waterside

14 miles NE of Norwich off the A149. turn off west into Catfield village and generally head south towards Catfield Hall.
O.S. grid ref: TG 382213
Post Code: NR29 5DB

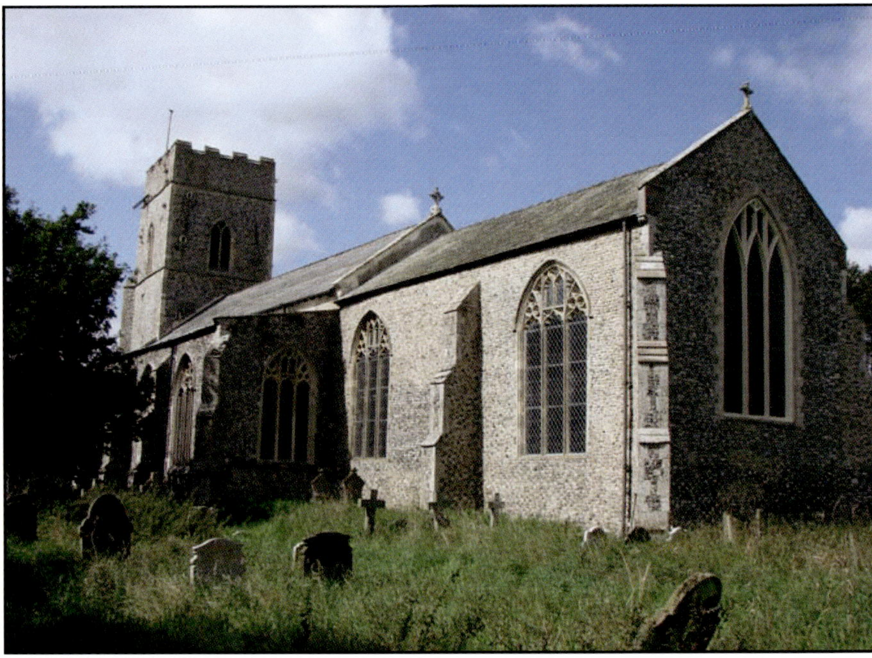

What is obvious from the exterior view is that this church has a large chancel. The early 14th c. tower is older than the church itself, which was rebuilt about 100 years later. The chancel too was rebuilt and completed in 1471. Also added at a later date was the south porch which has a parvise and the stairs leading to the parvise are open to the nave. On the opposite wall, a banner stave locker can be seen. The font is coeval with the nave, the bowl is battlemented and has quatrefoil and floriated tracery designs. The nave arcades have indistinct paintings on both sides. The screen, now minus its rood, has been horribly painted, probably with good intent. Thankfully, the sixteen figures on the panels are quite well preserved. Over the doorway hangs a large painting of the 'Deposition from the Cross'.

CHEDGRAVE All Saints

No of Bells:	1
19th c. Deanery:	Brooke
Hundred:	Loddon
Union house:	Heckingham
21st c Deanery:	Loddon
Benefice:	Chet Valley

9 miles SE of Norwich and 1 mile north of Loddon. In Chedgrave, turn right into Hardley Road. The church is on the right up an incline.
O.S. grid ref: TM 363993
Post Code: NR14 6NQ

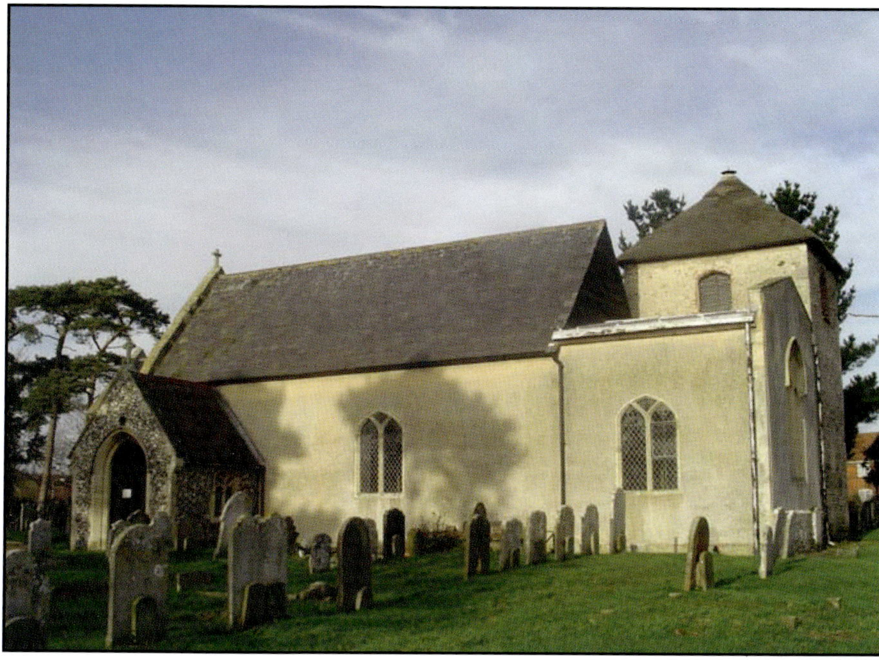

One of the most unusual positions for a tower can be seen here; situated northeast of the nave and north of the chancel. Both north and south doors are 12th c. as is the base of the tower. The south doorway has five orders of decoration and alone is worth a visit here. Above it a lozenge shaped plaque tells the reader that the porch was erected in 1880. Restoration took place here in 1819, the year Queen Victoria was born. Very little of the roof timbers are showing as all have been plastered over, leaving the interior with very little character. The modern pulpit stands only a foot off the floor. Angels holding shields surround the bowl of the slender octagonal font and the shaft is arcaded. The piscina is quite ordinary in comparison. If there ever was a sedilia there is no sign of it now.

CLAXTON	St Andrew
No of Bells:	3 unusable
19th c. Deanery:	Brooke
Hundred:	Loddon
Union house:	Heckingham
21st c Deanery:	Loddon
Benefice:	Bramerton

7 miles SE of Norwich, turn north off the A146 at Thurton and follow the road for 1 mile through Ashby St Mary.

O.S. grid ref: TG 327022
Post Code: NR14 7HY

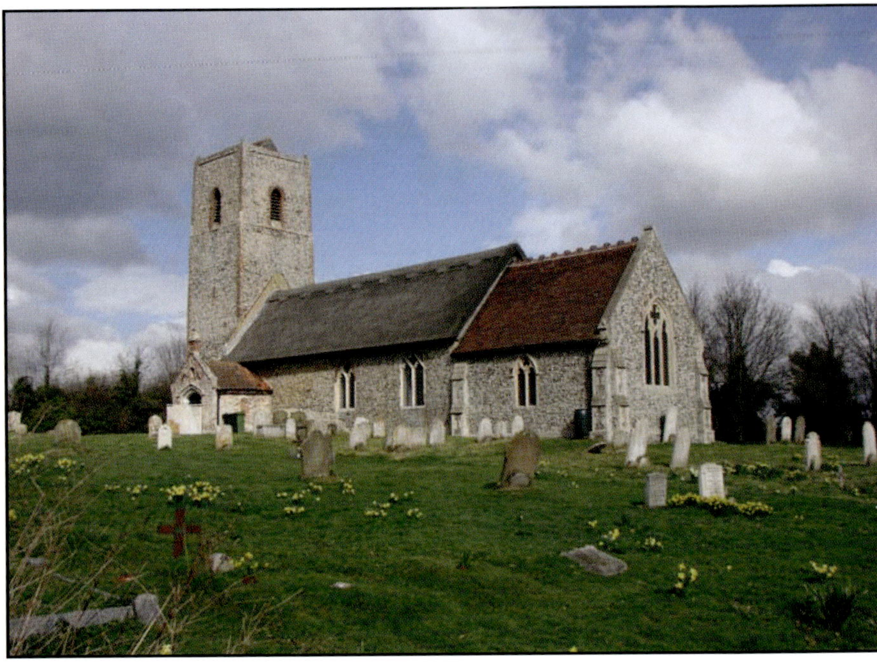

This is an out-of-the-way church set well away from the village which it serves, overlooking a tributary of the River Waveney. The nave is thatched and the chancel tiled. On the top of the west tower is what looks like a shed but is in fact the exit onto the roof. The Tudor brick-built porch has a niche over the entrance. Inside the church on the right is a niche for holy water and on the north wall is a series of blind arches through which once was a north aisle. The octagonal font is a typical East Anglian type from about the 15th c. The Royal Arms are George I and are dated 1715. In the chancel is a lovely 13th c. double piscina with a central column supporting two trefoiled arches. On the opposite wall is a memorial to Henry Goudy who died in 1620. The church also possesses a Bible dated 1617.

CLIPPESBY	St Peter
No of Bells:	1
19th c. Deanery:	Flegg
21st c Deanery:	Great Yarmouth
Hundred:	West Flegg
Union house:	Rollesby
Benefice:	Flegg

9 miles NW of Gt. Yarmouth. From the A1152 heading north, a few hundred yards north of the blue Clippesby Holidays sign, turn west.
O.S. grid ref: TG 428145
Post Code: NR29 3BJ

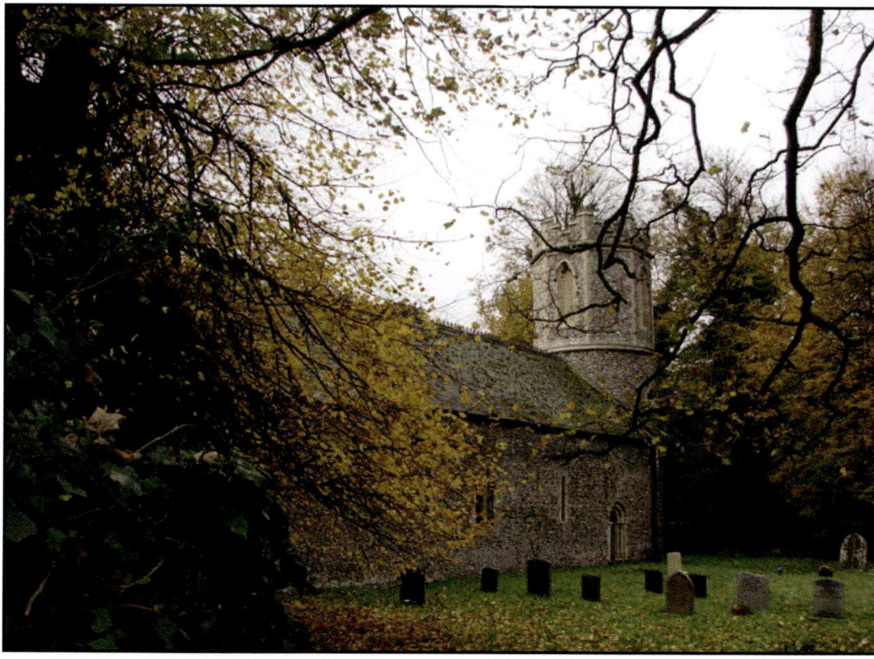

This lovely little Norman church is set well off the road and is hidden from it. The relatively modern octagonal belfry stage is immediately apparent. The north door is 13th c. and has an engaged column either side and three orders of moulding. It was restored in the 19th c. and is now sealed. Either side of the porch doorway is a small mass dial and above your head inside the reconstructed arch is more carved Norman stone. The octagonal font is very shallow and angels support the bowl from below. The 13th c. piscina is flanked by a dropped sill sedilia. There are beautifully carved benches with birds, animals and saintly figures. Some notable windows are to be seen here, one by Margaret Rope of Blaxhall. Monuments are chiefly to the Muskett family and there are nice floor brasses to John Clippesby and Thomas Pallyng.

COLTISHALL	St John the Baptist
No of Bells:	6
19th c. Deanery:	Ingworth
Hundred:	South Erpingham
Union house:	Aylsham
21st c Deanery:	Ingworth
Benefice:	Coltishall

7 miles NE of Norwich, take the B1150 then turn right at Horstead onto the B1354. The church is on the south side of the road.

O.S. grid ref: TG 272198
Post Code: NR12 7DJ

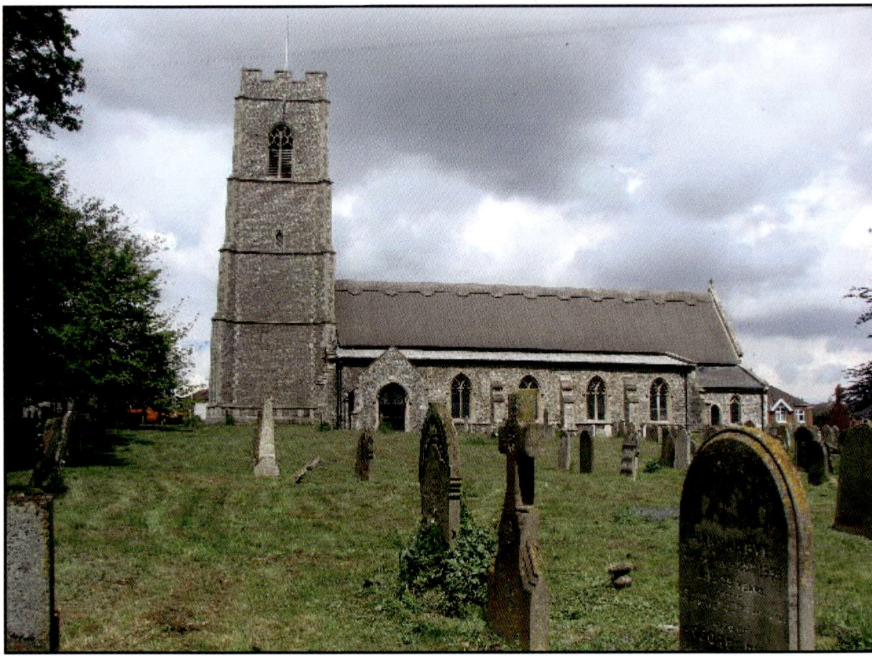

A pleasant entirely thatched church close to the road with a large well kept graveyard to the south. Around the base of the tower is a band of flushwork with shields and chalices, representative of St John. The unused north porch has labels above the windows with dog's heads as dripstones. Entry is gained through the west door. The square 12th c. Norman font is arcaded and supported on four columns around a central shaft. Its cover is an elaborate ogee design and is nicely coloured. Above, the roof of the nave is entirely plastered and barren of embellishment. Set into the north wall of the nave are two small round Saxon windows, the large one the more recent. The intricately traceried 15th c. screen has been restored and is looking very fresh and Victorian, and matches the carved reredos.

CROMER	St Peter & St Paul
No of Bells:	6
19th c. Deanery:	Repps
Hundred:	North Erpingham
Union house:	Sheringham
21st c Deanery:	Repps
Benefice:	Cromer

22 miles N of Norwich and 4 miles east of Sheringham on the coast. Situated in the centre of Cromer, large and imposing.
O.S. grid ref: TG 220423
Post Code: NR27 9HA

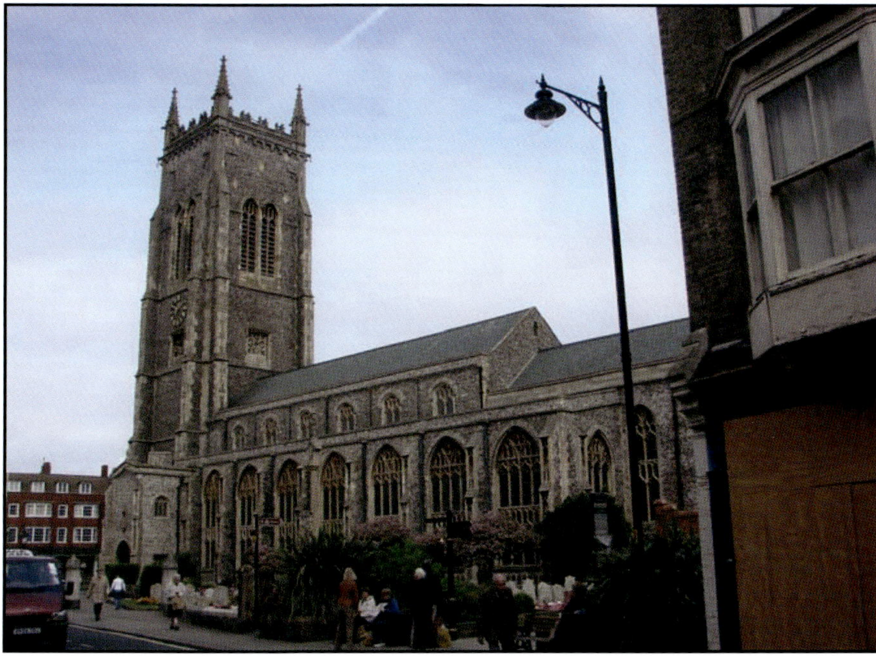

This lovely 15th c. church is right in the centre of town and always open during the day. I shall be brief. Note unusual decoration on the parapet of the tower. Every buttress has a niche with stool and canopy. The groined south porch has a parvise. Bar slots to south door. A fine carved Caen-stone font is a copy of the one at Yaxham. The tall 15th c. arcades are quite impressive. Most of the furnishings and fittings in the church are Victorian and very little of the old remains. In essence it is really a 19th c. church in a 15th c. shell. The chancel was almost completely rebuilt in 1889. The wall plates of the Victorian hammerbeam roof are supported on carved corbels. The Hanoverian Royal Arms hang on the north wall. The many and various windows are probably the church's most redeeming feature.

CROSTWICK	St Peter	4½ miles NNE of Norwich.
No of Bells:	1	From Norwich take the
19th c. Deanery:	Taverham	A1151 Coltishall Road, at 3
Hundred:	Taverham	miles turn right opposite the
Union house:	Horsham St Faith	Old Rectory Hotel.
21st c Deanery:	Norwich North	O.S. grid ref: TG 257159
Benefice:	Horsham	Post Code: NR12 7BG

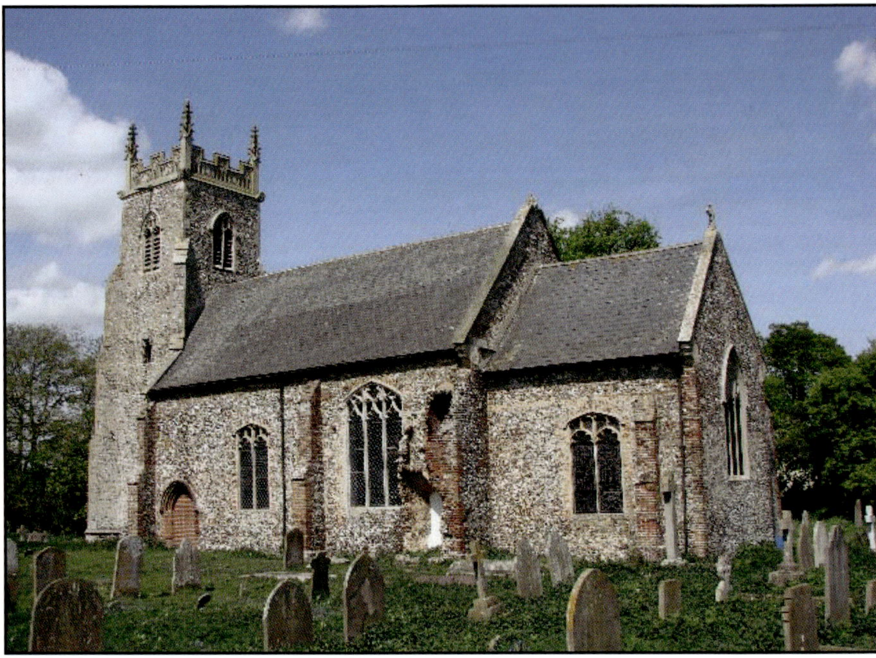

On the south side of the church is the collapsed rood loft turret, revealing the stairs within. The 15th c. tower has a 1998 parapet and part of the old one lies inside, beneath the tower. The font is of the 19th c. with carved figures on the bowl and shaft. There are seats beneath the windows, from when the congregation used to face inwards. The chancel roof is original but that of the nave has been replaced. A wall painting of St Christopher has seen better days. Benches were replaced by the Victorian restorers and lozenge-shaped ends are carved with faces, birds and foliage; the pulpit, reading desk and screen are all of the same period. At the same time the chancel was panelled and the simple piscina incorporated into the panels but the sedilia was eliminated. On the tower arch are the faces of bears.

CROSTWIGHT All Saints

No of Bells: 1
19th c. Deanery: Waxham
Hundred: Tunstead
Union house: Smallburgh
21st c Deanery: Norwich North
Benefice: Horsham

4 miles E of North Walsham. From Horning head north up Hall Road. ¼ m. after the Broom Lane crossroads turn right.
O.S. grid ref: TG 334300
Post Code: NR28 9UD

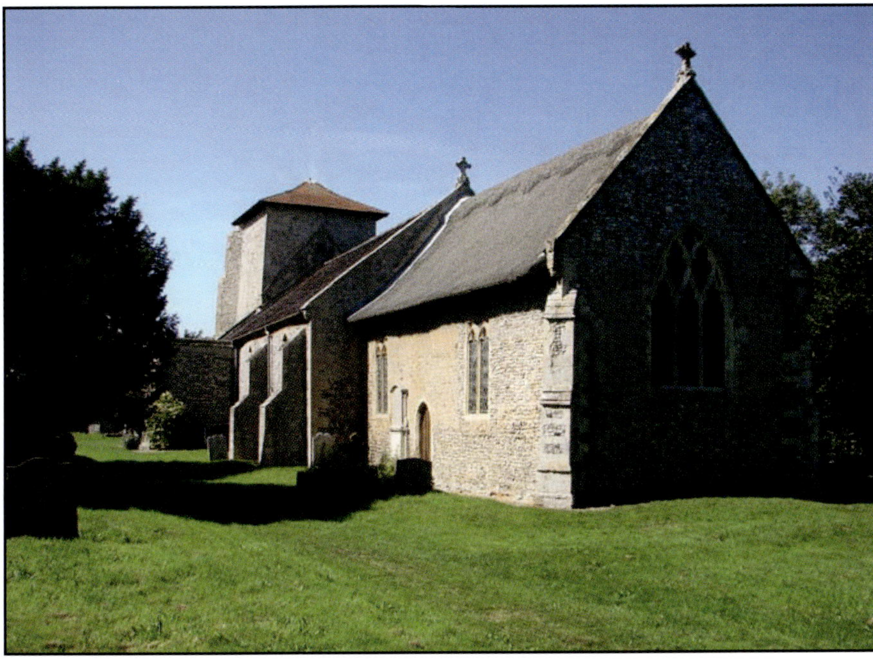

Do not confuse Crostwight with Crostwick near Norwich. Known locally as the Chinese church, there is a strange oriental-looking pyramidal cap to the tower which lost its upper story many years ago. The chancel is thatched. In the porch is a stoup-niche. A lovely 13th c. purbeck font is supported on eight columns around a central shaft. The wall of the nave has a significant wall painting divided into panels, depicting the life of Christ from his entry into Jerusalem to the Resurrection. Now faded and difficult to interpret, it was uncovered during Victorian restorations. The square-headed rood screen with tracery and minute detail in the spandrels is un-painted but is undoubtedly the work of a craftsman. The roof is a simple scissor frame construction, now plastered. Well worth a visit.

DENTON	St Mary	3½ miles W of Bungay.
No of Bells:	3	Leave Bungay on the A143,
19th c. Deanery:	Redenhall	after 2½ miles turn right
Hundred:	Earsham	and follow the road until
Union house:	Pulham St Mary	you come to the church.
21st c Deanery:	Redenhall	O.S. grid ref: TM 286873
Benefice:	Ditchingham (Earsham)	Post Code: IP20 0AD

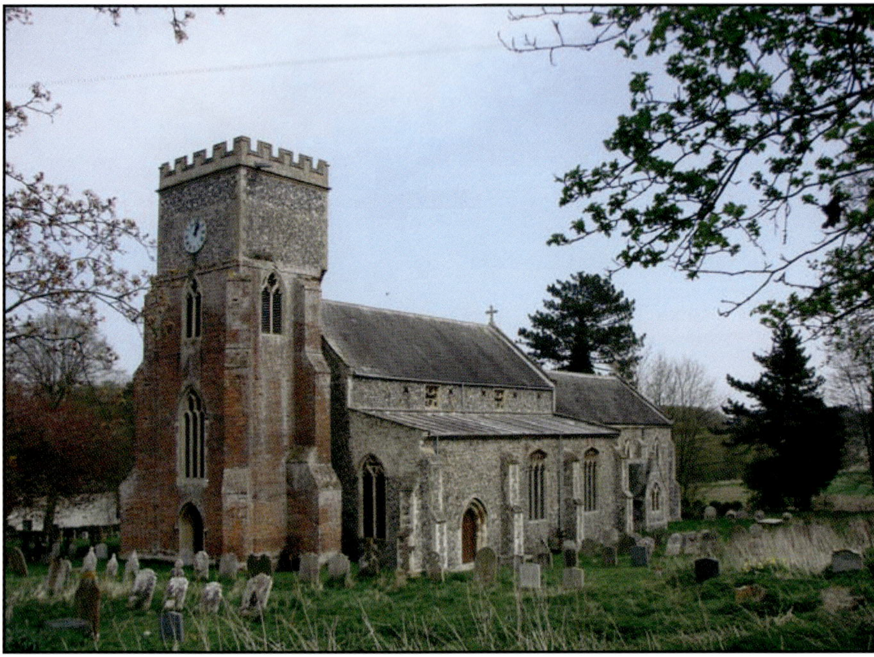

This church originally had a round tower, part of which can still be seen above the nave roofline. The tower was raised by ten feet in 1843, a clock installed and the embattlements added. The porch roof is vaulted with emblematic bosses at the intersections; there is a parvise above. There is quite a plain 15th c. font, except for the shields in quatrefoils around the bowl. The nave, north and south aisles all have arch-braced roofs; the former is plain, but with traceried spandrils in the two latter. The Jacobean pulpit has linen-fold carving on the lower panels. The piscina is very attractive with nice carving and a corbelled bowl. Adjacent to it is a sedile and dropped-sill sedilia beside that. There a two sets of Royal Arms, George III on canvas, and those of Queen Victoria are cast in plaster.

DILHAM St Nicholas

No of Bells:	1
19th c. Deanery:	Waxham
Hundred:	Tunstead
Union house:	Smallburgh
21st c Deanery:	Waxham & Tunstead
Benefice:	Smallburgh

5 miles SSE of North Walsham. From the A149 south of the village, take the road leading south and follow.

O.S. grid ref: TG 323259

Post Code: NR5 0EJ

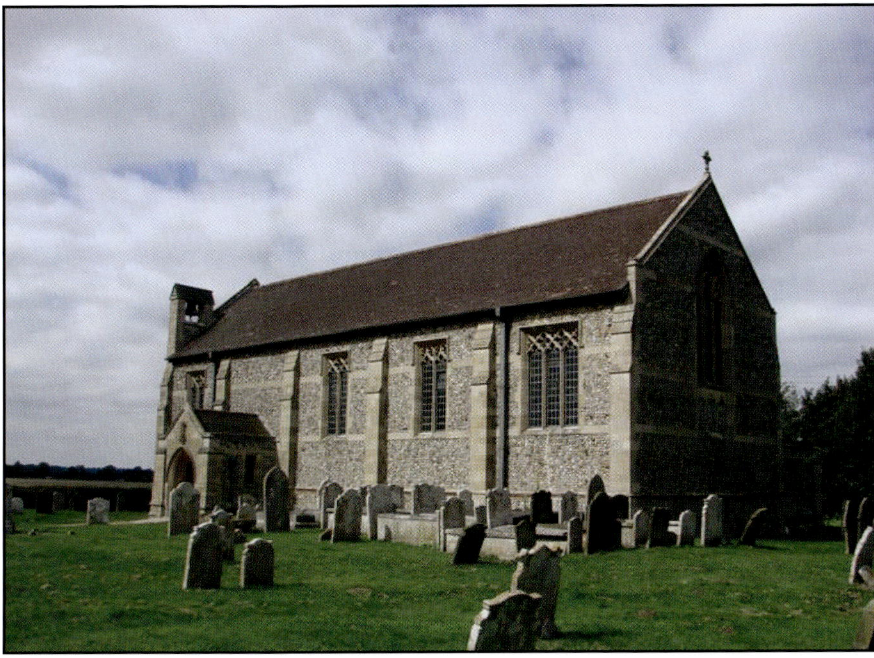

The round tower, which was originally embattled, was rebuilt in the mid-1820s using materials from an earlier one. Then, in 1931, the whole church was rebuilt and the top of the tower was demolished and a baptistery created beneath. Today, looking very much like a barn, it is no different inside apart from the fixtures and fittings. Only the 15th c. font stands witness to the date and history of this building. In the nave, a sheet of lead retrieved from the original roof has been made into a plaque telling the history of the church in Latin. The seating, pulpit and everything else in the church is modern but that does not seem to matter here. The church is well used and vibrant. It seems a pity that it looks so much like a barn from the outside. Being without a tower, its true identity is only revealed by the bell turret.

DITCHINGHAM St Mary
No of Bells: 8
19th c. Deanery: Brooke
Hundred: Loddon
Union house: Heckingham
21st c Deanery: Redenhall
Benefice: Ditchingham (Earsham)

2 miles N of Bungay. At the bottom end of Church Lane or Belsey Bridge Road off the B1332. Not far from All Hallows Convent.
O.S. grid ref: TM 329922
Post Code: NR35 2JS

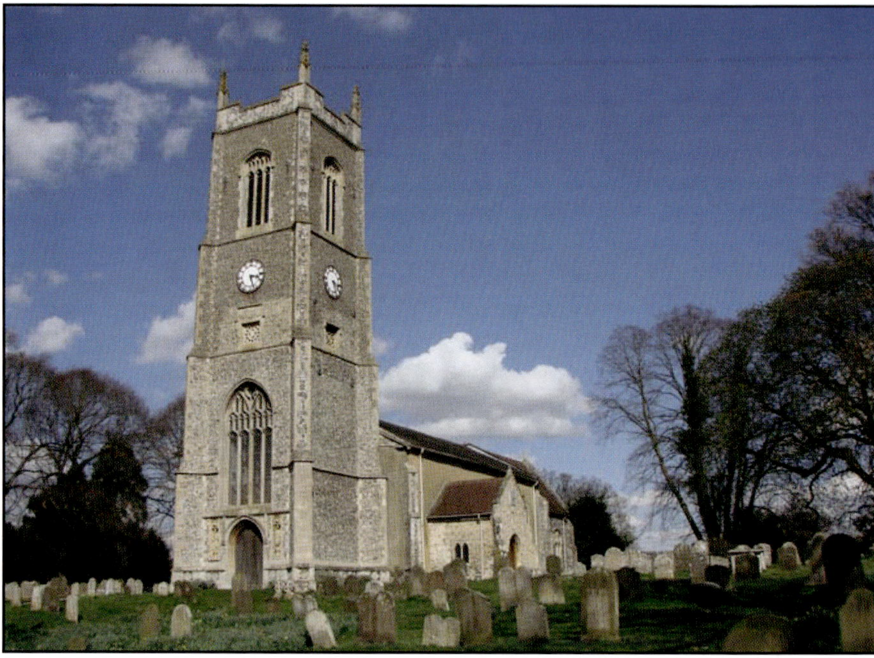

This massive tower, which dominates the church, has large niches either side of the west door and the base course has the Sacred Heart design. To the north is a vestry with a flint-clad chimney. Immediately in front of you as you enter is the War Memorial designed by Derwent Wood R.A. It is most unusual and beautiful. The 15th c. octagonal font has a traceried bowl and stands on a shaft with eight engaged columns on a quatrefoil base. A window in the north aisle is a memorial to Sir Rider Haggard who lived in Ditchingham. The chancel ceiling was entirely painted in 1862/3 by the hand of Albina Scudamore, wife of the rector at the time. A Victorian pulpit, its support and steps are made wholly from stone and is very unattractive, almost offensive in these surroundings.

EARSHAM All Saints
No of Bells: 3
19th c. Deanery: Redenhall
Hundred: Earsham
Union house: Pulham St Mary
21st c Deanery: Redenhall
Benefice: Ditchingham (Earsham)

1 mile W of Bungay near Earsham Mill. Turn off the A143 signposted Earsham Mill and follow into the village before turning south.
O.S. grid ref: TM 326888
Post Code: NR35 2TJ

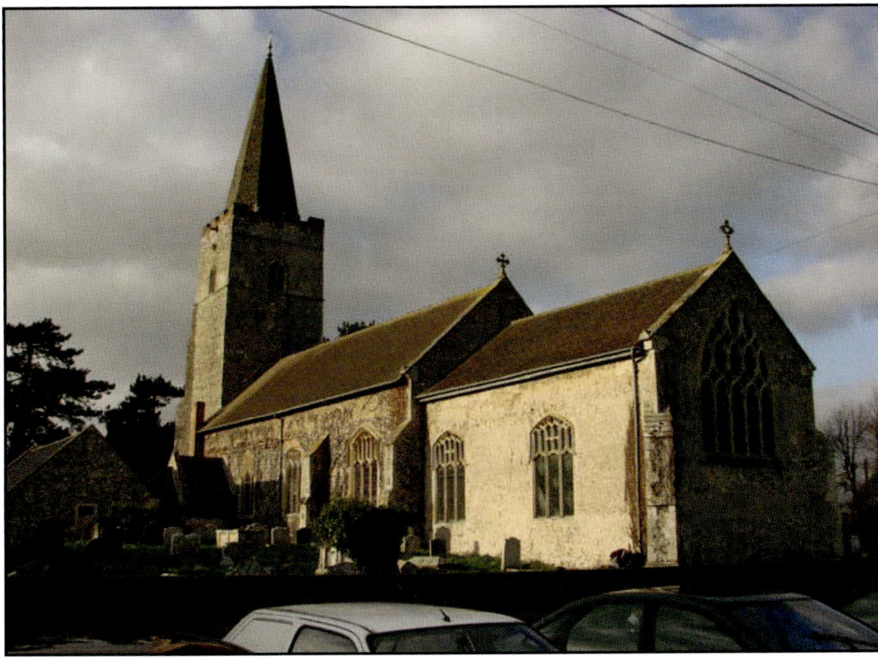

The 14th c. tower has an elegant wooden spire, which enhances the general appearance of the church. The south side is disappointingly drab. The Seven Sacraments font suffered at the hands of the Puritans but the panels are fairly intact. At one time, I believe, the nave roof was hammerbeam construction but is now quite ordinary. In the chancel, the single hammerbeam roof remains. Eight wooden columns support the pulpit, which is well decorated with traceried panels. The piscina has a traceried arch with a detached column between it and the split-level sedilia. On the walls of both nave and chancel are a number of wall-plaques, some to the Dalling family. The Hanoverian Arms are generous in proportion. The thing that will probably catch your eye is the beautifully decorated reredos; alone making a visit worthwhile.

EAST RUSTON St Mary
No of Bells: 1
19th c. Deanery: Waxham
Hundred: Happing
Union house: Smallburgh
21st c Deanery: Waxham & Tunstead
The Churches Conservation Trust

6 miles ESE of North Walsham. On the B1159, almost 2 miles east of the village standing on the brow of a hill.
O.S. grid ref: TG 364287
Post Code: NR12 9HR *

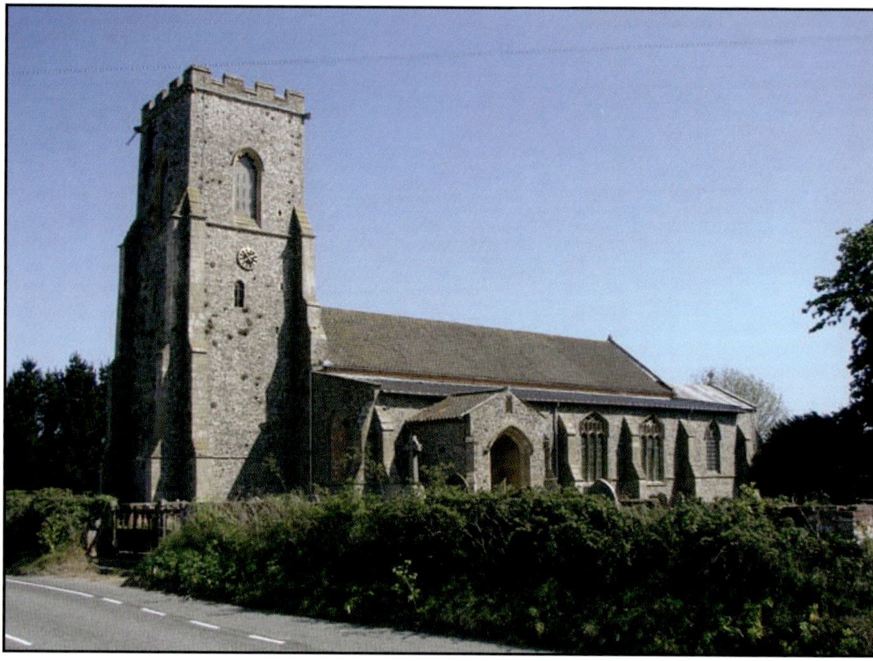

[From the postcode given go to the B1159 and then south ½ mile]
Sometimes called Riston. The church is basically 14th c. with arcades of that date in the nave. There was once a north aisle but it was demolished in the 19th c. and replaced with a brick wall. The octagonal font is most unusual with figures around the bowl and the corbel. On the shaft are ogee arches, below which are grotesque faces on the base. The upper section of the screen is virtually bereft of tracery but the treasure here is the lower portion. Eight painted panels, the four on the north depict the four evangelists, and to the south the Latin Doctors. The condition of the paintings is remarkable considering they were painted in the 15th c. The church is normally locked, unusual for a CCT church, but the key is not too far away.

EAST SOMERTON St Mary

No of Bells: -
19th c. Deanery: Flegg
Hundred: West Flegg
Union house: Rollesby
21st c Deanery: -
Benefice: -

8 miles N by W of Great Yarmouth, from Winterton Road turn right into Manor Farm Lane, turn left and park 25 yds on. Walk left.
O.S. grid ref: TG 480196
Post Code: NR29 4DZ

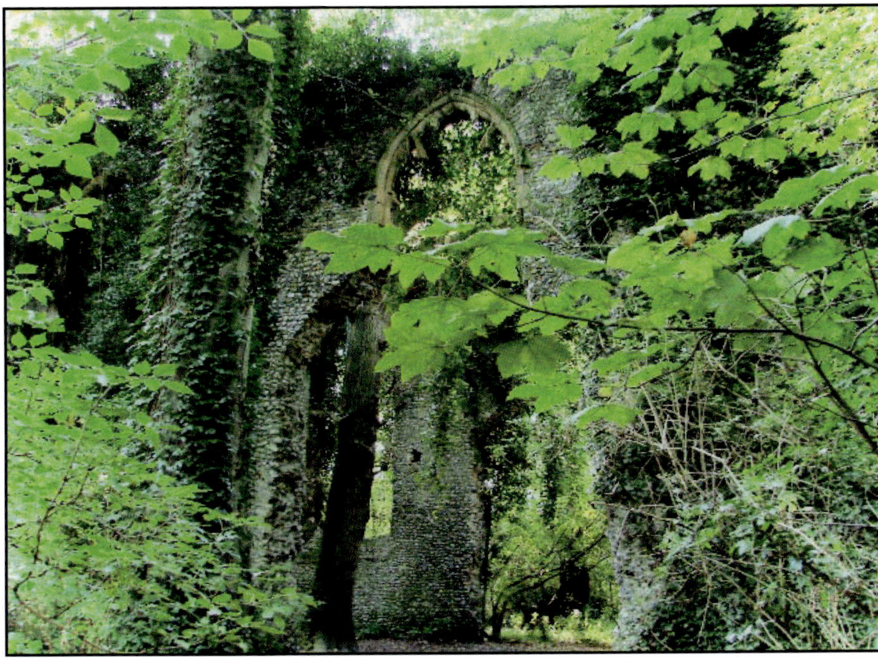

What can one say about East Somerton ruin? It is gracious and sits amid the trees retaining its elegance and beauty even in decay. Ivy climbs the flint walls and trees have sprung up in the nave, pigeons and jackdaws nest in the tower. It was about the time of the Commonwealth that the church ceased to exist as such. Surprisingly the parish was consolidated with Winterton and not West Somerton after the church fell into disuse, but was used for a short period as a chapel of ease. It is open to visit with not a locked door or fence anywhere in sight. It is a beautiful place to have a picnic after visiting West Somerton less than a mile away. Most of the headstones and other memorials have gone but those at rest here are surrounded by the beauty of an English woodland.

EATON	Christchurch
No of Bells:	1
19th c. Deanery:	Norwich South
Hundred:	Norwich
Union house:	Norwich
21st c Deanery:	Norwich South
Benefice:	Eaton Christchurch

1 m SW of Norwich Castle. Easily reached from the Mile End Road,. the A140. Turn towards Norwich City Centre into Church Avenue.
O.S. grid ref: TG 216073
Post Code: NR2 2AQ

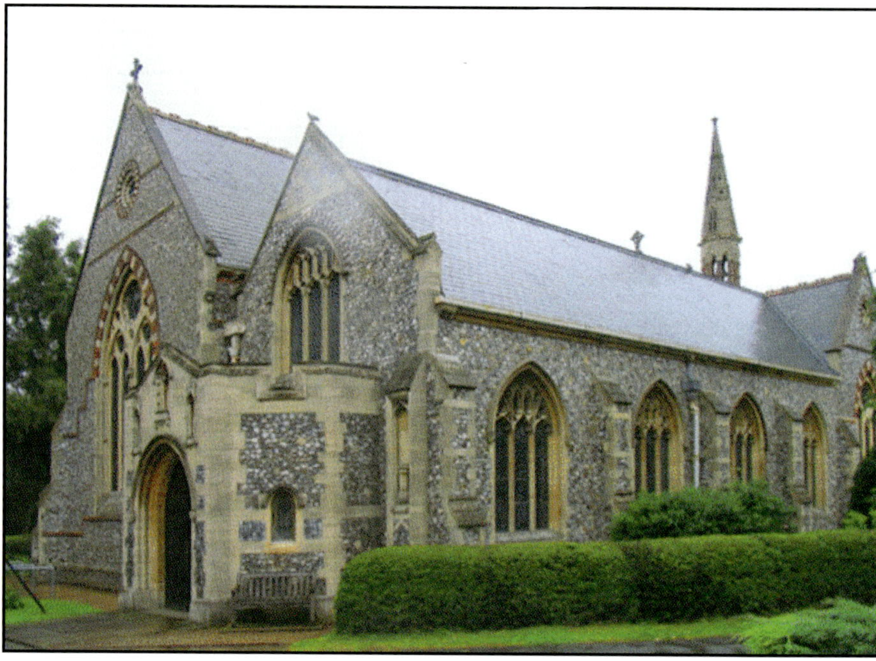

The church was erected in 1872 as a Chapel of Ease for St Andrew's Eaton in the Gothic Revival style. But in 2000 was consecrated as a Church in its own right. The small but highly decorated and traceried spirelet at the east end of the nave contains one bell. Just inside the porch there is a small window containing some good fragments of 15th c. glass. The circular Victorian font has simple decoration and stands on four slender columns and a thick central shaft. The arcades are decorated with jagged dragon-tooth decoration. A small window above the chancel arch does little to illuminate the rood or the scissor-beam roof trusses. All the furnishings and fittings are obviously Victorian and there is little to interest the historian, however, it is a very active and well attended church.

EATON	St Andrew	2 miles SW of Norwich city centre in Church Lane, Eaton just off the A11, Newmarket Road. Standing back off the road.
No of Bells:	3	
19th c. Deanery:	Norwich South	
Hundred:	Norwich	
Union house:	Norwich	
21st c Deanery:	Norwich South	O.S. grid ref: TG 202059
Benefice:	Eaton Christchurch	Post Code: NR4 6NH

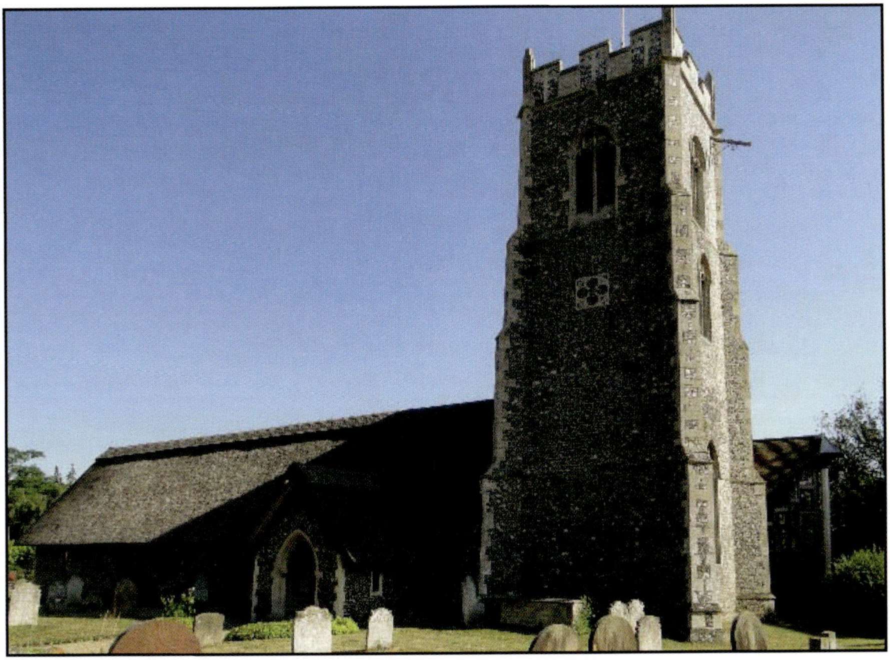

Entering the churchyard through the lychgate one encounters a more tranquil world away from the traffic. The church that greets your eye is quite unexpected in this setting on the edge of a large city and although it is not ancient, its origins are Norman. The building is entirely thatched and the tall embattled tower stands guard. Entry is gained through the north door and in the wall on the left is set a small stoup in a plainly arched niche. Inside you will find most of the fittings including the screen are modern as are the roofs. The font is a minimal octagonal from top to bottom with simple design around the bowl. The oldest thing to be seen is the pillar piscina which is late 13th c. and has a carved cap. The Holy table is Stuart dynasty and the Royal Arms are those of George III.

EDINGTHORPE All Saints

No of Bells:	3
19th c. Deanery:	Waxham
Hundred:	Tunstead
Union house:	Smallburgh
21st c Deanery:	Waxham & Tunstead
Benefice:	Coastal

3 miles NE of North Walsham on the Bacton road. After 2 miles at x-roads turn left, then 2nd right, the church is on the left.

O.S. grid ref: TG 309321

Post Code: NR28 9TN

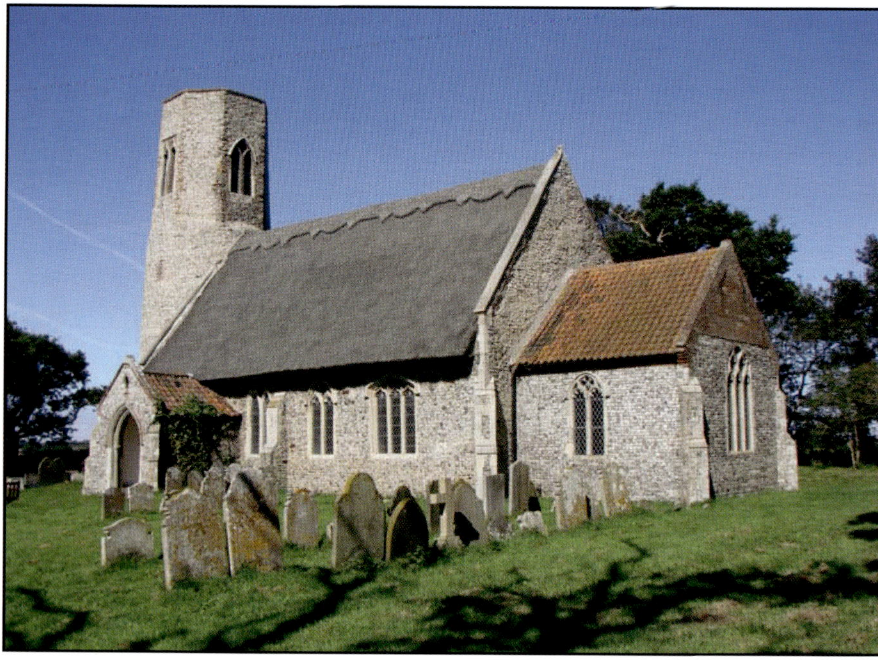

A lovely little country church, which is still partially thatched with an octagonal top on the otherwise Norman round tower. The north doorway is 12th c. Unfortunately, the roof of the nave has lost all character by being boarded and painted white, but the old tie-beams remain. That is unimportant compared with the other points of interest. The splendid 14th c. octagonal font bowl is decorated with quatrefoils and the shaft with double arcades. Some wall paintings are quite fragmented: they depict St Christopher and the Seven Deadly Sins. Wheel tracery in the screen is most uncommon and six panels in the base of the 14th c. screen are faded but the subjects can still be identified. Above the stairs of the rood loft is a painted niche with an unusual carved stool on which a figure would have stood.

ELLINGHAM St Mary
No of Bells: 5
19th c. Deanery: Brooke
Hundred: Clavering
Union house: Heckingham
21st c Deanery: Loddon
Benefice: Geldeston

4 miles S of Loddon south of the A143, quite close to Ellingham Water Mill on the Norfolk / Suffolk border.
O.S. grid ref: TM 366918
Post Code: NR35 2EP

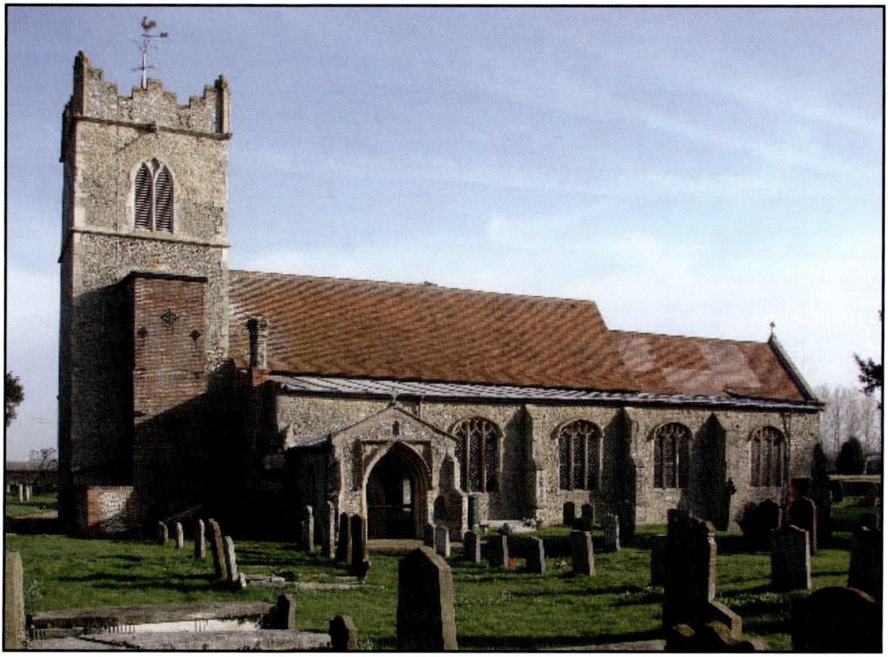

Built in the 13th c., this well buttressed church overlooks the River Waveney on the southern border with Suffolk. On the south of the slightly later tower is a 19th c. staircase to the belfry, built of brick. The porch, which has a niche for a stoup, is mediaeval, while the benches and box pews are Victorian and quite plain. The north wall is a mismatch of arches suggesting perhaps that there has been significant rebuilding at some time in the church's history. The 14th c. octagonal font has engaged columns supporting the bowl. On the west wall are the Royal Arms of George I dated 1721. An early carving of a bishop can be seen on the north wall; this is probably contemporary with the construction of the church and may be of the bishop who consecrated the church in the 1200s.

FELMINGHAM St Andrew

No of Bells:	9
19th c. Deanery:	Waxham
Hundred:	Tunstead
Union house:	Smallburgh
21st c Deanery:	Waxham & Tunstead
Benefice:	Coastal

2 miles WSW of North Walsham on the B1145 towards Aylsham on the left hand side at a sharp right-hand bend in the road.

O.S. grid ref: TG 252293

Post Code: NR28 0LQ

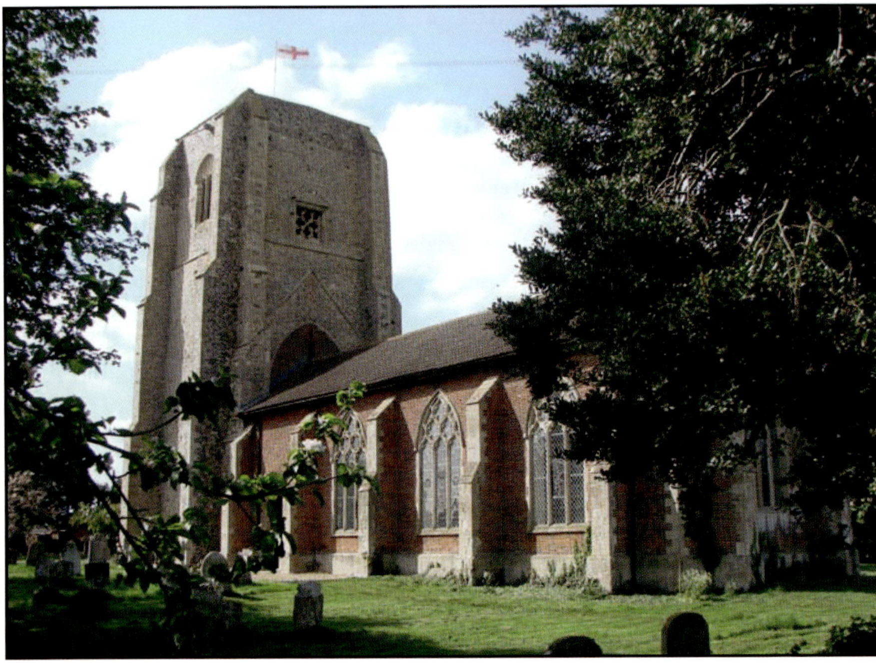

There was a fire in 1742 that destroyed the old church, which was much larger than the brick-built church we see today. I believe also that the truncated tower was planned to be at least one section higher. The old roofline can still be clearly seen on the east face. The 14th c. south door has been retained. Inside, the nave and chancel are as one with new roofs that cut badly into the magnificence of the tower arch. The splendid 13th c. purbeck font stands on an oversized 14th c. pedestal. In the chancel is a wonderful iron-bound parish chest which is used as a credence table. Some tracery, perhaps from the old rood screen, has been incorporated into the Victorian pulpit below the book rest. On the south wall, west of the door, are some old brasses salvaged from the floor and other monuments, most in bad Latin.

FILBY All Saints
No of Bells: 5
19th c. Deanery: Flegg
Hundred: East Flegg
Union house: Rollesby
21st c Deanery: Great Yarmouth
Benefice: Flegg (South Trinity Broads)

6 miles NW of Great Yarmouth on the A1064. In the centre of the village take a left turn, signposted 'CHURCH'.
O.S. grid ref: TG 468132
Post Code: NR29 3HW

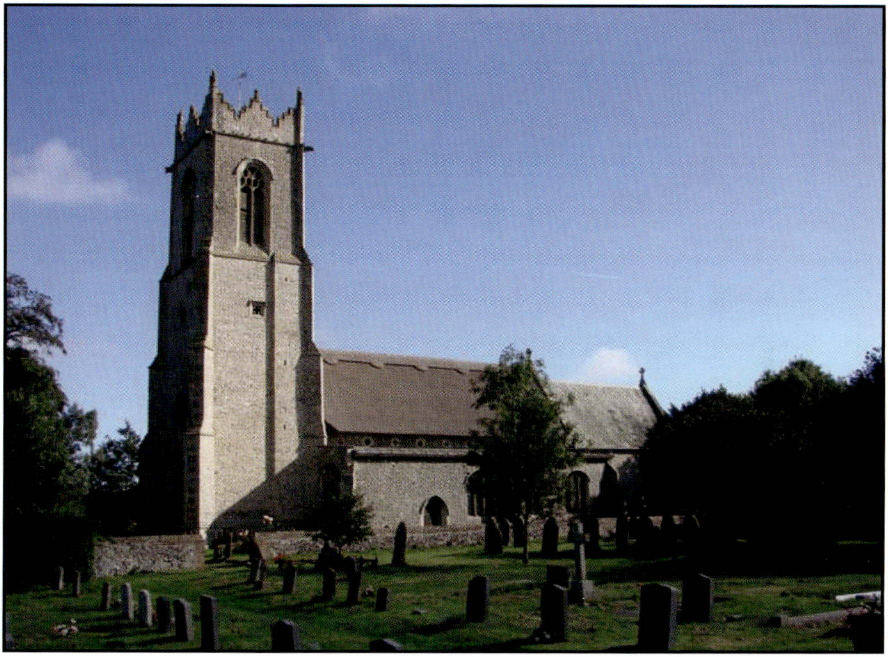

This church is elegant! The 15th c. tower stands dominant with its flush-panelled parapet looking like a crown. The figures at each corner are the Four Doctors. Around the foot is a flush-panelled base course. As you open the door, you hold the ring handle that was made in the 14th c. In front of you is the 13th c. octagonal font with shallow arcading around the bowl, which is supported by a central shaft and eight columns. Notice too the ancient iron-clad door to the tower with its seven locks. The 15th c. screen retains most of its colour and the Saints are easily recognised. Immediately in front of the screen is the 16th c. hexagonal pulpit. Like Spexhall in Suffolk, there are a few agricultural implements on display. Monuments to a former rector and other members of the Lucas family adorn the wall of the nave.

FISHLEY	St Mary	7½ miles WNW of Great Yarmouth. From Acle take the Sth Walsham road. The church can be seen on the right within ¼ of a mile.
No of Bells:	1	
19th c. Deanery:	Blofield	
Hundred:	Walsham	
Union house:	Acle	
21st c Deanery:	Blofield	O.S. grid ref: TG 398115
Benefice:	Acle	Post Code: NR13 6DA

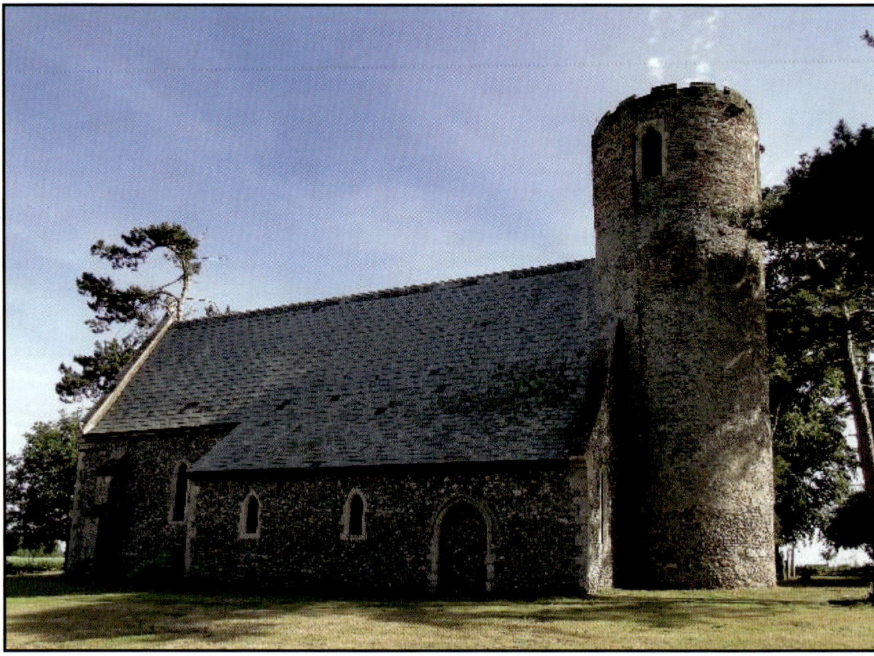

There is a lane signposted Fishley near the Hugh Crane complex. The church is at the top of the lane. This charming little Norman church is unrecognisable to the way it looked before 1861. The tower was then raised by ten feet with Tudor bricks and windows from the bottom were put in at the top and the holes bricked up. The pitch of the roofs were steepened and retiled. The church has never been thatched, as the pitch was originally too shallow. The Norman doorway is a very simple one and the windows are Early English. The font is unlike any I have seen before, resembling the top of an ice cream cone with rope decoration. It stands on a central column and four marble pillars. Beside it is a 'poor box' constructed from what was probably an old beam from the belfry. Only open on Fridays 10 am until 4 pm.

FRAMLINGHAM EARL St Andrew

No of Bells:	1
19th c. Deanery:	Brooke
Hundred:	Henstead
Union house:	Swainsthorpe
21st c Deanery:	Loddon
Benefice:	Poringland

4 miles SE of Norwich.
From Norwich on the A146 turn right at 'The Gull' P.H. Keep left, then 1 mile until you reach the T junction.
O.S. grid ref: TG 277027
Post Code: NR14 7SD

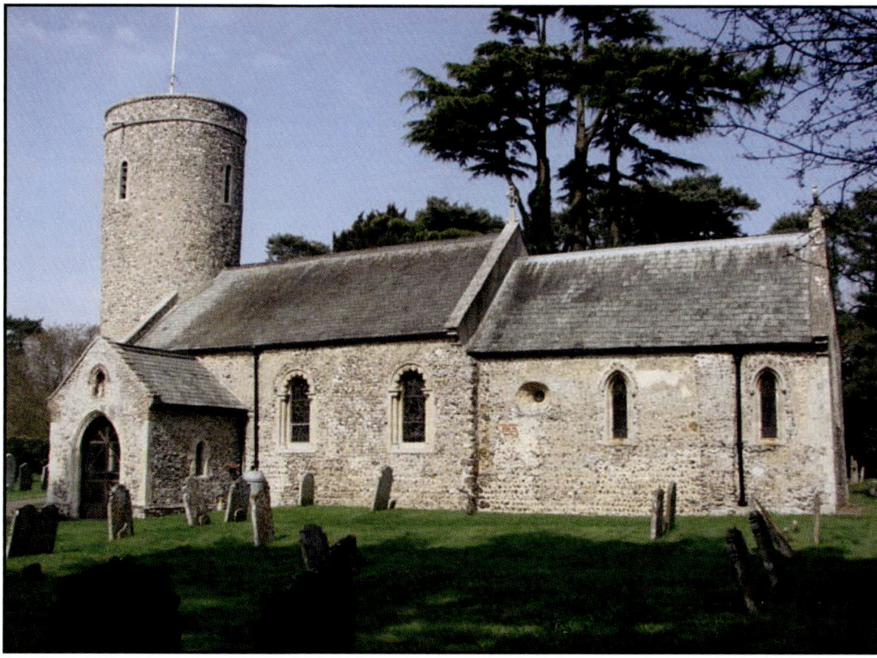

This very early Norman church on Saxon foundations has had some restoration but has retained the original design. The north doorway is rich in decoration, the south less so. In the north and south walls of the chancel are two circular windows deeply recessed on both sides. The nave windows with chevrons are replacements. The chancel arch is also Norman into which two very large squints have later been inserted. Housed in the western gallery is the organ, and from here there is a nice overview of the nave and chancel arch. The windows being small allow little light into the nave and it is rather dark except on the brightest of days. There are good examples of early glass here and worth a closer look. The pulpit is Jacobean and was originally at Sotterley St Margaret in Suffolk. The church is usually locked.

FRAMLINGHAM PIGOT St Andrew

No of Bells:	3
19th c. Deanery:	Brooke
Hundred:	Henstead
Union house:	Swainsthorpe
21st c Deanery:	Loddon
Benefice:	Thurton

4½ miles SE of Norwich. From Norwich on the A146 turn right at 'The Gull' P.H. then right again. Continue until you see the church.
O.S. grid ref: TG 277036
Post Code: NR14 7QJ

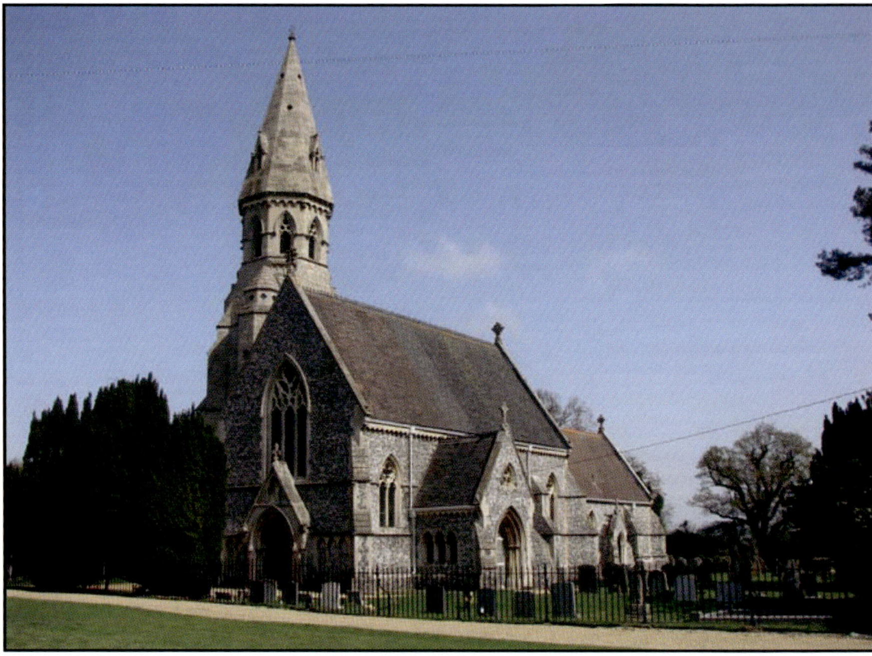

This church cost £4,500 to build. It is of unusual design with the strange looking tower and spire on the north side. It was designed by Robert Kerr, completed in 1859, and paid for by George Christie who lived at the Hall. It is inspired (no pun intended) with the base of the tower put to use. Of course, there is nothing old here. Nothing from the old small, thatched, towerless church which stood here before was saved or reused. The organ does seem to have been an afterthought and almost obscures the rear stalls. There is a pillar piscina and a single sedile, the pulpit is more like a walk-on stage accessed through a doorway cut into the chancel arch. It is 'fancy' and a good attempt at combining the practical with the traditional, but I'm not sure whether I like it or not. At least it is usually accessible.

FREETHORPE All Saints

No of Bells: 1
19th c. Deanery: Blofield
Hundred: Blofield
Union house: Lingwood
21st c Deanery: Blofield
Benefice: Freethorpe

8 miles W of Great Yarmouth. Turn south off the A47 at the windmill on the bend. Pass through Halvergate to Freethorpe.
O.S. grid ref: TG 408055
Post Code: NR13 3NP

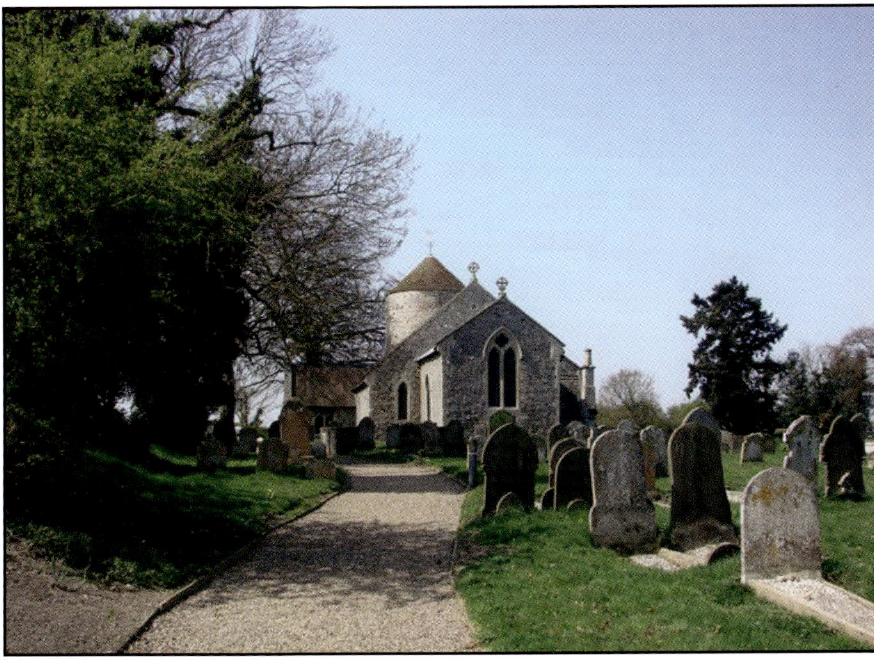

The Norman conical capped tower is the most striking part of the church. There is no doubt this was originally a Norman church but rebuilding has removed most of the evidence. It is rubble-built and little evidence of coursing exists. The chancel was added probably two centuries later as the flints are dressed. Much of what is to be seen inside the church is very good Victorian restoration. The restorers seem to have replaced the font and pulpit as well as the roof and no trace exists of a screen ever having been there. Even the corbelled piscina is 'new'. Interestingly to the north of the chancel is what seems to all intents and purposes a vestry, but is in fact a family pew, complete with fireplace, built by and especially for the benefactors, the Walpole family.

FRETTENHAM St Swithin

No of Bells:	2
19th c. Deanery:	Taverham
Hundred:	Taverham
Union house:	Horsham St Faith
21st c Deanery:	Ingworth
Benefice:	Frettenham

5 miles N of Norwich.
Church is ½ mile north of the village off the B1150.
Turn left at Crostwick, bear right, straight over x-roads.
O.S. grid ref: TG 244185
Post Code: NR12 7NW

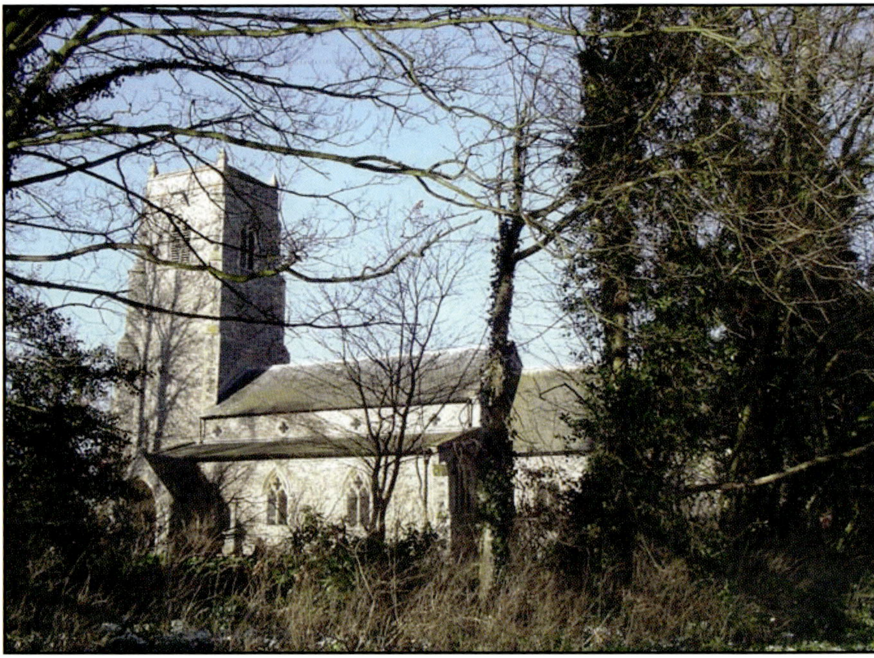

Almost hidden behind trees this is another of those churches with tiny coloured glass quatrefoil clerestory windows which let in so little light it makes you wonder if it was worth the effort. The church dates from the 14th c. although the chancel was rebuilt in 1869 in memory of the wife of the Rev. James Shirley. The original piscina and sedilia were retained and old brasses set into the latter. The font is typical of the 13th c. but the central shaft is much later. In the south aisle is a lovely 15th c. carved parish chest. The roofs are all part of the sympathetic Victorian restoration programme that was carried out here. The pulpit has nice tracery but that too is Victorian. A few old 15th c. backless benches with poppyheads still remain in the church and are worthy of admiration if only for those who had to sit on them.

FRITTON St Catherine *****

No of Bells:	3
19th c. Deanery:	Depwade
Hundred:	Depwade
Union house:	Pulham St Mary
.21st c Deanery:	Depwade
Benefice:	Hempnall

11 miles S of Norwich, and ½ mile north of Fritton Common, set well back off the road 100 yards up a short track.

O.S. grid ref: TM 227932

Post Code: NR15 2QU

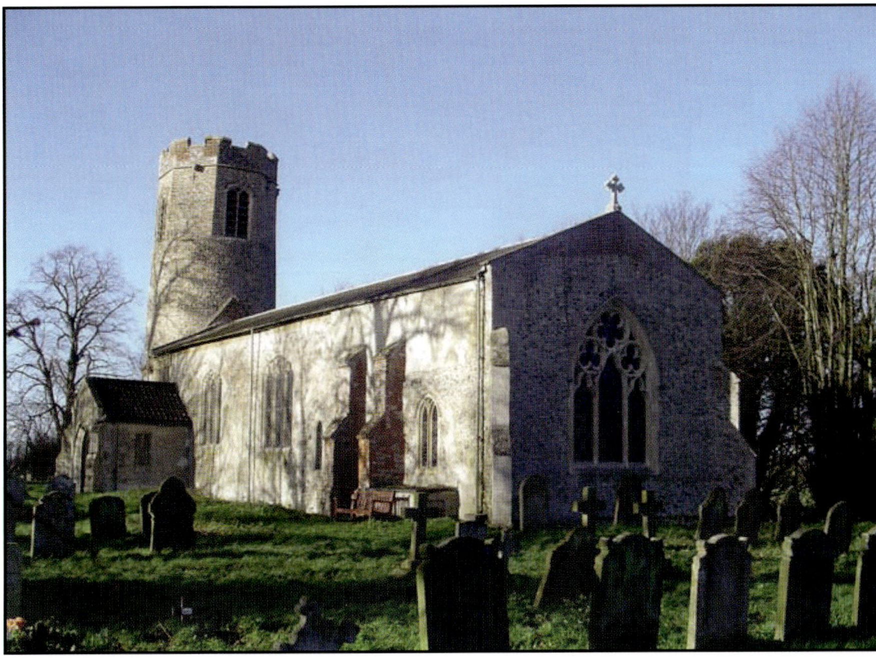

Situated about 150 yards off the road the entrance can be easily missed. This is a little gem of a church. The round tower is possibly pre-Conquest, the octagonal upper stage was added later. The roof does not differentiate between the nave and the chancel. Notice if you will the grinning lions on the base of the 15th c. typical East Anglian font. The entire roof is scissor-braced with tiebeams; the chancel is only defined by the lovely 100-year-old screen and rood loft. Although not ancient, it is a fine example of what a rood loft is all about. Depicted in the first (left) panel of the 16th c. screen are John Bacon and his family. He was the main benefactor of the church and had the screen made to his specifications. The remaining panels contain the Four Latin Doctors, St Simon and St Jude.

FRITTON	St Edmunds
No of Bells:	1
19th c. Deanery:	Lothingland
Hundred:	Mutford & Lothingland
Union house:	Oulton
21st c Deanery:	Lothingland
Benefice:	Somerleyton

7 m NW of Lowestoft between Haddiscoe & Great Yarmouth. From the A143 take Church Lane at the northern end of Fritton.
O.S. grid ref TG 473001
Post Code: NR32 5PE

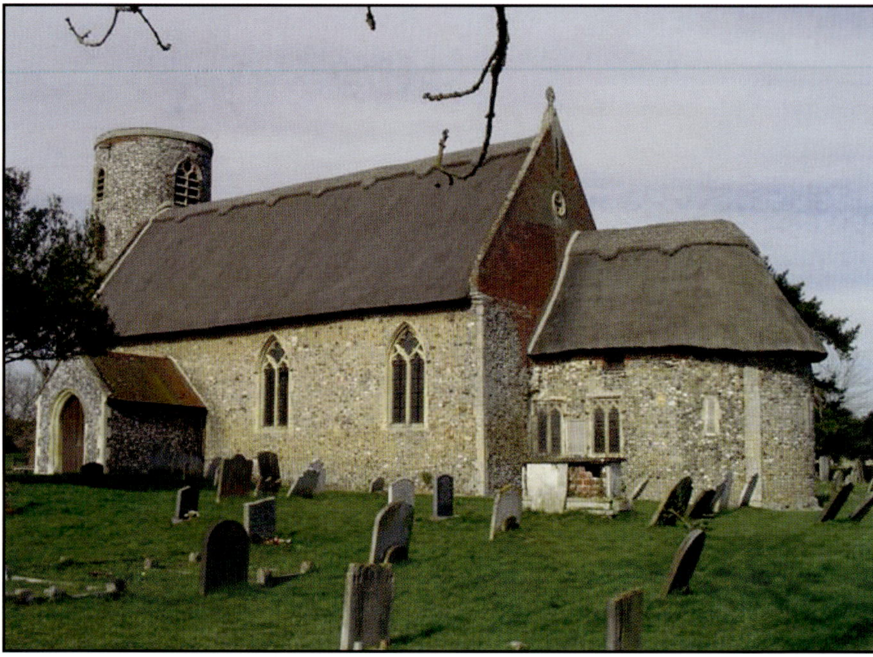

At one time in Suffolk, this lovely little thatched church has since been claimed by Norfolk along with six others in the Lothingland Deanery. There are a number of interesting points to interest the visitor. Roman tiles have been built into the fabric base of the Saxon tower. The top is 14th c. and tapers considerably east/west. Inside there are more examples of Saxon work: in the pilaster buttresses of the chancel and in the lower part of the tower, which is open and projects into the nave. The thickness of the walls can be seen by the reveals of the lancet windows. The best feature is the little 12 ft. wide apsidal Norman chancel which is not central to the nave and suggests that there was an earlier nave altar. There is a large 15th c. painting of St Christopher well worth close examination.

GELDESTON St Michael
No of Bells: 1
19th c. Deanery: Brooke
Hundred: Clavering
Union house: Heckingham
21st c Deanery: Loddon
Benefice: Geldeston

5 miles SSE of Loddon, on the old Gillingham to Kirby Cane road, north of the village street and next to the Rectory.
O.S. grid ref: TM 394922
Post Code: NR34 0LP

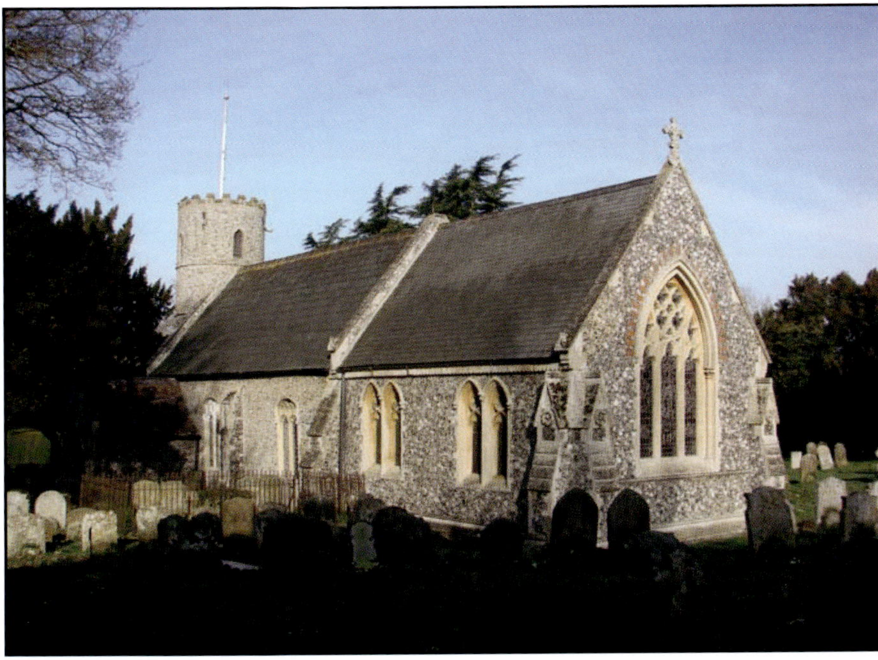

This rather remote church has a lovely round tower, which may be Norman, the base almost certainly is. I think most interesting is the drawing inside the nave along with three others of the proposed 'restoration' in 1835. All I can say is 'Thank God it never happened'. The 15th c. font, which is inscribed around the base, is octagonal and has armorial shields and roses around the bowl and lions around the shaft. The north transept with a double arch, supported by a marble column, has a bell in the gable. Behind the unusual skeletal pulpit are the rood loft stairs, still open. The windows and columns are a result of restoration and look somewhat out of place. There are no signs of a piscina or sedilia. There are one or two nice bench ends carved as poppyheads.

GILLINGHAM All Saints

No of Bells:	-
19th c. Deanery:	Brooke
Hundred:	Clavering
Union house:	Heckingham
21st c Deanery:	-
Benefice:	-

1 mile N of Beccles, a few yards from Gillingham St Mary's on the old Beccles to Norwich road. Direction as for St Mary's.

O.S. grid ref: TM 411923

Post Code: NR34 0ND

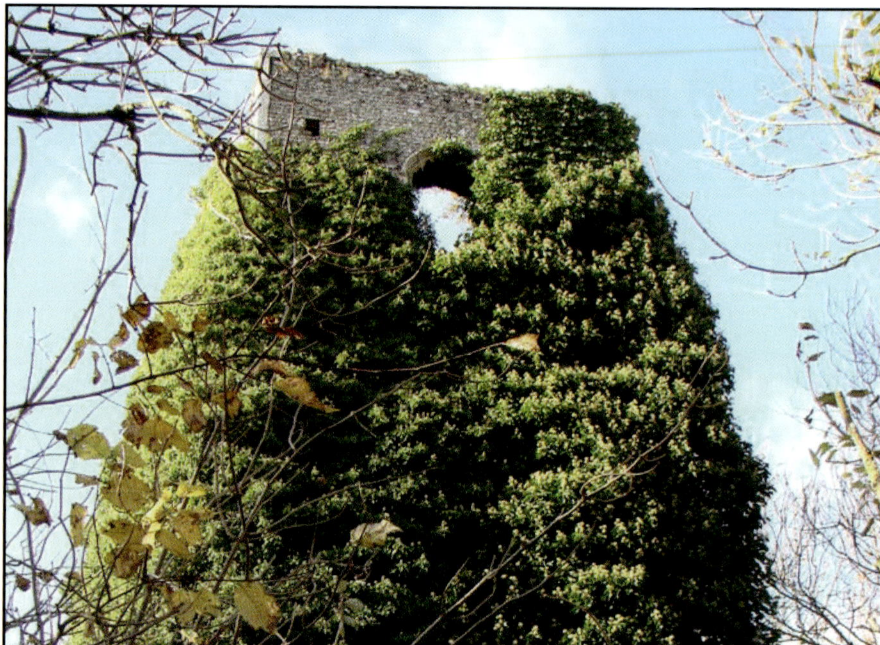

Locally this is known as Ivy Steeple. At one time serving three parishes, Winston, Wyndell and Gillingham, the church fell into disuse and was demolished in 1748. Only the tower survives. Two other churches suffered the same fate over the centuries. One was Winston St Andrew off the Norwich road, the other, Wyndell, just off the Yarmouth road. Both parishes were consolidated with Gillingham around the time of Elizabeth I and were demolished soon afterwards. Local legend has it that they were abandoned around the time of the Black Death but it is more likely that the diminished villages survived for about 200 years beyond this time. Very little remains of either except in the name of Winston Hall, now a game farm, and an area called Windle Hills half way to Toft Monks on the Yarmouth road.

GILLINGHAM St Mary

No of Bells: 3
19th c. Deanery: Brooke
Hundred: Clavering
Union house: Heckingham
21st c. Deanery: Loddon
Benefice: Geldeston

1 mile N of Beccles
signposted just off the A146
just before the roundabout
and turn left. The R.C.
church is on the right.
O.S. grid ref: TM 411923
Post Code: NR34 0ND

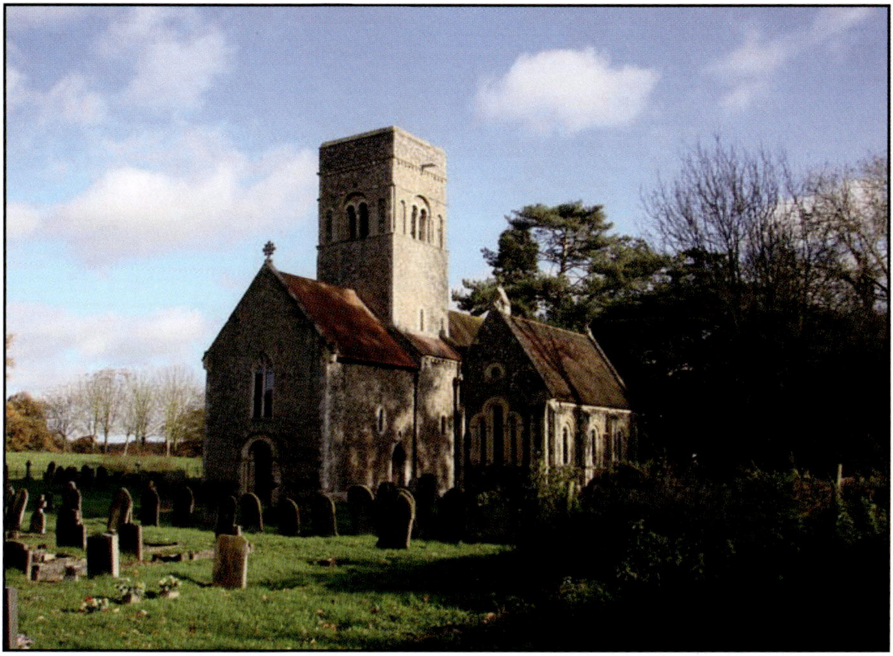

An ancient church built in the 12th c. which uncommonly has a central tower. There have been many changes over the centuries and it is difficult to work out what is original and what isn't. The tower is almost certainly how the Normans built it with only a few changes. The west porch was once part of the nave but the doorway is Norman and is probably in its original position. There was once a south transept which has been demolished to widen the aisle, probably when the nave was shortened. The font is square and rather uninteresting. Inside are lovely decorated Norman columns supporting the nave roof which form an arcade, but again whether or not they are original or replaced is debatable. Outside you will find the remains of the foot of a column discarded during remodelling of the interior.

GIMINGHAM All Saints
No of Bells: 3
19th c. Deanery: Repps
Hundred: North Erpingham
Union house: Gimingham
21st c. Deanery: Repps
Benefice: Trunch Team Ministry

4½ miles N of North Walsham. From North Walsham go to Trunch and continue on that road for 1½ miles.
O.S. grid ref: TG 285368
Post Code: NR11 8HF

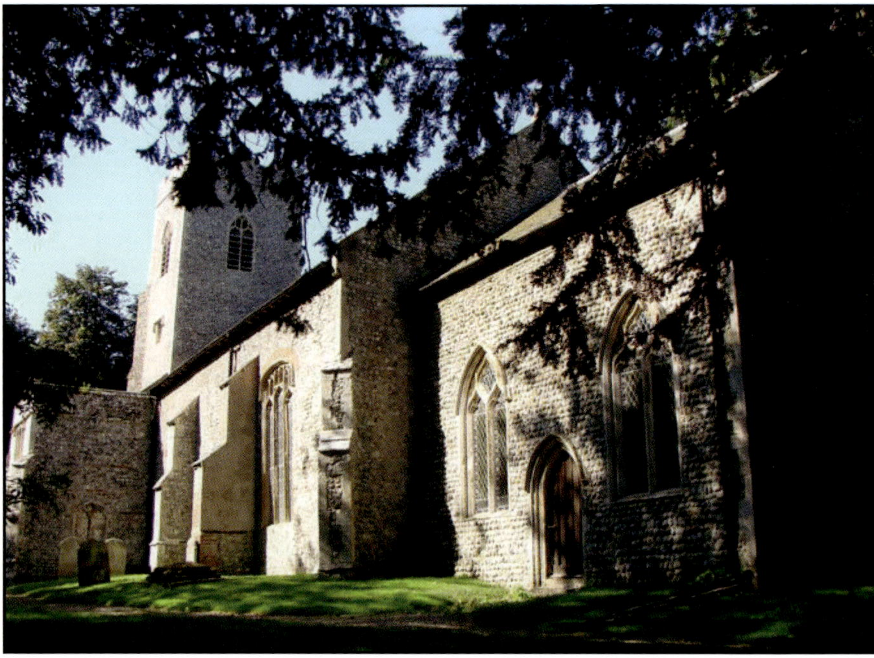

Partially obscured by trees this 15th c. church is worth a few minutes of anybody's time. The battlemented tower is in perfect proportion with the church. The south porch is coeval and has a parvise. Whilst the roofs are modern, some of the fittings are old and have been re-used. The prayer desk, for example, has been constructed using two old bench ends which still have the grotesques on them (more can be seen on other benches). The font is quite simple with quatrefoil design around the bowl and arcading on the shaft. Its conical cover is more elaborate with pierced tracery and crockets on the risers. The pulpit is quite ordinary, with some tracery on the panels, with steps leading up to it. The Royal Arms are Hanoverian and appear to be cast iron. It is impossible to make out to which monarch they belong.

GORLESTON St Andrew
No of Bells: 8
19th c. Deanery: Lothingland
Hundred: Mutford and Lothingland
Union house: Oulton
21st c. Deanery: Great Yarmouth
Benefice: Gorleston St Andrew

5 m N of Lowestoft
between Great Yarmouth & Lowestoft: near the roundabout of the B1370 in Church Road. Hard to miss.
O.S. grid ref TG 524043
Post Code: NR31 6LS

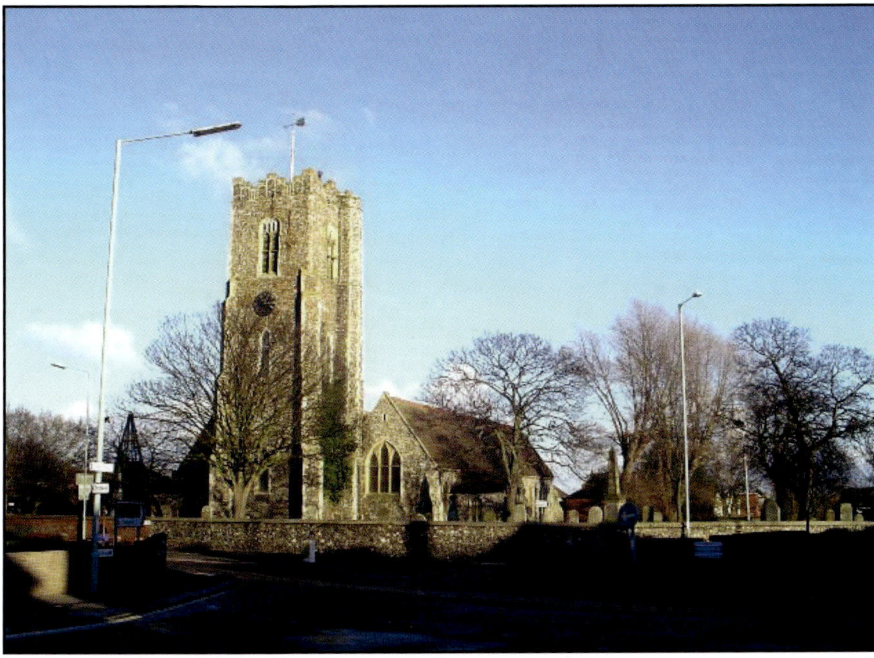

This church started its life as a small church established by the Bishop of Dunwich in the 7th c. and grew with the parish. At one time it stood in the middle of the countryside, the town of Gorleston has grown around it. A brass memorial to Sir John Bacon (1320) is in the chancel. Although somewhat defaced the font depicts the seven sacraments. The Arms of Charles I, dated 1644, are unique. Two 17th c. paintings of Moses and Aaron flank the tower. There are two piscinas, one 13th c. in the chancel with cusped arch and another in the chapel. The sedilia is a graduated dropped-sill type. The fine parish chest is iron-bound and dates from the 14th c.. The tower was restored last century as a memorial to the lifeboatmen of the parish, some of whom took part in the evacuation at Dunkirk in 1940.

GREAT HAUTBOIS Holy Trinity

No of Bells: 1
19th c. Deanery: Ingworth
Hundred: South Erpingham
Union house: Aylsham
21st c. Deanery: Ingworth
Benefice: Coltishall

8 m NNE of Norwich. From Coltishall take the Buxton road and the church is on the right within ½ mile of Coltishall village centre.
O.S. grid ref: TG 265203
Post Code: NR12 7JN

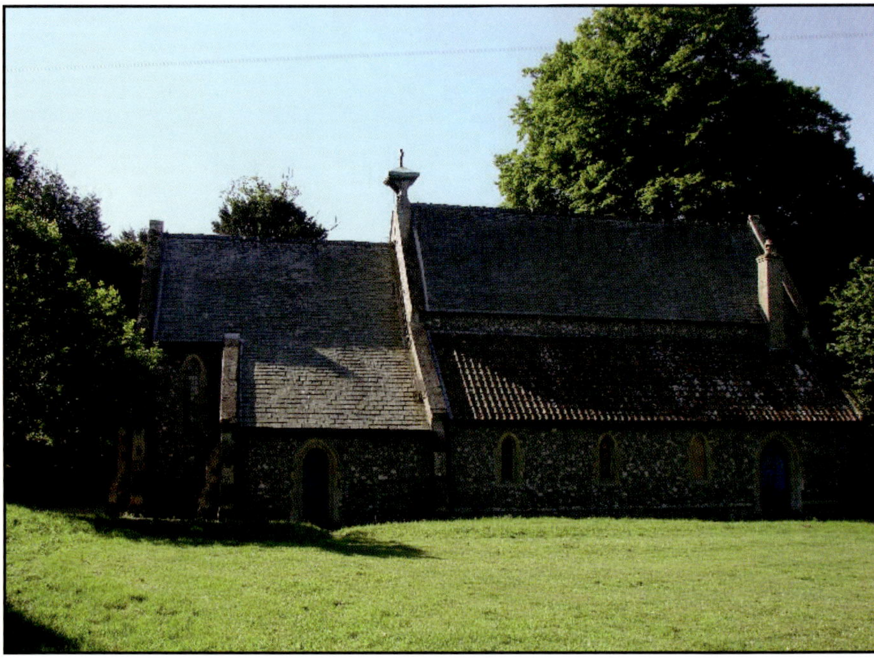

This is a humble little church, it has no tower and a strange Japanese style bellcote sits atop the eastern gable of the nave roof. I couldn't find a single headstone in the graveyard. I also couldn't find a keyholder so I was unable to gain access to the interior. However, the glass in the some of the windows is quite unique. There are three transfer-glass windows in Holy Trinity, that came from the ruined church of St Theobald (Great Hautbois). They are the only remaining examples of the type in Norfolk. The building was designed by Thomas Jekyll and constructed in 1860 to replace St Theobold's church the ruins of which are further north on the same side *(See page 73)*. You will feel more welcome there. As I have stated before: 'A locked church, with no keyholder, is no more than a shed.'

(GREAT) HAUTBOIS St Theobald

No of Bells: -
19th c. Deanery: Ingworth
Hundred: South Erpingham
Union house: Aylsham
21st c. Deanery: -
Benefice: -

8 m NNE of Norwich. From Coltishall take the Buxton road and the church is on the right within 1 mile of Coltishall village centre.
O.S. grid ref: TG 262204
Post Code: NR12 7JN

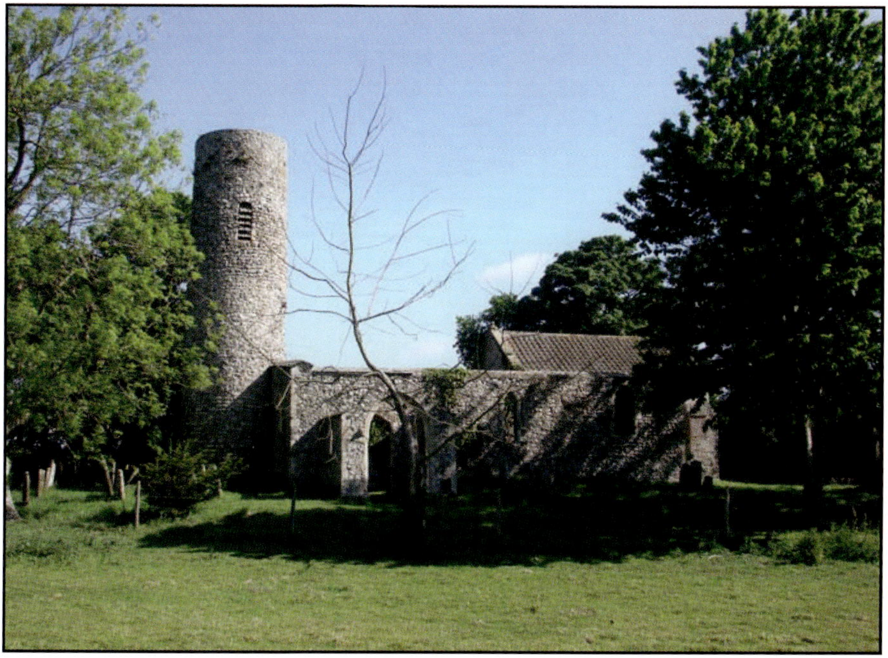

Hautbois is pronounced Hobbis. This lovely little Norman church was, in 1860, regarded as being too far gone to repair, so another was built just down the road. It was de-roofed and left to crumble into the ruinous state we see today. The chancel was used as a mortuary chapel for many years after its demise, but that too has now decayed. There used to be an early Norman font here, but that seems to have disappeared, unless it is secreted at Holy Trinity. The ruin has been consolidated and is quite safe to wander around. Burials still take place in the graveyard and some have even been interred in what was once the south aisle. The wild flowers, butterflies and bees give the whole place a sense of peaceful tranquillity. Take a picnic, park in the gateway and spend a little time here, surrounded by nature.

GREAT PLUMSTEAD St Mary

No of Bells:	1 (once 3)
19th c. Deanery:	Blofield
Hundred:	Blofield
Union house:	Lingwood
21st c. Deanery:	Blofield
Benefice:	Thorpe End

5 miles E of Norwich.
From Norwich take the A47 to Great Yarmouth and turn off left where signposted and follow road-signs.
O.S. grid ref: TG 302099
Post Code: NR13 5AB

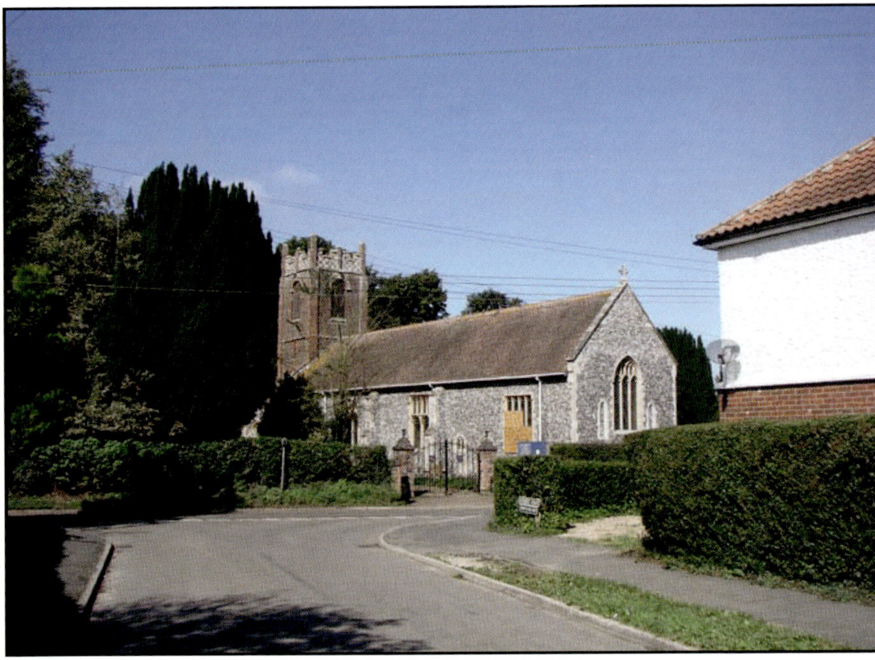

The church was originally built in the 15th c. and the brick tower was added in 1711. Just inside the south door is a niche with a Purbeck bowl for Holy water. The octagonal font is of no age, decorated with shields and tracery. In fact there is very little of any great age in the church at all, mainly due to a fire in 1891. The roof is modern scissor-beam, and the chancel is only distinguished from the nave by a large tie beam and wagon roof. Next to the 15th c. piscina with a simple trefoil arch is a dropped-sill sedilia. At the lower level, the rood loft stairs are still intact but lead nowhere. The pulpit and lectern I believe are late Victorian as are most, if not all, the fixtures and fittings. At the east end of the nave is a sketch of how the church used to look, rustic, but much nicer than the barn-like structure we see today.

GREAT YARMOUTH St Nicholas

No of Bells: 13
19th c. Deanery: Flegg
Hundred: Flegg
Union house: Northgate
21st c. Deanery: Great Yarmouth
Benefice: Gt Yarmouth Team Ministry.

19 miles E by S of Norwich in Great Yarmouth town centre at the north end of the Market Place near the Priory.
O.S. grid ref: TG 528076
Post Code: NR30 1NE

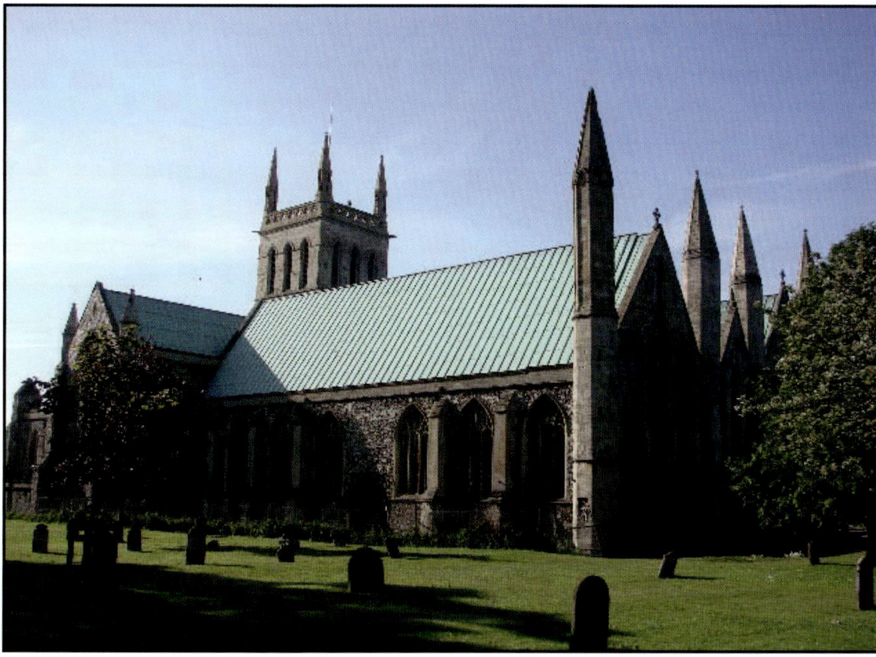

This may be an important church and second largest in the county, but unfortunately it is kept locked most of the time. Regrettably, because of this, the church has a cold and unwelcoming atmosphere. It suffered much bomb damage during WWII. The roofs of the nave and aisles are all boarded and uninteresting. The guidebook has much to say about the history of the church but visually all you will see is either restored or modern in comparison with the main structure of the building, which has been sadly neglected over the centuries. The font is small; the cover, originally the tester from the pulpit removed from St George's (now redundant), is suspended from the roof. The piscina and four seat sedilia have no great age. The east window is best seen with the morning sunshine filtering through it.

GUNTON St Andrew
No of Bells: 0
19th c. Deanery: Repps
Hundred: North Erpingham
Union house: West Beckham
21st c. Deanery: Repps
The Churches Conservation Trust

5 miles S of Cromer in Gunton Park. From the A140 turn left towards Suffield. Use the main entrance then bear left.
O.S. grid ref: TG 229342
Post Code: see below

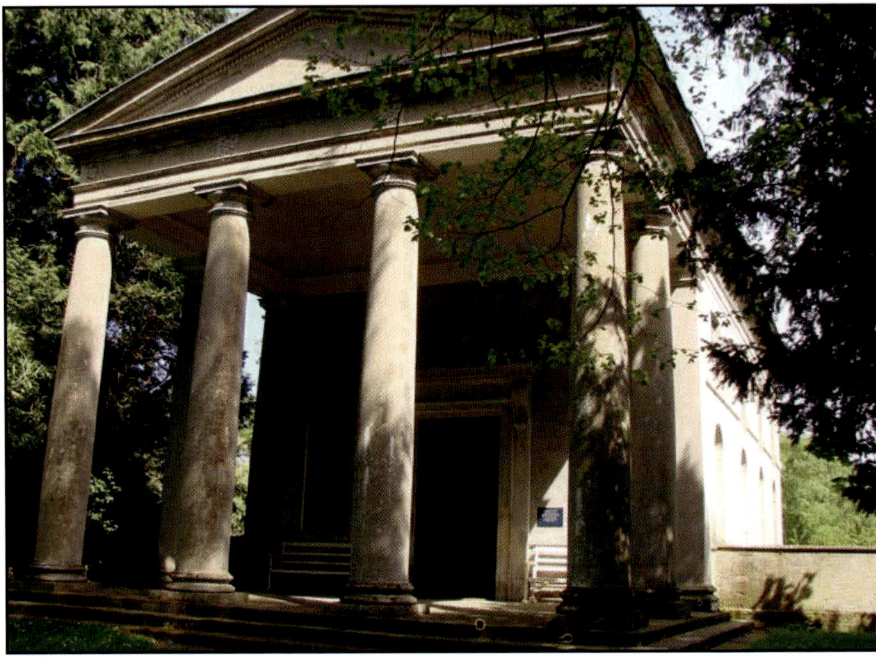

[Set Sat-nav for White Post Road, Suffield]. Enter by the west side of the estate at the sawmill and over the bridge bear right and past the front of the Hall, turn left, park and walk over the cattle grid. You will soon be faced with the Palladian colonnade pictured above. Built by Sir William Morden and designed by Robert Adams in 1742 (the only church he ever designed). Inside there are three doors, two to the gallery and the central one into the church. A wooden pedestal table and a marble bowl serve as a font. Small box pews on both sides with those on the right having memorials to members of the Harbord family. A carved marble memorial to Cecilia Annetta Suffield (1911) is especially poignant. Above, in the gallery, is the organ. On the wall among the hatchments are the Royal Arms of George I dated 1715.

HADDISCOE	St Mary
No of Bells:	5
19th c. Deanery:	Brooke
Hundred:	Clavering
Union house:	Heckingham
21st c. Deanery:	Loddon
Benefice:	Raveningham

6 miles E of Loddon. On the Beccles to Yarmouth road (A143). Easy to spot with the chequered parapet. Car park on north side.
O.S. grid ref: TM 439969
Post Code: NR14 6PB

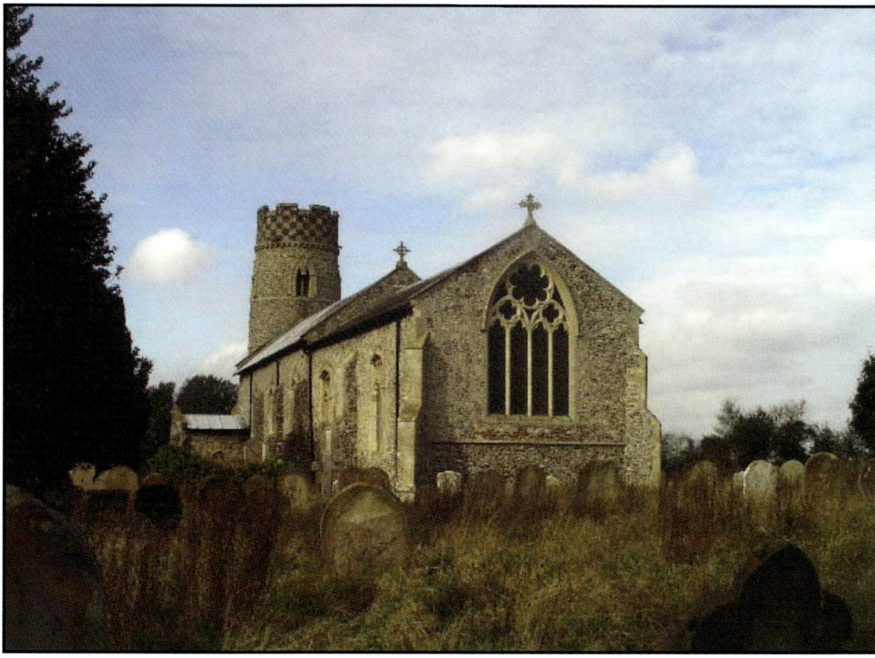

This is an ancient site. Many people pass this lovely church without ever going to look inside. A pre-Conquest tower with a refuge door sixteen feet above the ground is where the Saxon folk sought safety from invading forces. The upper chequered stage, which is so recognisable, is later. In the belfry stage are windows, which have triangular headed arches, and are most uncommon. The doorways are both Norman, the north has been altered but the south door is complete and, although not spectacular, was built by the Normans. Just inside the door is a stoup. A remarkably well preserved and crisp 15th c. font is the traditional East Anglian type. The 13th c. double piscina has trefoil arches with a central column. A rather plain pulpit has stone steps leading up to it.

HAINFORD All Saints

No of Bells: -

19th c. Deanery: Taverham

Hundred: Taverham

Union house: Horsham St Faith

21st c. Deanery: Ingworth

Now only used as a Burial ground.

6 m N of Norwich in Newton Road, Hainford. From the A140 turn onto the B1354, for ¾ mile then turn right for 300 yards.

O.S. grid ref: TG 234190

Post Code: NR10 3BG

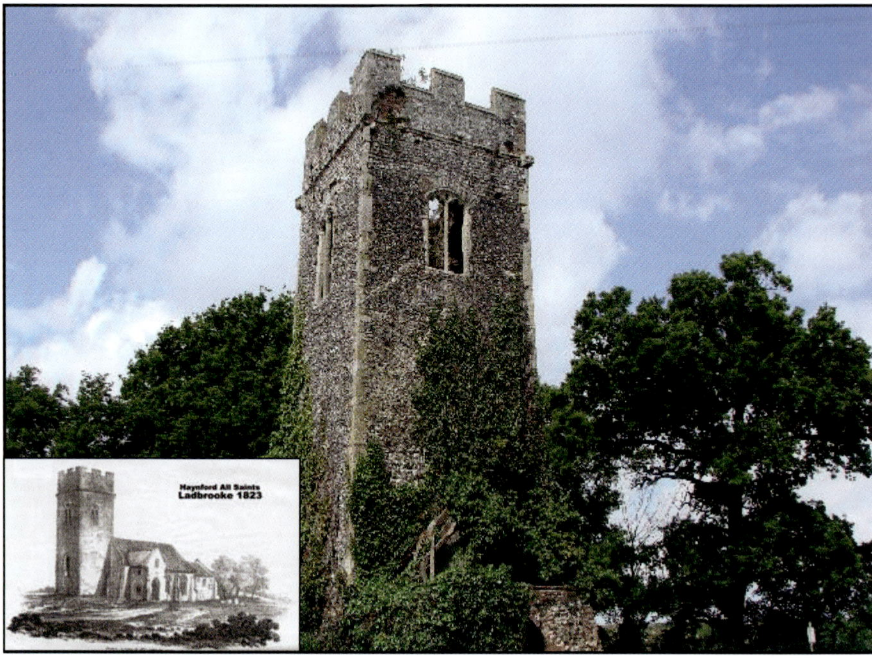

This lovely ruin stands over the graveyard of its former self, (inset, Ladbrooke 1823) which is still in use. When the new church was built in 1840 this church was unroofed and left to decay, leaving the tower as a landmark. That too has begun to crumble. A fence now surrounds the tower, with notices warning of falling masonry. The church dates from the late 13th c. and the tower from the 15th. The reason for its demise is not clear but it seems the architect concerned decided that there was more profit in building a new church rather than preserving the old one. It was decided to continue to use the burial ground and a mortuary chapel was constructed against the tower arch. This too has collapsed due to neglect, and the birds and other of God's creatures now make their home there. A fitting end to any church.

HAINFORD	All Saints
No of Bells:	1
19th c. Deanery:	Taverham
Hundred:	Taverham
Union house:	Horsham St Faith
21st c. Deanery:	Ingworth
Benefice:	Frettenham

6 m N of Norwich in Newton Road, Hainford. From the A140 turn onto the B1354 for ¾ mile then turn right for 300 yards.

O.S. grid ref: TG 224190

Post Code: NR10 3LY

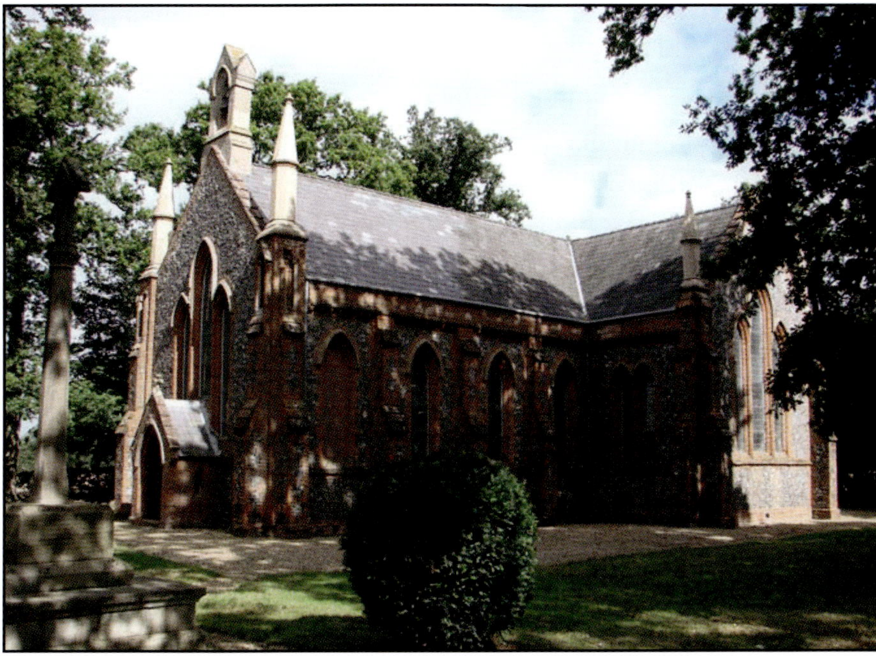

This 'new' church cost £1200 to build in 1838. It was consecrated in 1840. The flint was salvaged from the demolition of the old church (see previous page) and the bricks were made locally. It was built with a north and south transept and has a single bell turret over the west gable. A Victorian font replaced the old one but the parish chest, dated 1749, was recovered from the old church. Unusually the War Memorial takes the form of the altar rails. A memorial to those who lost their lives in WW1 is in the churchyard. While I am not a great lover of Victorian churches, this one I like; it is simple and austere in comparison with some I could mention. Parishioners' money has not been wasted on an assortment of unnecessary flamboyance and ornamentation. The Royal Arms are quite naturally those of Victoria.

HALES St Margaret *****
No of Bells: 2
19th c. Deanery: Brooke
Hundred: Clavering
Union house: Heckingham
21st c. Deanery: Loddon
The Churches Conservation Trust

2 m SE of Loddon, just east of the A146. 1 mile south of the village of Hales turn east at 'Hales Green' for 300 yards.
O.S. grid ref: TM 383961
Post Code: NR14 6NL

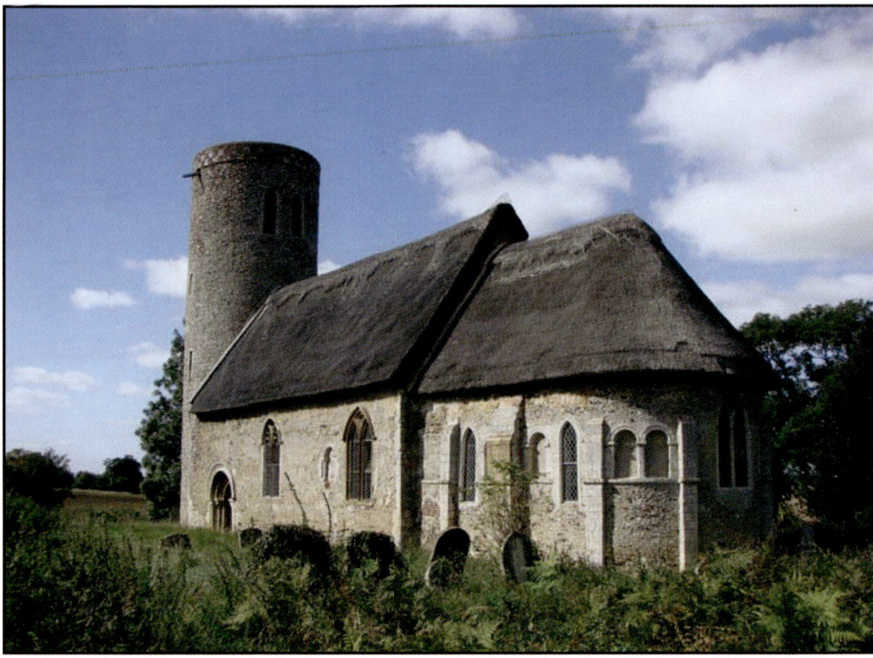

Carefully preserved by the Churches Conservation Trust it is always open. This is arguably the best-preserved Norman church in the county, looking remarkably like Heckingham, a mile or two away. The building is entirely thatched with an apsidal west end. The round tower was built by the Normans and a chequered parapet added later. The south door is superb and outstanding for such a small church. The north door is also Norman but with less decoration. Before you enter notice the crosses carved into the door jamb. They are graffiti thought to have been made by church wardens after a visitation by the Bishop. The font is a traditional East Anglian type with lions around the square foot. There are wall paintings, some of which are high up on the chancel arch. This church is must for all church-crawlers.

HALVERGATE St Peter & St Paul

No of Bells: 6
19th c. Deanery: Blofield
Hundred: Walsham
Union house: Acle
21st c. Deanery: Blofield
Benefice: Freethorpe

7 miles W of Great Yarmouth. From the A47 Yarmouth to Norwich road turn south at the windmill, turn right then left.
O.S. grid ref: TG 417067
Post Code: NR13 3PL

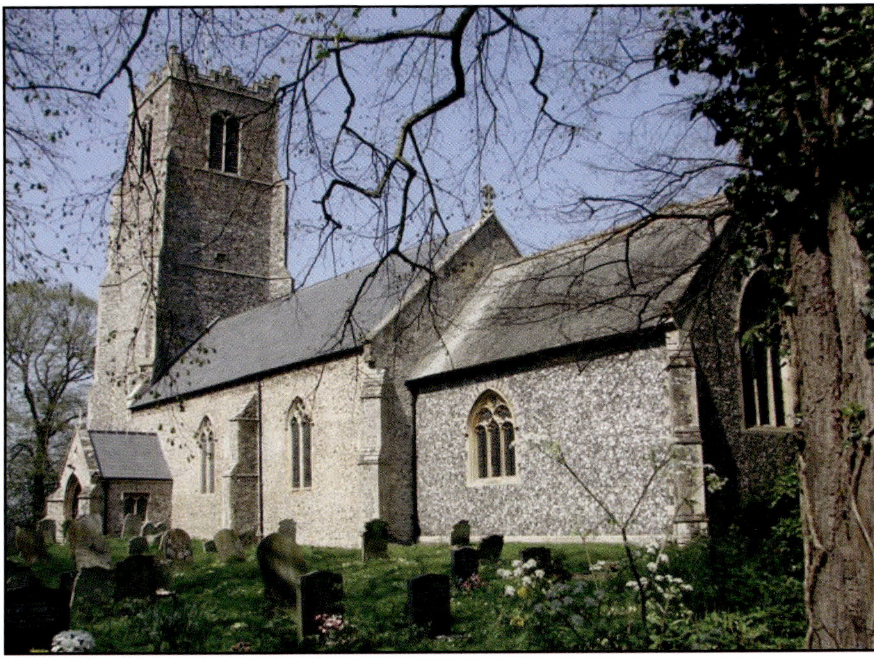

Always locked and I found no keyholder listed. This 14th c. church has been spoiled by restoration. The best part is just inside the porch. The arch with central and side pinnacles over the south doorway are all beautifully crocketted. The octagonal font has quatrefoil and rose designs around the bowl and trefoil arches around the shaft. A very dirty Royal Arms of George I hangs on the wall. There are 19th c. wall plaques to various members of the Gridley and Bately families but very little of real historical or architectural interest. It is unfortunate that the church is not left open. There is nothing here that can be stolen or damaged beyond repair except the windows. Churches die on their feet because they are kept sealed and secured from visitors except for Sunday services. Shame really!

HAPPISBURGH St Mary

No of Bells: 6
19th c. Deanery: Waxham
Hundred: Happing
Union house: Smallburgh
21st c. Deanery: Waxham & Tunstead
Benefice: Happisburgh

7 miles E of North Walsham. From the B1159 turn east towards Happisburgh and follow. The tower is easily seen.
O.S. grid ref: TG 380312
Post Code: NR12 0PN

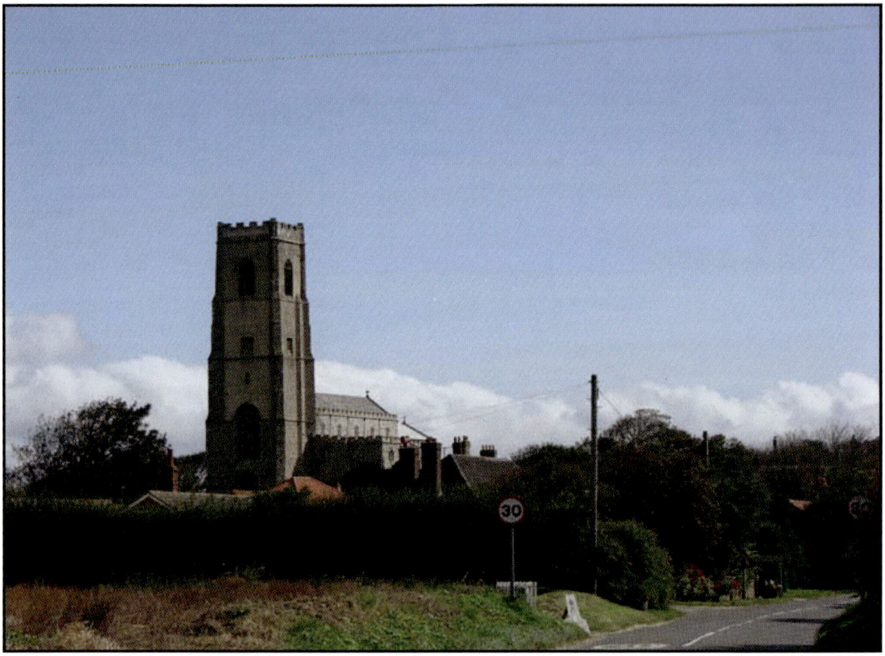

Pronounced Hazebrer. The 15th c. tower which is visible for many miles around is 110 feet tall. This magnificent 14th c. building is a gentle giant of churches. It was greatly enlarged 100 years later to what we see today, apart from Victorian restoration. The porch roof has a boss in the centre of the diagonal beams that support the parvise above. The clerestory, and a window above the chancel arch spill early morning sunlight into the interior. The 15th c. font is a fine example of the typically East Anglian style, with evangelistic symbols around the bowl and lions and wodewoses around the shaft. The piscina is 14th c. and the choir stalls are a century later. The roofs are arch-braced construction. There is much here to interest the visitor and the guidebook is quite comprehensive.

HARDLEY	St Margaret
No of Bells:	3
19th c. Deanery:	Brooke
Hundred:	Loddon
Union house:	Heckingham
21st c. Deanery:	Loddon
Benefice:	Chet Valley

2 miles NE of Loddon. Hardley is signposted from Chedgrave. Head towards Hardley Hall, not the village.

O.S. grid ref: TG 385007
Post Code: NR14 6BU

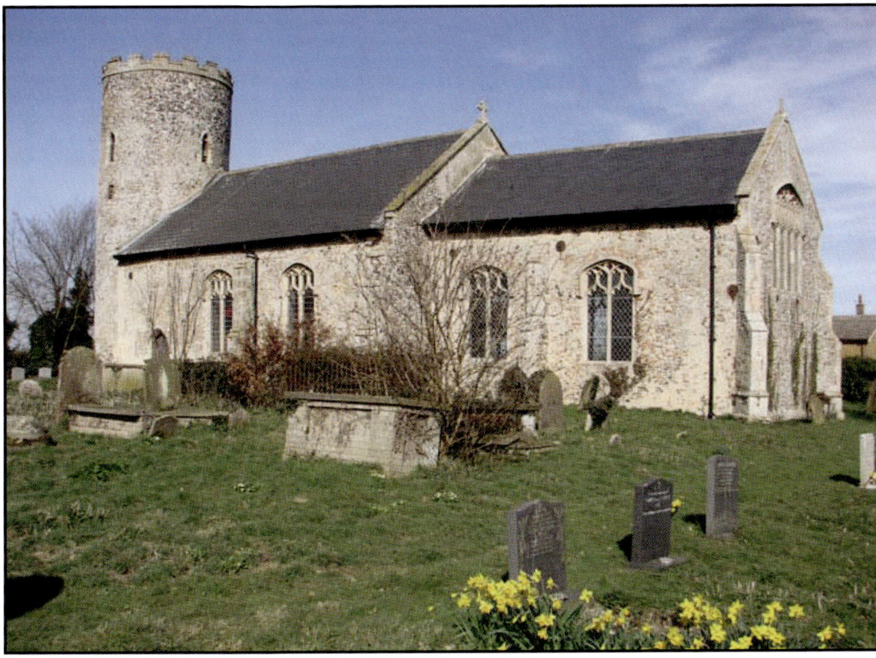

Hardley church is in general unspoilt by Victorian restoration. It is remote and set in lovely surroundings. The 13th c. embattled round tower dominates the west end of the nave that is entered through the 14th c. porch. A lovely 15th c. octagonal font is probably the most interesting item you will find here, carved with signs of the four evangelists in quatrefoil panels. Around the corona there is further decoration, with the familiar four lions around the shaft. The benches are rustic to say the least and plain pine, but unusual in their construction. Beside the small Jacobean pulpit are the blocked stairs to the rood loft, the traceried screen of which is still in place although very tired and bereft of further decoration. There are some wall paintings and a couple of the original poppy-head benches.

HARDWICK	St Margaret	5 m N of Harleston.
No of Bells:	1	Accessible by winding
19th c. Deanery:	Depwade	country roads from
Hundred:	Depwade	Harleston or Long Stratton.
Union house:	Pulham St Mary	Follow signposts.
21st c. Deanery:	Depwade	O.S. grid ref: TM 223900
Benefice:	Hempnall	Post Code: NR15 2AB

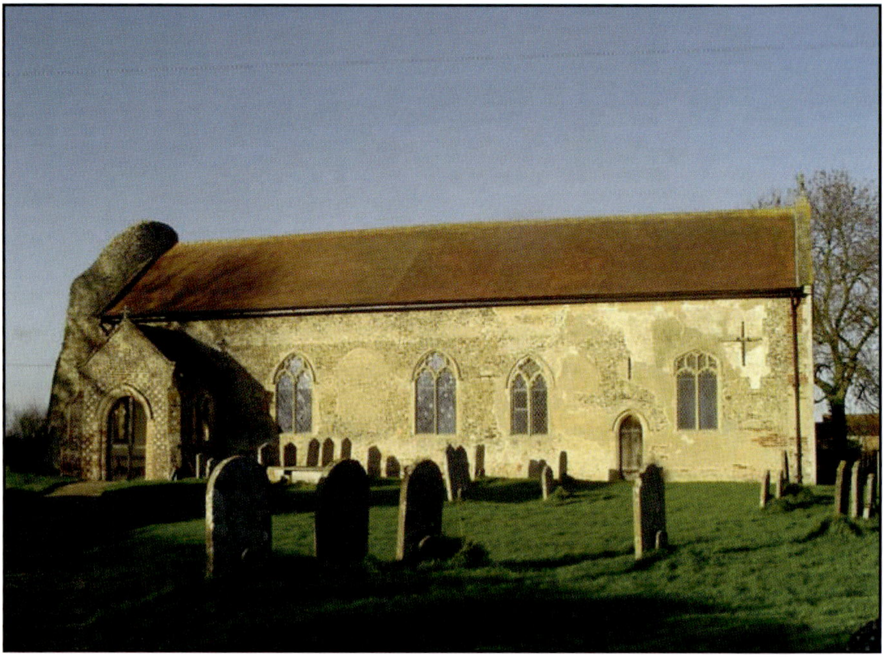

The church lost its round tower in 1770 but the ruin has been consolidated and contains the bell, which is rung from inside the nave. The south doorway is late 12th c. with engaged columns supporting a slightly pointed arch. On the door is a large sanctuary ring. The 15th c. font has quatrefoil designs around the octagonal bowl. On the north wall is a painting of St Christopher. The rood loft stairs ascend from the sill of a window in the north wall. The upper part of the 15th c. screen must have been beautiful with double filigree tracery, but alas it is much damaged and the lower panels have also suffered; but it is still possible to imagine how it used to be. The angle piscina has a carved face above it and the dropped-sill sedilia is adjacent to it. In the chancel is the painted tomb of Thomas Gleane (1666). Interesting!

HARLESTON St John the Baptist

No of Bells:	1
19th c. Deanery:	Redenhall
Hundred:	Earsham
Union house:	Pulham St Mary
21st c. Deanery:	Redenhall
Benefice:	Redenhall

7 miles SW of Bungay & 8 miles NE of Diss. In the town centre. On the Old Market at the junction with Briar Close.

O.S. grid ref: TM 246834

Post Code: IP20 9DX

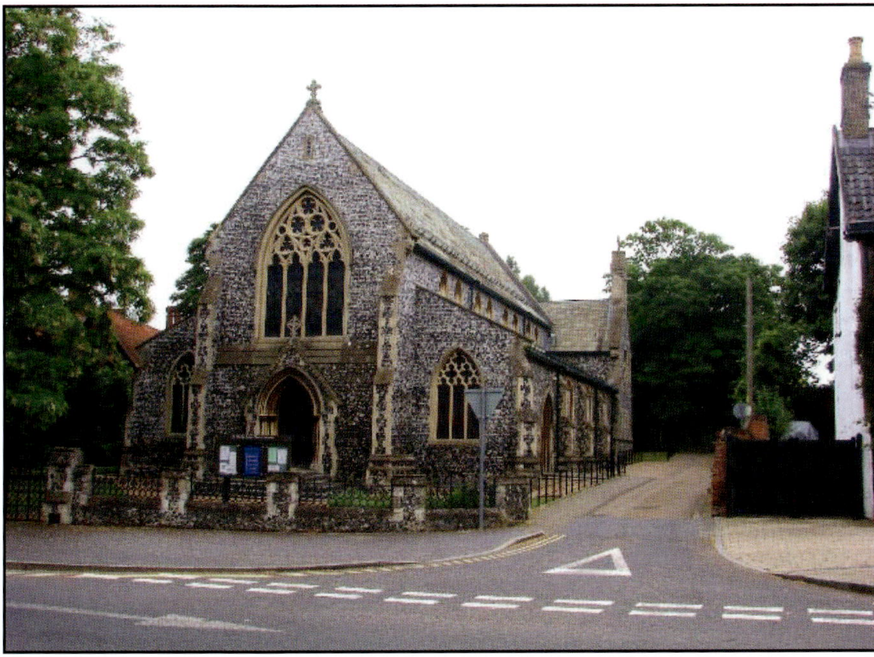

This is a modern church, which is really a chapel of ease for Redenhall, or more accurately a church of convenience for Harleston. It was built in the last quarter of the 19th c. to replace a mediaeval church that had been built as a chapel of ease in the market place. It was designed by diocesan architect Richard Philipson, who virtually had to rebuild St Mary le Tower at Ipswich. *[See East Suffolk].* There is no tower here and a small bell turret contains one bell. The interior is dark despite the clerestory, but by those who use it is well loved. North and south aisles give the spaciousness that is not apparent from the outside. There are some nice windows of painted glass, with religious and local themes. Coeval with the church is the font: the bowl is nicely carved and stands on four clustered columns.

HASSINGHAM St Mary

No of Bells: 1
19th c. Deanery: Blofield
Hundred: Blofield
Union house: Lingwood
21st c. Deanery: Blofield
Benefice: Lingwood

10 m ESE of Norwich in Church Road, Hassingham. Turn west off the B1140 north of Cantley and follow the road for about 1 mile.
O.S. grid ref: TG 369055
Post Code: NR13 4HH

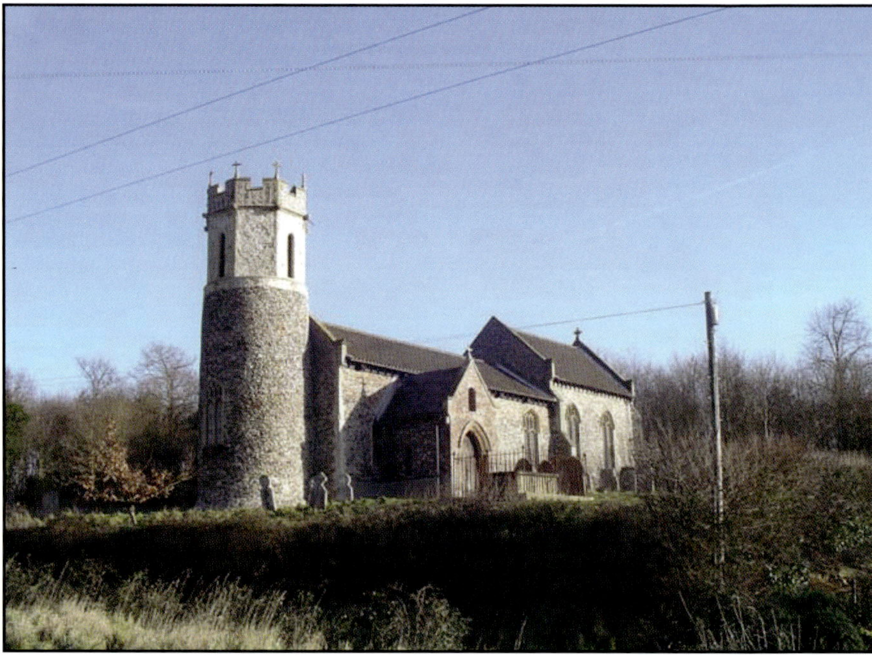

Two things distinguish this church. The most prominent is the lovely octagonal top to the Norman tower with crosses at each corner. The other is the extraordinary height of the chancel, towering about six feet above the nave. The porch is built in a similar fashion with its roof reaching the eaves of the nave. Inside the porch is a simple Norman doorway. Before the 1970s the roofs were thatched, but a fire gutted the interior and the roofs were rebuilt and tiled. For the same reason the inside of the building is stark and no attempt has been made to bring back the character of the past. Everywhere is painted white without enhancement or decoration. Seating is individual chairs and the Holy table looks as if it came from IKEA. The church is always locked, but there's little worth seeing inside anyway.

HECKINGHAM St Gregory *****

No of Bells:	2
19th c. Deanery:	Brooke
Hundred:	Clavering
Union house:	Heckingham
21st c. Deanery:	Loddon
Benefice:	Chet Valley

2 miles E of Loddon off the B1136. Follow the Loddon to Norton Subcourse road. The church is on the left down a short track.

O.S. grid ref: TM 384988
Post Code: NR14 6QU

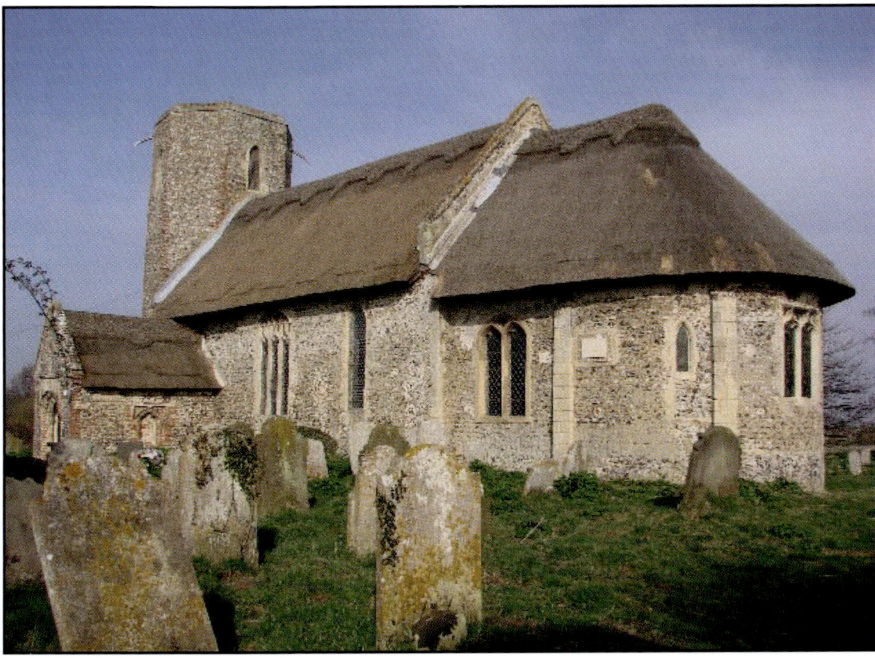

This beautiful church is maintained by The Churches Conservation Trust and is always open. Totally thatched with an apsidal end, it looks very similar to Hales church a few miles away. The porch protects a spectacular Norman doorway with five orders of decoration and is one of the finest in the county. Every part of the church is Norman except for the octagonal upper stage of the tower which was added a few centuries later. Just inside the south door is a broken ancient stone coffin. The original 12th c. font is square, standing on four columns and a central shaft. Nearby is an old bier, once used to carry coffins up to the church. The roof of the nave is panelled, that of the apsidal chancel is plastered. Two old backless benches with crude poppy-head type ends occupy the front of the nave. Wonderful!

HEDENHAM St Peter
No of Bells: 6
19th c. Deanery: Brooke
Hundred: Loddon
Union house: Heckingham
21st c. Deanery: Redenhall
Benefice: Ditchingham (Earsham)

3 miles NW of Bungay.
From Bungay turn right at the Mermaid PH or large Tudor Manor House and follow the road.
O.S. grid ref: TM 312933
Post Code: NR35 2LF

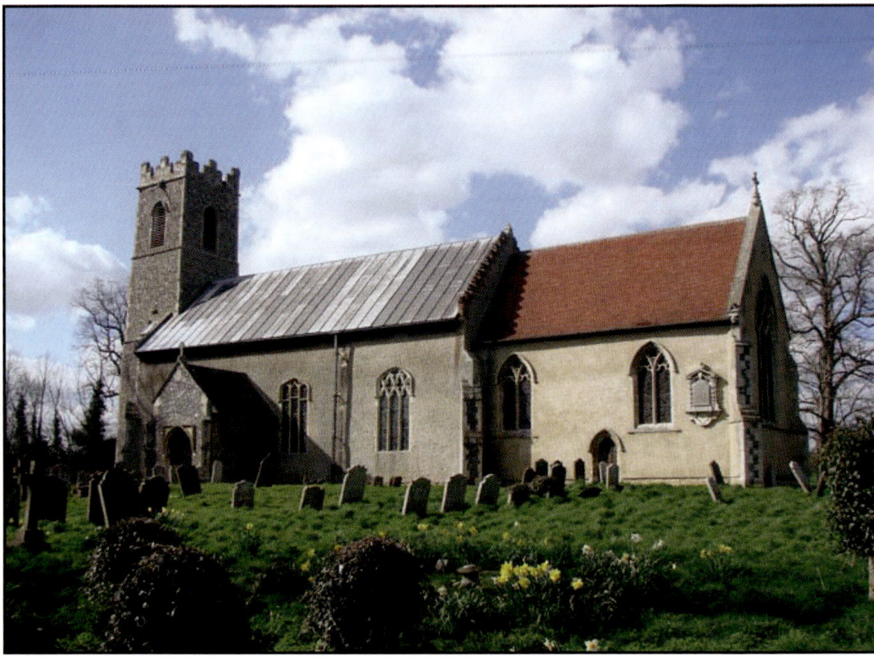

The church was built on high ground overlooking the parish to the south. Steps leading to the church are foot-stones, deliberately robbed from graves. The tower is without buttresses and has a stepped crenulated parapet. Cement-rendering on the outer walls does little to enhance the appearance, although I have seen much worse. The octagonal 15th c. font is deeply carved with Tudor roses and shields, and clustered columns around a narrow shaft. Above the nicely carved chancel arch is a Victorian wall painting. The piscina and three-tier sedilia have also been touched by over-enthusiastic Victorian hands and are ornamented with gaudy tiles and heraldic devices. The walls are liberally splattered with monuments to the Bedingfield, Garney and Spendlove family members, some dating as far back as the 16th c.

HEIGHAM	Holy Trinity
No of Bells:	1 (unusable)
19th c. Deanery:	Norwich
Hundred:	Norwich
Union house:	Norwich
21st c. Deanery:	Norwich South
Benefice:	Heigham Holy Trinity

1 mile as the crow flies SW of Norwich castle in Trinity Street, Heigham. Between Newmarket Road and Unthank Road.
O.S. grid ref: TG 222080
Post Code:110A, NR2 2BJ

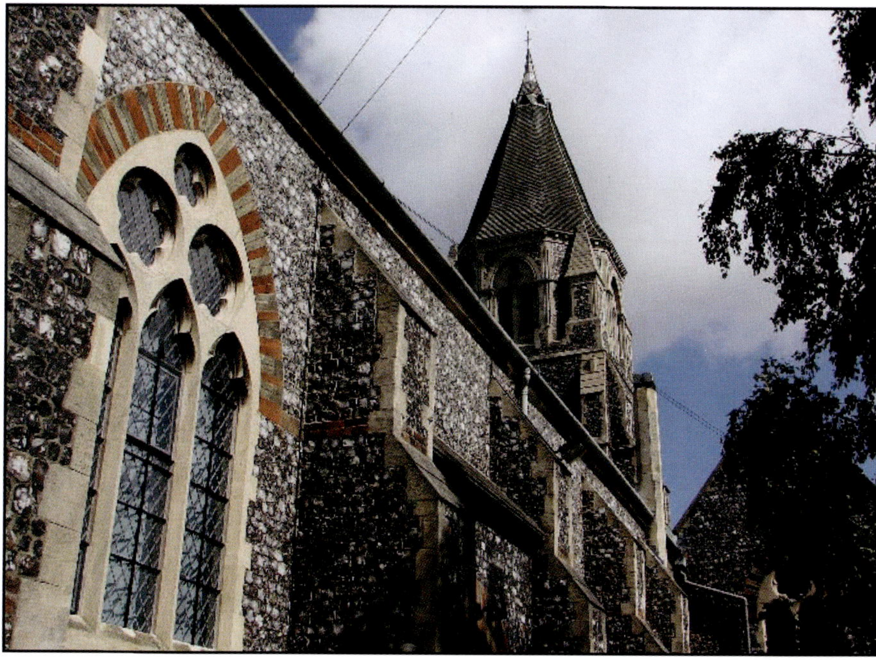

Holy Trinity was consecrated in 1861. It is a typical Victorian church with embellishments to the structure added wherever possible. Entering the church is like entering a cinema, with a foyer containing a lending library and kitchen facilities. Double glass doors lead through into the carpeted nave, which is bright and airy. In the northwest corner is the stark square white font, supported on four-rust coloured marble columns with decorated capitals around a central shaft. A small portable pillar font is situated in the chancel. The coeval pulpit has carved panels and looks brand new. A nice brass eagle lectern looks out of place surrounded by so much varnished wood. Behind the holy table is a reredos depicting the Last Supper, beautifully carved in wood. Always open and welcoming to visitors.

HEIGHAM St Thomas
No of Bells: 1
19th c. Deanery: Norwich
Hundred: Norwich
Union house: Norwich
21st c. Deanery: Norwich South
Benefice: Heigham St Thomas

1 mile as the crow flies SW of Norwich castle. In Earlham Road at the Junction with Edinburgh Road.
O.S. grid ref: TG 214086
Post Code: NR6 5NU

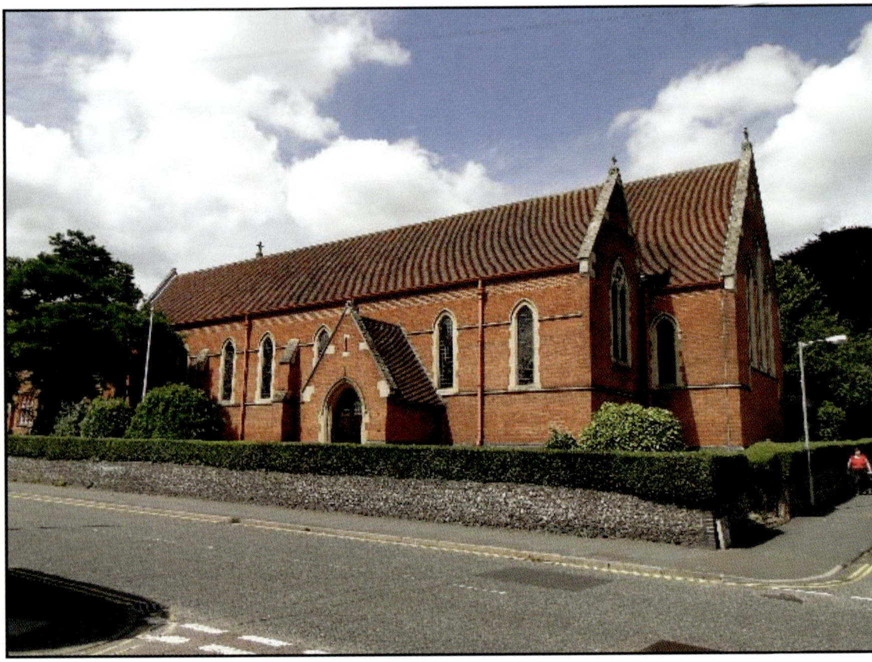

First built in 1888 with a hammerbeam roof, it was bombed in 1942 and had to be completely rebuilt and in 1954 it was rededicated. Since then it has become one of the most successful churches in the city. The huge expanse of the nave and north and south aisles is beautifully lit by the windows, many of which have stained glass featuring Sts. Withburga, Juliana, Edmund and Felix. St. Thomas features in the east window. The benches and fittings are all in a light oak colour and very agreeable. The broad arcades are very pleasing and give the impression of openness without the feeling of being a barn as many Victorian churches seem to do. The modern slim-line font is in the traditional style I am pleased to say. My usual dislike of Victorian churches has certainly found an exception here.

HELLESDON	St Mary	2 miles from the centre of Norwich. From Dereham Road (A1074) take 1st on the right from the ring road and follow ¾ mile on Low Road.
No of Bells:	3	
19th c. Deanery:	Taverham	
Hundred:	Taverham	
Union house:	St Faith's	
21st c. Deanery:	Norwich North	O.S. grid ref: TG 200106
Benefice:	Hellesdon	Post Code: NR6 5AE

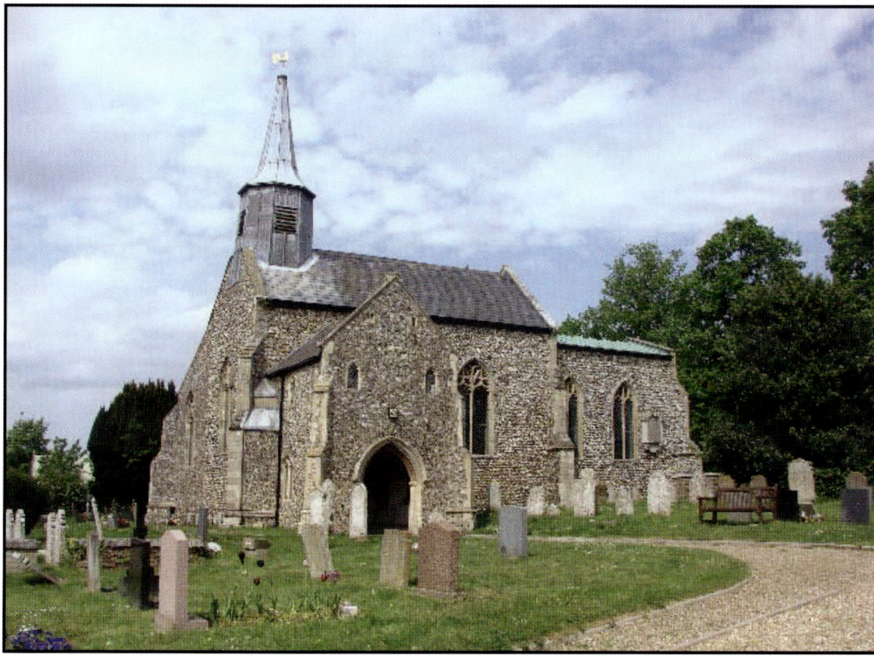

This is not one of the prettiest churches I have seen. Every part seems disproportionate to the other. The tall porch is groined and has a parvise above with two quite small windows. Access to it is via an external stair turret and seems to be a later addition. The bell turret is making every attempt to look like a spire above a short 'stumpy' nave that is not helped by the addition of a north aisle. Inside there is a late 14th c. font with tracery decoration and engaged columns to the central shaft. The internal arcade is 15th c. relating closely to the date of construction. The Victorians have replaced the roofs and most of the furnishings and fittings. In the narrow chancel is a simple double piscina with traceried heads. A chancel chapel is the only unusual feature in an otherwise quite uninteresting church.

HELLINGTON St John the Baptist
No of Bells: 1
19th c. Deanery: Brooke
Hundred: Loddon
Union house: Heckingham
21st c. Deanery: -
The Churches Conservation Trust

7 miles SE of Norwich. Turn left off the A146, 7 miles S of Norwich at the crossroads. Then first left and follow to destination.
O.S. grid ref: TG 313030
Post Code: NR14 7BS

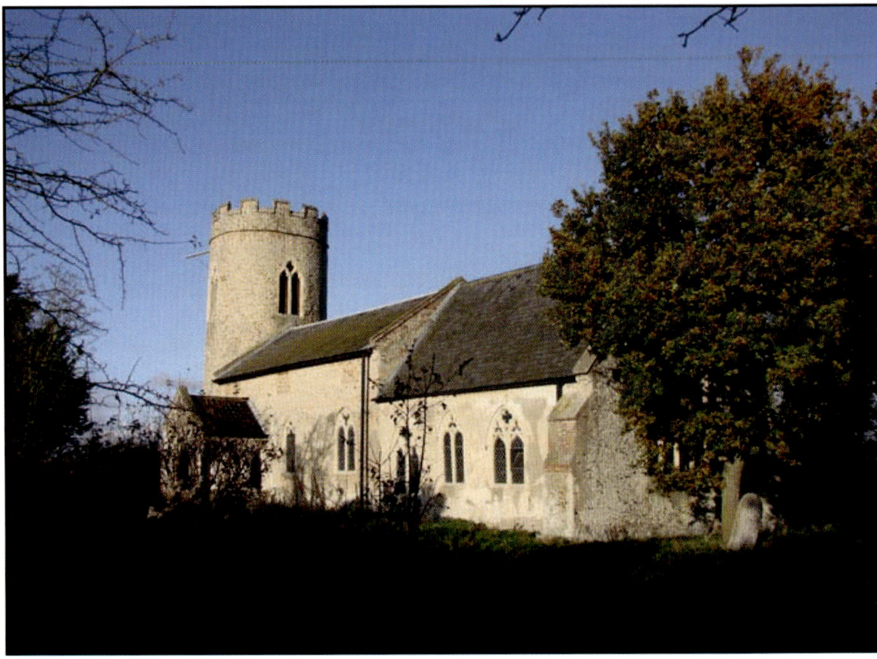

The Churches Conservation Trust is responsible for the upkeep of this lovely little church. Although all valuables have been removed it is still a splendid example of an early Norman church. The 13th c. porch with its three canopied niches around the doorway gives a hint of its past importance. Inside the porch the wonderful Norman doorway with six orders of decoration (although partially hidden by the porch which was obviously added later) is revealed in all its splendour. The north doorway is also Norman. Inside the nave there are carved heads all over the place peering down at the visitor. The font is relatively plain and unimportant. Poppyheads on the benches are ordinary but all different. The later double drain piscina and dropped-sill sedilia are quite plain. Well worth a visit for its curiosity value, however.

HEMBLINGTON All Saints

No of Bells:	1
19th c. Deanery:	Blofield
Hundred:	Walsham
Union house:	Acle
21st c. Deanery:	Blofield
Benefice:	Blofield

8 miles E by N of Norwich.
From the A47 turn north west of Burlingham, go left, right, left, until you reach the Hall then turn right.
O.S. grid ref: TG 353115
Post Code: NR13 4EF

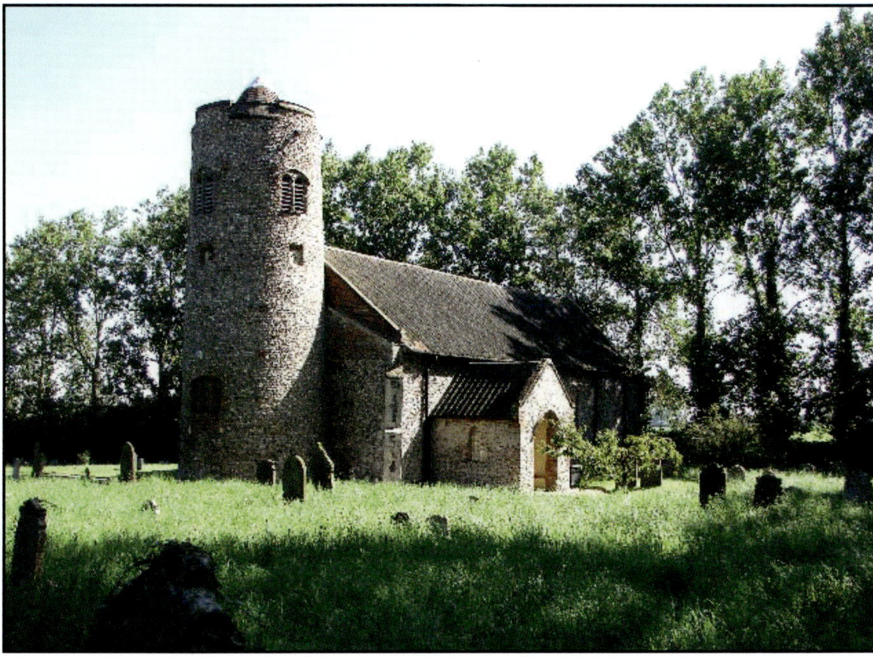

Hemblington is a lovely little church and the keyholder is never far away. The tower may be as early as Saxon and has seen little change in its history, probably originally as a defendable shelter in the event of invasion. In the rubble-built porch is a niche for a stoup. The church fabric is a little later. Immediately inside the door on the right is a semi-intramural burial. The stone coffin lid bears a foliated cross (but it is maybe just a seat). The font is quite unusual, depicting saints and the Trinity. It has been coloured in pastel shades and is quite pleasing. Wall paintings are still in vivid colour and have not suffered the usual fading. Above the nave is a simple arch-braced roof; the chancel has a wagon roof. Steps that once led to the rood loft are still visible. The pulpit complete with back-board and tester is 18th c.

HEMPNALL St Margaret of Antioch

No of Bells:	1
19th c. Deanery:	Depwade
Hundred:	Depwade
Union house:	Pulham St Mary
21st c. Deanery:	Depwade
Benefice:	Hempnall

9 m S of Norwich in 'The Street', Hempnall. Beside the road on a bend midway between Woodton and Tasburgh on the B1527.
O.S. grid ref: TM 241944
Post Code: NR15 2AD

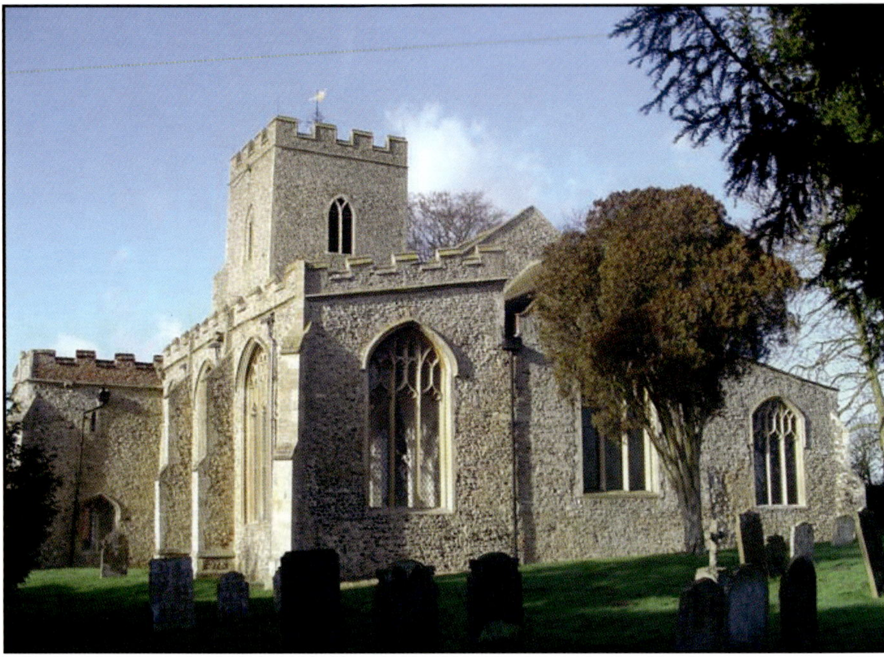

This is a monster of a church and it is full of chairs. Column arcades create the 13th c. north and 14th c. south aisles. The font is typical of the East Anglian style but the decoration around the octagonal bowl is a little unusual. A gallery has been constructed accessed by a spiral staircase beneath the tower. There is no pulpit; instead, there is a stage in front of the chancel. Above, the roof has arch-braced tiebeams. The clerestory windows are attractive, but tiny and somewhat ineffective. The parish chest is locked away out of sight in the parvise, but it ought to be on show. The church looks more like a theatre than a church, but I have nothing but praise for the Hempnall Team Ministry, who keep every church in the benefice open. It was a joy to visit all eight of them. Thank you. May others follow your example.

HEMPSTEAD	St Andrew ****	8 miles E of North Walsham. From the coast road turn east at Lessingham and follow the road signs to Hempstead.
No of Bells:	3	
19th c. Deanery:	Waxham	
Hundred:	Happing	
Union house:	Smallburgh	
21st c. Deanery:	Waxham & Tunstead	O.S. grid ref: TG 404284
Benefice:	Happisburgh	Post Code: NR12 0SH

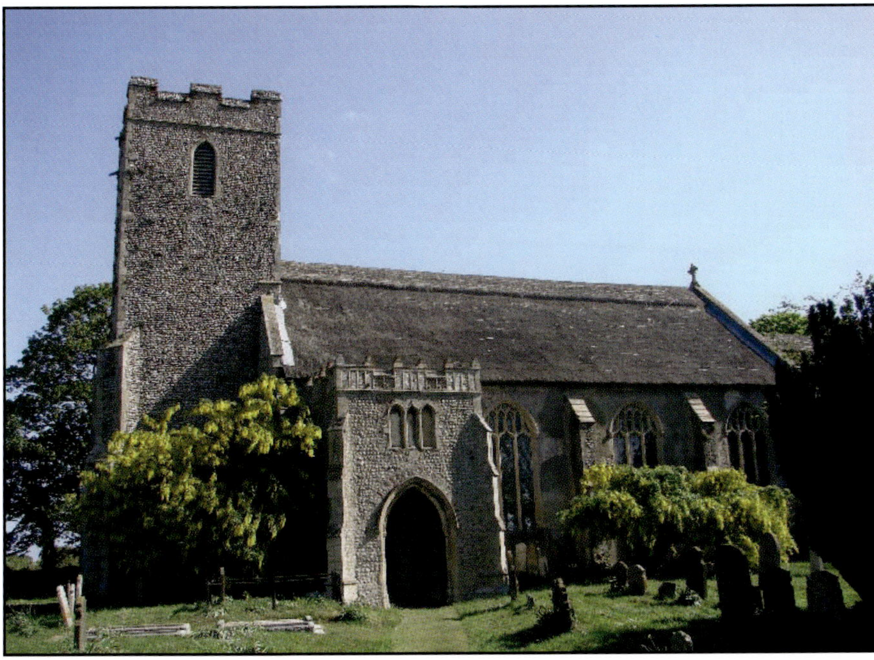

The nave and chancel are continuous and both are entirely thatched. This is a typical country church, with perhaps the exception of having a chamber over the embattled porch. Built in the 15th c. it has remained almost unaltered. The south doors have the original tracery. There is a simple coeval octagonal font with roses and shields and four lions around the shaft. There are some unusual baroque bench ends and a Jacobean pulpit. The screen however is what makes this church special. It has delicately carved fine tracery including the arch, some of which is missing, but it is the panels painted with beautiful representations of eleven named saints which makes is so unique *[The twelfth, St Eligius, was stolen in 1982]*. Arguably exceeds Ranworth in quality. Quite special and worthy of a visit.

HEMSBY	St Mary the Virgin	6 miles N by W of Great
No of Bells:	1 usable 2 on display.	Yarmouth. From
19th c. Deanery:	Flegg	Yarmouth turn right after
Hundred:	West Flegg	the stadium and follow to
Union house:	Rollesby	Hemsby for 4½ miles.
21st c. Deanery:	Great Yarmouth	O.S. grid ref: TG 494173
Benefice:	Flegg (Coastal)	Post Code: NR29 4EU

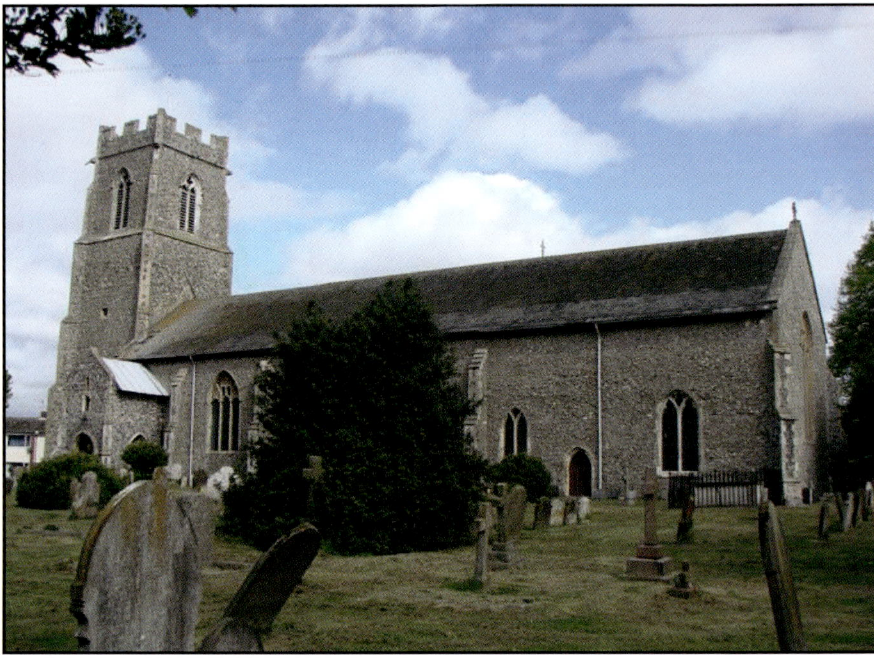

A deeply embattled parapet atop this fine 15th c. tower and single roofline distinguish this church. The 15th c. south porch has a parvise over the groined ceiling which has some interesting carved bosses. The entrance however is by the north door. The font is a typical East Anglian type standing on two octagonal plinths. The modern roof is arch-braced resting on large corbels. Also in the chancel are two of the original five bells, but only one remains to strike the hours. Modern benches have reproduction poppyheads, in fact most of the furnishings are Victorian or later, including the rood loft and screen. Stairs to the rood loft are still usable. A piscina in the south aisle indicates a one-time chapel. The chancel piscina has been filled in but the dropped-sill sedilia remains with a new wooden seat.

HICKLING St Mary
No of Bells: 5
19th c. Deanery: Waxham
Hundred: Happing
Union house: Smallburgh
21st c. Deanery: Waxham & Tunstead
Benefice: Waterside

18 miles NE of Norwich. From the A149 turn east at Sutton and follow to Hickling. The church is north of the village centre.
O.S. grid ref: TG 414243
Post Code: NR12 0BQ

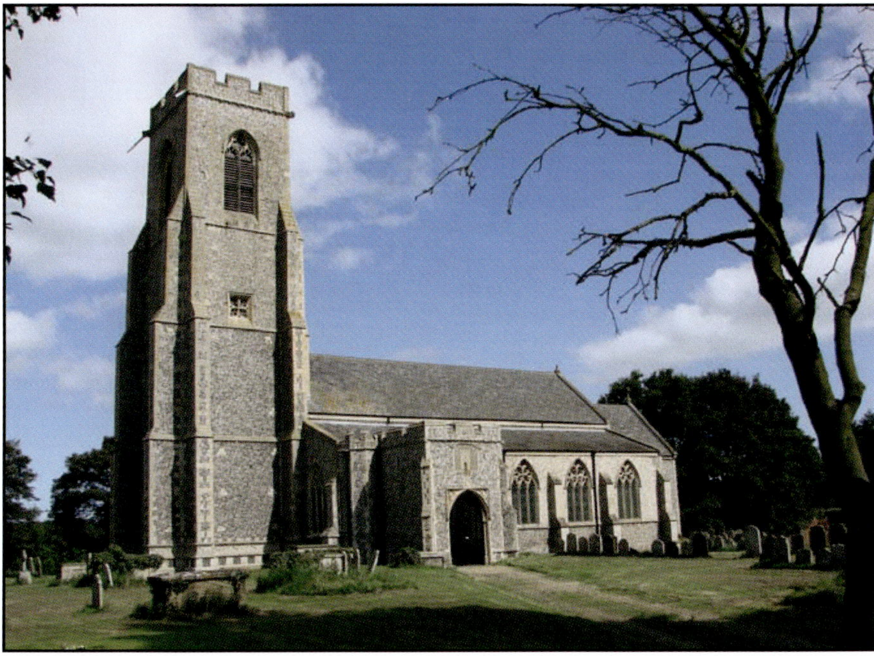

A quite splendid embattled tower dominates the church which has a porch with a parvise above, leading into the south aisle. The 14th c. font has floriated designs in the panels around the octagonal bowl and shaft. Close by stands a fine large-wheeled bier with a canopy and T handle. The north and south aisles are divided from the central aisle by magnificent arches. The chancel is small and might suggest that the church was once much smaller than it is today. The Victorians have certainly left their mark here. Ancient graffiti can be seen on the fine tomb at the east end of the north aisle. See if you can make out what is written there! The Holy table has a fine pair of legs and is from the Stuart period. All the roof timbers are modern and were part of the Victorian restorations.

HONING	Sts Peter & Paul	4 miles SE of North Walsham.
No of Bells:	5	From the A149 at Nth
19th c. Deanery:	Waxham	Walsham turn left at the x-
Hundred:	Tunstead	roads and follow the road
Union house:	Smallburgh	through Briggate for 2 miles.
21st c. Deanery:	Waxham & Tunstead	O.S. grid ref: TG 325280
Benefice:	Smallburgh	Post Code: NR28 9PF

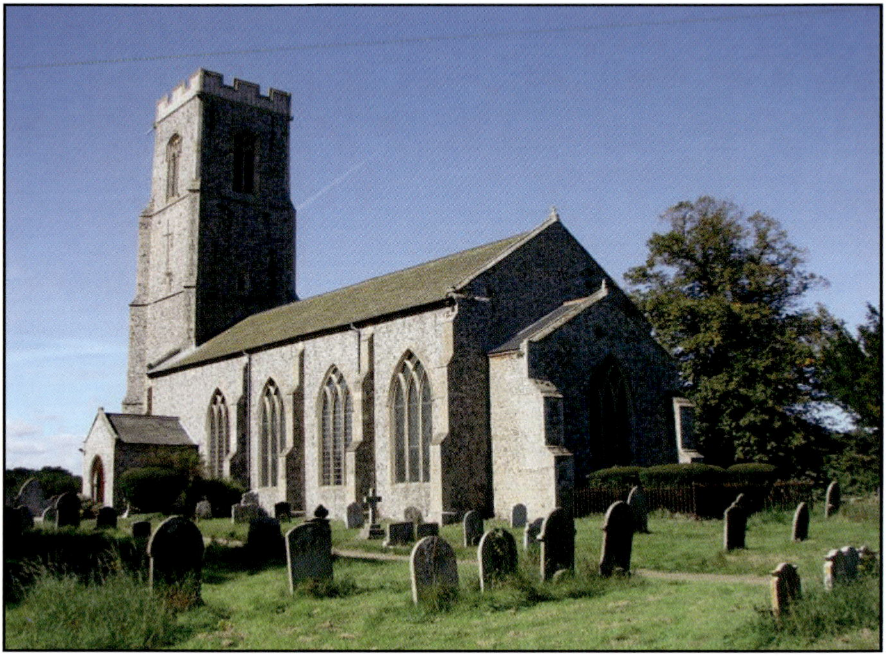

The tall nave and tiny heavily buttressed chancel of this church are obvious from the external view. The 15th c. embattled tower is in perfect proportion with the nave. The church was originally a Norman construction but in 1795 the whole building was restructured. The four-feet-deep chancel was intentional to give greater effect to the east window. The north and south aisles are very narrow and have elongated octagonal columns that give support to the arch-braced beams, with king posts supporting the single roof. The font bowl is octagonal with arcading, and dates from the 13th c. It is decorated with heads beneath, but the beautifully decorated shaft on which it stands is 200 years later; a pleasing combination. The Holy table, which is almost as wide as the chancel, is Stuart in date.

HOPTON with BROTHERTON St Margaret

No of Bells: (2) removed
19th c. Deanery: Lothingland
Hundred: Mutford & Lothingland
Union house: Oulton
21st c. Deanery: -
Benefice: -

4 m N of Lowestoft
between Lowestoft & Gt. Yarmouth, turn east off the A12 at Hopton into village.
O.S. grid ref TM 530999
Post Code: NR31 9BT

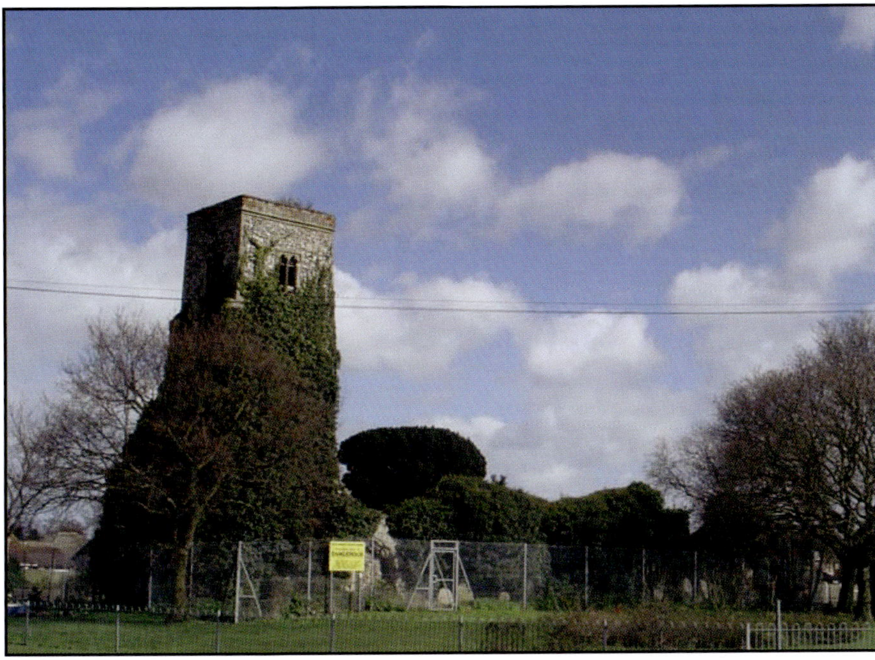

This ruin was created when the church burned down (the heating stove went out of control) on a cold January 2nd 1865. The church and tower is 14th c. and the east window shows typical tracery for that period. The roof was thatched, which obviously contributed to the ferocity of the fire. Although the tower still stands at its full height the structure is covered in ivy and detail cannot be seen. The nave was served by a north door without a porch. An unobstructed west nave window was achieved by the west tower being offset to the south corner of the nave. The font was described as 'curiously sculptured': it would be nice to know where it is today, if it survived. The hamlet of Brotherton, which was to the west of Hopton, was consolidated with Hopton many centuries ago.

HOPTON-ON-SEA St Margaret
No of Bells: 2
19th c. Deanery: Lothingland
Hundred: Mutford & Lothingland
Union house: Oulton
21st c. Deanery: Great Yarmouth
Benefice: Corton

4 m N of Lowestoft
between Lowestoft & Gt. Yarmouth, turn east off the A12 at Hopton & then turn left
O.S. grid ref TG 524000
Post Code: NR31 9AH

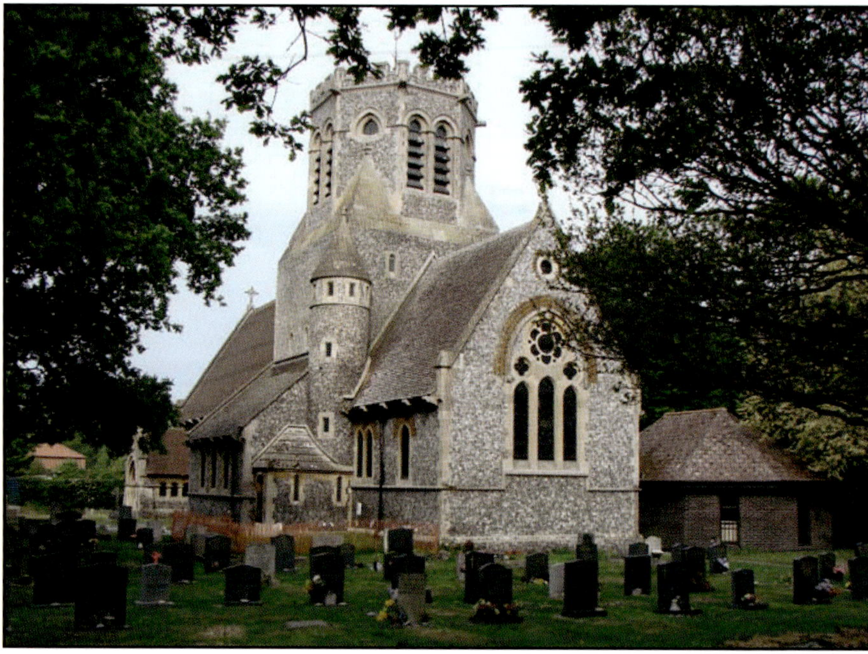

This church is Victorian and was built in 1865/ 66, replacing the mediaeval church which was destroyed by fire *(see previous page)*. It was designed by S.S.Teulon and built by Brown & Bailey of Norwich. The design is revolutionary and has a central square tower which becomes octagonal above the roof-line. The belfry is accessed by the turret staircase with a conical roof. The interior is mainly red and white brick dressing with stonework around the windows. Everything in the church is modern and nothing was retrieved from the old church. St. Margaret's has been acclaimed as 'a fine example of a Victorian church in which everything is boldly executed'. To me it is trying to look like something it has no business to look like. A town church in a village just doesn't sit comfortably with me.

HORNING	St Benedict
No of Bells:	1
19th c. Deanery:	Waxham
Hundred:	Tunstead
Union house:	Smallburgh
21st c. Deanery:	Waxham & Tunstead
Benefice:	Ashmanhaugh

9 miles NE of Norwich. between Hoveton & Potter Heigham. Turn south off the A1062 east of Horning near Grove Farm.

O.S. grid ref:	TG 355166
Post Code:	NR12 8PZ

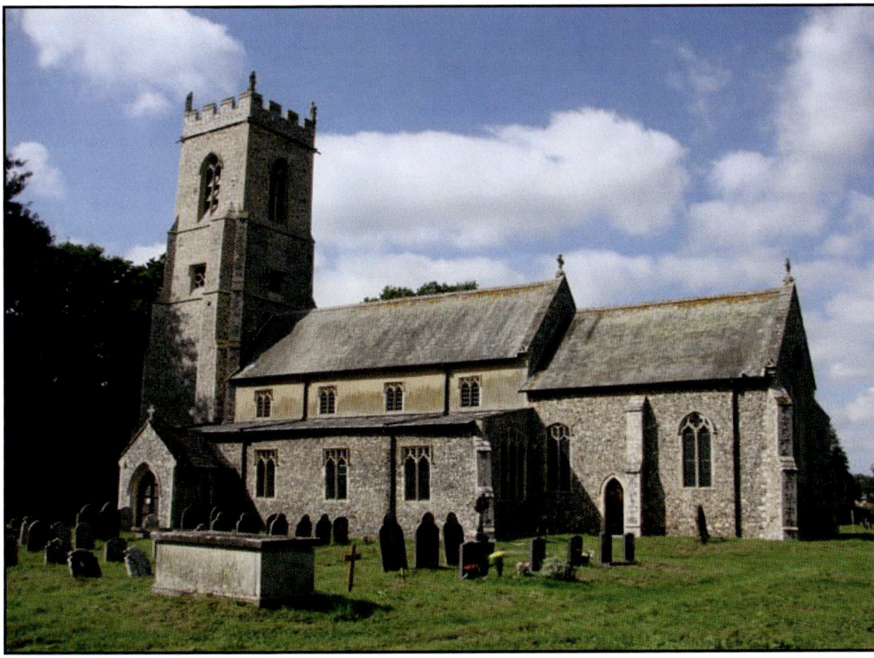

When entering the churchyard through the lychgate you will see that the arches of the north aisle are noticeable in the external wall. Standing upon the embattled parapet of the 15th c. tower are four evangelists seemingly guarding the churchyard. The nave has an eight-window clerestory which still leaves the interior quite gloomy, but with its small windows the south aisle is the real culprit here. The pulpit is on the left of the nave, to the right the rood loft stairs remain open. The octagonal font has simple designs around the bowl with an embattled rim, the shaft has columns extending all the way up to the bowl. In the chancel there are consecration crosses on the walls and the 16th c. benches have various carvings of grotesques. The church also possesses a 13th c. chest with a fine example of early ironwork.

HORSEY-NEXT-THE-SEA All Saints

No of Bells:	1
19th c. Deanery:	Waxham
Hundred:	Smallburgh
Union house:	Smallburgh
21st c. Deanery:	Great Yarmouth
Benefice:	Flegg (Coastal)

11 miles NE of Great Yarmouth. Midway between West Somerton & Sea Palling. turn left in Horsey at right hand bend.

O.S. grid ref: TG 457231

Post Code: NR29 4EF

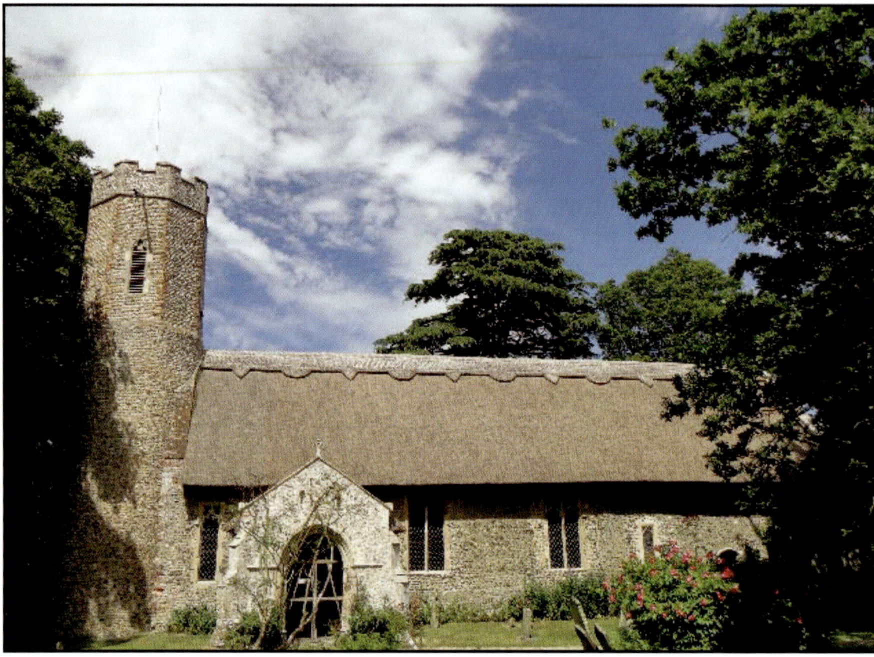

In 2010 the church was re-thatched. This church is a little gem with a good Norman tower with an octagonal upper stage. Situated in a lovely setting, it is partially hidden by trees particularly on the north side. The 14th c. font has simple arcading around the bowl and shaft. Bench ends with poppy-head carvings on the ends fill the aisle. A rowel hangs in front of the simple screen behind which, in the chancel, are three aumbries set into the wall. The piscina has a round arch that once had tracery decoration, and a dropped-sill sedilia, behind which a later small window has been inserted. The Victorians have made some changes and inserted new windows, but it has been sympathetically carried out. Behind the pulpit it is believed there is a second piscina, indicating an earlier chapel. A pleasure to visit.

HORSHAM ST FAITH St Mary & St Andrew

No of Bells:	5	3 m N of Norwich. Turn right off the A140 out of Norwich. The church is within 400 yards.
19th c. Deanery:	Taverham	
Hundred:	Taverham	
Union house:	Horsham St Faith	
21st c. Deanery:	Norwich North	O.S. grid ref: TG 215152
Benefice:	Horsham	Post Code: NR10 3JJ

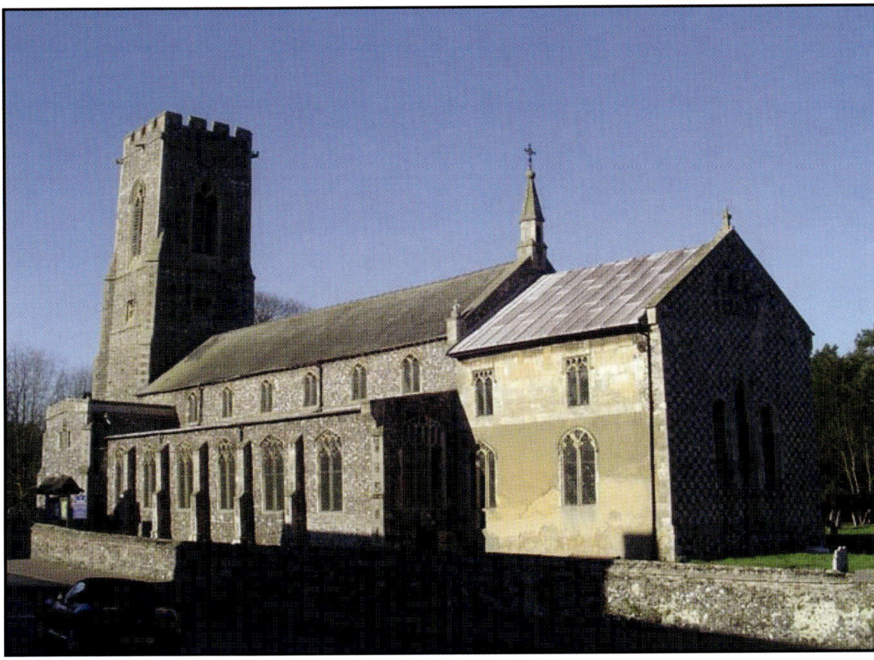

Standing within a few feet of the road this church is worth a visit. Over the groined porch is a parvise. There are more paintings of saints here than most. Not only are there twelve on the vaulted screen, but a further eight on the pulpit. The former is dated 1528, the latter 1480, and is quite exceptional. The 15th c. font has tracery around the bowl and animal heads on the base. The font cover has four pillars rising to a canopy and an ogee pyramidal top, terminating in a pinnacle, similar to the one at St Michael at Plea. A squint has been cut into the chancel arch for the south aisle chapel to view proceedings at the altar. The double piscina is quite plain, with trefoil arches and a central pillar. The sedilia has been removed. At the west end of the south aisle stairs lead to the ringing chamber. The parish chest is about 17th c.

HORSTEAD with Stanninghall All Saints

No of Bells:	3	7 m NNE of Norwich.
19th c. Deanery:	Taverham	Leave Norwich on the
Hundred:	Taverham	B1150 for 5½ miles, then at
Union house:	Horsham St Faith	the Y junction turn left.
21st c. Deanery:	Ingworth	O.S. grid ref: TG 262199
Benefice:	Norwich North	Post Code: NR12 7EP

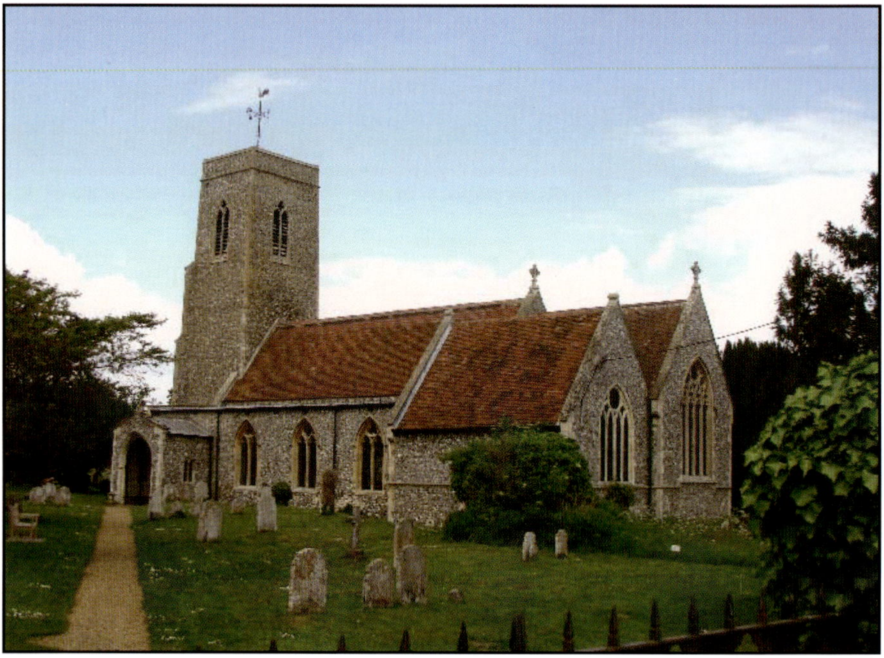

The addition of a chancel chapel beside the chancel has given this church an asymmetric appearance. The Victorian 'restorers' almost rebuilt the church. Everything of historical interest has been discarded except the Royal Arms of Queen Anne, which are filthy. A plain 13th c. octagonal font is supported on eight columns around a central shaft. The lovely wooden pulpit has been replaced with one of cold stone. What is exceptional here is the 19th and 20th c. painted glass in the windows. Glass is quite specialised and I usually avoid the subject, but here it is rather impressive. Many of the saints are represented, as they should be in a church dedicated to All Saints. Why the church is locked amazes me because the value is in the windows that could so easily be smashed, but the key is very close by.

HOVETON St John

No of Bells:	1
19th c. Deanery:	Waxham
Hundred:	Tunstead
Union house:	Smallburgh
21st c. Deanery:	Waxham & Tunstead
Benefice:	Wroxham

7½ miles NE of Norwich. From the A1151 go through Wroxham and turn right onto the A1062. The church is 300 yards on the right.

O.S. grid ref: TG 309183

Post Code: NR12 8JE

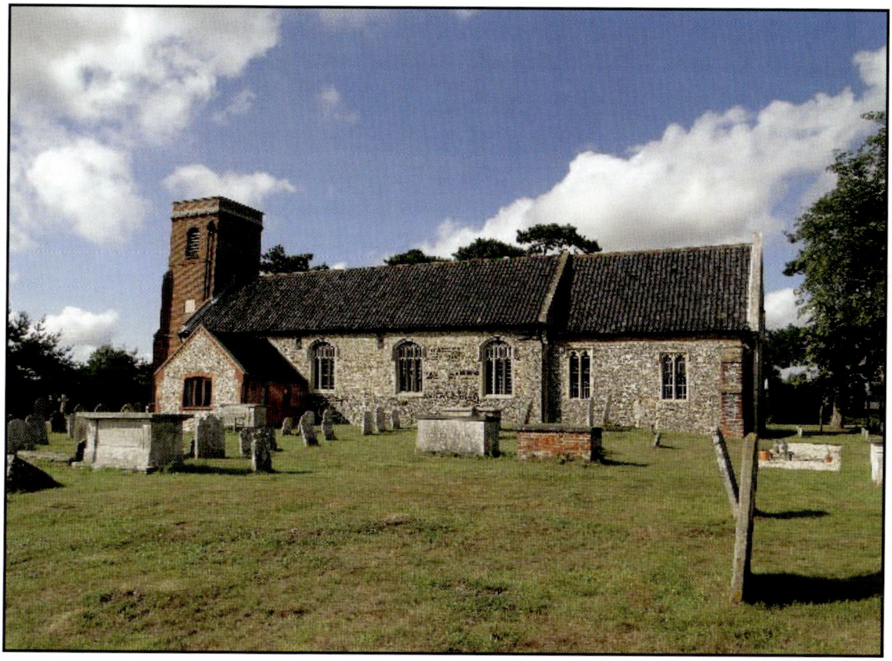

Looking slightly out of character is the brick tower which was built in 1765 to replace the earlier one which fell. The roof was replaced in Victorian times and the benches and the seating were probably replaced at the same time. The south porch is also a modern addition. The 15th c. octagonal font has shields on each facet and faces looking down from around the corbel. The square headed traceried screen has a rowel suspended from the ceiling to light the now non-existent rood. Light spills into the nave on a sunny day from the large 16th c. Perpendicular windows. The pulpit is octagonal and has tracery in the panels. The Royal Arms are Stuart and probably those of Charles II although they are unattributed to a monarch. The church possesses a 14th c. chest with a good example of ironwork of the day.

HOVETON	St Peter	9 miles NE of Norwich.
No of Bells:	1	From the A1151 go north
19th c. Deanery:	Waxham	through Wroxham and turn
Hundred:	Tunstead	left at the x-roads 1¼ miles
Union house:	Smallburgh	north of Hoveton village.
21st c. Deanery:	Waxham & Tunstead	O.S. grid ref: TG 314096
Benefice:	Wroxham	Post Code: NR12 8RL

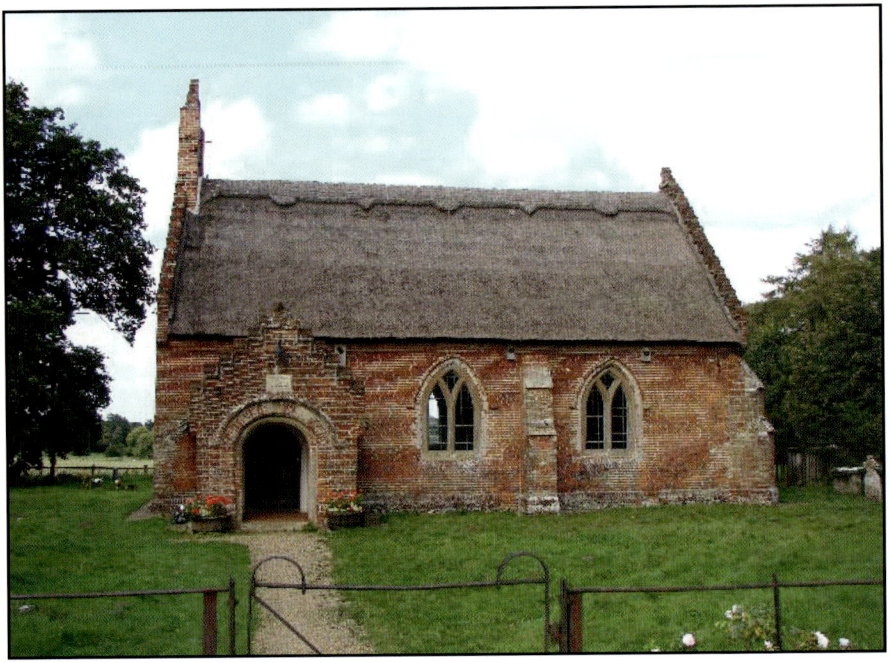

This tiny church was built in the early Stuart period about 1624. It is entirely thatched and has a lovely crow-step gable. It replaced an earlier church on the site. Above the roof at the west end is a single turret. Immediately inside the door stands the coeval round font very simply decorated with four Maltese crosses, one at each of the four compass points. On the wall are the unattributed Arms of the Royal Stuarts, and hatchments of the Blofeld family hang profusely around the nave. Worthy of note is a wall monument carved from marble giving the appearance of cloth, surmounted by cherubs and the family crest. It is to Mary Aufrere (1760) and her daughter Catherine aged 8 years who died in 1738. In the churchyard you will encounter a host of wildlife in the summer months; a beautiful and tranquil place.

HOWE	St Mary the Virgin
No of Bells:	1
19th c. Deanery:	Brooke
Hundred:	Clavering
Union house:	Heckingham
21st c. Deanery:	Loddon
Benefice:	Poringland

5 miles S of Norwich outskirts turn west off the B1332 1½ miles south of Poringland and follow the road to Howe Lane.

O.S. grid ref: TM 275999

Post Code: NR15 1HD

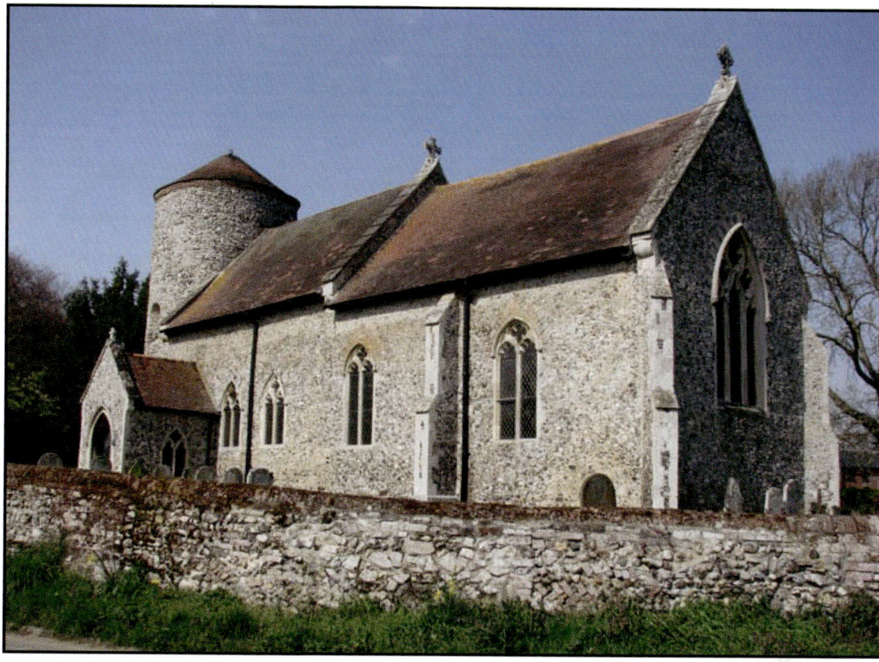

According to Pevsner this tower is one of the oldest in England. It is certainly pre-Conquest, with deep splayed circular windows. Even the church, in part, may be 11th c., although most of what you see is 14th or 15th c. A good deal of restoration took place in 1895 when the chancel arch and roofs were constructed. Earlier restoration saw new windows and the hanging of a bell, when the pyramidal cap was put on the tower. The roof is arch-braced with long wall-posts and figures on the corbels. Both pulpit and the square font are quite modern in comparison. The rood loft stairs are still open to the top although no trace remains of the loft or screen. One thing I did find very pleasing was the 100-year-old lectern which, carved from walnut, is in the form of an angel.

INGHAM	Holy Trinity	1¾ miles NE of Stalham.
No of Bells:	2	From Stalham church take
19th c. Deanery:	Waxham	the Ingham / Sea Palling
Hundred:	Happing	road. Church is at 2nd
Union house:	Smallburgh	crossroads.
21st c. Deanery:	Waxham & Tunstead	O.S. grid ref: TG 391240
Benefice:	Stalham	Post Code: NR12 9TB

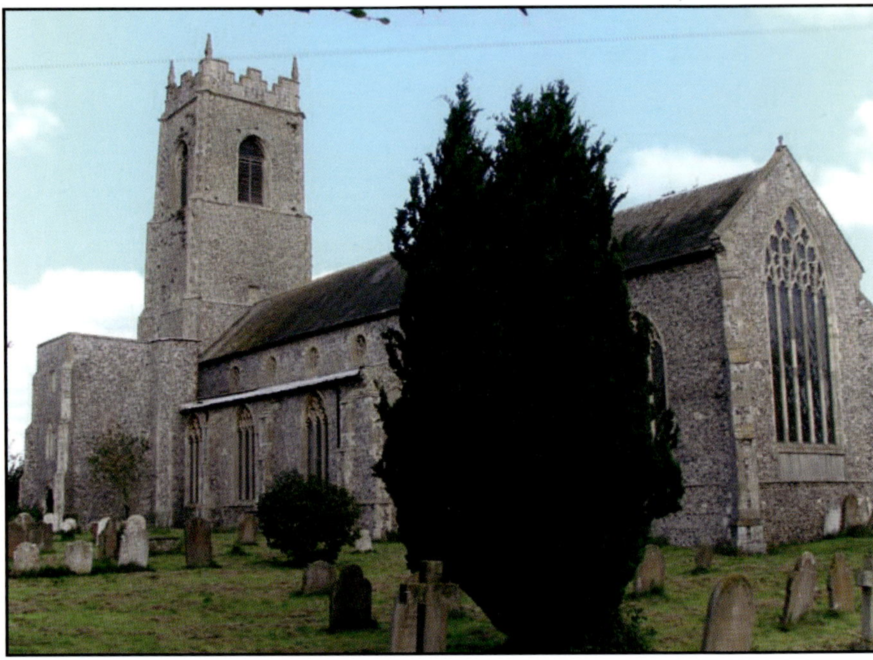

The 15th c. tower is very elegant, with its stepped battlements and tall pinnacles. Entry to the church is by the south porch which is simply groined and has two stories above, once used as a schoolroom. The large church used to be a conventual church to a priory; inside, the cloisters can still be seen in the north aisle. Unusually too, the clerestory has coloured glass in circular windows creating a lovely effect. The font is a large arcaded octagonal bowl supported by eight detached marble columns. Many of the fittings and the roofs are modern but the fine monumental effigies make up for that. The best is that of Sir Oliver de Ingham (1344). On the north wall is another knight, Roger le Blois, and his wife. The piscina and sedilia, on three different levels, are beneath four conjoined traceried arches.

IRSTEAD	St Michael
No of Bells:	1
19th c. Deanery:	Waxham
Hundred:	Tunstead
Union house:	Smallburgh
21st c. Deanery:	Waxham & Tunstead
Benefice:	Ashmanhaugh

11 miles NE of Norwich. From the A1062 turn north at Horning, turn right and follow road signs to Irstead. Go through Irstead Street.

O.S. grid ref: TG 365205

Post Code: NR12 8XR

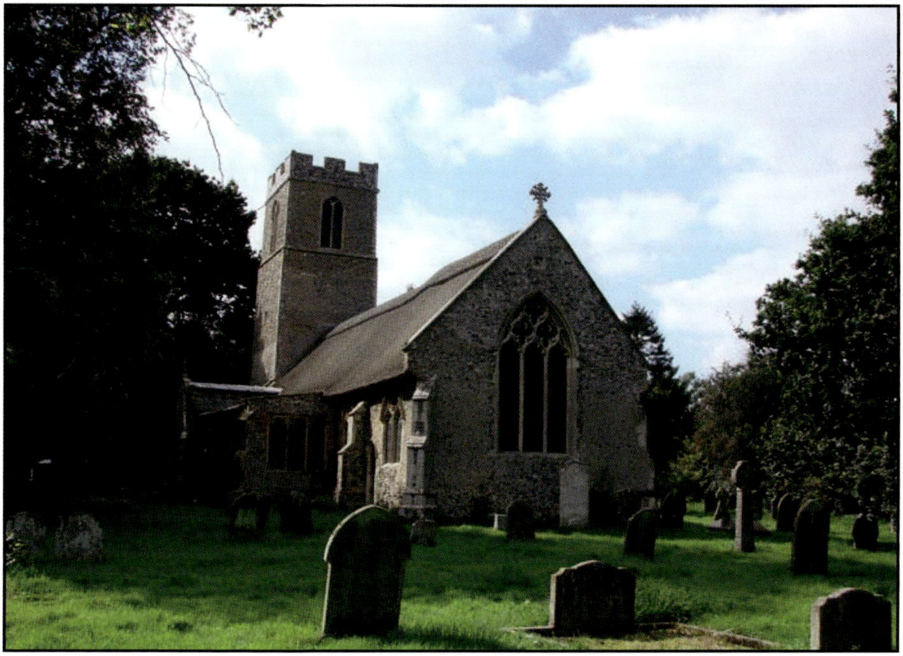

Built in the 14th c. the church remains entirely thatched to this day. The roof shows only slight differentiation between the nave and chancel, there being no chancel arch. The door handle is a quite rare surviving example of 14th c. ironwork. An embattled parapet tops the 14th c. square tower. The 14th c. font is quite intriguing having the usual carvings of lions but with figures between them. Around the bowl are other carved religious emblems. Original paintings showing the twelve apostles can still be seen on the screen that remains in good condition. On the wall is a much damaged painting partially obscured by two wall plaques and a window. The Elizabethan pulpit has linen fold panels and the Holy table is from about the same period. A few grotesques can be seen on some of the benches.

KIRBY BEDON St Andrew	
No of Bells:	3
19th c. Deanery:	Waxham
Hundred:	Tunstead
Union house:	Smallburgh
21st c. Deanery:	Waxham & Tunstead
Benefice:	Ashmanhaugh

3 miles SE of Norwich. Leave Norwich on the A146 and turn left at 3rd set of traffic lights at top of the hill and follow for 3 miles.
O.S. grid ref: TG 278054
Post Code: NR14 7DX

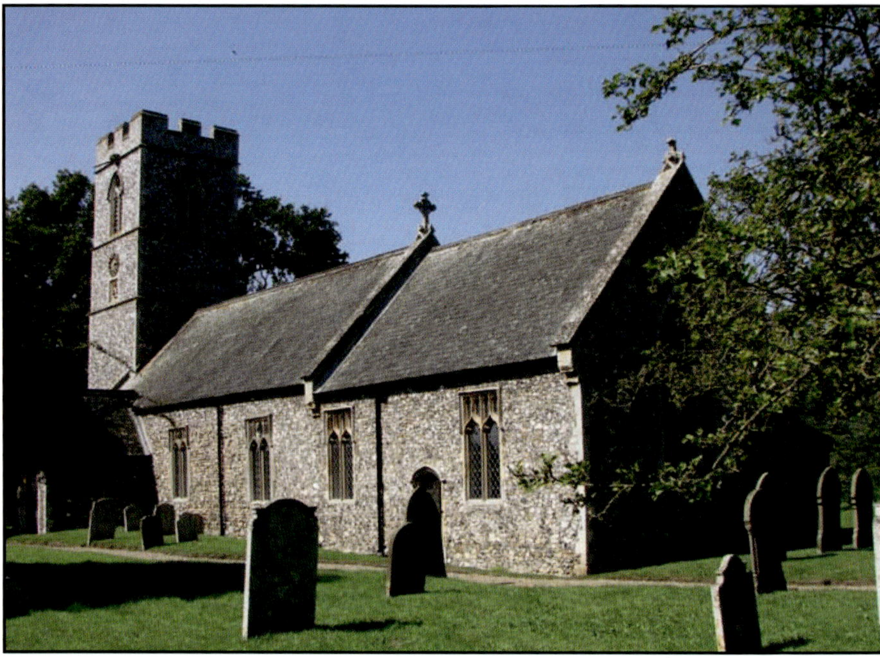

During the Spring this churchyard is a mass of daffodils. The church has a simple Norman doorway and the door and ironwork are contemporary. Beside the door is a stoup. Immediately inside the door is the early arcaded font and matching pedestal. Inside the base of the tower are the weights for the clock, which chimes every quarter. Most of the fixtures and fittings are Victorian, replaced during the period of restoration. A few poppy-head bench ends have been reproduced and a small piscina in the chancel is juxtaposed to the dropped-sill sedilia. Plaques and memorials adorn the nave and chancel walls; most are to the Brooke family. Knipe, Ward, Coleman and Randall are among the others recorded here. The nicest, with two figures kneeling in front of one another, is regrettably unreadable, I think due to over-polishing.

KIRBY BEDON St Mary

No of Bells: -

19th c. Deanery: Brooke

Hundred: Henstead

Union house: Swainsthorpe

21st c. Deanery: Loddon

Benefice: Bramerton

3 miles SE of Norwich.
Leave Norwich on the A146 and turn left at 3rd set of traffic lights at top of the hill and follow for 3 miles.

O.S. grid ref: TG 280054

Post Code: NR14 7DX

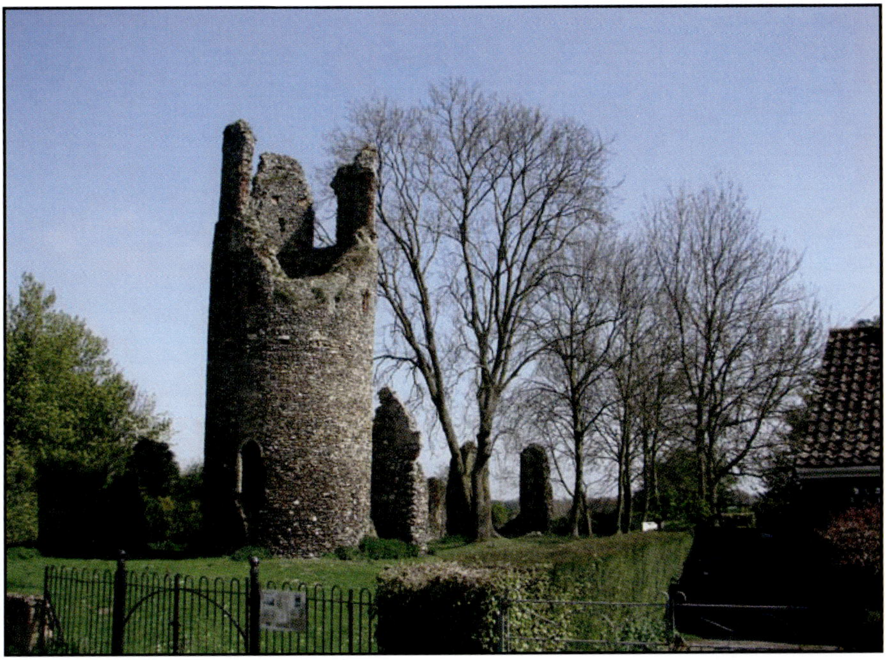

St Mary's is one of the ruins the visitor can stroll around at leisure. The walls have been consolidated and it is unfenced. The church, which is from between the late Norman and Early English period, fell into disuse after the Commonwealth and the reinstated Monarchy. About this time many of the parishes were uniting, and when two churches were as close together as these two were *(see previous page)* and with a depleted population at the end of the Civil War, the most favoured church won over the congregation. In many instances the fabric of the redundant church was used to repair the other. This happened in some cases, but not all, as there were many other reasons why churches were abandoned. Queen Elizabeth ordered many to be demolished, presumably those which adhered to Catholicism.

KIRBY CANE All Saints
No of Bells: 5
19th c. Deanery: Brooke
Hundred: Clavering
Union house: Heckingham
21st c. Deanery: Loddon
Benefice: Geldeston

4 miles S of Loddon and north of the village on the Loddon to Kirby Cane road. Quite close to Kirby Cane Hall.
O.S. grid ref: TM 373941
Post Code: NR35 2HN

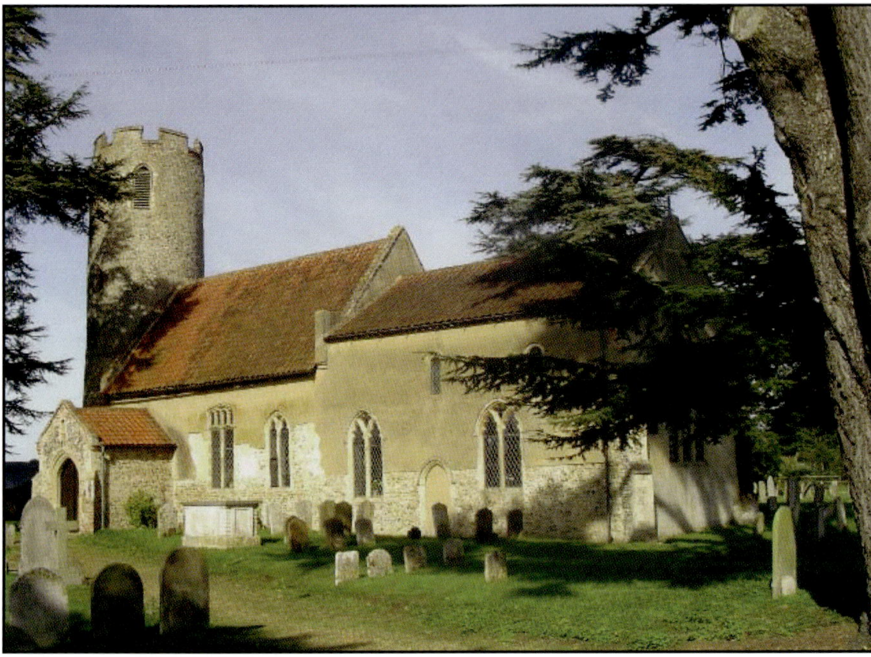

An early church, built in the 12th c. and little has changed here over the years. It has an elegant crenulated round tower, possibly pre-Conquest and was used as a defendable watch-tower. Around the base are pilaster strips about 4 feet high. The porch has a niche above the doorway and a stoup; the south doorway is Norman and has two engaged columns either side. The font is 14th c. with engaged columns around the shaft, angelic faces around the corbel and shields on the traceried bowl. A bier stands at the back of the church behind the pews. The pulpit is from the Stuart period as is the holy table. The rood stairs ascend from the reveal of a window within the wall of the nave. Near the chancel is an old tomb with undecipherable writing. Memorials include members of the Catelyne and Bacon families.

KIRSTEAD	St Margaret
No of Bells:	1
19th c. Deanery:	Brooke
Hundred:	Loddon
Union house:	Heckingham
21st c. Deanery:	Depwade
Benefice:	Brooke

8 miles SSE of Norwich. On the B1332 in Brooke turn left at crossroads and right after 300 yds. Ignore signs for Kirstead Green.

O.S. grid ref: TM 296985

Post Code: NR15 1ER

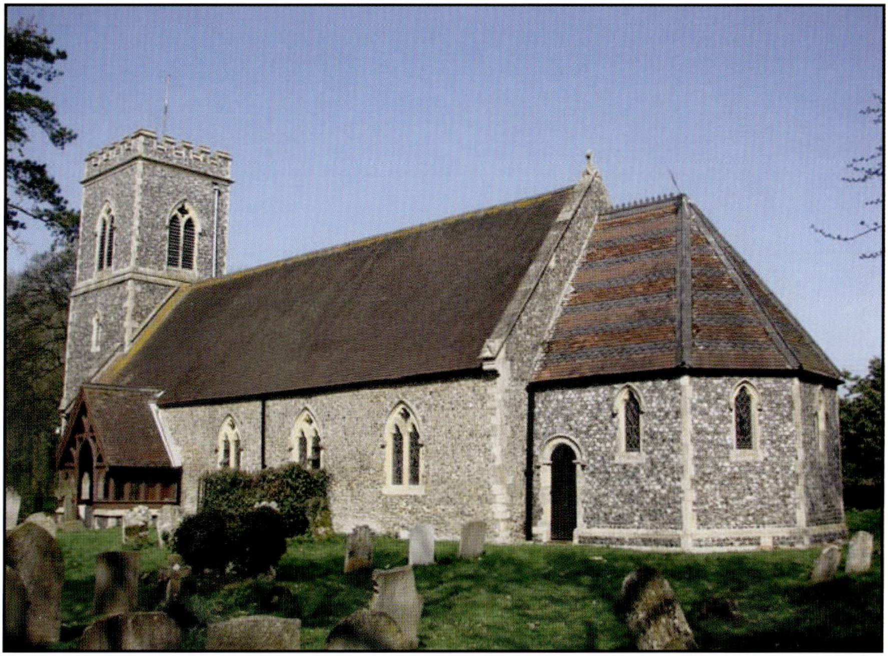

Kirstead has a lovely little church in a beautiful village setting but it has been so rebuilt only the original nave and a 12th c. doorway remain. Even the font is new and is very uninteresting. The skeletal style pulpit which stands on a stone base, seems completely inappropriate. Bench ends are decorated with poppy-heads but even this doesn't really help to make this church appealing to the historian or those looking for interesting architecture. Before the rebuilding, financed by the Kerrison family, the church was thatched and had two bells in a bellcote (a drawing in the church confirms this). My personal opinion is that it would have been more pleasing left as it was. However, what we see here today, albeit essentially a Victorian church, is better than an ivy-mantled ruin surrounded by nettles.

KNAPTON St Peter & St Paul *****

No of Bells: 5
19th c. Deanery: Repps
Hundred: North Erpingham
Union house: Gimingham
21st c. Deanery: Repps
Benefice: Trunch Team Ministry

3 miles NNE of North Walsham off the road to Mundesley (B 1145). At the second sharp bend after the water tower go straight on.
O.S. grid ref: TG 307342
Post Code: NR28 0AD

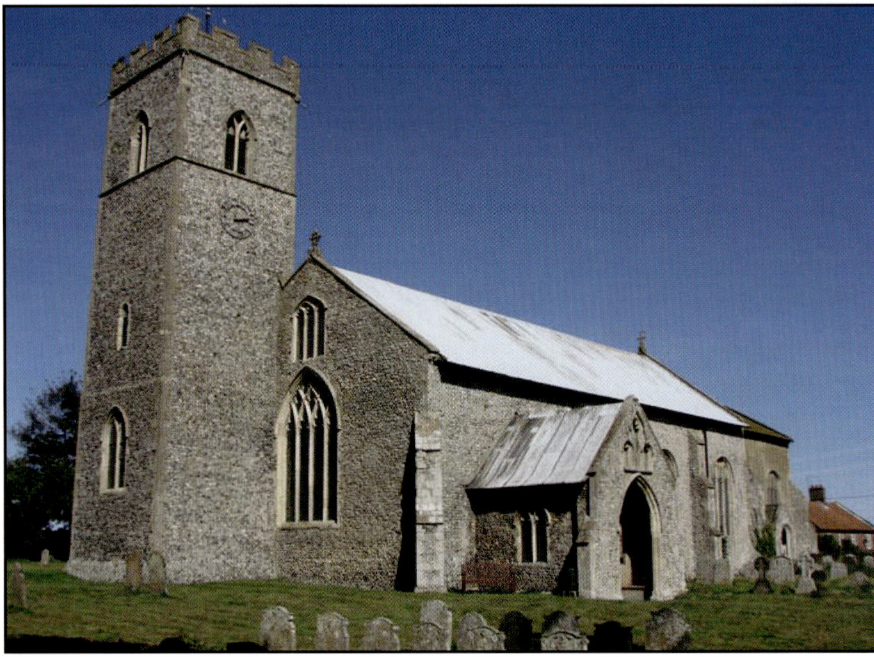

The 14th c. tower is offset to the northwest of the nave allowing a four-light window at the west end of the nave. A real rarity is the porch over the priest's door into the chancel. Inside, you will be delighted by the magnificent double hammerbeam roof of the nave. Winged angels adorn the hammers, and the paintwork is very subtle and not at all over the top. If you can cast your eyes away from the roof, you will see the font which has a very rare permanent cover with a Greek palindrome. The 13th c. Purbeck bowl itself (which stands on a central shaft and eight columns) is quite plain, with only shallow arcading. The piscina has double quatrefoils in the tracery of the arch. At the east end of the nave by the chancel arch are some very old sepulchral stones, and in the chancel is an Easter sepulchre recess.

LAKENHAM	St John the Baptist	1½ miles S of Norwich city centre, in Harwood Road, Old Lakenham. Turn south off the ring road at lights into Lakenham.
No of Bells:	3	
19th c. Deanery:	South Norwich	
Hundred:	Norwich	
Union house:	Norwich	
21st c. Deanery:	Norwich East	O.S. grid ref: TG 234061
Benefice:	Lakenham (St John)	Post Code: NR1 2NG

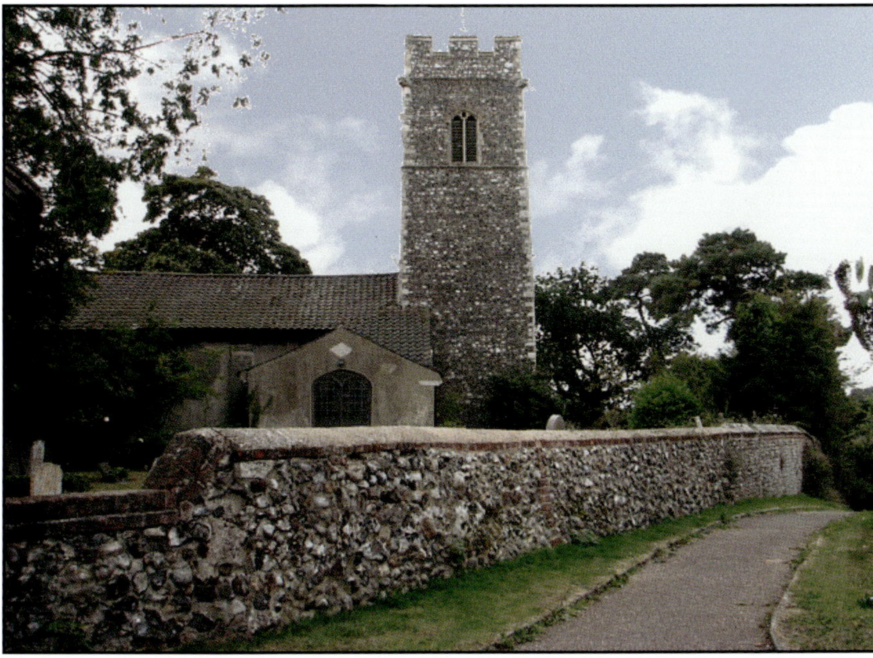

A hamlet of Norwich, which has its own church. Mentioned in the Domesday Book it was a much smaller, probably wooden, church at that time. The present church is built on the same site. Although it is a mediaeval church, it has been much restored. The south aisle was added in 1825. In 2002 iron columns (encased in wood) replaced, the original wooden ones which had suffered the ravages of death-watch beetle. The lovely and unusual 15th c. font originally came from Knettishall in Suffolk; one panel depicts the instruments of the Passion. A small corner piscina is set into the chancel wall. It is a shame that the old benches have been ripped out and more comfortable 'dining' chairs have been installed, but that's progress. The church is surrounded by trees and suffering from dampness.

LAKENHAM	St Mark	About 1 mile from Norwich castle between Hall Road and City Road in New Lakenham. Just south of St John Sepulchre church.
No of Bells:	1	
19th c. Deanery:	City of Norwich	
Hundred:	Norwich	
Union house:	Norwich	
21st c. Deanery:	Norwich East	O.S. grid ref: TG 235075
Benefice:	Lakenham (St Mark)	Post Code: NR1 3HP

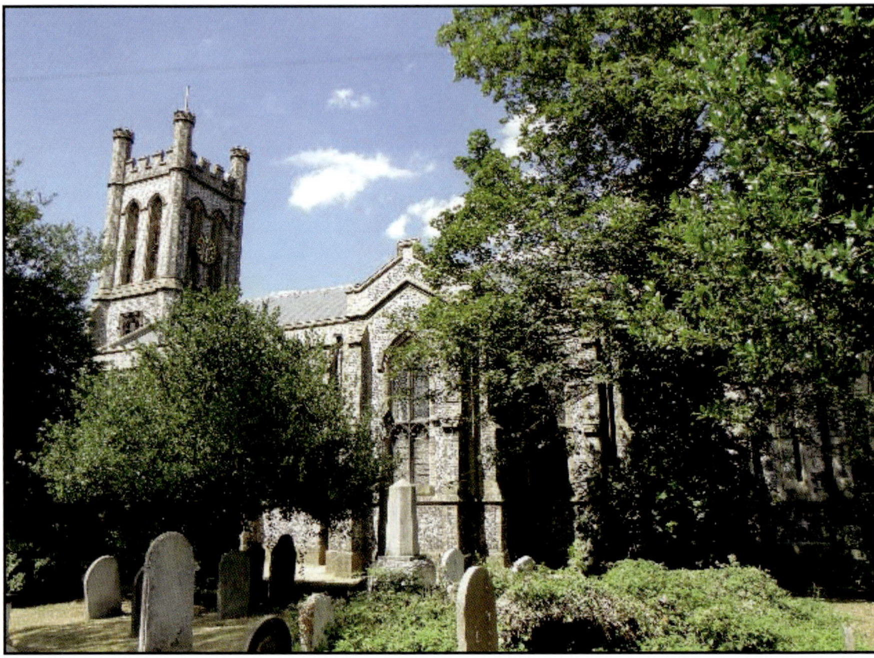

The second of Lakenham's two churches, and like St John's, almost hidden by trees. Built in 1844 by the architect John Brown it has all the usual trappings of a Victorian church. The apsidal east end is something not often seen in a Victorian church and was added ten years later. There is a gallery at the west end, and from there a closer examination of the roof is possible; painted in red blue and green foliate designs. The font although decorated is very ordinary and uninteresting. Various scenes from the life of Jesus can be seen on the screen, upon which is a rood. A contemporary pulpit stands on a carved stone base looking for all the world like the bowl of a font. The Hanoverian Royal Arms are on the west wall above the gallery. For a Victorian church this appears, in some respects, traditional.

LAMMAS or LAMAS St Andrew

No of Bells:	5
19th c. Deanery:	Ingworth
Hundred:	South Erpingham
Union house:	Aylsham
21st c. Deanery:	Ingworth
Benefice:	Bure Valley

4 m SE of Aylsham. Between Buxton and RAF Coltishall on the left by the River Bure. On the opposite side to the houses.

O.S. grid ref: TG 245233
Post Code: NR10 5EJ

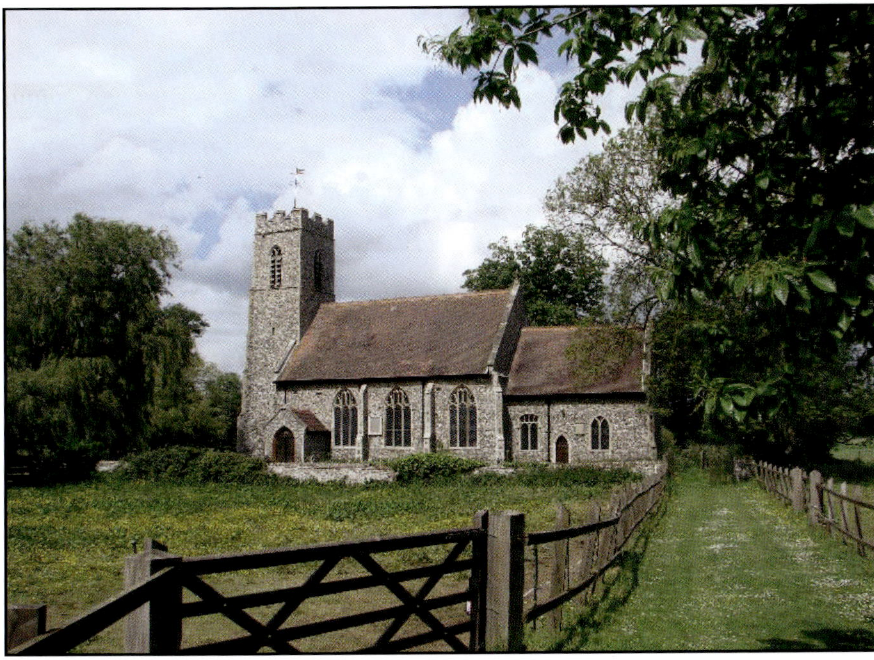

A lovely little church in a rural setting. Only a few yards from the gently flowing River Bure. The church was built at the end of the 13th c. but was restructured 200 years later when the tower was added. Until 1887 the roof was thatched. On the 15th c. octagonal font are decorative shields and roses; the matching shaft is decorated with crocketted buttresses. The 20th c. pulpit is very simple, devoid of any form of decoration. This church is noted for the dramatic 'weep' of the chancel to the north. The roofs are Victorian, as is the small porch. The Holy table is of the Tudor period and the parish chest is likely to be similar in date. A basic trefoil arch trims the piscina. The sedilia has been recently lined with wooden seating. Queen Elizabeth the Queen mother visited here in 1998 and signed the Visitors Book.

LANGLEY St Michael
No of Bells: 5, unused
19th c. Deanery: Brooke
Hundred: Loddon
Union house: Heckingham
21st c. Deanery: Loddon
Benefice: Chet Valley

1½ miles N of Loddon. From Loddon go north through Chedgrave, past Langley School and turn left. Church is on the left.
O.S. grid ref: TG 355009
Post Code: NR14 6BL

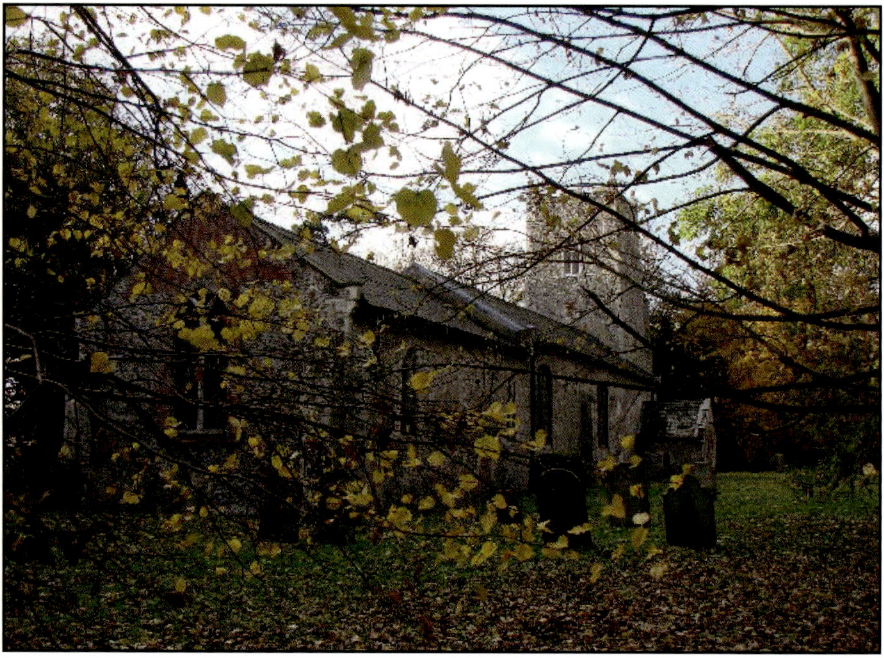

The key is at Langley School. Despite numerous attempts I was never able to see inside. A late 14th c. carved font is coeval with the building of the church. In the nave the roof is arch-braced but the chancel roof has been plastered at the expense of the local Beauchamp family and their Arms have been incorporated into the plasterwork. Above the chancel arch are hung the Hanoverian Arms denoting when earlier restorations took place here. Considerable preservation work has taken place more recently particularly on the ceiling of the chancel which had started to collapse. Four hatchments and memorials to the Beauchamp family adorn the walls of nave and chancel alike. An iron-bound parish chest, probably 600 years old, is another of the possessions of the church. Information via other sources!

LESSINGHAM	All Saints
No of Bells:	3
19th c. Deanery:	Waxham
Hundred:	Happing
Union house:	Smallburgh
21st c. Deanery:	Waxhan & Tunstead
Benefice:	Coastal

8 miles E of North Walsham. Probably best approached from Stalham, through Ingham to north of Lessingham village.

O.S. grid ref: TG 392285
Post Code: NR12 0DL

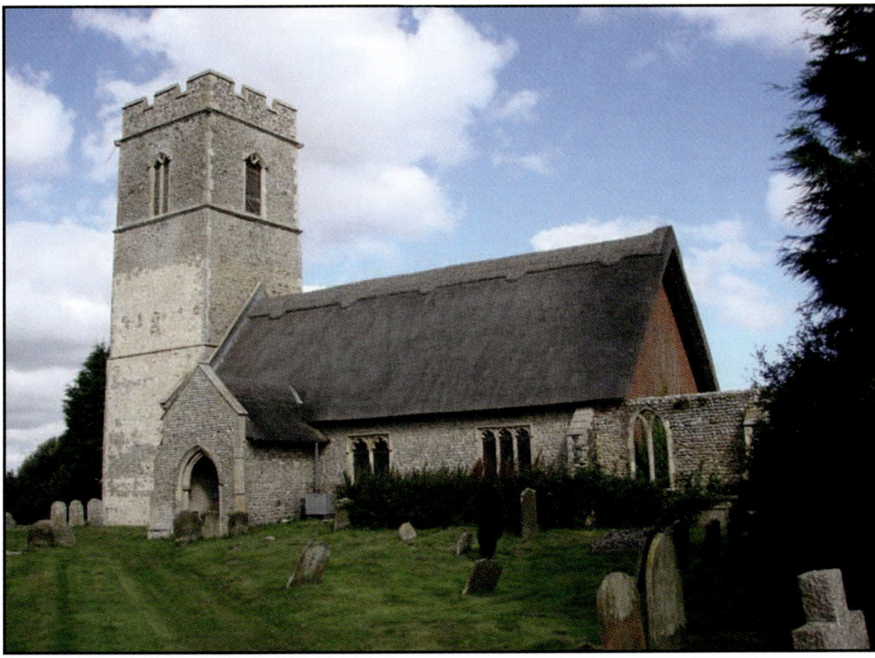

There is now no distinction in the thatched roof between the nave and chancel. It was once a longer church, reduced in length in 1961 as a result of a storm when the chancel collapsed. A new east wall was constructed and the old chancel left ruinous. Inside the church there is no chancel arch, part of the nave has now become the chancel. At the west end, the lovely 13th c. Purbeck font is typical of the period with shallow arcading around the bowl. It is supported by a central round column and eight very slender smaller ones. The pulpit is Jacobean and still retains its backboard and tester. This is a typical Norfolk church and can only be found if you are looking for it. It is at the end of a remote trackway but you will find a warm welcome here. Unlike some other churches I could mention, it is always open.

LIMPENHOE St Botolph
No of Bells: 1
19th c. Deanery: Blofield
Hundred: Blofield
Union house: Lingwood
21st c. Deanery: Blofield
Benefice: Freethorpe

11 miles ESE of Norwich. Probably best accessed by the B1140 from the A47, through Cantley and on to Limpenhoe.
O.S. grid ref: TL 982897
Post Code: NR13 3JE

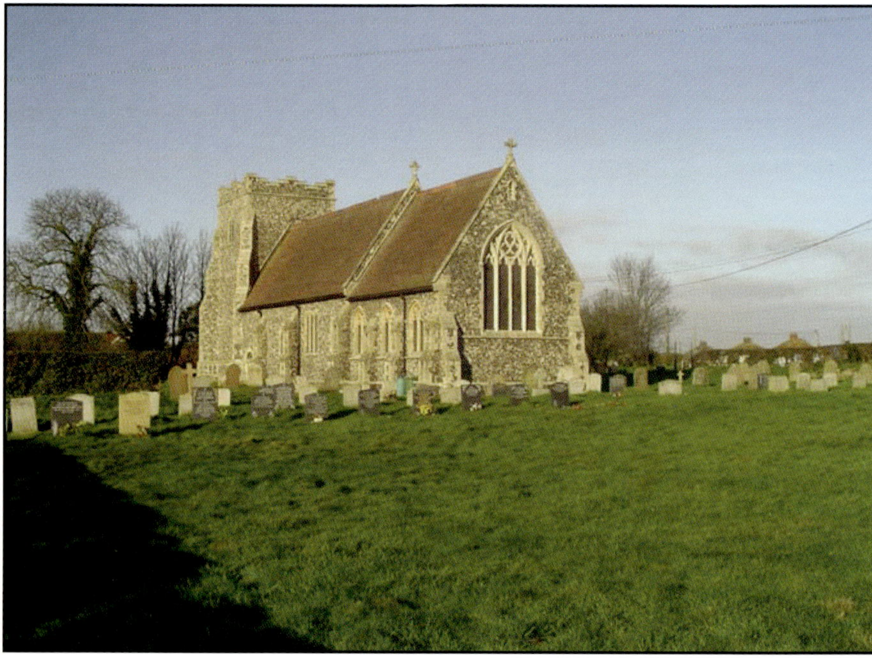

The stump of a tower makes this church quite distinctive. Before the parapet was added it had a tiled pyramidal roof and was thatched, as the drawing in the church shows. On the south side there is a blocked Norman doorway with two columns and three orders of decoration. Around the base of the tower are panels of flushwork. Entry is by the wooden north porch with a traceried gable. This is obviously an early church but it has been somewhat over-restored. The Purbeck font is 13th c. with shallow arcading around the bowl, which is supported on eight detached columns surrounding a central shaft. The nave roof is scissor construction. A corbelled piscina set into a window sill can be found in the chancel. A stone reredos matches the hideous stone pulpit. A tapestry, which hangs in the nave, is from Southwood.

LINGWOOD	St Peter
No of Bells:	1
19th c. Deanery:	Blofield
Hundred:	Blofield
Union house:	Lingwood
21st c. Deanery:	Blofield
Benefice:	Lingwood

8 miles E of Norwich. Easily accessible from the A47. Turn south in North Burlingham opposite the telephone box.

O.S. grid ref: TG 361091
Post Code: NR13 4PB

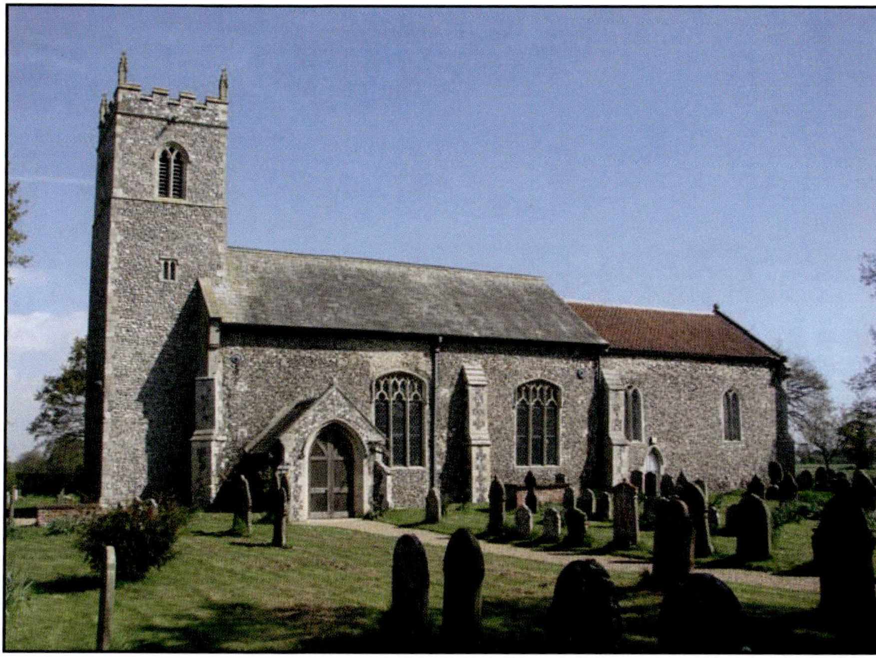

The church dates back to the 14th c. Carved faces greet you as you enter the south door. The octagonal font is plain and uninteresting. On the north wall is St Christopher looking a bit worse for wear. Whoever varnished the pulpit and reading desk should be made to pay to have them restored to their proper condition, they look awful. Fortunately, he stopped before destroying the 15th c. benches with figures on the armrests, they are delightful. I believe the corbel has been cut off the simple piscina. The adjacent sedilia is of the dropped sill variety. Laudian style baluster altar rails divide the sanctuary from the chancel. The George IV Royal Arms were made on a budget, cut from a piece of wood, and painted. A simple 19th c. wall plaque remembers Richard Ayers (1820) and Elizabeth his wife (1844).

LITTLE PLUMSTEAD Sts Protase & Gervase

No of Bells:	1	6 miles E by N of Norwich. From Norwich on the A47, turn north at radio masts. Over cross roads, then right & right again.
19th c. Deanery:	Blofield	
Hundred:	Blofield	
Union house:	Lingwood	
21st c. Deanery:	Blofield	O.S. grid ref: TG 307109
Benefice:	Thorpe End	Post Code: NE13 5EW

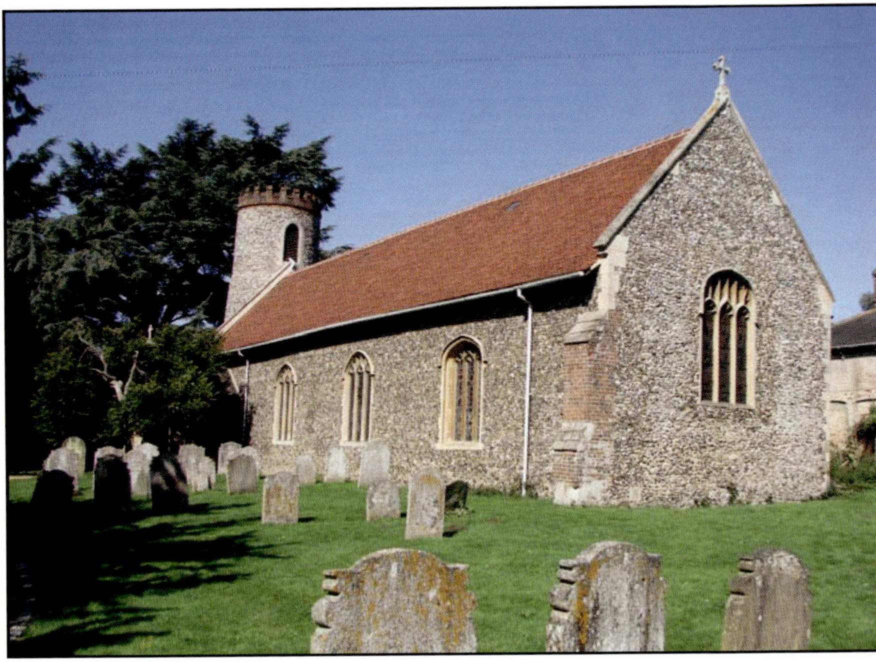

You will find the church to the right of the hospital. The round tower is Norman and badly constructed. It does however still have a squint giving a clear view of the altar. Take a flash photo through it to see it properly. The church itself has been somewhat over-restored. A billeted arch spans the Norman doorway. The font is a modern replacement, the old one serves as a birdbath outside. The pulpit is no more than a reading desk on a stone base. A modern scissor-beam roof runs the length of nave and chancel and, like Great Plumstead there is no distinction between the nave and chancel, except a tie beam. A marble monument to Thomas Penrice (1816) and his following generation takes up a large chunk of the chancel wall. No piscina, no sedilia, no character, just a well-loved and over-protected church.

LODDON	Holy Trinity
No of Bells:	8
19th c. Deanery:	Brooke
Hundred:	Loddon
Union house:	Heckingham
21st c. Deanery:	Loddon
Benefice:	Chet Valley

10 miles SE of Norwich. Turn off the A146 and into the centre of Loddon; the church is a little way back off the road to the east.
O.S. grid ref: TM 363987
Post Code: NR14 6EY

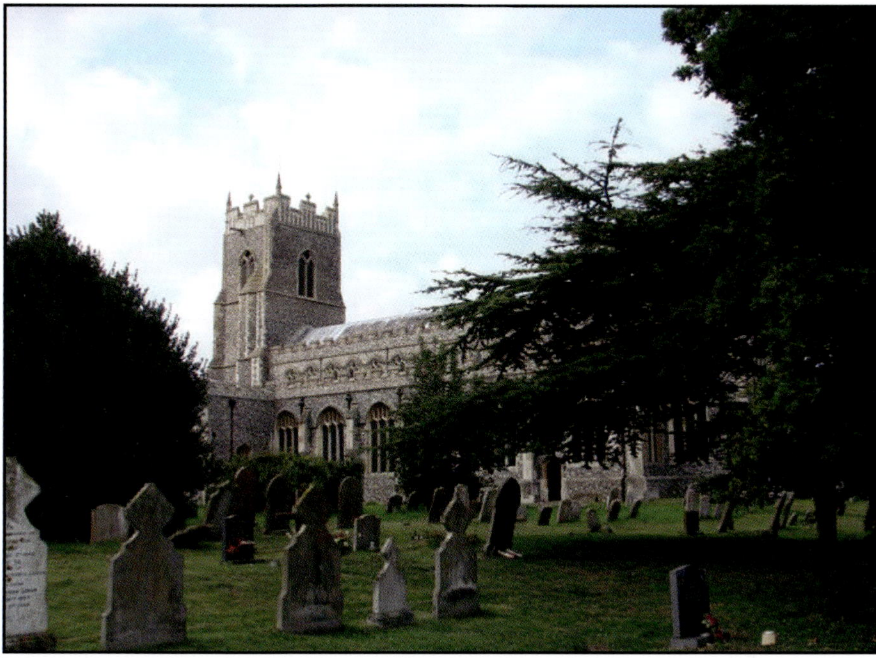

This grand 15th c. church has many interesting features. The external detail provides much to admire: note the intricacy of the mason's craftsmanship in the stone. Above the porch is a parvise currently used as an information centre. The single hammerbeam and arch-braced roof is a treat, but the 30-odd small windows of the clerestory fail to allow enough light into the nave except on the sunniest of days. A 'poor-man's box' is attributed to the Saxon era but is probably late Norman. However, the gem here is the font displaying the Seven Sacraments; it was badly mutilated during the Puritan era but is still beautiful, standing on three tiers of steps. The 15th c. screen too is well worth close examination; the paintings are original and still in good condition. There is no dampness here to despoil the fabric.

LUDHAM	St Catherine *****	13 miles NW of Great Yarmouth. From the A149 go right at Potter Heigham onto the A1062 and follow into Ludham.
No of Bells:	5	
19th c. Deanery:	Waxham	
Hundred:	Happing	
Union house:	Smallburgh	
21st c. Deanery:	Waxham & Tunstead	O.S. grid ref: TG 387183
Benefice:	Waterside	Post Code: NR29 5AB

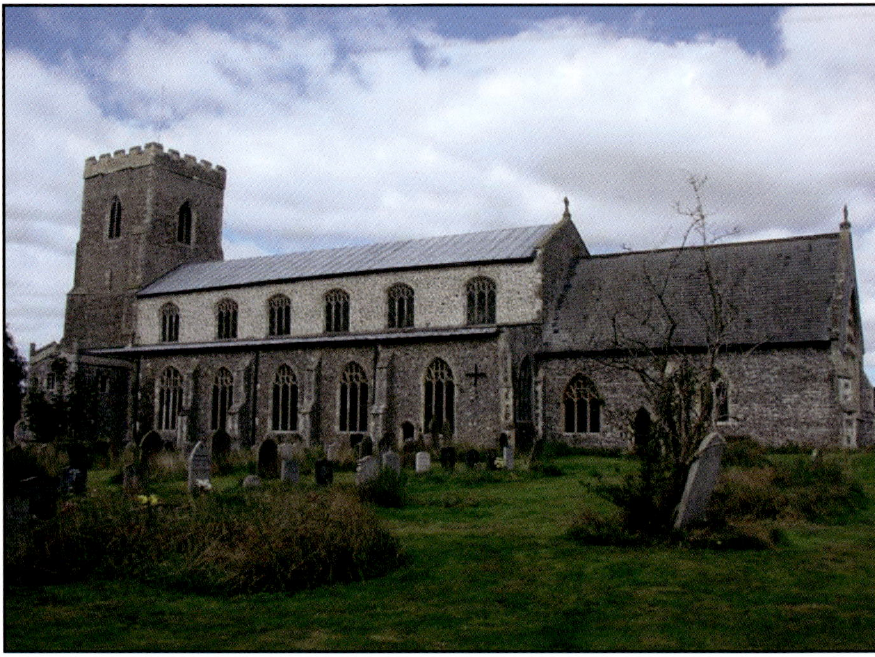

The church as you see it today is 15th c. but with a 14th c. tower, which would suggest an earlier 13th c. church stood on this site. This is borne out by the Norman doorway into the nave. The clerestory has twelve large three-light windows that spill sunlight into the nave. The panelled screen is exceptionally fine and one of the best in the county. The painted figures are well preserved. Above that, in the tympanum is a painting of the Rood group; and above that is the lovely hammerbeam roof with the wheels of Catherine in the spandrils. The font is a typical East Anglian type with wodewoses and lions around the base. The piscina and sedilia have beautiful trefoiled and crocketted arches and are on three levels. This is a fine church and well worth a visit. More information is available in the church.

MARTHAM St Mary ****

No of Bells: 6
19th c. Deanery: Flegg
Hundred: West Flegg
Union house: Rollesby
21st c. Deanery: Great Yarmouth
Benefice: Flegg Group

9½ miles NNW of Great Yarmouth. From Yarmouth on the A149, turn right at Rollesby. Bear left in centre of Martham.
O.S. grid ref: TG 454184
Post Code: NR29 4PR

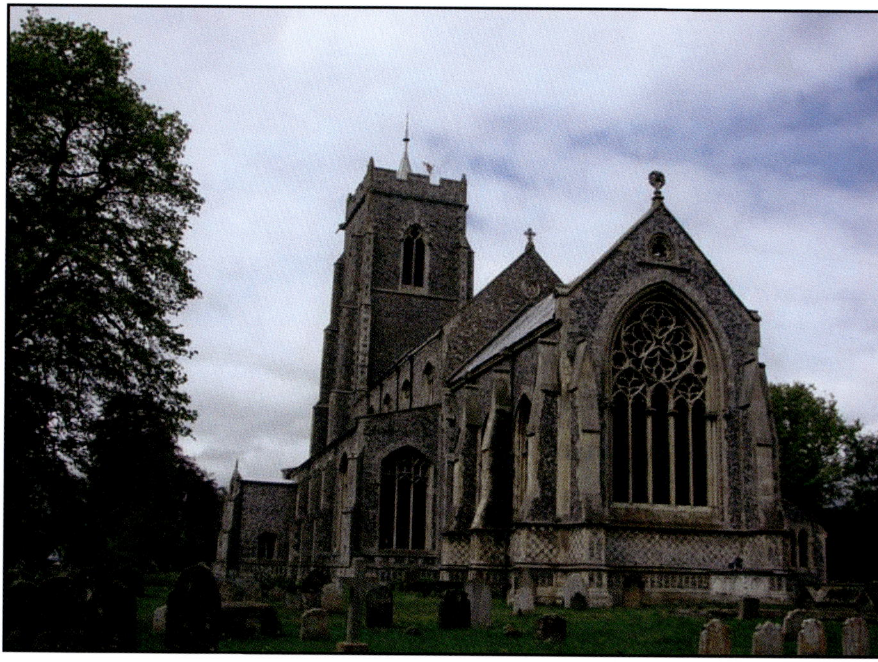

This is one of the great 15th c. wool churches that are typical of east Norfolk. Above the groined ceiling of the porch is a parvise. A lovely Seven Sacraments font stands just inside the door. The hammerbeam roof with angels on the hammers is Victorian, as is much you will see around you. The poppyheads on the benches are 15th c. and have been cleverly worked into the modern benches. The pulpit is carved stone. The chancel arch is a good example of Victorian over-indulgence; but the carving is very good. Everything beyond it is coeval, the chancel having been completely rebuilt around the 1850s. An imitation Easter sepulchre is dedicated to the memory of Rev Jonathan Dawson who ordered the work. Opposite is a triple-seat, arched sedilia. A chapel in the south aisle dedicated to St. Blide, is now a prayer corner.

MAUTBY St Peter & St Paul
No of Bells: 1
19th c. Deanery: Flegg
Hundred: East Flegg
Union house: Rollesby
21st c. Deanery: Great Yarmouth
Benefice: Flegg (Sth Trinity Broads)

5½ miles NW of Great Yarmouth. Leave Yarmouth on the A1064 and turn left at x-roads before Filby, then left at next junction.
O.S. grid ref: TG 480123
Post Code: NR29 3JA

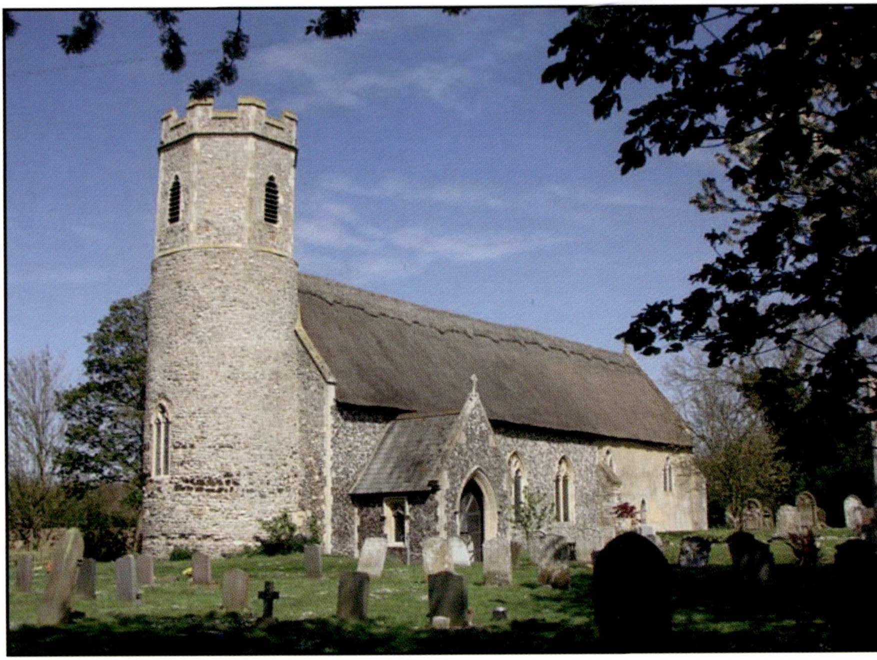

The octagonal top to the round tower is Mediaeval, but the rest is Norman. There is no distinction between the modern thatched nave and chancel roof. The church itself is a little later in the Early English style. Quatrefoils and shields decorate the octagonal 15th c. font. The shaft has eight engaged pillars and arches between, the cover is a crocketted conical design. The pulpit appears to have been made in the woodwork class at school. A squint has been cut into the base of the screen which is otherwise stripped of its figures. In the chancel, the matching 14th c. piscina and sedilia have cusped arches. Set into the south wall is a 600 year old stone carved figure of a knight lying cross-legged on his semi-intra mural coffin, his identity unknown. On the wall is a handwritten Paston family pedigree.

MORNINGTHORPE St John the Baptist

No of Bells: 3
19th c. Deanery: Depwade
Hundred: Depwade
Union house: Pulham St Mary
21st c. Deanery: Depwade
Benefice: Hempnall

11 m S of Norwich. From the A140 turn left after Long Stratton church for 1½ miles then left.
O.S. grid ref: TM 218925
Post Code: NR15 2QL

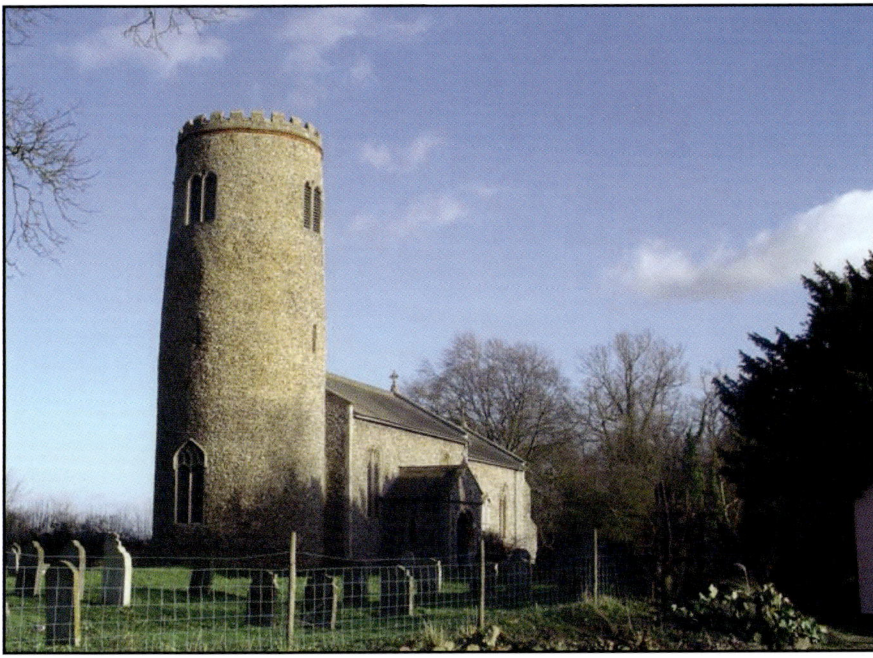

The church stands close to the road and is easy to find. The tower, which may be pre-Conquest, tapers inwards a little at the top which is finely crenulated. A traditional East Anglian octagonal font has a crown-like cover with eight crocketted ogee arches coming to a point surmounted by an angel. In the south aisle is a small piscina, but the one in the chancel has crocketted ogee arches and in the spandrils are the emblems of the De la Pole's *(a rose and leopard's head)*. Ledger slabs set into the floor are mostly for members of the Garneys family dating from 1654. A carved set of George III Royal Arms is supported by brackets in the form of two heads on the west wall; another set hangs over the door. The remaining fittings and furnishings are Victorian and were all part of the 'restoration'.

MOULTON	St Mary	9 miles W of Gt. Yarmouth.
No of Bells:	1	From the B1140 make your
19th c. Deanery:	Blofield	way to Beighton then
Hundred:	Walsham	follow road to Freethorpe.
Union house:	Acle	Midway is Moulton church.
21st c. Deanery:	-	O.S. grid ref: TG 402066
The Churches Conservation Trust		Post Code: NR13 3NW

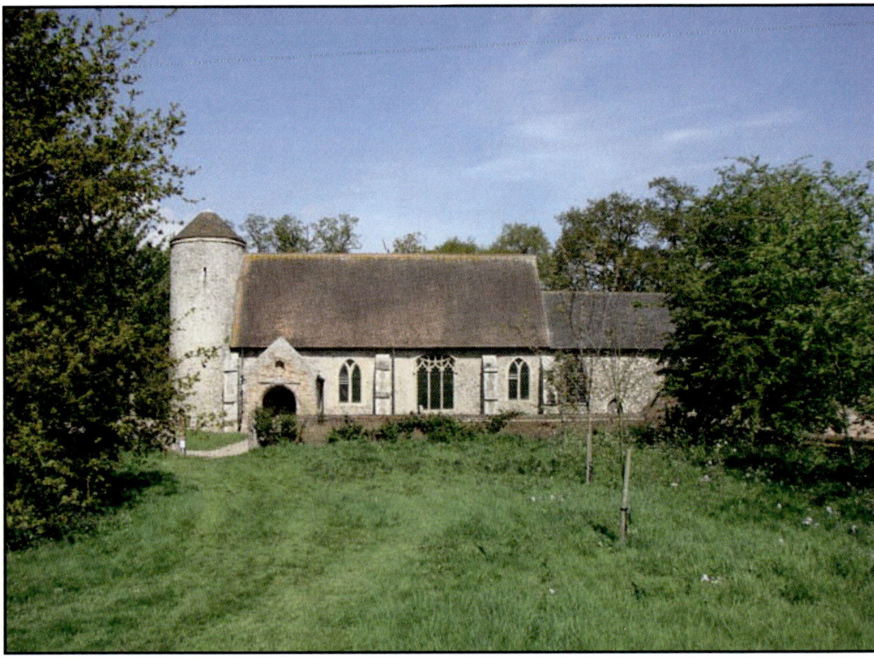

Set a mile away from the village this 13th c. church is close to Manor Hall. The Norman round tower has a later conical cap giving it an unusual appearance. A scratch dial inside the porch indicates that the porch was added later. The octagonal Purbeck font is typical of the Norman period with shallow arcading stands on a central shaft surrounded by eight columns. Wall paintings of the Seven Works of Mercy and St Christopher are quite clear and in good condition. A prayer desk is clearly dated 1619. The pulpit, backboard and tester seem to be late 17th c. Set into the south wall is a double piscina with a central column, beside which is a dropped-sill sedilia. There is a fine wall monument to Edmond Anguishe (1616) and later Richard, his brother (1626) and Richard's wife Abraha (1627).

MUNDESLEY All Saints
No of Bells: 1
19th c. Deanery: Repps
Hundred: North Erpingham
Union house: Gimingham
21st c. Deanery: Repps
Benefice: Trunch Team Ministry

8 miles ESE of Cromer.
Enter Mundesley from the B1145 and turn left. The church is on your right within 200 yds.
O.S. grid ref: TG 301369
Post Code: NR11 8DB

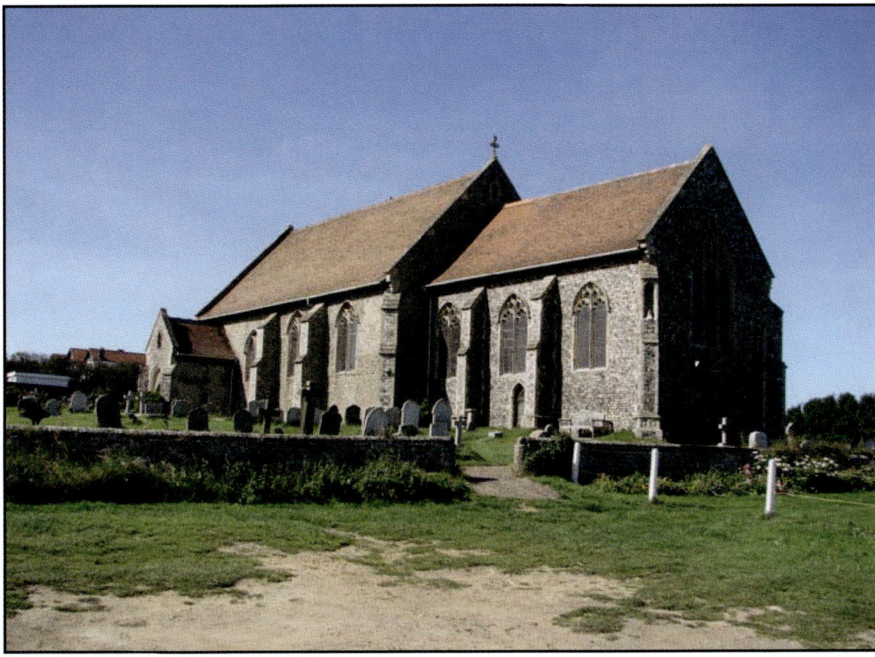

William White says in the 1864 edition 'the tower gone ...has been a noble edifice, but the chancel and part of the nave are in ruins'. There is a drawing in the nave, showing how the church was, with a pyramidal roof, in the period between the ruin and the almost complete rebuilding. Some of the walls however, are original with new roofs and fittings. The work took place in the early 1900s before the outbreak of WW1. The porch too is original having survived the ravages of time. Although there is no tower as such, there is a 'belfry' chamber at the west end. The 14th c. font is octagonal and bereft of any design or embellishment. The interior fittings belie the mediocre external appearance; it is plush and wonderfully light. The pulpit has survived intact, complete with its backboard and tester.

MUNDHAM	St Ethelbert
No of Bells:	-
19th c. Deanery:	Brooke
Hundred:	Loddon
Union house:	Heckingham
21st c. Deanery:	-
Benefice:	-

9½ miles SE of Norwich in Loddon Road, Mundham. In private woodland. Please do not trespass. Ask for permission at the farm.
O.S. grid ref: TM 331976
Post Code: NR14 6EJ

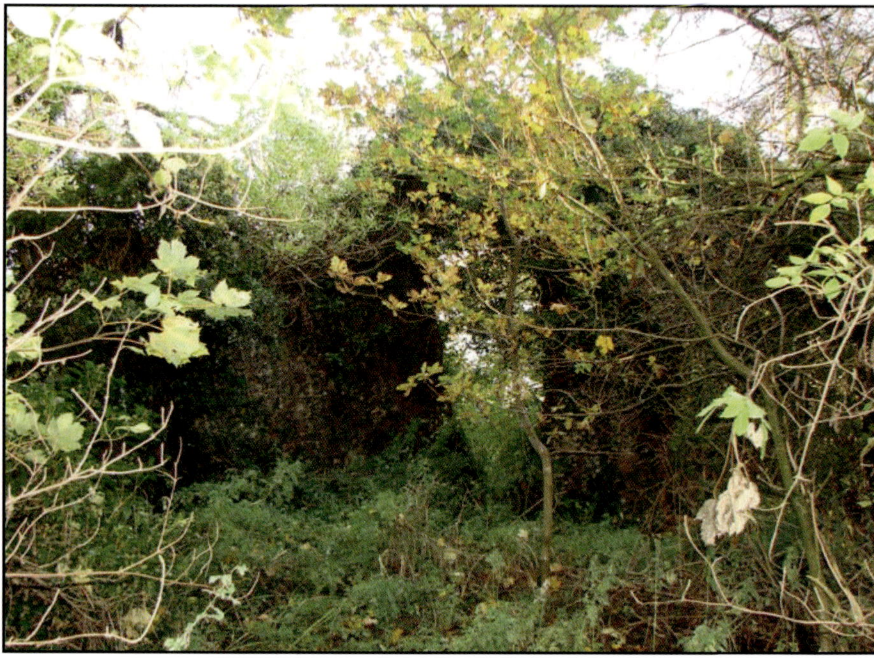

The reader may just be able to make out the shape of a wall with an arch in the photograph above. There is not much remaining of this little church. What does remain is part of the east and north chancel walls. Set among trees in the middle of a copse, it is home only to rabbits and pheasants. How rapidly decay can set in! It was only 1749 that the church was declared redundant and surplus to the needs of the parish. The church, which was originally built in the 13th c., served the parish for more than of 500 years. As far as I can ascertain there are no accurate records of how the church appeared when it was in use. Despite the brambles, it is easier to access than St Peter's a half mile away to the west (See overleaf). The church is locked and the keyholders are very helpful; if you can find them at home.

MUNDHAM St Peter
No of Bells: 3
19th c. Deanery: Brooke
Hundred: Loddon
Union house: Heckingham
21st c. Deanery: Depwade
Benefice: Brooke

9½ miles SE of Norwich.
In Loddon Road, Mundham, ⅓ mile east from Seething church. There is no good place to park a car here.
O.S. grid ref: TM 325980
Post Code: NR14 6EJ

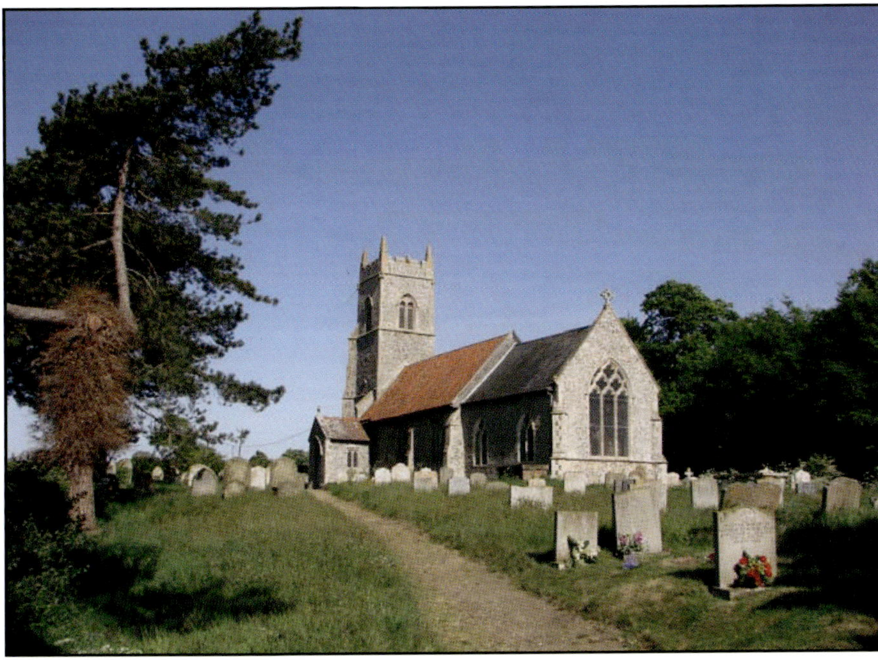

An earlier church probably stood on this prominence before the Normans built this one. There are fine gargoyles on the tower. The south door is a good example of its kind, having three engaged ornamented columns and five orders of decoration. Just inside is a niche for a stoup. The font is a modern one but behind it is the broken Purbeck Norman font. Nearby is an oven for baking wafers and a banner stave locker. The Norman north door, now in the vestry, has one column and is very simple. The trefoil piscina still retains its credence shelf, which, unusually, has notches for draining the chalices. To the side is a dropped-sill sedilia. In the floor is a brass to William Harborne (1617). A simile hangs on the wall nearby. A plaque to Robert Grimer (1809) covers much of a mediaeval wall painting.

NEATISHEAD St Peter
No of Bells: 1
19th c. Deanery: Waxham
Hundred: Tunstead
Union house: Smallburgh
21st c. Deanery: Waxham & Tunstead
Benefice: Ashmanhaugh

10 miles NE of Norwich. Leave Hoveton on the A1151. Turn right at Beeston St Lawrence church and follow, 1 mile.
O.S. grid ref: TG 343219
Post Code: NR12 8BT

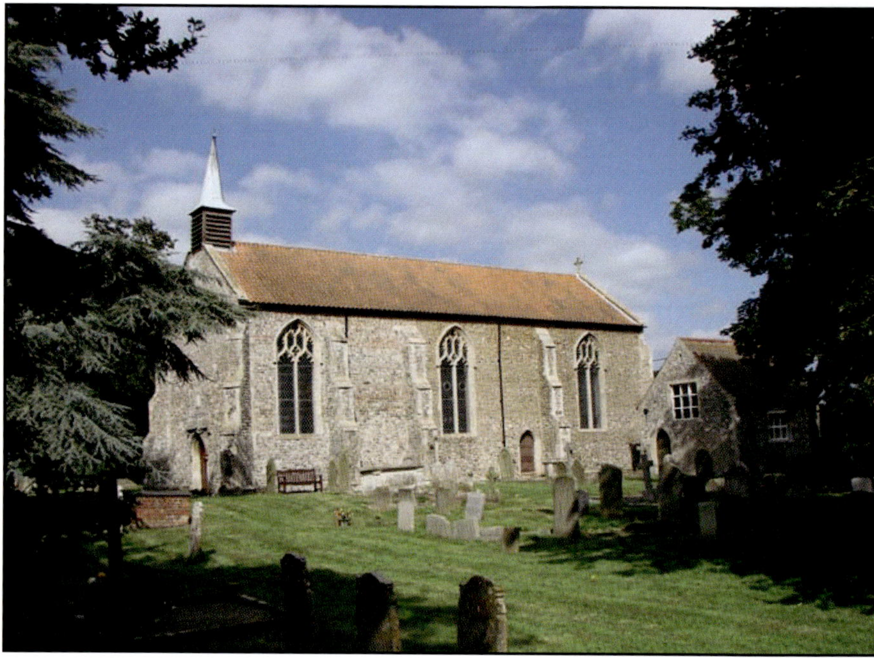

This church looks somewhat incomplete without a tower and only a small bellcote with a spirelet at the west end to break the roofline. What the reader may not realise is that this is just the chancel of a considerably larger, earlier church. The great tower collapsed and the nave was demolished; the chancel became what is now the nave and chancel. Obviously, there is now no chancel arch. Over the west doorway is a carved panel with tracery design, probably salvaged from the ruins. Inside is a portico before the main doorway in to the 'nave'. The octagonal font is 14th c. the bowl decorated with simple tracery. The conical cover is relatively recent. A lovely Elizabethan goblet style linen-fold pulpit must be admired. There are some nice old carved bench-ends with grotesques and poppyheads.

NEEDHAM	St Peter
No of Bells:	3
19th c. Deanery:	Redenhall
Hundred:	Earsham
Union house:	Pulham St Mary
21st c. Deanery:	Redenhall
Benefice:	Redenhall

2 m SW of Harleston.
From the A143 south of Harleston take the exit to Needham, church is about 500 yds on the right.
O.S. grid ref: TM 230819
Post Code: IP20 9LB

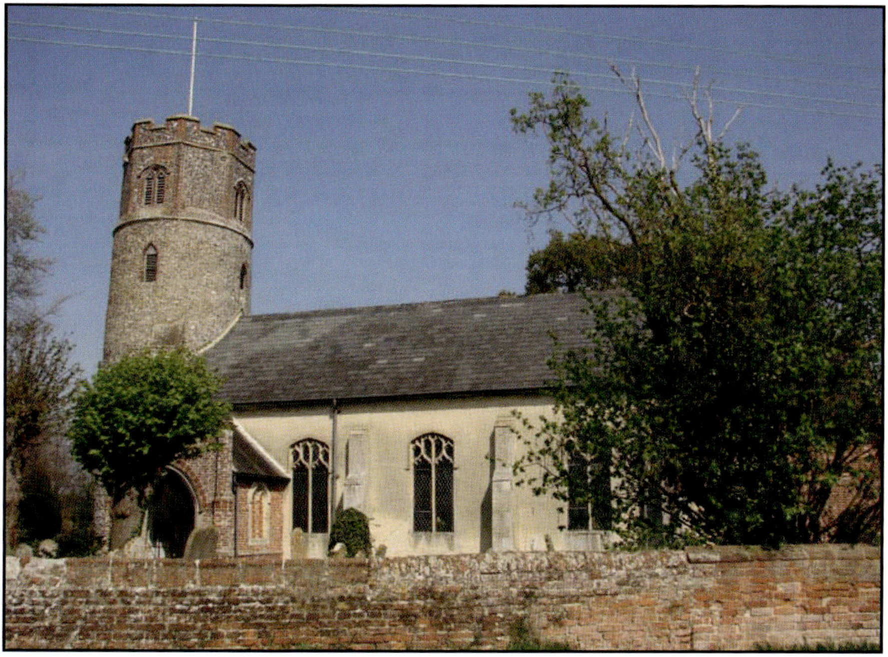

This quaint little church with its brick and flint octagonal top to the tower is right beside the road. Octagonal piers rise above the 15th c. brick porch which has a crow-stepped gable. Above the doorway is a niche containing a statuette of St Peter with a huge key in his left hand. 1735 saw the rebuilding of the chancel. In contrast the nave has been cement-rendered. A 15th c. traditional East Anglian font with lions around the base, and some traces of colour still remain. The arch-braced roof is of the same period. Fresh flowers decorated the old rood loft stairs when I visited; a nice touch! A quite rare table of affinity hangs in the base of the tower. Some of the bench ends have poppy-heads. On the wall is an 18th c. memorial to William Freston (1739) and his wife Margaretta (nee Kedington) (1741).

NEW CATTON Christchurch

No of Bells:	1
19th c. Deanery:	Norwich
Hundred:	Norwich
Union house:	Norwich
21st c. Deanery:	Norwich North
Benefice:	New Catton

From the centre of Norwich exit on the B1150, the North Walsham Road. The church is on the right hand side near the Royal Oak P.H.

O.S. grid ref: TG 239118
Post Code: NR6 7QH

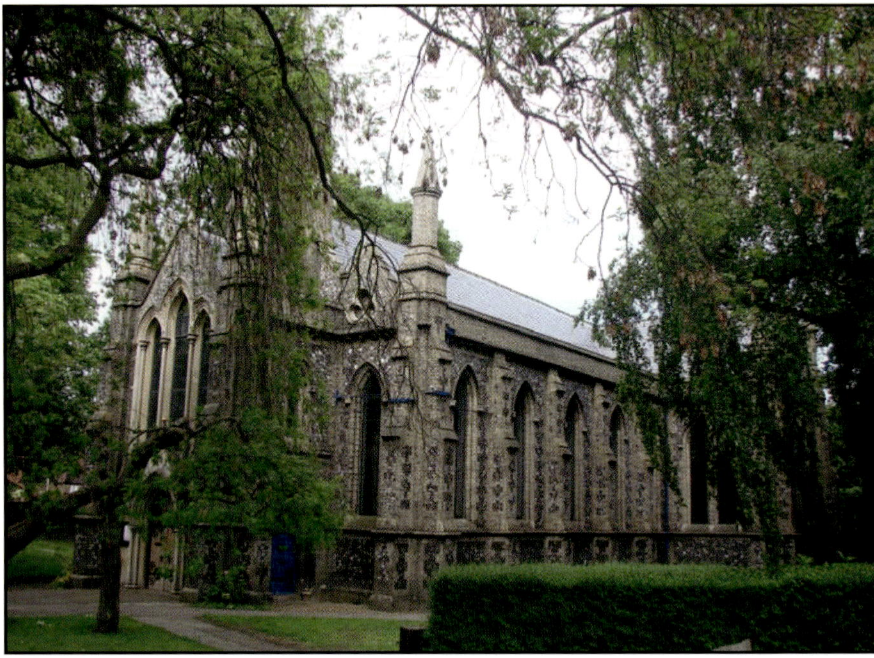

A Victorian built church in 1842 and designed by John Brown, and has all the trimmings; spirelets and pinnacles and a bell turret with a clock beneath which is partially covered by the west gable of the grand entrance. Inside it reminded me of an aircraft hanger with seats. Everything is painted in two shades of blue-green. The octagonal font is coeval with the building. The triple arch of the chancel and the altar behind and an organ, gives it some semblance of a church The war memorial window bears many names lost to the parish during WWI and II. To me it lacks any character, but you must form your own opinion. It is however well used, well loved and open every weekday morning. It is a pity other churches don't follow its example in this respect. Well done, despite my indifference for Victorian churches.

NORTH BURLINGHAM St Andrew

No of Bells: 3
19th c. Deanery: Blofield
Hundred: Blofield
Union house: Acle
21st c. Deanery: Blofield
Benefice: Acle

8½ m E of Norwich. The church is easily seen from the A47. Turn off the A47 at Burlingham slip road onto the old road.
O.S. grid ref: TG 365101
Post Code: NR13 4TA

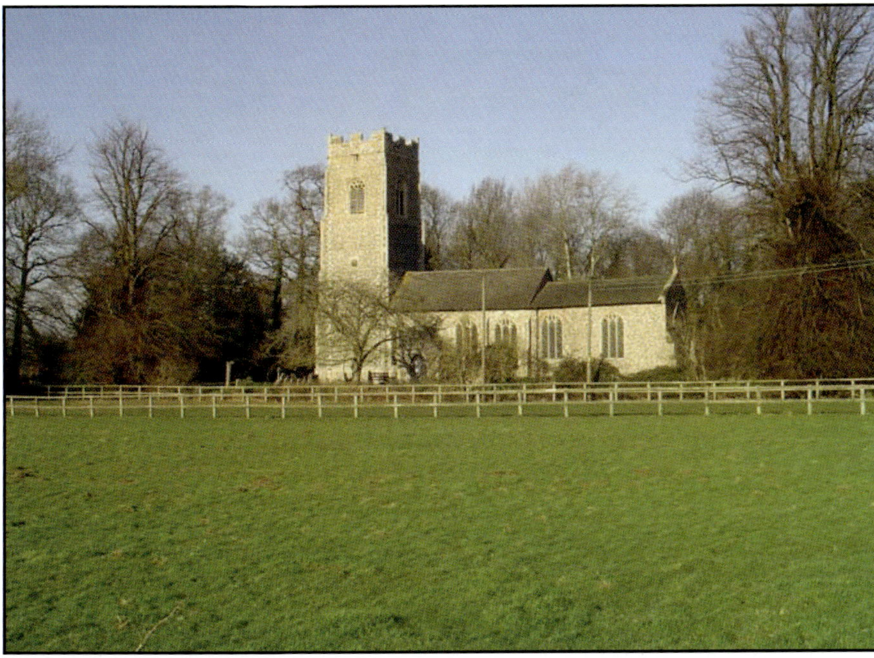

Always locked and the keyholder will accompany you during your visit. Set into the tall tower arch is the screen from St Peter's *(See page 35)* a hundred yards or so towards Yarmouth. The tracery is intricate with feathered angels bearing shields with the keys of St Peter. Carved into the delicate tracery are small faces, some grotesque. The 15th c. un-restored screen is another of the interesting items to see here. On it are depicted ten saints, mutilated but otherwise un-retouched. The nave roof is a single hammerbeam with coloured angels on the hammers and carved corbels. The octagonal font is simple with four clustered columns forming a shaft. A wall monument with two cherubs records the death of Robert Mileham de Burgh (1615); notice also the small floor-brass to Will Gilman.

NORTH WALSHAM St Nicholas

No of Bells: 2
19th c. Deanery: Waxham
Hundred: Tunstead
Union house: Smallburgh
21st c. Deanery: Waxham & Tunstead
Benefice: North Walsham

15 miles NNE of Norwich. Situated in the Market Place in the centre of North Walsham. Plenty of parking available.
O.S. grid ref: TG 284303
Post Code: NR28 9BT

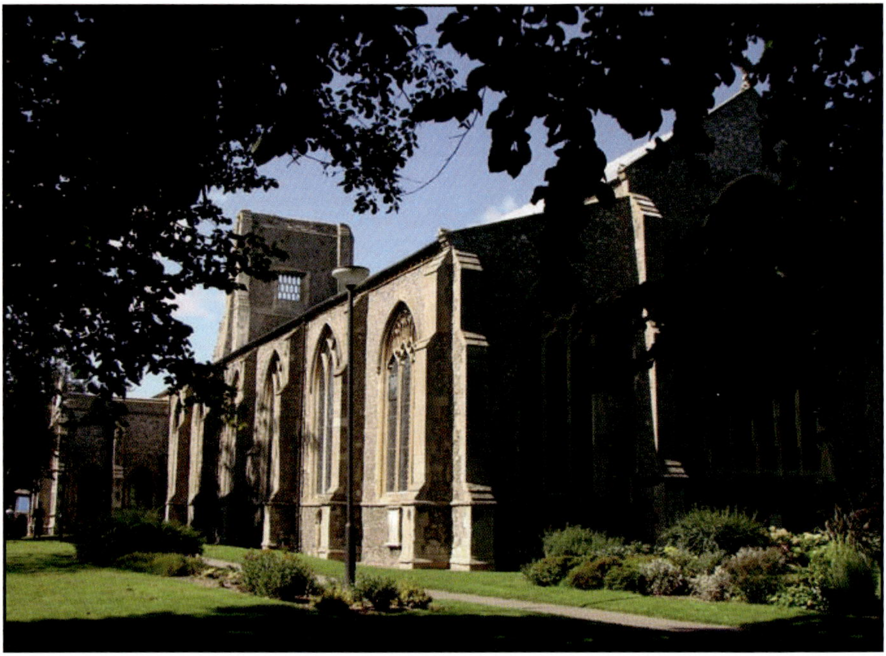

From the east, the church looks like any normal church, but from the west what remains of the 147-feet tower can be clearly seen. It partially collapsed in 1724 and suffered a further fall in 1835. The original line of the tower arch is visible. The wooden structure at the top houses two small bells. Inside, the 15th c. tabernacled font cover immediately catches the eye. It is suspended from a beam set into the arch. Apart from the organ, looking into the chancel, a huge wall monument to Sir William Paston (1608) is very noticeable. The screen has some unusual features, and the piscina and sedilia have cusped ogee arches and detached columns. A 15th c. iron bound chest with seven locks and a gargoyle from the tower is also on display. There is much of interest here for the visitor to see.

NORTHREPPS St Mary

No of Bells:	8
19th c. Deanery:	Repps
Hundred:	North Erpingham
Union house:	Gimingham
21st c. Deanery:	Repps
Benefice:	Overstrand

3 miles SE of Cromer. The church is to the south of the main village. Easy access from the A140 or A149. Follow the road signs.

O.S. grid ref: TG 245391
Post Code: NR27 0LG

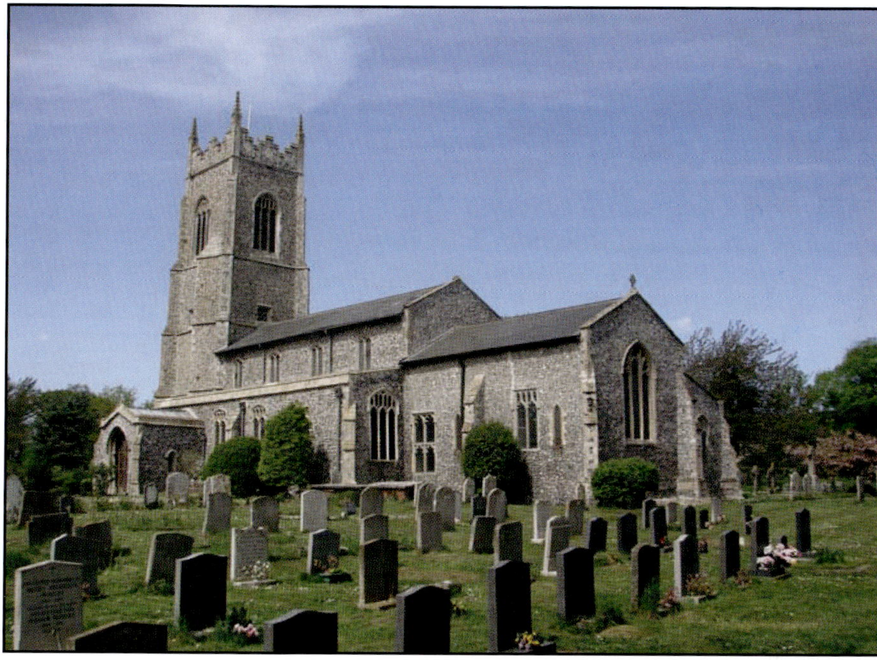

The lofty 15th c. tower can be seen from some distance away, generously crocketted pinnacles and deep crenulations add to the effect. Large louvers and quatrefoil sound-holes appear on all four sides. The 14th c. font also has quatrefoils on the bowl and arcades around the shaft. Both nave and chancel roofs are arch-braced with long wall-posts. Box pews fill the central aisle. Tall 15th c. arcades support the four-windowed clerestory. A small piscina indicates that the south aisle was once a chapel; now a prayer corner. The fine coved screen was restored in the 1860s and has the lovely patina of old wood. A pedestal pulpit stands before it. An aumbry has been created from the chancel piscina, and the walls are panelled. The Royal Arms are of George III but are in fact Stuart, and over-painted.

NORTON SUBCOURSE St Mary

No of Bells: 6
19th c. Deanery: Brooke
Hundred: Clavering
Union house: Heckingham
21st c. Deanery: Loddon
Benefice: Raveningham

3 miles E of Loddon . Follow the road through Heckingham. Situated on a crossroads on the Loddon to Thurlton road.
O.S. grid ref: TM 407986
Post Code: NR14 6RU

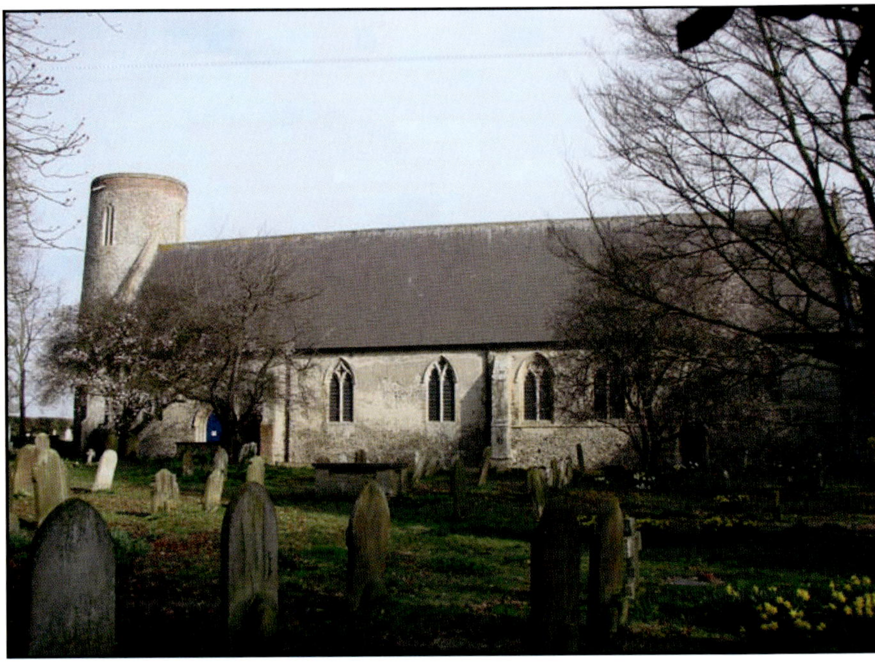

This is one of the 'barn roof' churches where no external distinction is obvious between the nave and the chancel. The round tower is un-crenulated and appears rather stumpy as a result. The defensive doorway, half way up the tower, has been blocked, but nevertheless suggests an earlier, perhaps Saxon date. Adjacent to the doorway are the Royal Arms of William IV. The exterior is unremarkable but inside one or two treats await the visitor. The 13th c. font is of Purbeck stone with eight columns around a central shaft supporting the bowl. In the arch-less chancel the double piscina and matching sedilia have clustered columns surmounted by cinquefoil ogee arches and floriated finials. Opposite is a semi intra-mural tomb, too low I believe to be an Easter sepulchre.

NORWICH All Saints
No of Bells: 6
19th c. Deanery: Norwich
Hundred: Norwich
Union house: Norwich
21st c. Deanery: Norwich South
Benefice: -

5 minutes walk from the castle, in Westlegate Street at the Northern end of Ber Street on the edge of All Saints Green.
O.S. grid ref: TG 232083
Post Code: NR1 3LT

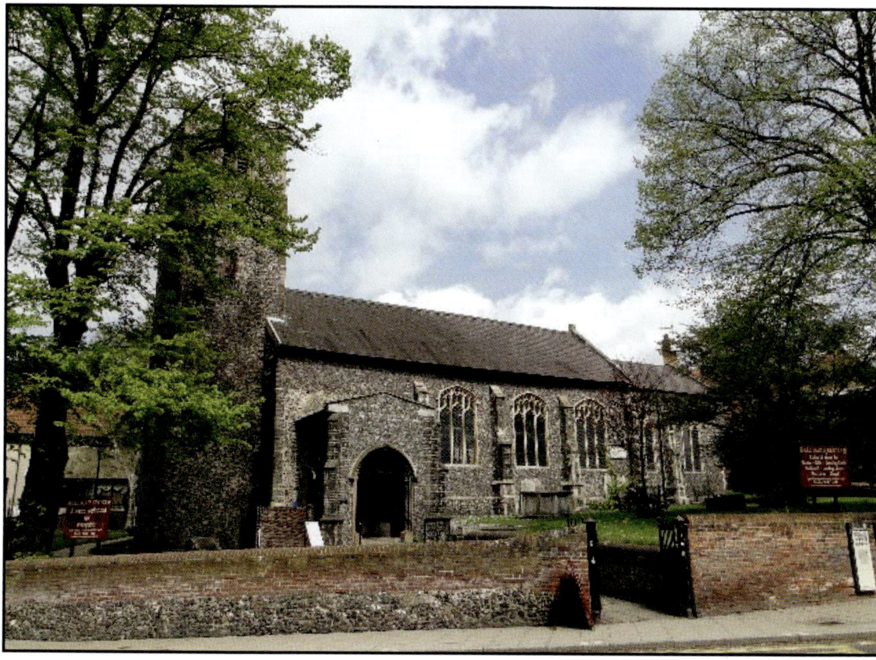

Entering Norwich by Ber Street this church is straight ahead. You may find somewhere to park, but Norwich is a very car-unfriendly city. I must be honest I don't know if it is a church or a café. Both I think. Everything has been obliterated with white emulsion paint. The altar is in place for use as a chapel. There are chairs, books, cards and goods for sale everywhere. The roofs of both 'nave' and chancel are arch-braced with wall posts and 16th c. arcade. The 15th c. font was removed to St Julian's to replace the one damaged during WWII. The wall monuments have been left in situ, fortunately devoid of paint. That to William Clabburn (1812) is one; another is to John Morse (1837) and his wife Sarah (1829). A friendly face and a nice cup of freshly made tea are far better than a locked church! Well done!

NORWICH	St Andrew	A short distance from the castle. In St Andrew's Street, near the junction of Prince's Street and St George's Street.
No of Bells:	7	
19th c. Deanery:	Norwich	
Hundred:	Norwich	
Union house:	Norwich	
21st c. Deanery:	Norwich East	O.S. grid ref: TG 231087
Benefice:	St Andrew (Norwich)	Post Code: NR2 4AQ

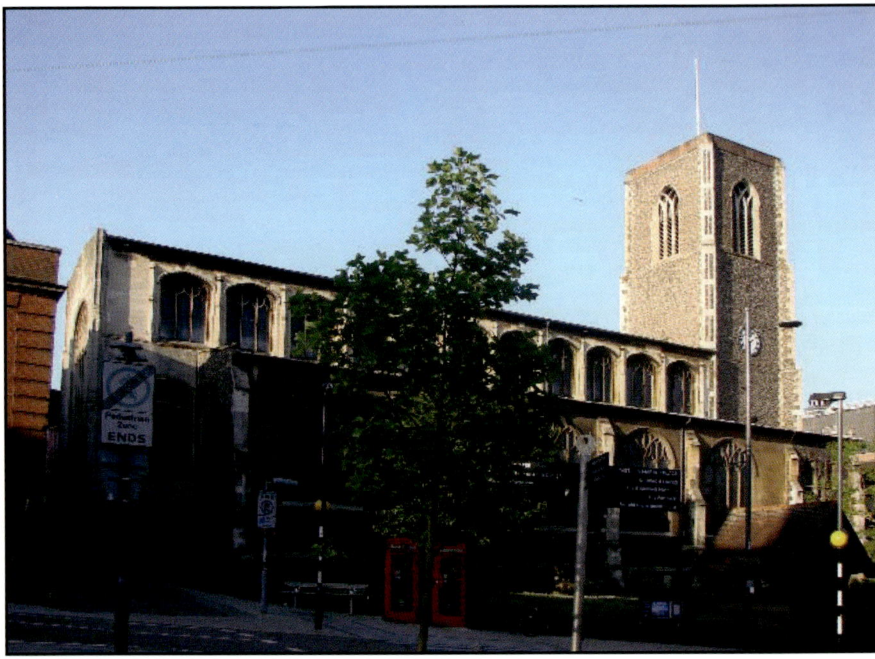

This is the second largest mediaeval church in the city. The tower has a plain parapet and was built in 1478 to a height of 96 feet. Looking around the outside there are shields and carved decoration around the base course, particularly at the east end, which is probably earlier than the rest of the church. The west door has tracery decorating the upper part incorporating the cross of St Andrew. Both porches have a parvise over them. A cambered tie-beam roof covers the nave. The modern font has a cover dated 1637. In the chancel is the restored sedilia, very elaborately decorated with multi-cusped ogee arches with buttressed and crocketted shafts. The Suckling chapel is impressive with effigies of John Suckling (1613) and his wife. Much more to see than mentioned here; a really splendid church which is worth visiting.

NORWICH St Augustine
No of Bells: 3
19th c. Deanery: Norwich
Hundred: Norwich
Union house: Norwich
21st c. Deanery: -
The Churches Conservation Trust

Situated about a ½ mile north of the castle. In St Augustine Street, opposite Rose Yard before reaching Aylsham Road.
O.S. grid ref: TG 228092
Post Code: NR3 3BY

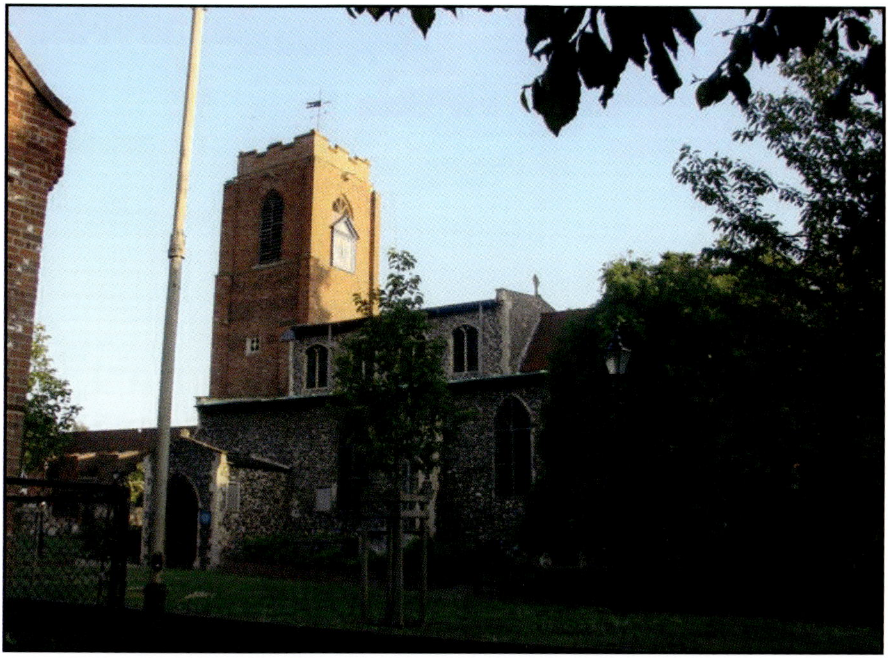

This is the most northerly of the 15th c. mediaeval churches of the city. The brick tower, complete with a clock, was started in 1682 and completed five years later. The 16th c. roof is arch-braced and there are both north and south aisles, parts of which are richly carved. The Victorian 'restoration' was more like a complete refurbishment, and took place in the 1880s. Everything within the church apart from some of the monuments and the font are from that date. The pulpit and reading desk are integral with the otherwise simple screen, which was erected as a memorial to those who lost their lives in the Great War. The church was declared redundant in 1997. Although the church is open there is not much of historical interest to see, unless your interest is Victorian architecture.

NORWICH St Bartholomew
No of Bells: -
19th c. Deanery: -
Hundred: -
Union house: -
21st c. Deanery: -
Norwich City Council

Situated fairly centrally in Ber Street near the junction to Horn's Lane and opposite Scott's Yard, in front of some flats.
O.S. grid ref: TG 233081
Post Code: NR1 3ER

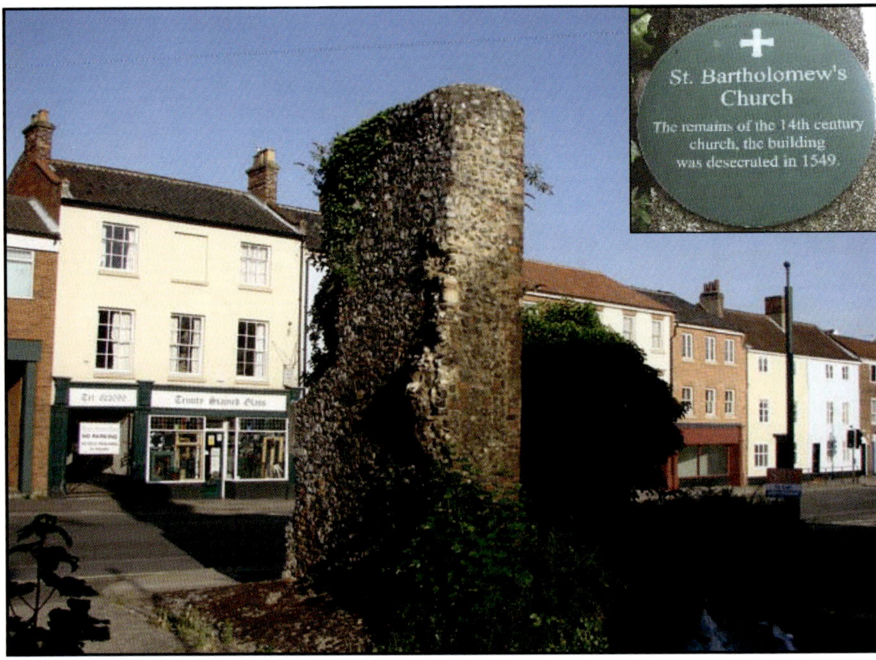

Ruins are all that remain of St. Bartholomew's 14th c. church. Before WWII there was more of the church to see, but the site was cleared for factories and housing in 1939. It was one of the nine parish churches that used to serve Conesford, the most southern part of the walled city. The plaque *[inset]* attached to the remains of the tower indicate the church was desecrated in 1549. Today desecrated has a distinctly different meaning to deconsecrated. It is a good thing that the City preserves ruins like this, and others, St Bartholomew's in Heigham and St Benedict near St Giles. The ivy-covered ruin though is only a small representation of the important buildings that used to dominate this area of the city. There were a number of monasteries in the area and it was home to rich merchants before it became industrialised.

NORWICH	St Benedict
No of Bells:	3 - removed
19th c. Deanery:	Norwich
Hundred:	Norwich
Union house:	Norwich
21st c. Deanery:	-
Norwich City Council	

At the western end of St Benedict's Street, on the right, near Ten Bells Lane. Between St Benedict's Street and Pottergate.
O.S. grid ref: TG 225088
Post Code: NR2 1HE

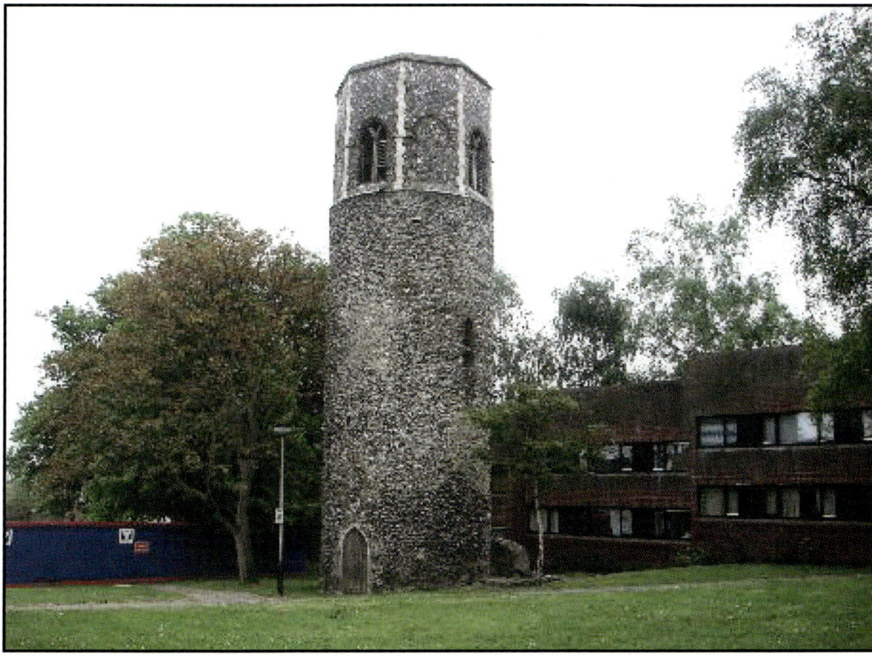

Before the night in 1942 when the Germans bombed Norwich, this was a failing church. It was restored by the Victorians in 1869, but within 35 years was almost in ruins again. Cast iron eventually replaced the stone columns of the north arcade. Bombing completely destroyed the chancel and nave, the font that once stood there was also destroyed. It was beautifully carved and quite unique, with seated figures around the octagonal bowl. The underside was groined, forming canopies in recesses around the shaft, in which there were small statuettes on column-like stools. There were small clerestory-like windows high in the nave, which would have been extending to the right in the picture above, which was taken facing north-west. Today, only, the tower remains like a sentinel over a graveyard cleared of monuments.

NORWICH St Clement Colegate
No of Bells: 3
19th c. Deanery: Norwich
Hundred: Norwich
Union house: Norwich
21st c. Deanery: -
Norwich Historic Churches Trust

Situated a few yards north of Fye Bridge north of Tombland and at the junction with Colegate and Fye Bridge Street.
O.S. grid ref: TG 232091
Post Code: NR3 1HZ

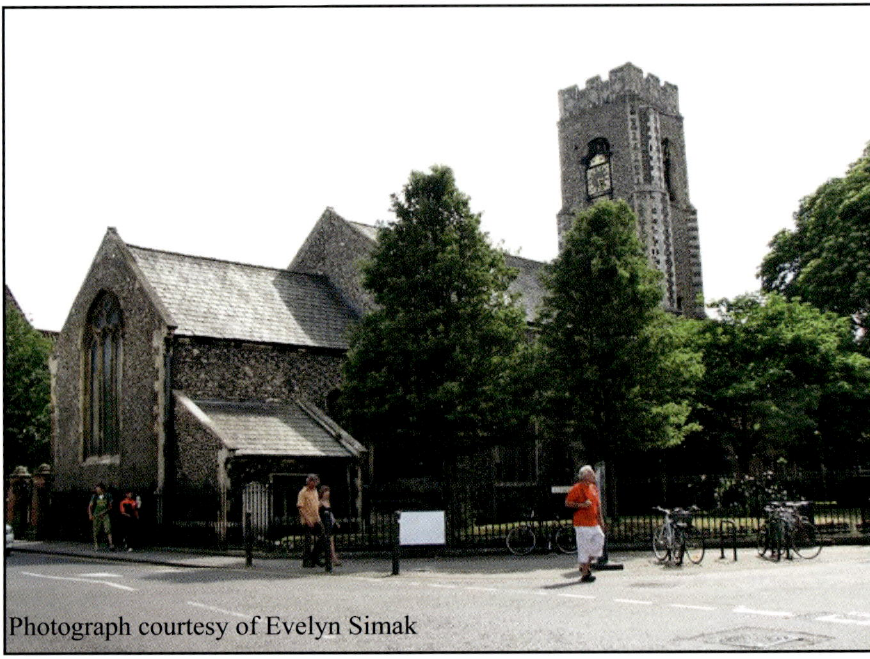

Photograph courtesy of Evelyn Simak

A pink wall plaque on the gate informs that the church is in the care of the Norwich Historic Churches Trust. So, this is another of Norwich's many redundant churches and currently utilized as a dance school. The tower is 15th c. and is simply crenulated, but the nave and chancel are a little later. The octagonal font is 16th c. and probably coeval with the church. It is most unusually decorated (as many of the Norwich fonts seem to be), mainly floriated and very Renaissance in appearance. An overall width of 29 feet made it unnecessary to create aisles either side of the nave. Within the nave is a floor-brass to Margaret Petwode, dated 1514, and on the wall a plaque to William Hayward (1622). The dark appearance is created by the copious use of black flint as well as the dirt and grime of passing traffic.

NORWICH	St Edmund
No of Bells:	1
19th c. Deanery:	Norwich north
Hundred:	Norwich north
Union house:	Norwich
21st c. Deanery:	-
Norwich Historic Churches Trust	

In Fishergate, just off Whitefriars and Blackfriars Street. East of Magdalene Street. A car park is very close by.

O.S. grid ref:	TG 231091
Post Code:	NR3 1SE

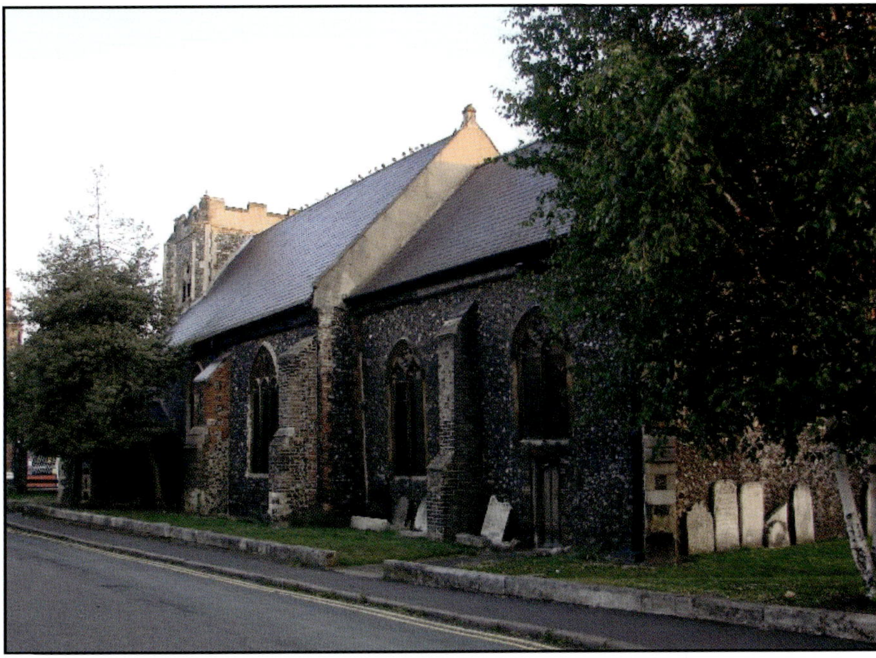

For many years this 15th c. redundant church has been used as a store. Only wall plaques remain. Although it was renovated in 1882 it never really recovered its congregation and rapidly went into decline. There is a south aisle and arcades which have been described as 'strange' because solid walls partially infill the lower portion of some of the arches, which themselves differ in size. Some damage was caused by bombing during WWII but is mainly superficial. The roof was repaired and utilised as storage for a nearby factory which had been bombed. Like many other churches in Norwich it is now in the care of the Norwich Historic Churches Trust. There was once a crystal box kept here, containing (it is said) a piece of the shirt of St Edmund, King and Martyr. Its present whereabouts is unknown to me.

NORWICH	St Etheldreda	At the southern end of King Street, near the junction with Rouen Road. Now an Artists Studio. Restricted parking.
No of Bells:	1	O.S. grid ref: TG 235079
19th c. Deanery:	Norwich	Post Code: NR1 1QP
Hundred:	Norwich	
Union house:	Norwich	
21st c. Deanery:	-	
Norwich Historic Churches Trust		

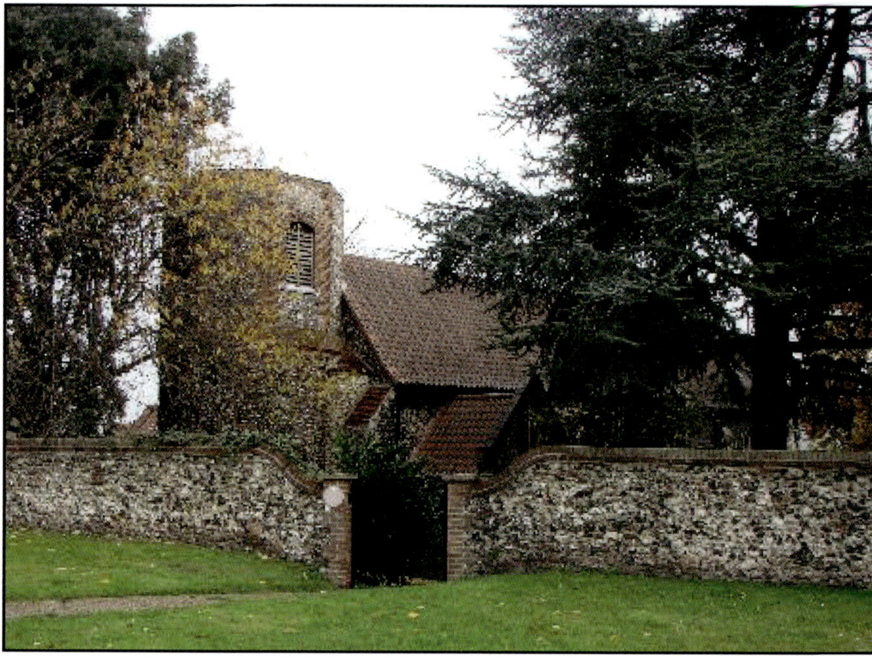

This is the oldest intact church in Norwich. A round Norman tower with an octagonal top west of the nave confirms an early date as does the southern doorway. In fact, traces of Norman handiwork can be seen in many aspects of the structure. Some restoration took place in the 19th c. when St Peter Southgate was abandoned. All fittings and fixtures that could be moved have gone. New floors have been laid and inside it is almost unrecognisable as a church. The font that used to be here was 15th c. decorated with shields around the octagonal bowl. In 1865 White recorded the piscina as Norman and had been mutilated, and that a slab set on a low window sill formed a sedilia. He also mentions a wall monument to William Johnson 1611), which depicts his wife and four children.

NORWICH St George, Colegate

No of Bells:	3	On the north side of the Wensum over Fye Bridge. At the Colegate and St. George's Street junction off Magdalen Street.
19th c. Deanery:	Norwich	
Hundred:	Norwich	
Union house:	Norwich	
21st c. Deanery:	Norwich East	O.S. grid ref: TG 230091
Benefice:	Tombland (Norwich)	Post Code: NR3 1DJ

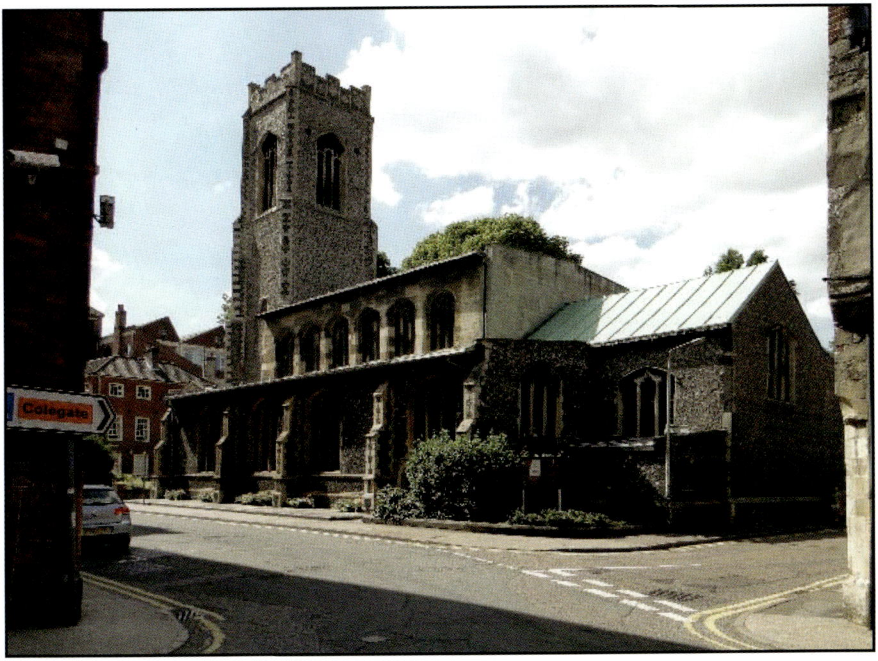

St Margaret's Colegate in 1349 and St Olave's in 1546 were both united with St George's which was built around the mid-15th c. The chancel and north and south aisles were added a short time after. There is a fine clerestory which permeates plenty of light into the interior. Furnishings and fittings are mainly of the Georgian period, when modifications were made to the interior. The Victorian restorations were minimal. The pulpit is quite exceptional with spiral stairs, above which is a backboard and tester. St Saviour's church contributed the octagonal font when it was declared redundant. The original font was given to St Peter Hungate as an exhibit in the museum. Some bomb damage was caused during WWII but good sympathetic repairs ensured its continued use right up to the present.

NORWICH	St George, Tombland
No of Bells:	5
19th c. Deanery:	Norwich
Hundred:	Norwich
Union house:	Norwich
21st c. Deanery:	Norwich East
Benefice:	Colegate (Norwich)

Situated right in the heart of the city in Princes Street, almost directly opposite Norwich cathedral in Tombland.

O.S. grid ref: TG 234088

Post Code: NR3 1AE

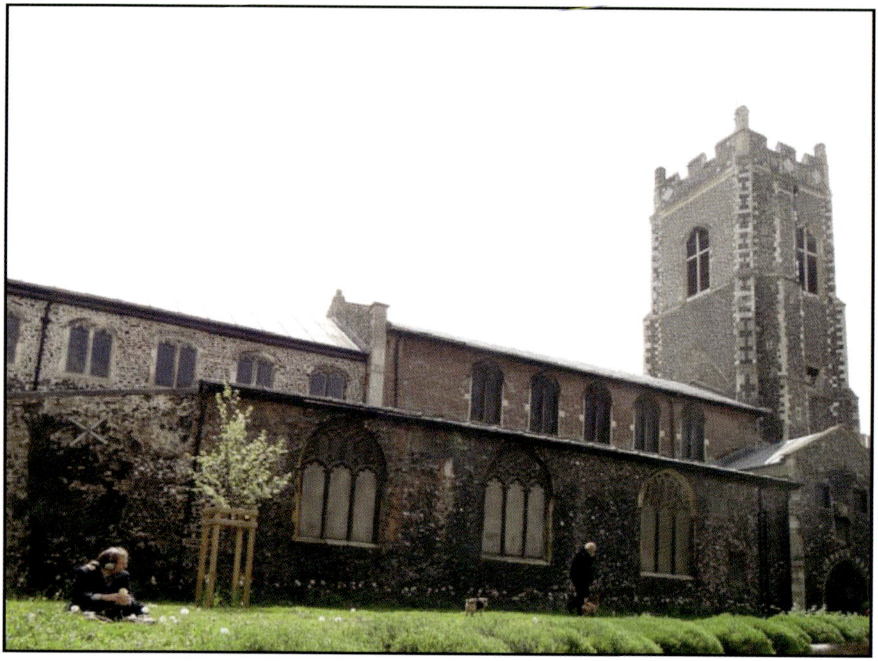

In 1597 a lead-covered wooden spire was erected and remained the only spire on any church until 1806 when it was declared unsafe and removed. The building is recognisable by the brick clerestory and the large blue clock face on the tower. It was erected in the 17th c., an earlier church having stood on this site for many years. Both north and south aisles and the vaulted porch were added a short time after, above the latter there is a parvise. Originally the elaborate pulpit was a 'three-decker' but has been reduced in size and retains its backboard and tester. Probably from the earlier church is the 13th c. font with a beautiful 17th c. cover surmounted by George and the Dragon in gold. There are many monuments here to earlier prominent citizens of Norwich. Visitors may be able to avail themselves of a guided tour.

NORWICH	St Giles	At the western end of St Giles Street from the city, or from the RC cathedral turn into Cleveland Road at the roundabout.
No of Bells:	8	
19th c. Deanery:	Norwich	
Hundred:	Norwich	
Union house:	Norwich	
21st c. Deanery:	Norwich East	O.S. grid ref: TG 226086
Benefice:	Norwich St Giles	Post Code: NR2 1EU

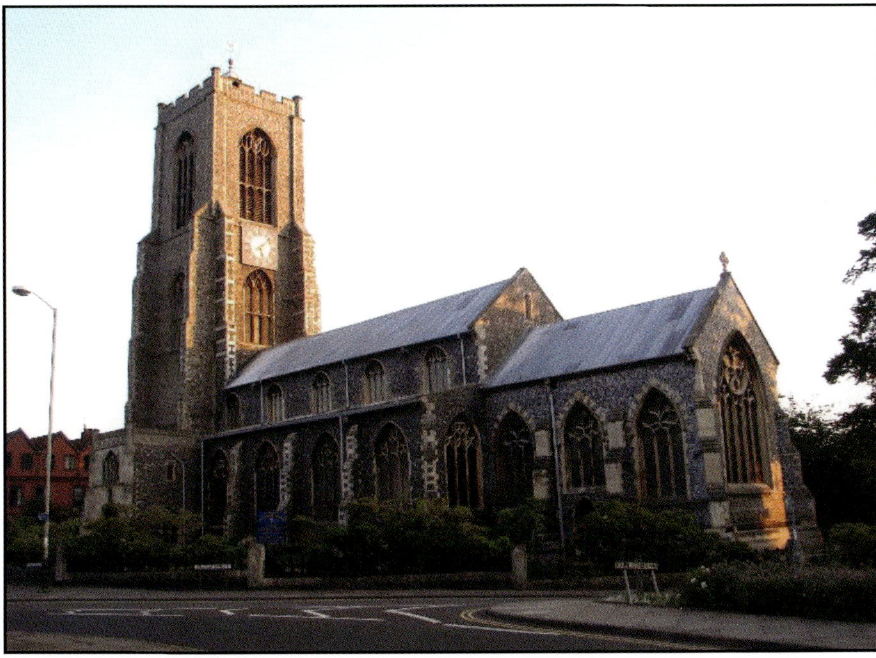

A church has stood on this sight since before the Conquest. This church however was built in the late 14th and early 15th c. The tower is 120 feet tall with a cupola centrally situated on the top. Above the finely fan vaulted roof of the porch is a parvise, and was once a chapel to St Christopher. There is a clerestory and an east window above the nave. A new chancel was added in 1866 when it was decided to replace the one demolished in 1581. A hammerbeam roof above the nave has angels holding shields of England and France. This was part of the French Borough and the richest in the city. Victorian restoration has gone over the top here. The eagle lectern is large, as one might expect in such a church. There is a notable wall monument to Thomas Churchman (1781). Very interesting church.

NORWICH St Gregory *****
No of Bells: 6 (now removed)
19th c. Deanery: Norwich
Hundred: Norwich
Union house: Norwich
21st c. Deanery: -
Norwich Historic Churches Trust

In Pottergate, near the Maddermarket Theatre (south). Or (north) Charing Cross, next to Strangers Hall museum.
O.S. grid ref: TG 229087
Post Code: NR2 4AX

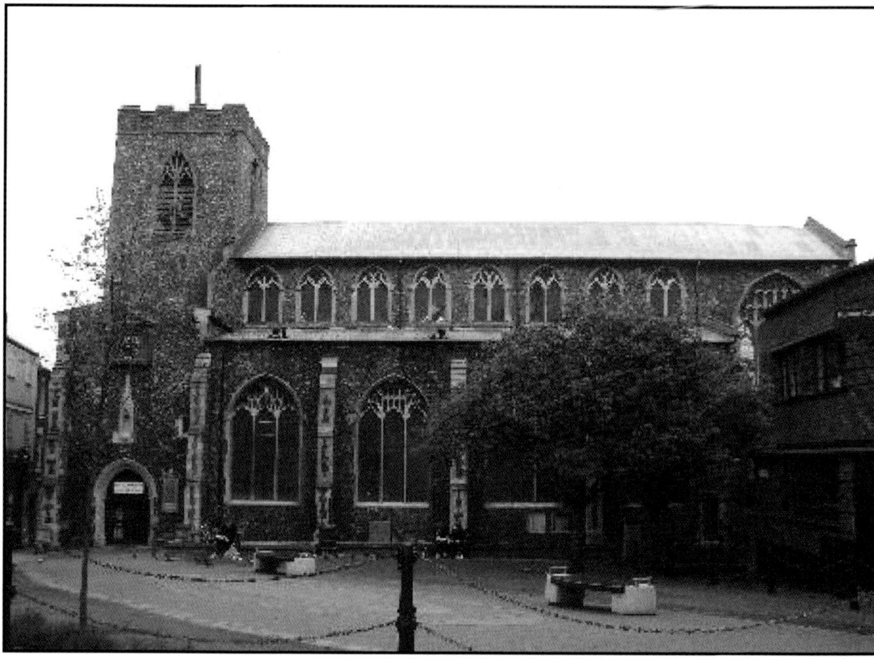

This is a church which should be visited more often. There is so much to see here it is impossible to mention everything. From its strange high sanctuary, underneath which is an alleyway, to the unusual configuration of the porches either side of the tower. Looking up from beneath the tower is a beautiful groined ceiling, above which is the ringing chamber. The sixteen windows of the clerestory permeate light into the nave through the tall, graceful 15th c. arcades and the nave. Also of the same period is the font with its unusual carved heads squashed by the shaft. Wall paintings, one of George and the Dragon are the speciality of the church and more paintings of saints on the ancient screen. In the choir are four misericordes, which are well carved, and the lectern dated 1493. Full of interesting things to see.

NORWICH St Helen

No of Bells: 1

19th c. Deanery: Norwich

Hundred: Norwich

Union house: Norwich

21st c. Deanery: Norwich East

Benefice: Norwich St Helen

From Tombland take Palace Street, then into Bishopgate next to the Great Hospital, behind and east of Norwich cathedral.

O.S. grid ref: TG 238090

Post Code: NR1 4EJ

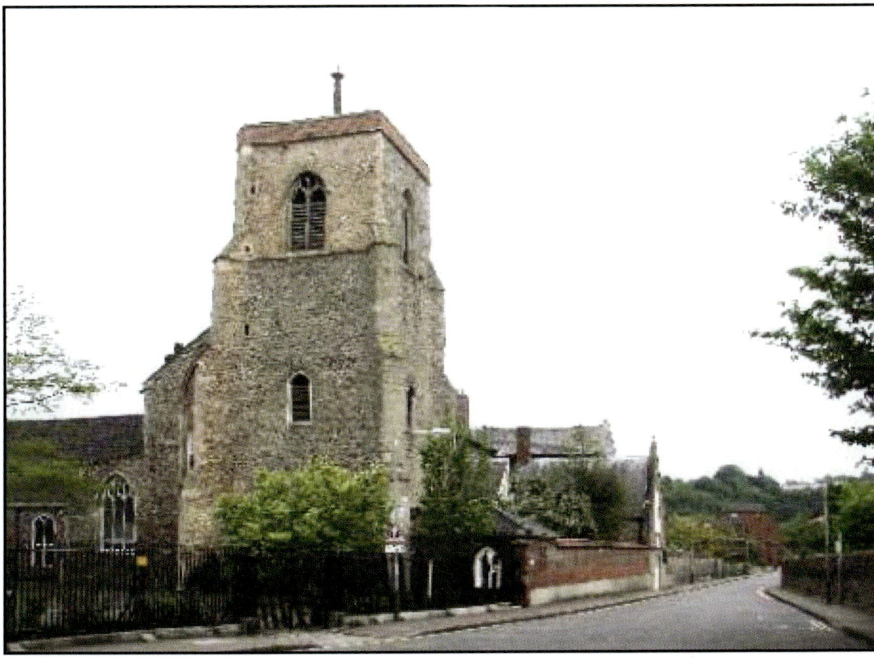

In 1249, St Helen's was built close to here, and demolished sometime before the time when this church was completed in the 15th c. The layout of the building is confusing as parts of it were utilised as wards for the Great Hospital. Patients were separated from the church itself by partitioning. Part of the chancel was used as a chapel for the Hospital and screened off before eventually a wall was erected. In the south transept the ceiling is beautifully groined with elaborately carved bosses at the intersections depicting religious themes. Brightly painted in blue and white it stands out as something special. Some of the bench ends are 16th c. and carved, one shows St Margaret emerging from the mouth of the dragon. The church stands behind Derlynton's Tower which is now detached from it.

NORWICH	St James, Pockthorpe
No of Bells:	1
19th c. Deanery:	Norwich
Hundred:	Norwich
Union house:	Norwich
21st c. Deanery:	-
Norwich Historic Churches Trust	

A half mile NNE of the castle. In Barrack Street near the Whitefriars, St Crispin's Road - Charlton Road roundabout.
O.S. grid ref: TG 234093
Post Code: NR3 1TY

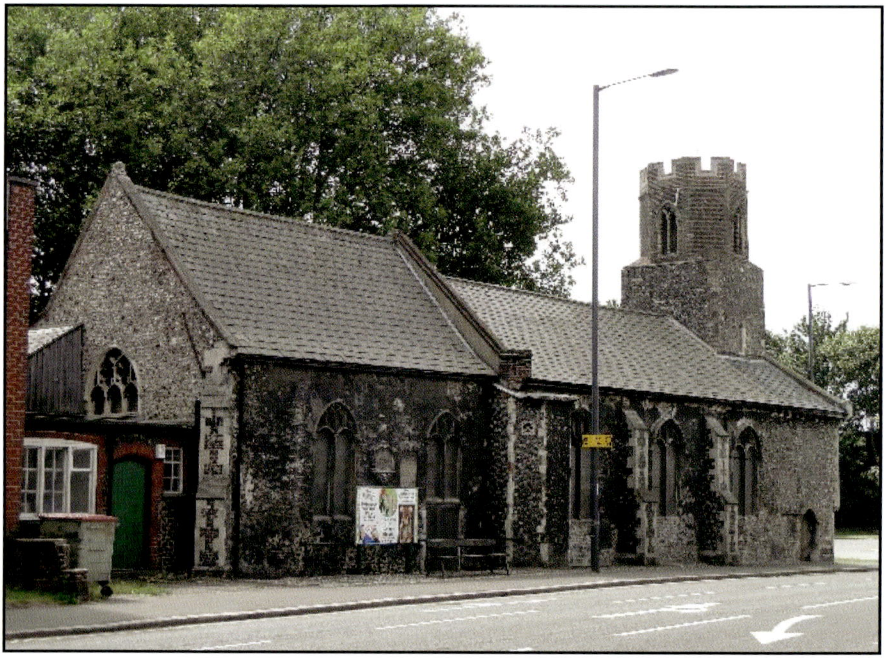

Pockthorpe, a small hamlet of Norwich, was united with St James in 1201 when it was acquired by the cathedral and became a peculiar of the Dean and Chapter. This church was built around 150 years or so later. The tower is supported by two piers (NE and SE) forming three arches and only the west wall is solid. In 1743 the brick-built octagonal top was added. Entry is gained by the south porch which is at the western end of the south aisle. Having been made redundant in 1972 it was emptied of religious artefacts; the 14th c. font and the base of the painted screen with 10 depictions of saints are now in St Mary Magdalene in Silver Road. It became a night shelter but was found to be too small. Eventually it became a puppet theatre which has been very successfully operating here for a number of years.

NORWICH St John Maddermarket
No of Bells: 6
19th c. Deanery: Norwich
Hundred: Norwich
Union house: Norwich
21st c. Deanery: -
The Churches Conservation Trust

North of St Peter Mancroft. Next to the Maddermarket theatre in Pottergate, very close to St Gregory's Church
O.S. grid ref: TG 229087
Post Code: NR2 1DR

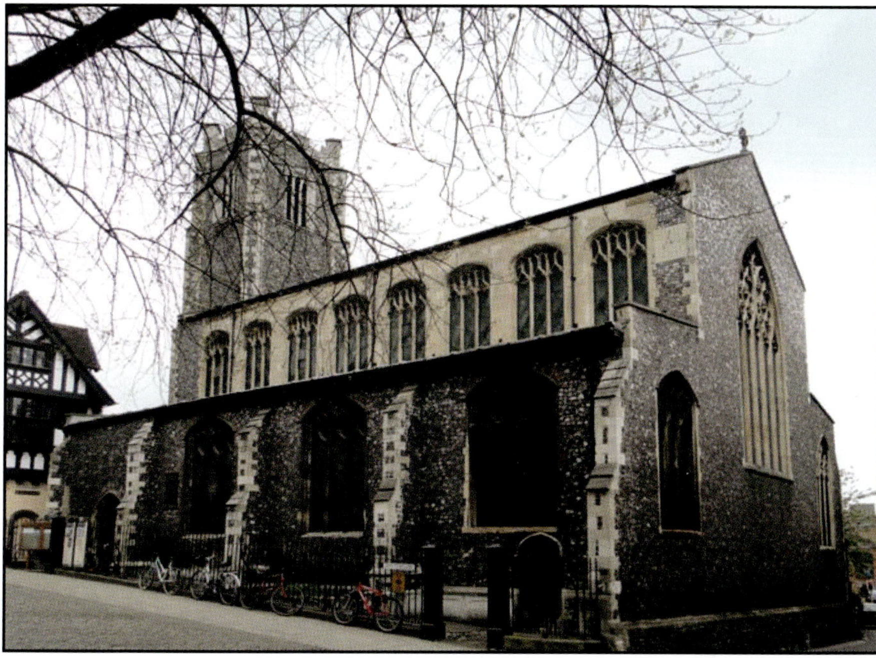

Built in the Perpendicular period and a classic example of mid 15th c. design this lovely church stands south of the Guildhall. Beneath the tower is a walkway for pedestrians and the south door to which there are steps down, retains its mediaeval hinges. Above the north porch is a large parvise. The clerestory is built of stone whereas the rest of the church is of knapped black flint. There is no chancel, the south aisle contains a Lady Chapel, and mediaeval carving can be seen in the painted roof. The roof of the nave is also painted with fan vaulting but is part of the Victorian restorations. The 18th c. font looks as if it has come from Egypt. Above the 1863 pulpit is a 17th c. tester, suspended from the ceiling. Many impressive monuments of notable citizens are here including that of Alderman Thomas Sotherton (1608).

NORWICH St John the Baptist and the Holy Sepulchre

No of Bells: 5 (all removed)
19th c. Deanery: Norwich
Hundred: Norwich
Union house: Norwich
21st c. Deanery: -
Currently unused

Situated at the northern end of Bracondale and the southern end of Ber Street, at the junction with Finkelgate.
O.S. grid ref: TG 234077
Post Code: NR1 3HF

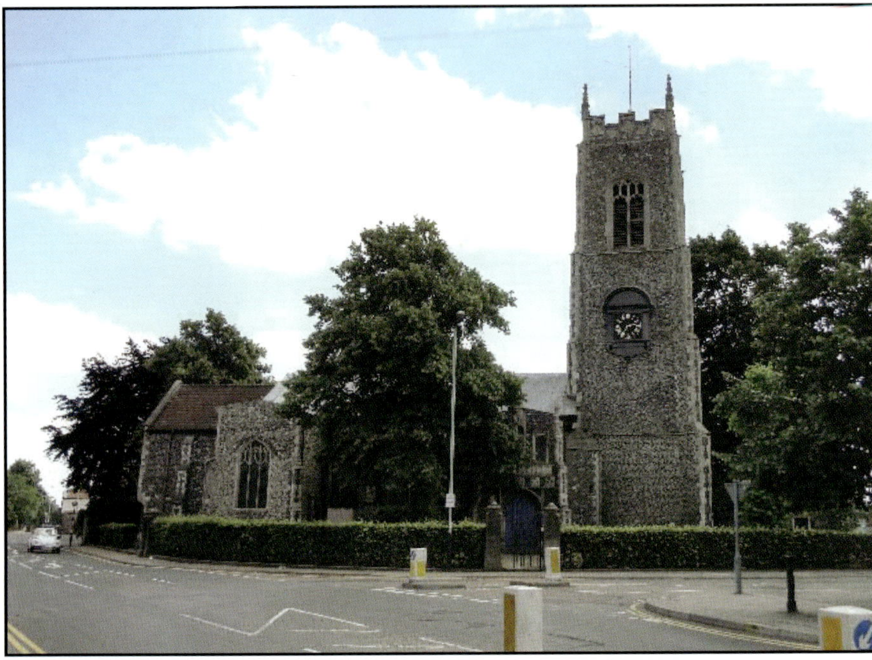

Now called St John the Theologian this is a very prominent church as you enter Norwich from the south. An earlier church was built here just after the Conquest. The present edifice was built in the 15th c. It has north and south transepts and a fine tower. It was declared redundant in 1970 along with scores of other churches in the county. Above the porch is a parvise and there is some good tracery on the door into the nave. A well-decorated East Anglian style font is coeval with the building of the church. Many of the fixtures and furnishings came originally from St Bartholomew's a short distance away when it was deconsecrated in 1549. A very basic piscina remains but most of the moveable paraphernalia has gone. There is also a really good reredos. It may be taken on by The Churches Conservation Trust.

NORWICH St John the Baptist, Timberhill

No of Bells:	1 - (5) see text	At the northern end of Ber Street in Timberhill at the junction with Golden Ball Street.
19th c. Deanery:	Norwich	
Hundred:	Norwich	
Union house:	Norwich	
21st c. Deanery:	Norwich (East)	O.S. grid ref: TG 232082
Benefice:	Timberhill	Post Code: NR1 3LA

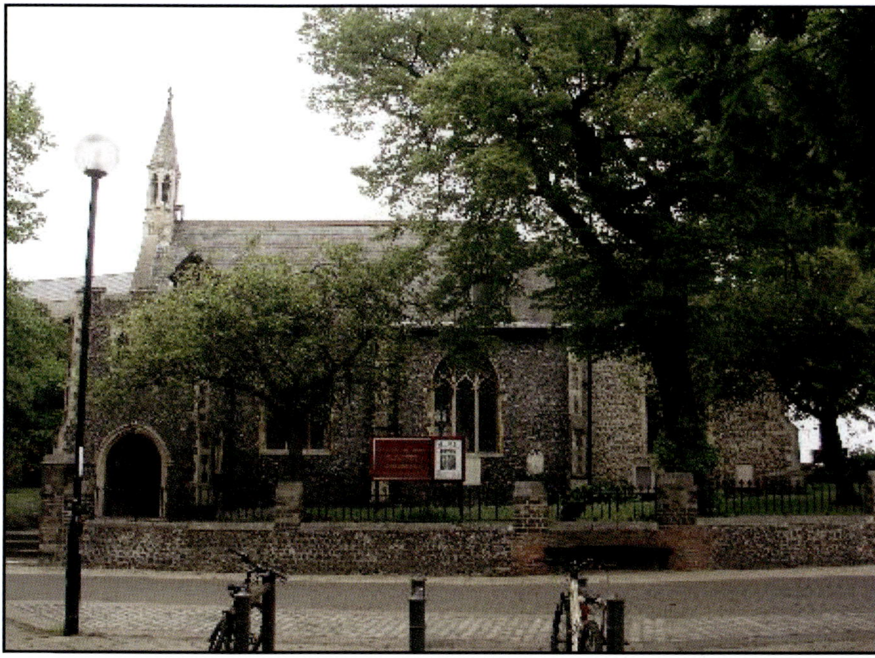

There was once a splendid tower at the west end but it fell onto the nave in 1784. The base was rebuilt as a vestry and the bellcote with a spirelet housing one bell was erected. The bells were sold to pay for repairs. At one time the church was known as 'St John at the Castle Gates' for obvious reasons. Much of what we see today is Victorian, although some long and short work remains at the east end indicating early origins. Inside, at the west end, the font cover is striking and unusual in that a door within it is opened instead of raising the cover. The font itself is quite plain. A Bishop stands in one corner gesticulating! A rood beam separates the nave from the chancel and the reredos is painted and gilded, triptych style. In the north aisle is a small chapel and a modest organ, which is elevated to permit access.

NORWICH	St Julian	South of the castle, situated in St Julian's Ally off King Street and between Rouen Road. Opposite Old Barge Yard.
No of Bells:	1	
19th c. Deanery:	Norwich	
Hundred:	Norwich	
Union house:	Norwich	
21st c. Deanery:	Norwich (East)	O.S. grid ref: TG 235081
Benefice:	Timberhill	Post Code: near NR1 1QU

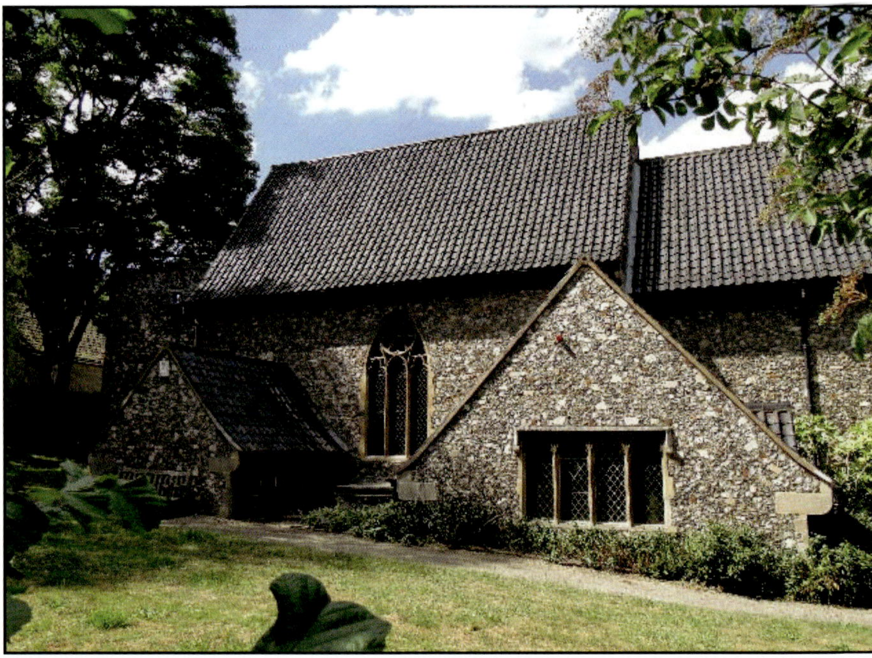

This is one of Norwich's smallest churches. It has a round tower the base of which probably dates back to the Saxon period. The church itself is more Norman than Saxon, or was before it was bombed in 1942. In 1845 the beautiful Norman south doorway was restored at the same time the chancel was restructured. The original font was Norman but it too was destroyed in the bombing. The original Norman work can still be recognised today under the excellent rebuilt nave and chancel. The tower, however, was never rebuilt and remains just a suggestion of its former glory. The replacement font is from All Saints. It was here that Dame Juliana, a devout recluse, spent much of her life in a flea-ridden cell during the 14th c. A modest painted and gilded reredos makes a beautiful backdrop for the altar.

NORWICH St Laurence
No of Bells: 6
19th c. Deanery: Norwich
Hundred: Norwich
Union house: Norwich
21st c. Deanery: -
Norwich City Council (Viking Trail)

West of the castle. Close to the intersection of St Benedict's Street and Westwick Street. Close to Charing Cross.
O.S. grid ref: TG 228088
Post Code: NR2 4AX

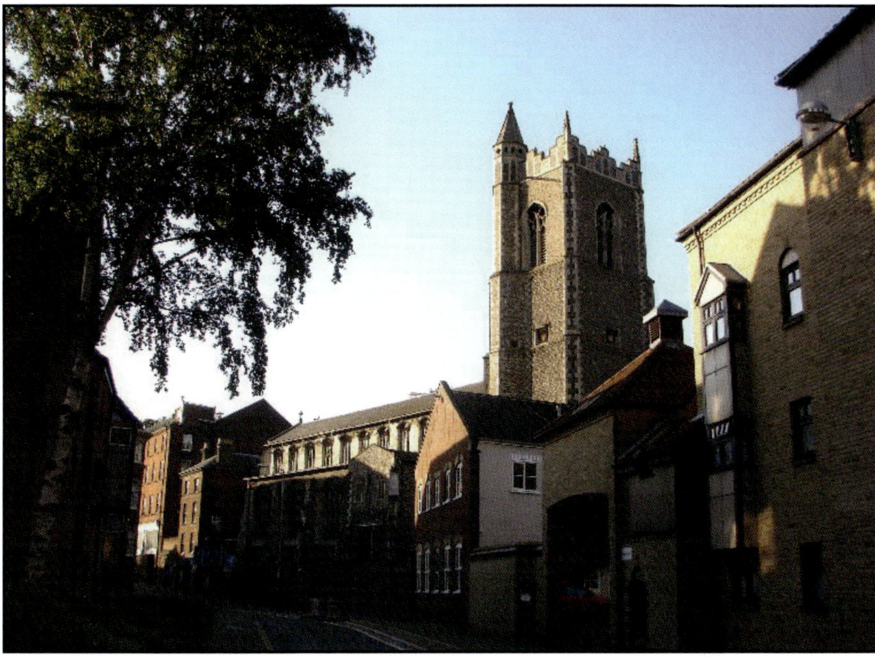

This 15th c. church replaced a Saxon church built in the early 11th c. The tower was raised to a height of 112 feet including the spirelet above the stair turret. It's worth studying the outside, because you will be disappointed by the interior. Above the west door are carved spandrels depicting the martyrdoms of St Laurence and St Edmund and a frieze of shields around the base of the tower. Set into the buttresses are stooled and canopied niches. Eleven windows each side of the clerestory permeate plenty of light into the nave. Around the 15th c. unusual octagonal font are angels holding shields. An original door still has its tracery in the upper part. The piscina is uncommonly plain and the sedilia made unusable by the raising of the chancel. The pulpit, reredos and even the rood beam are all early 20th c. additions.

NORWICH St Margaret de Westwick

No of Bells: 1 originally 5
19th c. Deanery: Norwich
Hundred: Norwich
Union house: Norwich
21st c. Deanery: -
Norwich Historic Churches Trust

A few hundred yards west of the castle. Situated in St Margaret's Street between St Benedict's Street and Westwick Street.
O.S. grid ref: TG 227088
Post Code: NR2 1TX

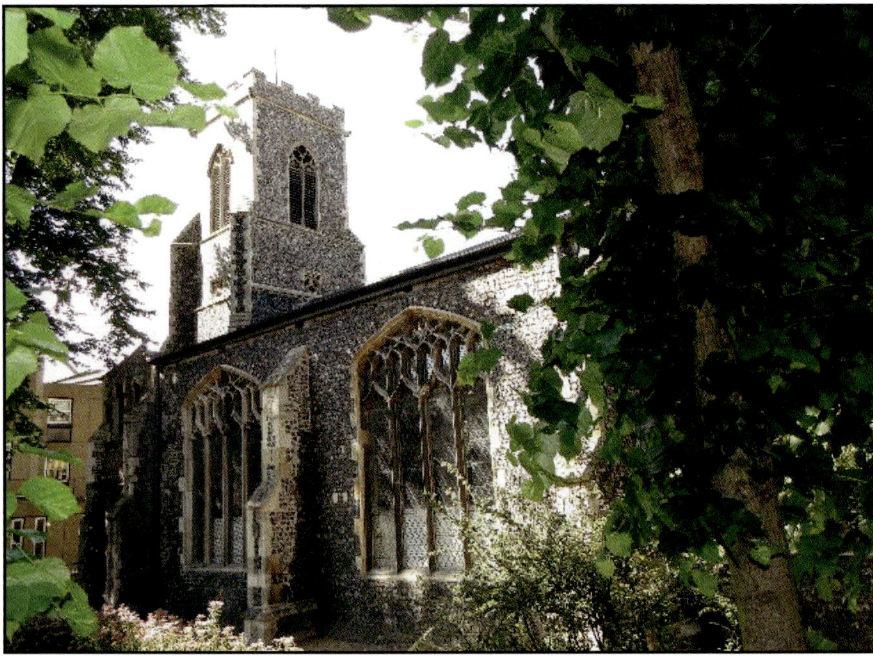

Since 1975 the church has been redundant, destined to be demolished as recommended by the Brooke Report. Thankfully today the exterior of this 14th c. church is just as it was then. The lovely pair of Perpendicular windows of the narrow south aisle give this smallish church a grace of its own. Inside however, is a different story. The 14th c. traceried font has gone, the reredos, screen, pulpit and benches have all been removed and the place is now an art gallery, and ideally suited for the purpose. Because it is itself a piece of art, Moses and Aaron flank the Decalogue board above the south door. Wandering about the nave and aisles, it becomes obvious that the church was cobbled together over a long period of time. Nothing seems to line up with anything else and a mish-mash of re-structuring is evident.

NORWICH	St Martin at Oak	North of the castle. Off the western end of St. Crispin's Road and at the northern end of Oak Street in St. Martin's Lane.
No of Bells:	3	
19th c. Deanery:	Norwich	
Hundred:	Norwich	
Union house:	Norwich	
21st c. Deanery:	-	O.S. grid ref: TG 227092
Norwich Historic Churches Trust		Post Code: NR3 3AG

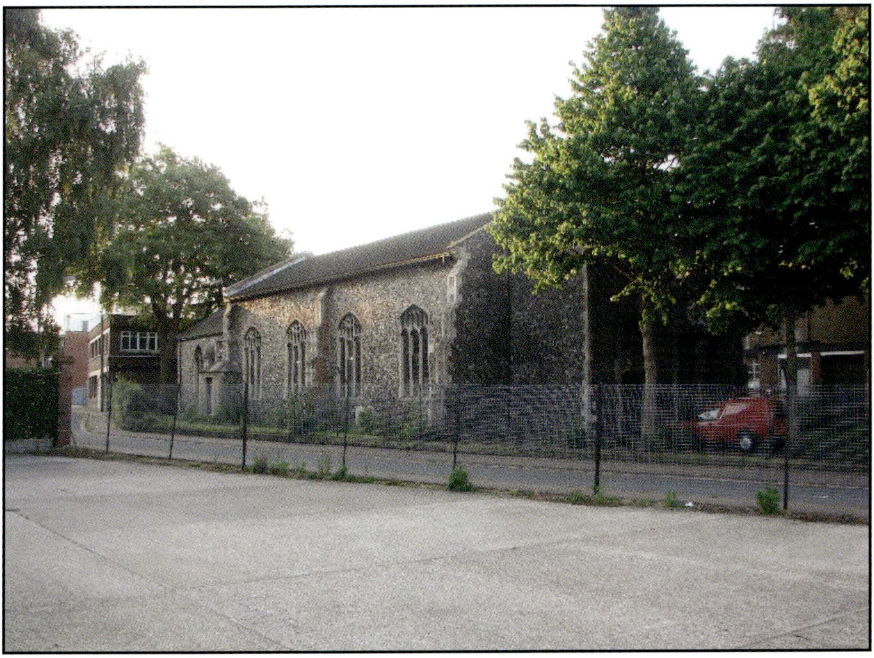

Like most churches in Norwich, this one too was bomb damaged in 1942. Some were cleared away, some were repaired, this is one such church. It lay derelict until 1953 when it was rebuilt, not as a place of worship but as a community hall. In 1978 it became a night shelter for the homeless after St James was found to be inadequate. More suitable accommodation was found and it closed as such in 2004. What was the tower has been truncated with a west stepped gable. A door was inserted into the west wall of the south aisle and the south porch with its canopied and stooled niche, sealed. Everything except a few wall memorials have been removed. The one to Jeremiah Revans (1727) was so damaged it was removed and the considerable figures on it are now in the castle museum. St. Martin's is currently an art centre.

NORWICH	St Martin at Palace
No of Bells:	5
19th c. Deanery:	Norwich
Hundred:	Norwich
Union house:	Norwich
21st c. Deanery:	-
Norwich Historic Churches Trust	

Situated in Palace Street where it joins Bishopgate at the southern end of Whitefriars. Opposite the cathedral's north Gate.
O.S. grid ref: TG 237091
Post Code: NR3 1RT

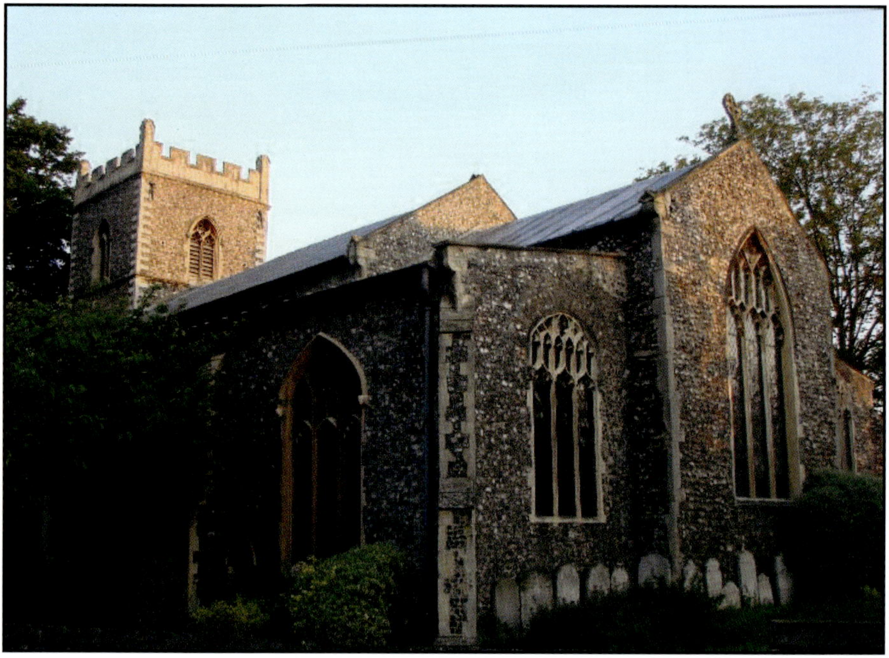

This little 15th c. church (now offices) is surrounded by trees and still has its own graveyard, whereas most in the city have lost theirs. Many of the headstones however, are sadly just propped against the walls. Excavations revealed that at least one Saxon church stood here before this one was erected, and possibly a Norman church too, but nothing more is known about either. The tower has collapsed twice and the north aisle once in its history. Much Victorian restoration has taken place as well as the rebuilding. There are north and south aisles and the porch has a parvise. Quatrefoil lights in the low clerestory have little effect in lighting the nave. The chest tomb and wall monument combination to Elizabeth Caltrop (Calthorpe) (1578) is at the east end of the north aisle. Admission to look around is permitted.

NORWICH	St Mary, Coslany
No of Bells:	6
19th c. Deanery:	Norwich
Hundred:	Norwich
Union house:	Norwich
21st c. Deanery:	-
Norwich Historic Churches Trust	

Situated ¼ mile north of the castle, between Oak Street and the northern end of Duke Street on St. Mary's Plain.

O.S. grid ref:	TG 228092
Post Code:	NR3 3AF

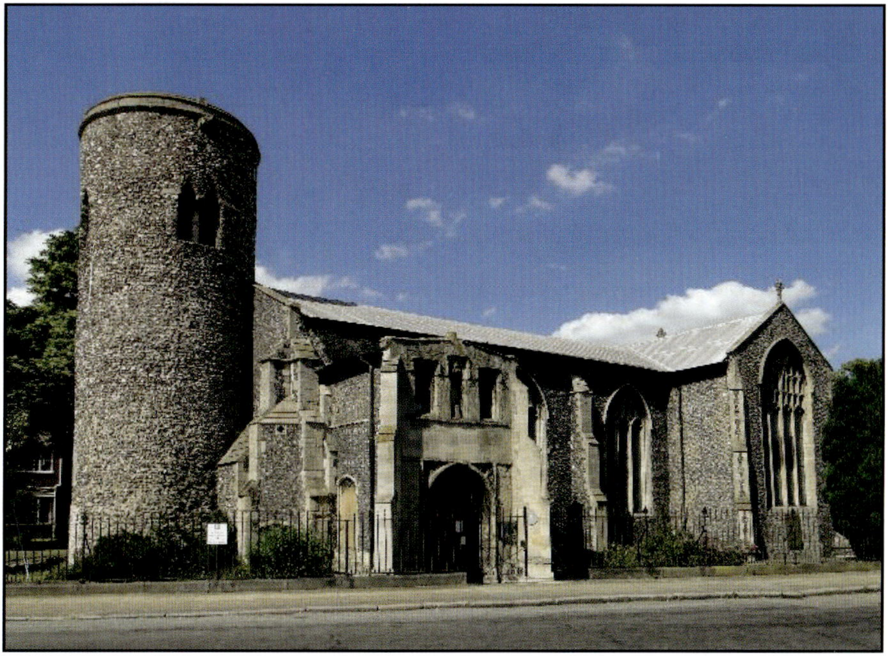

Here is the oldest tower of any of the Norwich churches dating from before the Conquest. The double triangular-headed windows with a central column are reminiscent of the period. There used to be a 15th c. octagonal belfry stage, which was constructed at the same time. The Saxon church was demolished and the one we see today erected. The south porch has a parvise and a canopied niche over the entrance. An arch-braced roof over the nave is decorated with bosses and mostly original; chancel and transept ceilings are also highly decorated. All furnishings and fittings have been removed since it was declared redundant in 1974, including the linen-fold pulpit, 15th c. font, screens, 14th c. ironbound chest, Jacobean holy table, hour-glass and stand. Only the wall monuments and traceried piscina remain.

NORWICH	St Mary the Less
No of Bells:	5 (removed)
19th c. Deanery:	Norwich
Hundred:	Norwich
Union house:	Norwich
21st c. Deanery:	-
Norwich Historic Churches Trust	

Situated opposite and to the right of the cathedral main gate between buildings on the Queen's Street and Tombland junction.
O.S. grid ref: TG 233089
Post Code: NR2 4SG

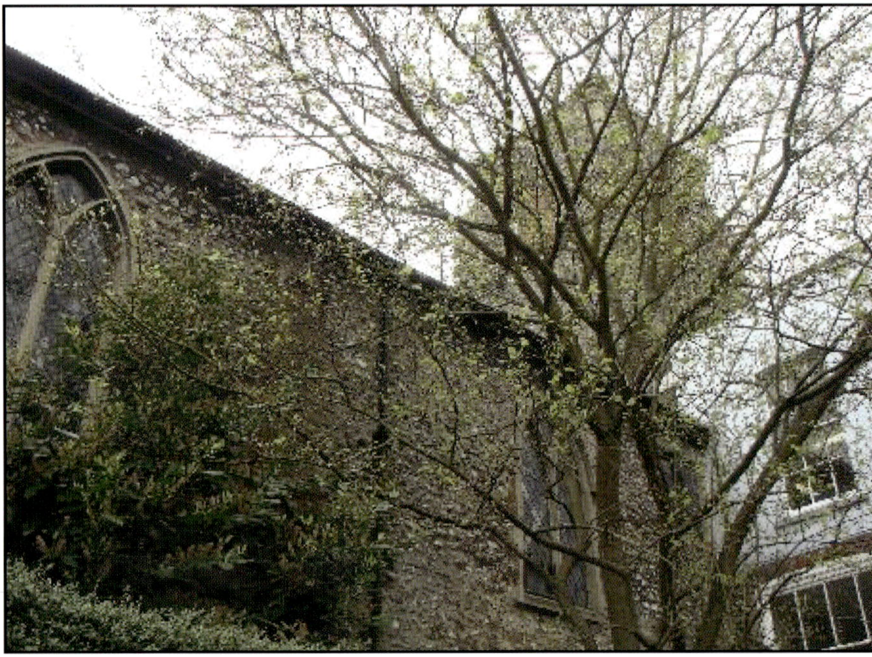

Otherwise known as 'The French Church'. Concealed behind other buildings it is not easy to find. Secreted behind restraints and offices it has been built onto and against, to such an extent only the tower is visible above the roofs of the surrounding buildings. Even Cautley couldn't find it and it is not included in his volume. It does however, have a very interesting history. Believed to date from the 13th c. it has obviously undergone major changes over the centuries. It was virtually made redundant as early as 1544 after which time it was used as a saleroom for cloth. In 1637 it was taken over by French protestants for use as a church and continued as such for 200 years. Today it is privately owned. I wonder what the next 200 years will have in store for this, the most unusual of all the churches in the city.

NORWICH	St Matthew
No of Bells:	-
19th c. Deanery:	Norwich
Hundred:	Norwich
Union house:	Norwich
21st c. Deanery:	-
In private ownership	

About a ½ mile east of the castle. Turn east off Riverside Road into St Matthew's Road or half way along Rosary Road.

O.S. grid ref: TG 240086
Post Code: NR1 1SP

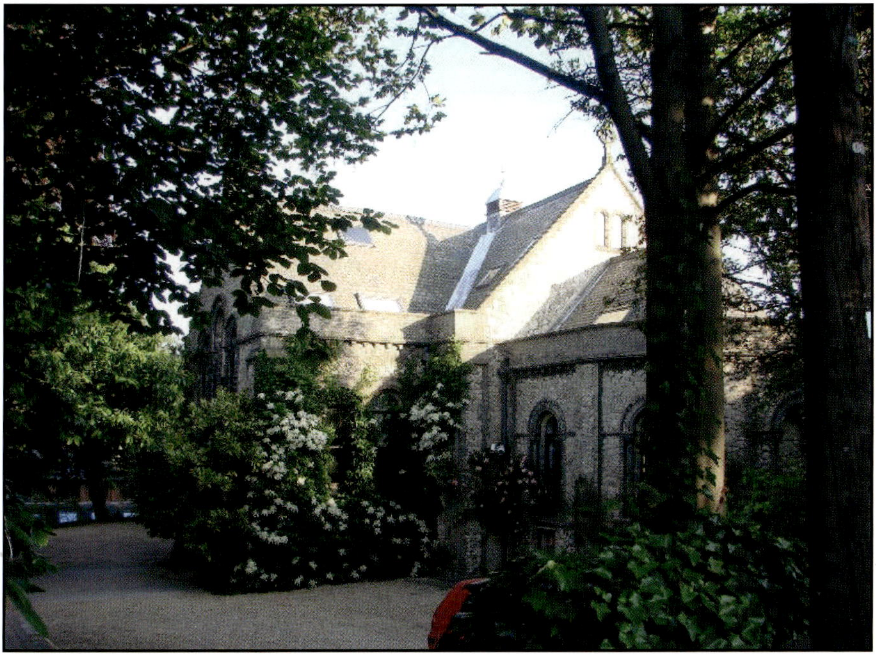

This Victorian church was erected mid-century and opened in 1851. Designed by John Brown, it was built in a pseudo-Norman style and lasted little more than 100 years before it was declared redundant and set to be demolished. It is, however, an attractive addition to the landscape and is currently used as offices. Architecturally it is a very interesting edifice. Although attractively decorated and once filled with all the paraphernalia of a Victorian church it holds little interest for the historian. Basically, it is a cruciform church with an apsidal chancel at the east end and an attractive bellcote on the west gable in lieu of a tower. The windows are attractively arranged in pairs, with three engaged columns for each. Entry is gained through a fine copy of a Norman doorway in the south transept.

NORWICH St Michael at Plea
No of Bells: 2
19th c. Deanery: Norwich
Hundred: Norwich
Union house: Norwich
21st c. Deanery: -
Norwich Historic Churches Trust

Situated within the bounds of Redwell Street, Queen's Street, Prince's Street and Tombland, and close to the Post Office.
O.S. grid ref: TG 233087
Post Code: NR2 4SN

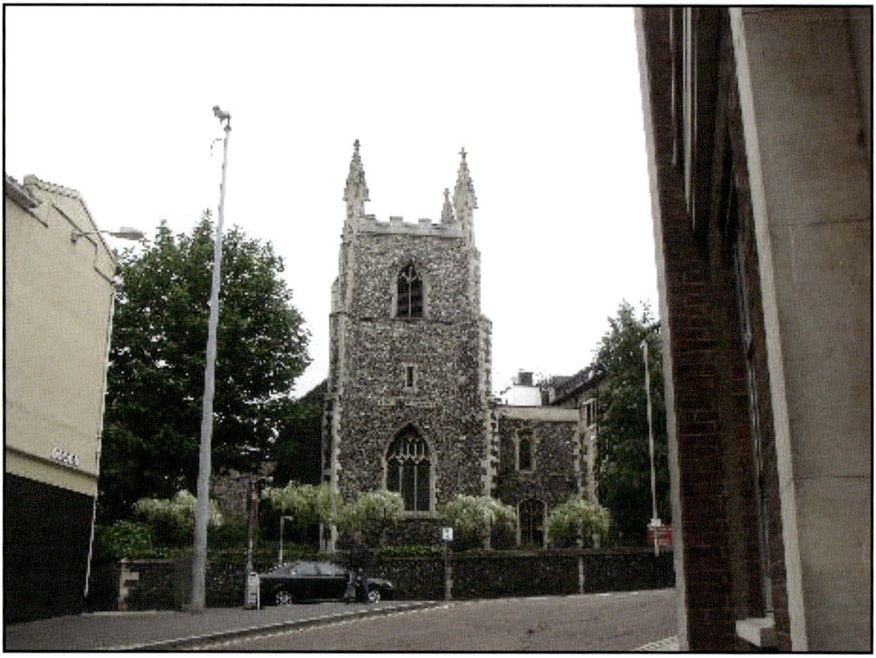

So called because the Archdeacon of Norwich used to hold his pleas or courts here. The top of the tower was removed late in the 19th c. and the oversized pinnacles erected; on the south is a clock face. Over the entrance to the splendid south porch is a niche between the windows of the parvise, with St George, having slain the dragon. Either side of the entrance are two more canopied niches. Through the traceried door into the base of the tower, on the right, is the nave and the 15th c. octagonal font with panelled bowl shaft, upon which is the 17th c. cover with a dove sitting on top of the pinnacle. A traceried screen replaces the original, now in the cathedral. Gilded angels look down from the nave roof onto the NCRC bookshop. In the chancel is the 'Forget-Me-Not Café' where you can get a nice cup of tea.

NORWICH	St Michael, Coslany
No of Bells:	8
19th c. Deanery:	Norwich
Hundred:	Norwich
Union house:	Norwich
21st c. Deanery:	-
Norwich Historic Churches Trust	

About 500 yards NNW of the castle. In Colegate just off Oak Street with St. Mary's and St. Martin's churches close by.
O.S. grid ref: TG 230090
Post Code: NR3 3DP

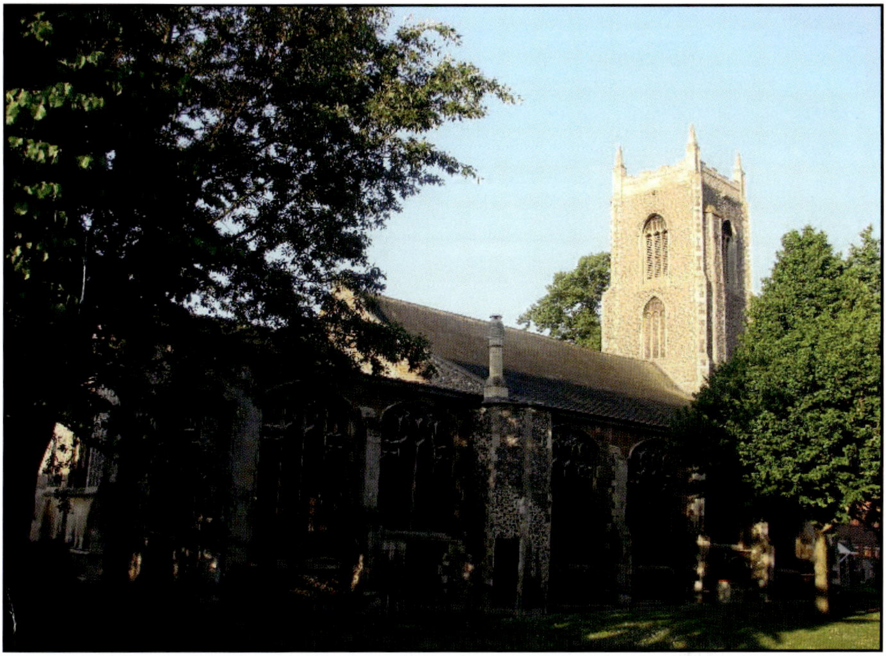

Probably the most interesting feature about this church can be seen from the outside. The 15th c. flushwork which covers the south aisle or Thorpe chapel is for the most part original. That on the east end (the chancel) was restored in 1884 when a new east window was inserted. Compare it with the plainness of the north aisle. The west door has some nice tracery work and above is a band of shields and escutcheons, above that are two fine canopied niches. Because of the unusual height of the aisles there is no clerestory. Although the church was made redundant in the 1970s, the eight musical bells are still rung on special occasions. The font was moved to Reedham after theirs was damaged by fire. Like other redundant churches, it is now used for a different purpose, this one as a Discovery Centre.

NORWICH	St Peter, Hungate
No of Bells:	2 (removed 1906)
19th c. Deanery:	Norwich
Hundred:	Norwich
Union house:	Norwich
21st c. Deanery:	-
Norwich Historic Churches Trust	

West of the cathedral & north of St Michael at Plea. At the southern end of Elm Hill at the junction of Prince's Street.

O.S. grid ref: TG 233087
Post Code: NR3 1HN

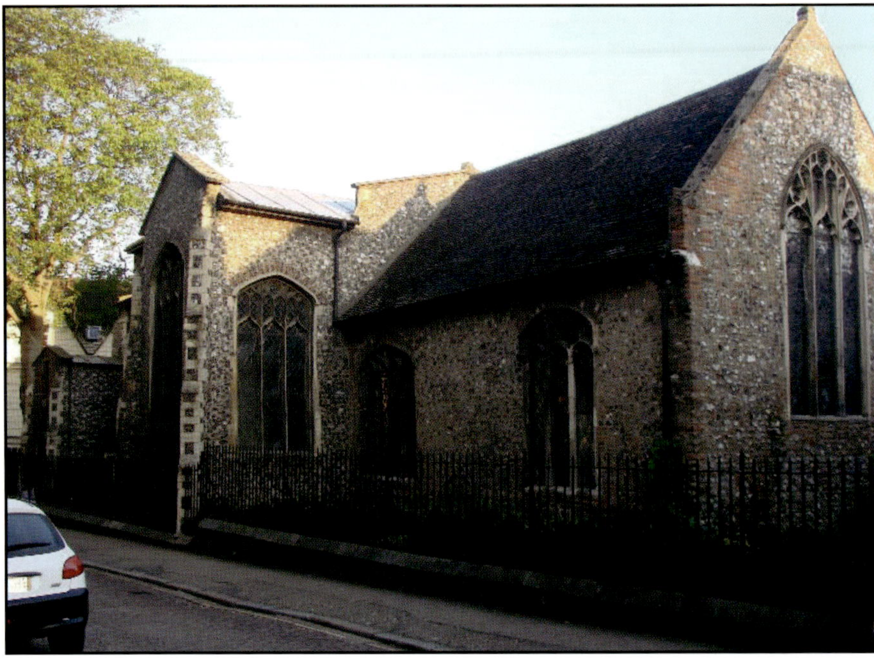

For many years the church stood unused, having been built on the site of an earlier church. It was financed by John Paston in 1460. Nicholas Ingram built the north porch in 1497 so he could be buried beneath it. Most parts of the church have been rebuilt since. The latest was the removal of the belfry and topping off the tower with the pyramidal roof. There is little to see in this now empty church. In 1936 until 1995, when it was closed to save money to be spent on the castle modifications for the millennium, it was a museum of church ephemera, housing many unique items of ecclesiastical interest. Now the exhibits are in the dungeons of the castle, and rarely ever seen. Today it is an exhibition and interpretation centre for the medieval arts focussing mainly on stained glass.

NORWICH St Peter Mancroft *****

No of Bells: 12
19th c. Deanery: Norwich
Hundred: Norwich
Union house: Norwich
21st c. Deanery: Norwich East
Benefice: St Peter Mancroft

At the side of the Market Place where Gentleman's Walk meets Haymarket. In front of and to the right of City Hall
O.S. grid ref: TG 229084
Post Code: NR2 1QD

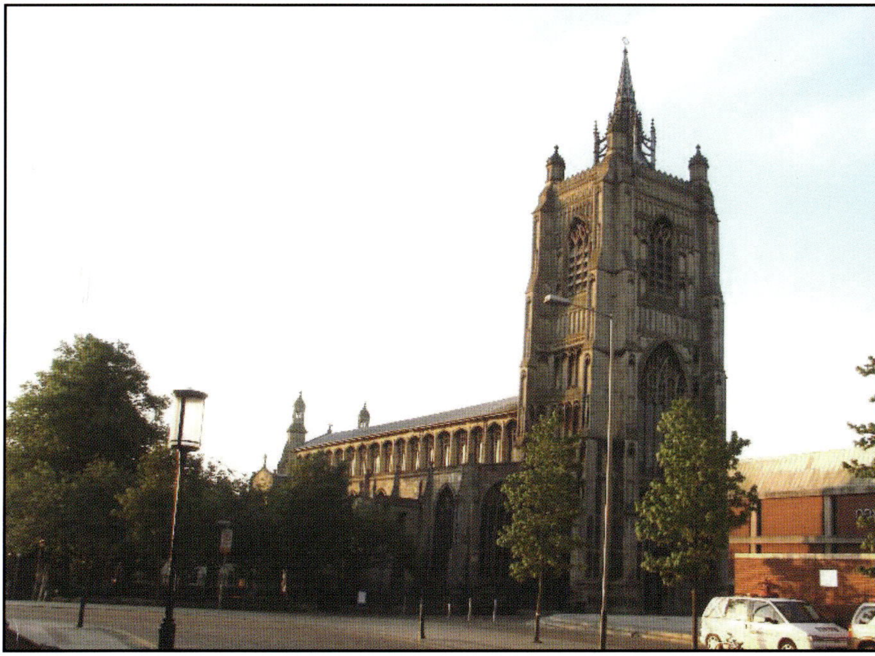

Unsurprisingly this is the most impressive church in the county. Completed in 1455 it displays the opulence of the City of Norwich, probably originally dedicated to St. Peter and St. Paul. It stands on the site of an earlier church, which probably had a central tower, built just after the Conquest by Earl Ralph Waiet. The Victorians had to have their piece of the action and added the spire and 'pepper-pot' turrets in 1895. The crenellations in the parapet are triangular and so small they have little decorative effect. The peal of twelve bells amounts to over nine tons. Behind the sanctuary is the 'Treasury', unique to this church. The church is always open for looking around. There is little point in adding detail to this page as the magnificence of the church's interior must be seen to be fully appreciated.

NORWICH St Peter Parmentergate
No of Bells: 5
19th c. Deanery: Norwich
Hundred: Norwich
Union house: Norwich
21st c. Deanery: -
Norwich Historic Churches Trust

Situated south of the castle, at the northern end of King Street. South of Cattle Market Street and east of Rouen Road.
O.S. grid ref: TG 234084
Post Code: NR1 1PD

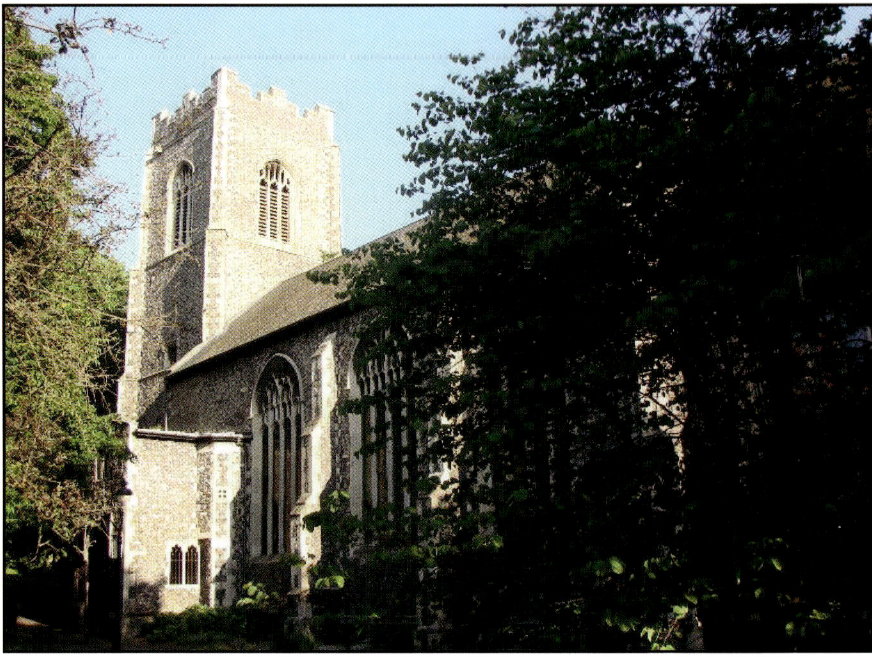

A much earlier Saxon or Norman church stood on this site of which we know very little. This is a good solid 15th c. church with a coeval tower with double crenulated parapet. The very simple south porch has a parvise. Set into the east wall is a large stooled niche, presumably once with St Peter in residence. The building was made redundant in 1981 and in 2005 an academy of martial arts took over the lease. A typical East Anglian font (if it's still there) has two wodewoses and two lions around the base. The rood screen has been removed but the stairs and external turret remain. All moveable furnishings and fittings have been removed, including the bells from the tower. A tomb with effigies of R. Berney esq. and his wife (circa 1625) is against the south wall. It was restored in 2007.

NORWICH St Saviour *(a misnomer)*
No of Bells: 2
19th c. Deanery: Norwich
Hundred: Norwich
Union house: Norwich
21st c. Deanery: -
Norwich Historic Churches Trust

South of Tombland, over the Wensum at Fye Bridge and towards the centre of Magdalene Street, just before the flyover.
O.S. grid ref: TG 233093
Post code: NR3 1TA

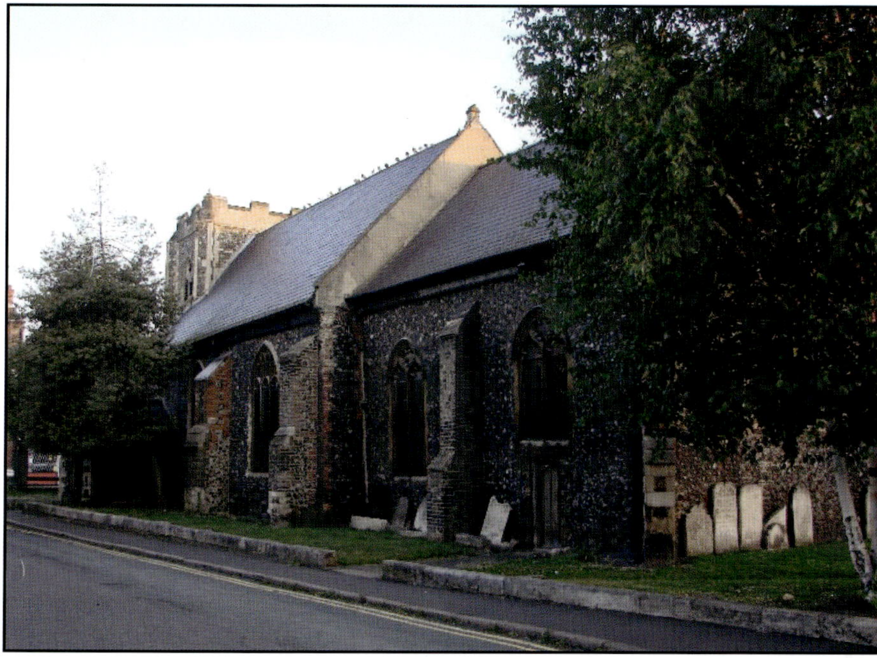

'The Transfiguration of our Saviour' is the true dedication. The truncated tower of St. Saviour's is quite distinctive with a clock on the west face. The previously thatched roof was tiled in the 19th c. For some time the south porch was used as a baptistery and contained the octagonal font which is now in St George's Colegate. The nave roof is scissor braced with tie beams. Monuments have been left in situ on the walls but all that can be removed has gone, including the gallery that found its way to All Saints in Westlegate. It is however still serving a useful spiritual purpose as a centre for young Christians to meet an make music. It is unfortunate that this otherwise lovely church is in such a neglected area of the city. The headstones leaning against the outer walls do nothing to help in that regard.

NORWICH	St Simon & St Jude
No of Bells:	0 (5 before tower fell)
19th c. Deanery:	Norwich
Hundred:	Norwich
Union house:	Norwich
21st c. Deanery:	-
Norwich Historic Churches Trust	

200 yards south of the cathedral. In Wensum Street and at the top of Elm Hill. Just south of Fye Bridge.

O.S. grid ref: TG 233088
Post Code: NR3 1JP

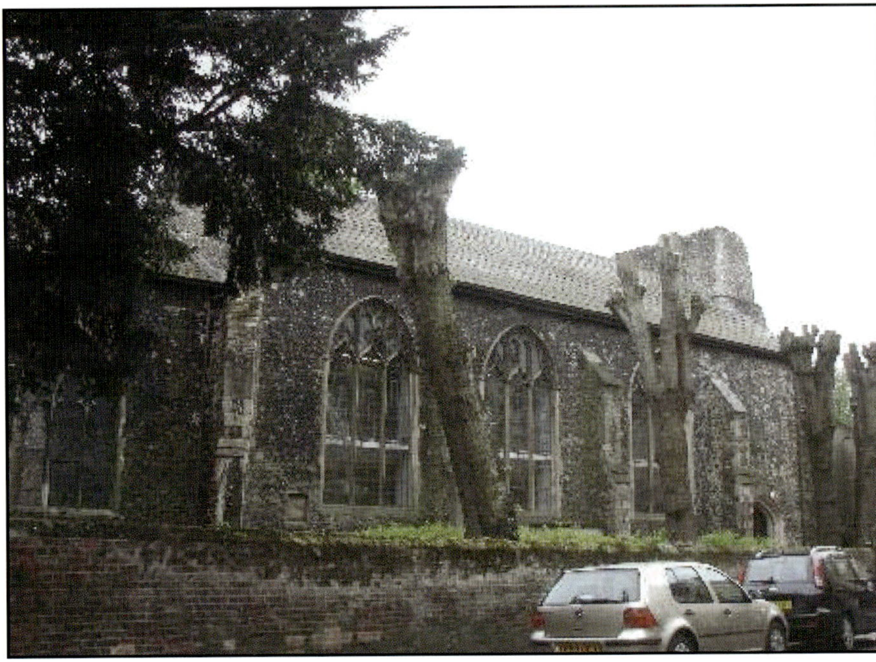

What is quite certain is that a church has stood on this site since Saxon times. This church, built in the 15th c. and was declared superfluous to parish requirements in 1892. In 1911 the tower collapsed. Subsequently it was used as a Sunday school until 1939, when extensive repairs took place financed by The Norwich Society. In 1952 it was leased as a scout HQ, until 1997. Concrete floors have been integrated into the structure and partitions put up to divide the interior into rooms. The only thing the church has to offer the historian, apart from its recent history, are the Pettus monuments. Sir Thomas Petus *(sic)* (1597) prays at a prayer desk with his wife and children. Sir John Pettus (1614) reclines in full armour and Augustus Pettus (1613) lies alongside his wife Abigail. It is now a dance school.

NORWICH	St Stephen
No of Bells:	3
19th c. Deanery:	Norwich
Hundred:	Norwich
Union house:	Norwich
21st c. Deanery:	Norwich East
Benefice:	Norwich St Stephen

Not in St Stephen's Street but in Malthouse Road which is just off Rampant Horse Street. Quite close to the Theatre Royal.

O.S. grid ref: TG 229083
Post Code: NR2 1QY

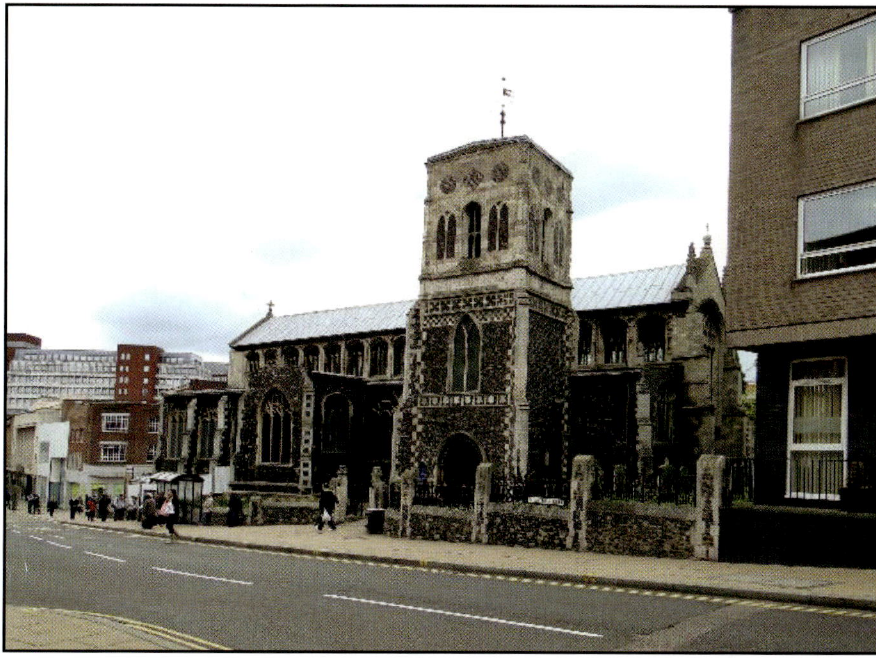

From before the Conquest a church has stood on this site. This may account for the tower being north of the nave. The building we see today is mainly 16th c. Cautley believed the porch beneath the northwest tower to be two centuries earlier, obviously that of an earlier church. The porch is finely vaulted, Sts. Laurence and Stephen are represented in the ceiling bosses. The nave and chancel are very tall and a sixteen-window three-light clerestory is supported by the lofty arcades. The lovely hammerbeam roof over the nave and chancel has angel corbels. Most of the interior fittings date from around the 1860s after the church was re-ordered, although a few items of interest remain such as the iron-bound chest and misericordes. Many grand monuments to various Norwich worthies adorn the walls.

NORWICH St Swithin Holy Apostle
No of Bells: 1
19th c. Deanery: Norwich
Hundred: Norwich
Union house: Norwich
21st c. Deanery: -
Norwich Historic Churches Trust

The most westerly of the three remaining churches in St Benedict's Street opposite Ten Bell Lane. On the north side.
O.S. grid ref: TG 226088
Post Code: NR2 4TX

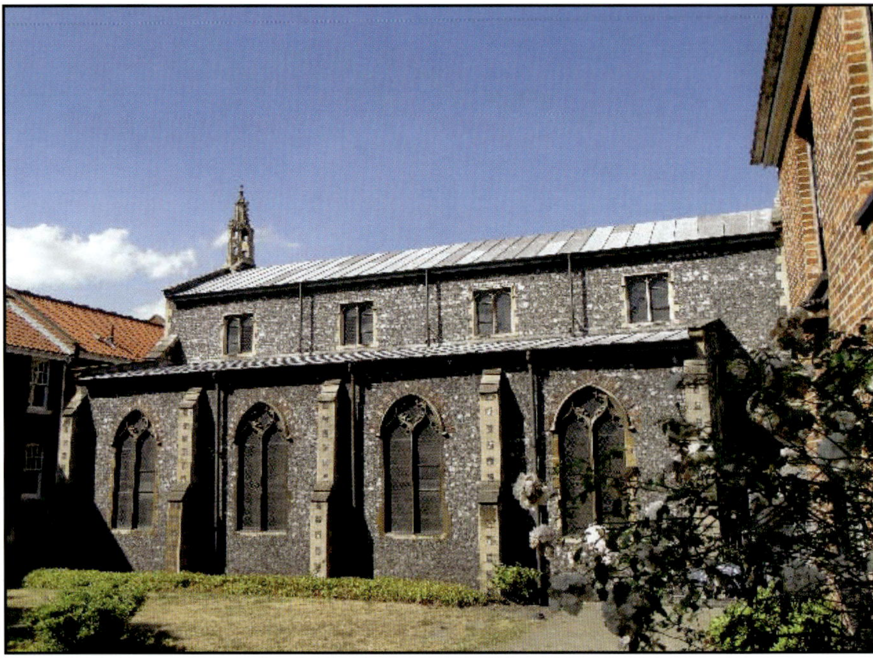

The square tower was demolished in 1882; a bell turret containing a single bell was erected on the west gable. The porches have also been demolished giving it a village hall appearance. There is no defined chancel. It was closed in 1881, reopening in 1883 for just 8 years, eventually falling into disrepair. It was thoroughly restored in 1905. It closed for the last time in 1951 and was taken over as an Arts Centre in 1980. Little remains except a few wall plaques. Entry to the stage of the Arts Centre is now through the east wall via a new lobby. The traditional East Anglian font which once baptised so many has gone, as have the screen, pulpit and seating. We must be thankful that demolition of the churches of Norwich has been limited to those damaged by bombing in WWII, despite Brooke's recommendations.

OLD CATTON	St Margaret
No of Bells:	1
19th c. Deanery:	Taverham
Hundred:	Taverham
Union house:	Horsham St Faith
21st c. Deanery:	Norwich North
Benefice:	Old Catton

2 m N of Norwich centre. From Boundary Road take St Faith's Road & turn right, or Spixworth Road & left into Church Street.

O.S. grid ref: TG 231123
Post Code: NR6 7DR

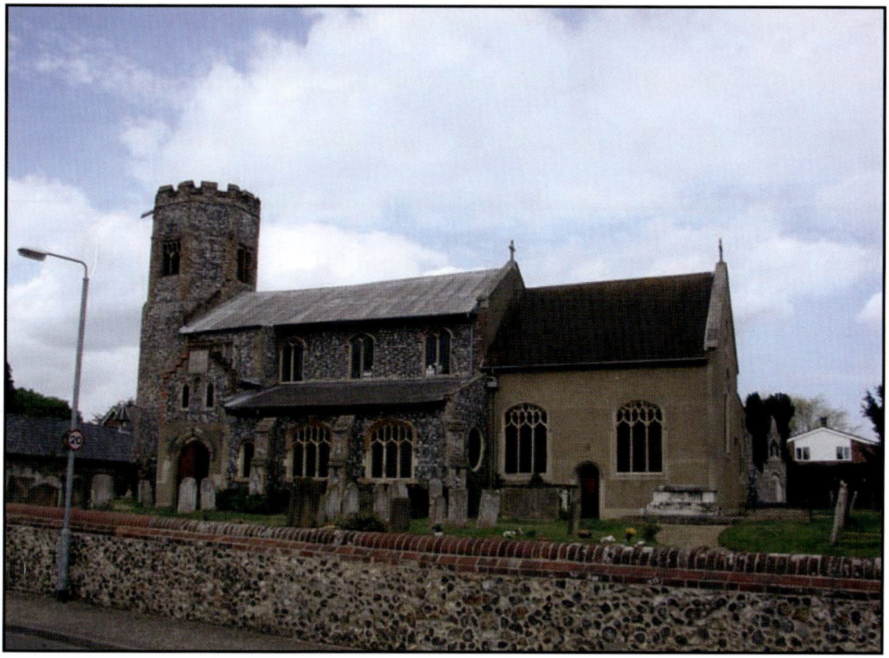

This church is so different on the inside from its outward appearance. The round part of the tower is Norman with an octagonal belfry added in the 15th c. The south porch has a sundial on the gable and a parvise above. The interior is large and dark despite the clerestory, A 19th c. transept on the north aisle creates a sense of spaciousness yet there are Victorian benches squeezed into all available space. The font is early 15th c., being decorated only with quatrefoils and no religious emblems, remains undamaged. The lovely linen-fold carved pulpit is the real treasure here and is dated 1537. It was originally in St George, Colegate. Behind the pulpit is what remains of a groined canopied niche. The screen is decorated with twenty shields. There is a lovely colourful Bignold memorial rose window in the south aisle.

ORMESBY ST MARGARET St Margaret of Antioch

No of Bells: 1 + digital peals
19th c. Deanery: Flegg
Hundred: East Flegg
Union house: Rollesby
21st c Deanery: Great Yarmouth
Benefice: Ormesby St Margaret

5 miles N by W of Great Yarmouth turn off the A149 into the village centre. Car park 75 yds west of the church.
O.S. grid ref: TG 498145
Post Code: NR29 3QB

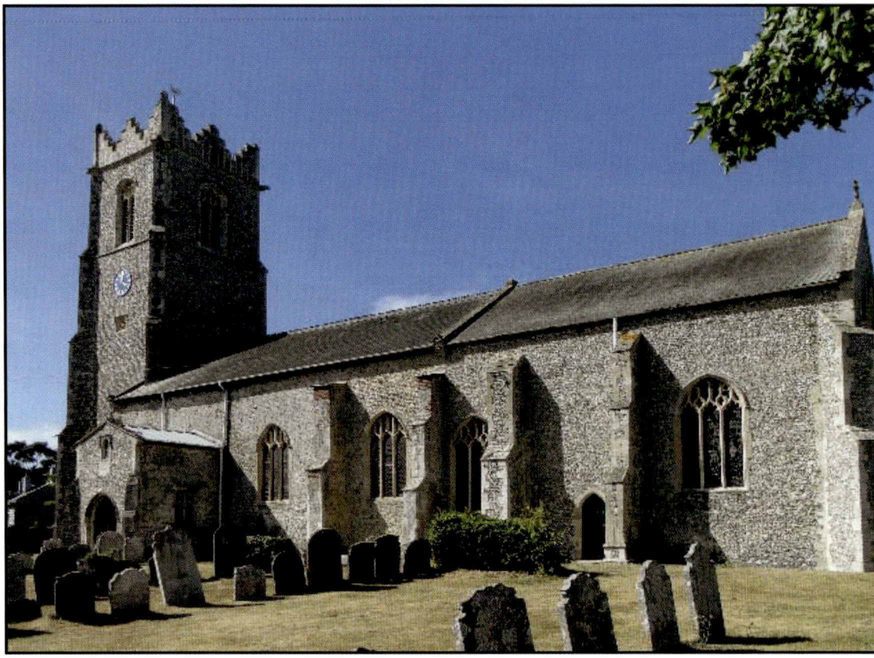

Standing tall and proud beside the road through the village the church dates from the 15th c. The tower with stepped battlements has unfortunately lost the pinnacles, which were in the form of monks. The coeval south porch has a parvise and inside is a fine Norman doorway with four orders of decoration and engaged columns either side. The font is disappointingly somewhat plain with little in the way of decoration. Much of what is to be seen is Victorian. The roof is arch-braced with wall struts resting on carved corbels. Set into the north wall of the sanctuary is a tomb with multi-cusped decoration. The bells here were recorded in Cork, Ireland and played through speakers in the belfry. In the nave is a memorial to Lady Caroline Home who died aged 25 in 1794. The inscription is very poignant.

ORMESBY ST MICHAEL

No of Bells: 5
19th c. Deanery: Flegg
Hundred: East Flegg
Union house: Rollesby
21st c Deanery: Great Yarmouth
Benefice: Ormesby St Margaret

6 miles NNW of Great Yarmouth on the A149 on the side of the road at the eastern end of the parish. Ample car parking at the side.
O.S. grid ref: TG 480149
Post Code: NR29 3LN

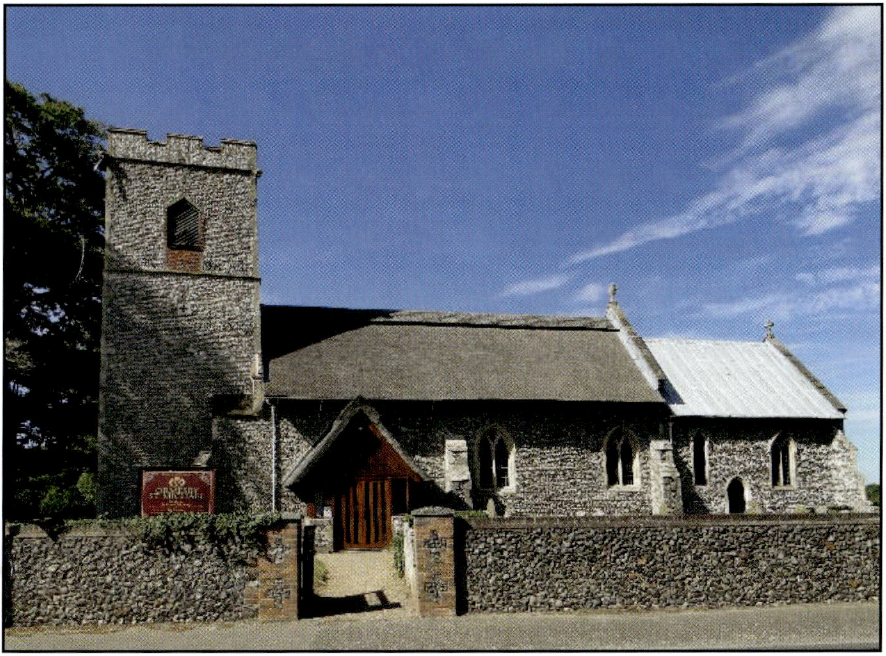

Standing next to the road, this 13th c. partly thatched church is difficult to miss. The stumpy tower was built a century later and the lack of buttressing is apparent. The southwest buttress has a scratch dial. The thatched porch is modern. Above the entrance are the Royal Arms of Elizabeth II, dated 1952. Much restoration (particularly in the 1970s) has taken place, the building is in good condition, and there is little to see here that is ancient. The roof is 15th c. and at the intersections, are small bosses of floral design, which are richly painted. The 13th c. plain octagonal font looks almost brand new and the pulpit is of stone with some tracery decoration. On the terminals of the hood-moulds of the north window there are carvings of a grotesque and a unique representation of a Norfolk horned sheep.

OVERSTRAND St Martin

No of Bells: 1
19th c. Deanery: Repps
Hundred: North Erpingham
Union house: Gimingham
21st c. Deanery: Repps
Benefice: Overstrand

1 mile ESE of Cromer on the coast road at the western end of the parish. The church stands very close to the road.
O.S. grid ref: TG 241408
Post Code: NR27 0NX

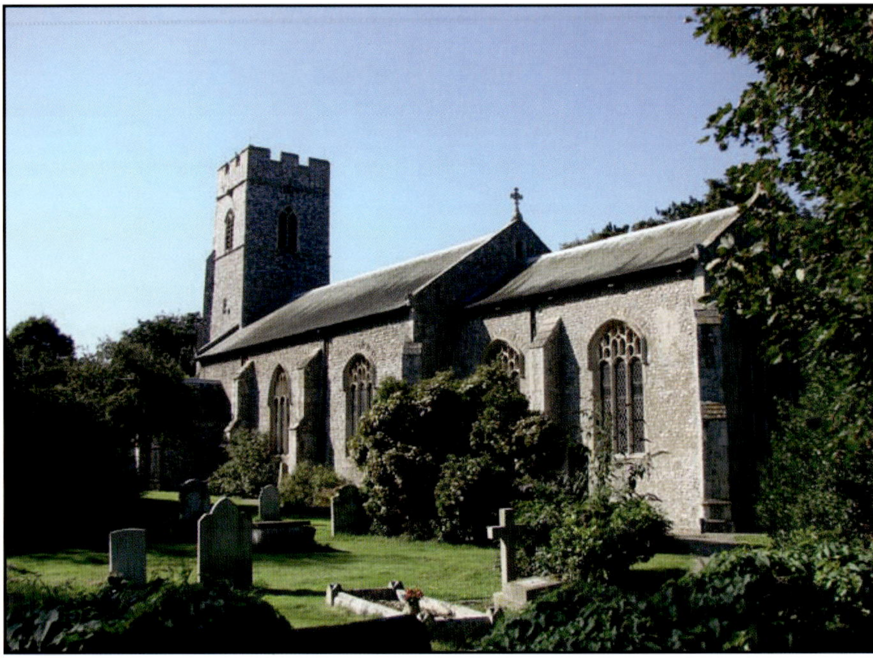

The original church was washed into the sea in the 14th c. Another church was built, but was a ruin by the late 18th c. A further church, Christchurch, was built, but it was soon demolished and the old ruin restored. Apart from the undeniably Victorian guardian angel in a niche outside, the church is 15th c. The interior is quite austere and apart from the ancient font which has a rare side drain-hole, a lovely bowl stoup set into a pillar, a doorway and the angle piscina, all is Victorian restoration. A lovely trefoiled arch over the sedilia has been mutilated by the addition of a lower chancel window. It still has the steps up to a rood loft, behind the plain oak pulpit. This is a strange mixture of the old and the new but I like it. A real effort has been made here to show the continuity of the church through the ages.

PANXWORTH	All Saints
No of Bells:	(2) removed
19th c. Deanery:	Blofield
Hundred:	Walsham
Union house:	Acle
21st c. Deanery:	-
Benefice:	-

9 miles ENE of Norwich. Just off the B1140 west of South Walsham. In Church Road, Panxworth, at the 4-x-ways take the Ranworth road.
O.S. grid ref: TG347136
Post Code: NR13 6JQ

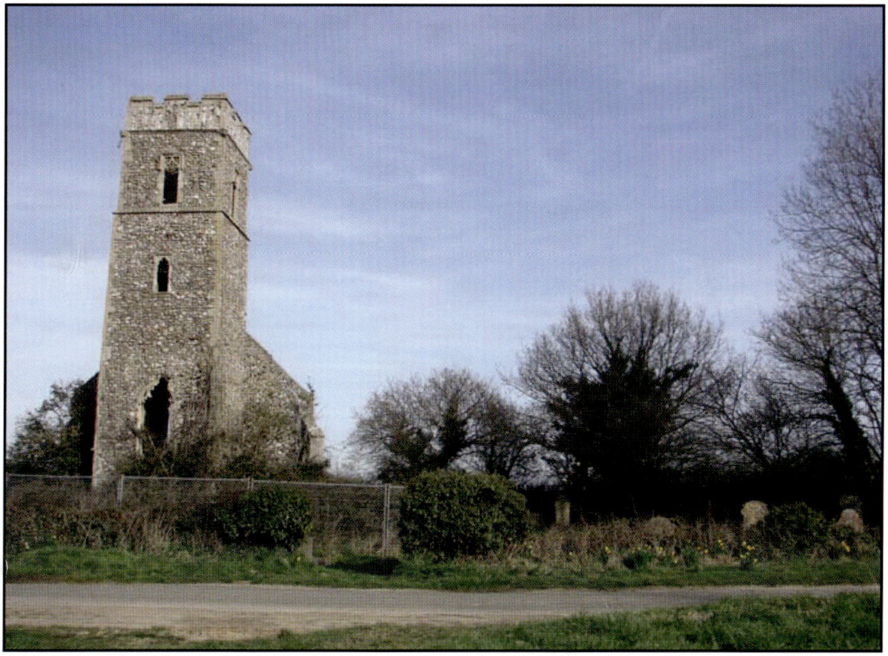

The ruin of Panxworth church is surrounded by a fence to protect the visitor from falling masonry. In 2006 the tower was struck by lightning and a hole blasted in the eastern face of the parapet. The church had been ruinous for many years and was eventually rebuilt in 1847 by the Victorians, who seem to have had money to burn. It was used for a century or so, but was eventually made redundant in the 1970s through lack of use, and became a place of worship for Satanists. Hearing of this (it made national news) the C of E decided that the building should be demolished. Thankfully the 14th c. tower remains as a picturesque landmark which incidentally can be clearly seen from the tower of nearby Ranworth. The graveyard has been left untouched and fresh flowers still appear on some of the graves.

PASTON	St Margaret	4 miles NE of North Walsham, and 1½ miles south of Mundesley. Follow the signs to Paston Barn. The church is next door.
No of Bells:	5	
19th c. Deanery:	Waxham	
Hundred:	Tunstead	
Union house:	Smallburgh	
21st c. Deanery:	Repps	O.S. grid ref: TM 028876
Benefice:	Trunch Team Ministry	Post Code: NR28 9TA

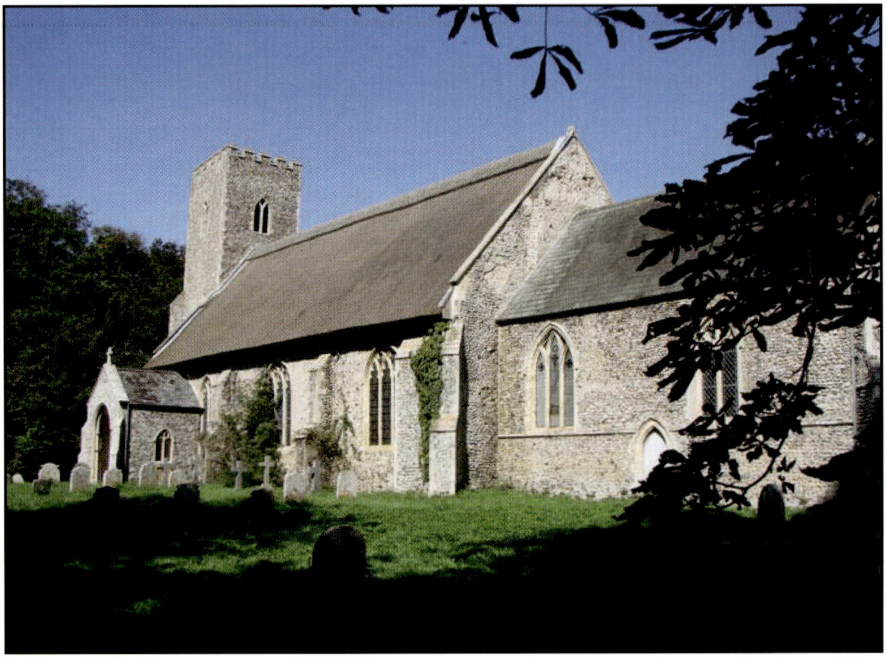

Thatch still covers the nave of this lovely church, although the graveyard is overgrown and the lych gate inaccessible. Inside, the scissor-beam roof is the last thing that will catch your eye. Some wall paintings are faded but discernible, the 'three living and the three dead' is one difficult to decipher. St Christopher is much clearer. A 14th c. font stands at the west of the nave and the parish chest is from the same period. The screen is 15th c. but has been repainted and spoilt. What are most remarkable are the railed-off monuments to members of the Paston family: the one to Lady Katherine (1628) is particularly splendid. A sarcophagus tomb has been set into the sedilia recess, another is placed against the north wall, both are half in the nave and half in the chancel. The piscina still has a credence shelf.

PORINGLAND All Saints

No of Bells: 1
19th c. Deanery: Brooke
Hundred: Henstead
Union house: Swainsthorpe
21st c Deanery: Loddon
Benefice: Poringland

4½ miles SSE of Norwich on the B1332. The church is situated near the shops at the southern end of the village.
O.S. grid ref: TG 271017
Post Code: NR14 7AD

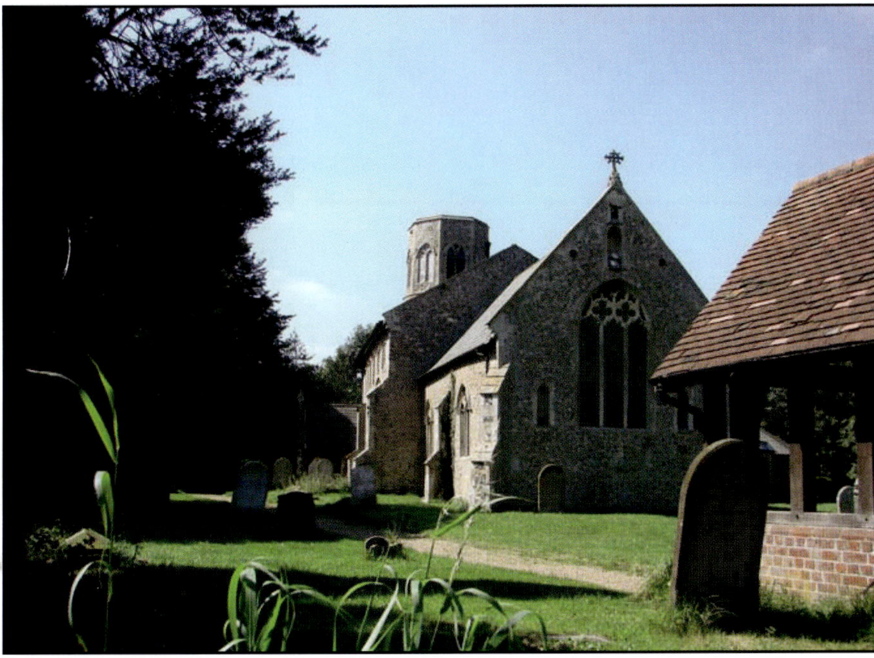

Originally there were two parishes, Great and Little Poringland, but they were consolidated as one parish about 1540 when the church of the latter (St Michael's) was demolished. The lower part of the tower is Norman; the upper octagonal stage is a later addition. The east wall uncommonly has three niches; and notice the little creature at the south corner. This is a very well lit church with the 12 windows of the clerestory affording plenty of light to enter. There is additional seating in the base of the tower which is most unusual, probably used at baptisms at the lovely typical East Anglian style font which stands close by. The nave, which has no aisle, has a late 15th c. arch-braced hammer-beam roof, that of the chancel is plastered. There is a nice trefoil piscina and a bench in the window recess replaces the sedilia.

POSTWICK	All Saints
No of Bells:	3 hanging, 1 usable
19th c. Deanery:	Blofield
Hundred:	Blofield
Union house:	Lingwood
21st c. Deanery:	Blofield
Benefice:	Brundall

4 miles ESE of Norwich. Turn off the A47 signposted Postwick, bear right at the fork and follow to the T junction. Difficult parking.
O.S. grid ref: TG 296078
Post Code: NR13 5HL

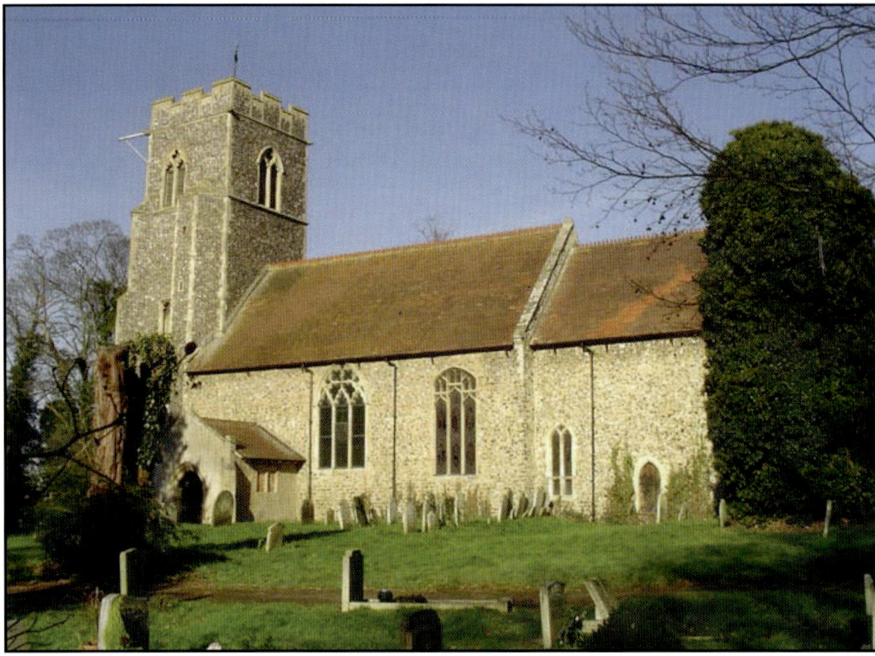

Pronounced Pozick. I was fortunate to find the church being cleaned when I made my call. It is usually locked. The church has ancient, probably Early English origins. The square tower has a stair turret on the south side and the parapet is embattled. The octagonal font has quatrefoil and tracery designs and faces for corbels at each corner. As much as I dislike Victorian stone pulpits, this is the nicest I have come across, colourful and pictorial. The arch-braced hammerbeam roof to the nave is relatively modern, but the double-arched piscina is 13th or 14th c. although it has been restored. The adjacent single level sedilia is of the dropped-sill type. A shorter window has been inserted here at a later date. An aumbry on the opposite wall has a modern door. Above the tower arch is a sanctus bell window, now blocked.

POTTER HEIGHAM St Nicholas

No of Bells: 3
19th c. Deanery: Waxham
Hundred: Happing
Union house: Smallburgh
21st c. Deanery: Waxham & Tunstead
Benefice: Waterside

15 miles ENE of Norwich. From the A149 turn into 'Potter' opposite the A1062 turnoff. At the T junction turn right and follow.
O.S. grid ref: TG 419199
Post Code: NR29 5LL

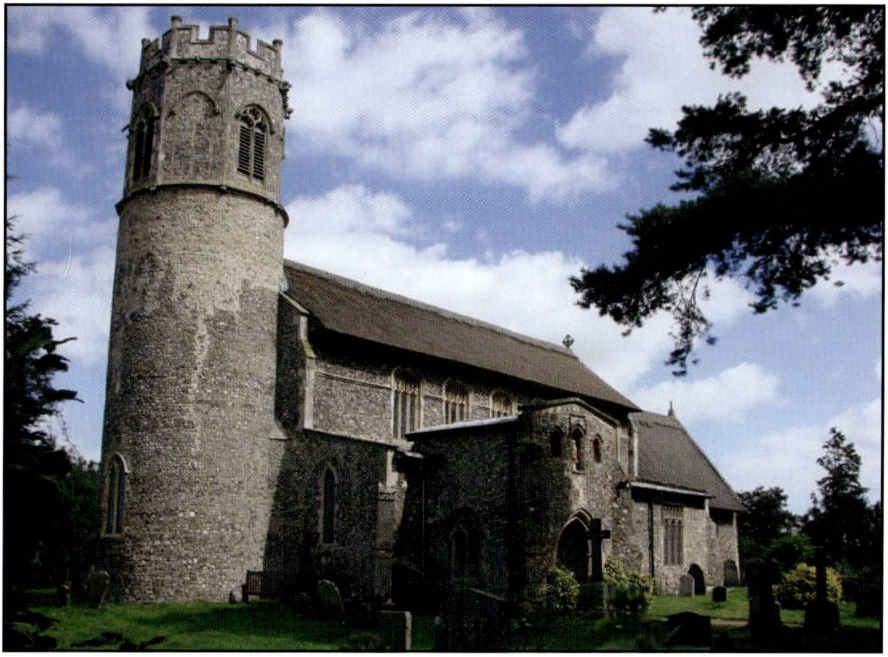

Not the easiest of churches to find. It was built against a Norman tower and had an octagonal top added in the 14th c. Both nave and chancel are thatched, the former being unusually tall with windows inserted above the south aisle. One of the most unusual fonts in the county can be seen here, made of brick in the 15th c. and standing on a brick and stone plinth. At one time it had a considerable cover and the pulley to raise it can still be seen above. The parish chest and the old bier are nearby. A hammerbeam and arch-braced roof is supported by carved corbels and extra long wall posts. On the screen are eight saints easily discernible. Perhaps the most interesting items are the splendid collection of wall paintings, still in very good condition considering their age. Well worth a visit and an hour of your time.

PULHAM MARKET St Mary Magdalene

No of Bells: 8
19th c. Deanery: Redenhall
Hundred: Earsham
Union house: Pulham St Mary
21st c. Deanery: Redenhall
Benefice: Dickleburgh & The Pulhams

4½ m NW of Harleston and 1½ east of the A140, on the village green, in the village centre.
O.S. grid ref: TM 197861
Post Code: IP21 4TD

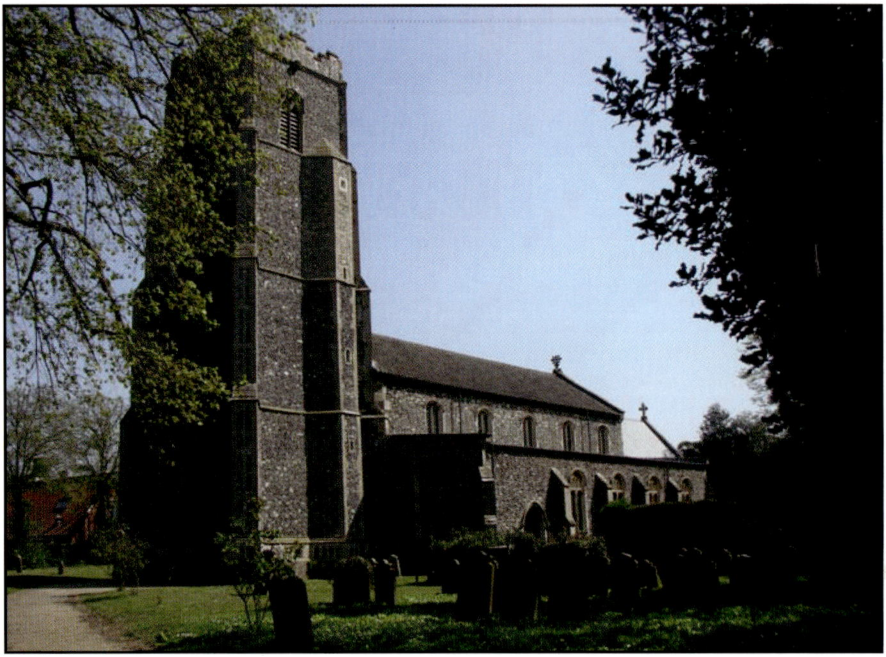

The chancel was originally built in the 14th c. as a chapel of ease for neighbouring St Mary the Virgin. In the 15th c., it was expanded into this magnificent church. Above the west door are two niches with small figures within. The north porch has three empty niches and a parvise above. The font is Victorian. The south arcade is slightly older than that of the north. Between them on the chancel arch is a large mural, above which on the arch-braced roof is a restored painting acting as a canopy of honour for a screen that is now in the tower arch. A piscina in the south aisle indicates that it was once a Lady chapel, probably dedicated to St Nicholas. The chancel piscina is a simple cusped arch, the adjoining dropped-sill sedilia shows that the chancel floor was once lower than it is today. Much more to see here.

PULHAM ST MARY St Mary the Virgin ****

No of Bells: 6
19th c. Deanery: Redenhall
Hundred: Earsham
Union house: Pulham St Mary
21st c. Deanery: Redenhall
Benefice: Dickleburgh & The Pulhams

3 m NW of Harleston on the main road, just as you enter the village from the south.
O.S. grid ref: TM 212853
Post Code: IP21 4RE

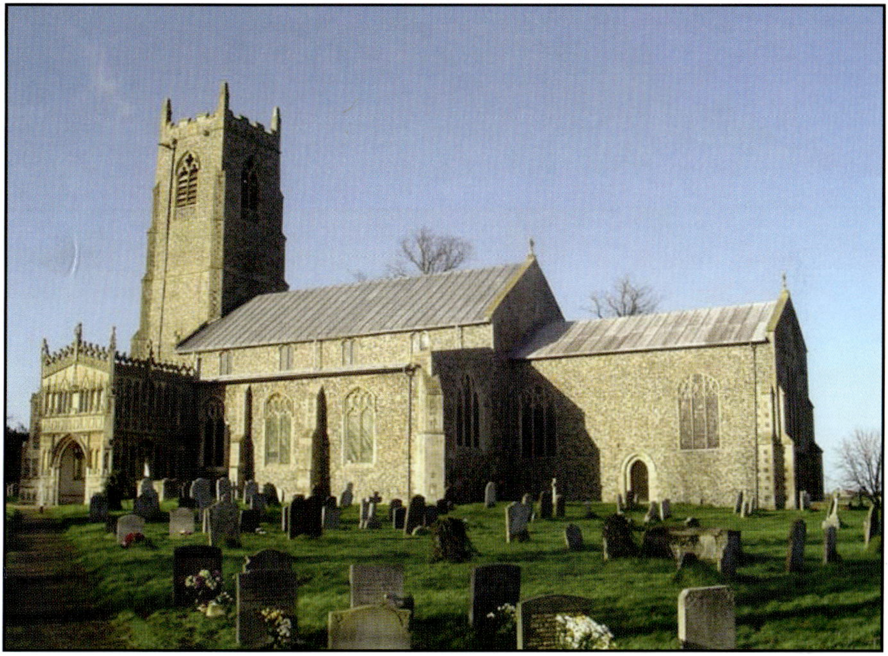

The 15th c. south porch is really special with tracery, shields, figures and the Annunciation in the spandrels of the doorway. Above is a parvise surmounted by a pierced parapet and grotesques. An unusual feature is the wooden staircase leading to the ringing chamber in the tower passing through the south arcade. The font is 15th c. and without damage, it has been painted quite tastefully. Angels encircle the base of the bowl and saints surround the shaft. Some of the 15th c. benches have mutilated figures. The traceried, canopied screen has been skilfully repainted in original colours, and in front hangs a rowel, now with an electric light instead of candles. The double arched piscina is quite unusual with one square and one quatrefoil basin, the three tier sedilia is adjacent. Well worth a look round.

RACKHEATH	All Saints	4 m NE of Norwich. On the opposite side of the A1151 to the parish. Turn left nth of Rackheath and down a single track lane.
No of Bells:	3, disengaged	
19th c. Deanery:	Taverham	
Hundred:	Taverham	
Union house:	Horsham St Faith	
21st c. Deanery:	-	O.S. grid ref: TG 284126
The Norfolk Churches Trust		Post Code: NR13 6NF

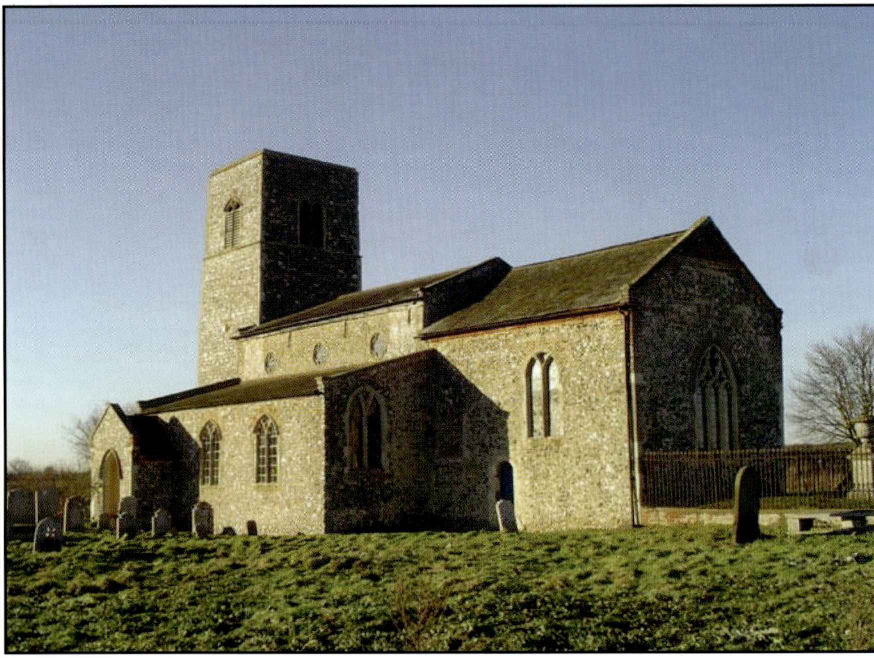

Rackheath was once two parishes, Great and Little, these were consolidated many centuries ago. This lonely little redundant church has a three quatrefoil window clerestory and south aisle. On the north side, the redundant rood loft stairs have been revealed and turned into a window. Unusually, the font is hexagonal and is dated 1639 and quite different from most. In the north wall of the chancel is a large arch, which may have been a tomb or Easter sepulchre. The piscina and sedilia are contemporary with the 13th c. arcades and bulk of the church. On the walls are many memorials from more affluent times, mostly to members of the Pettus and Stracey families Other families mentioned are Knyvet, Batcheler and Dashwood. A black ledger slab to Sir Thomas Pettus (1654) is the oldest.

RANWORTH St Helen

No of Bells:	5
19th c. Deanery:	Blofield
Hundred:	Walsham
Union house:	Acle
21st c. Deanery:	Blofield
Benefice:	Ranworth Broadside

9 miles ENE of Norwich and 3½ miles SE of North Walsham. Well signposted from the B1140 near Ranworth Broad.

O.S. grid ref:	TG 356148
Post Code:	NR13 6HT

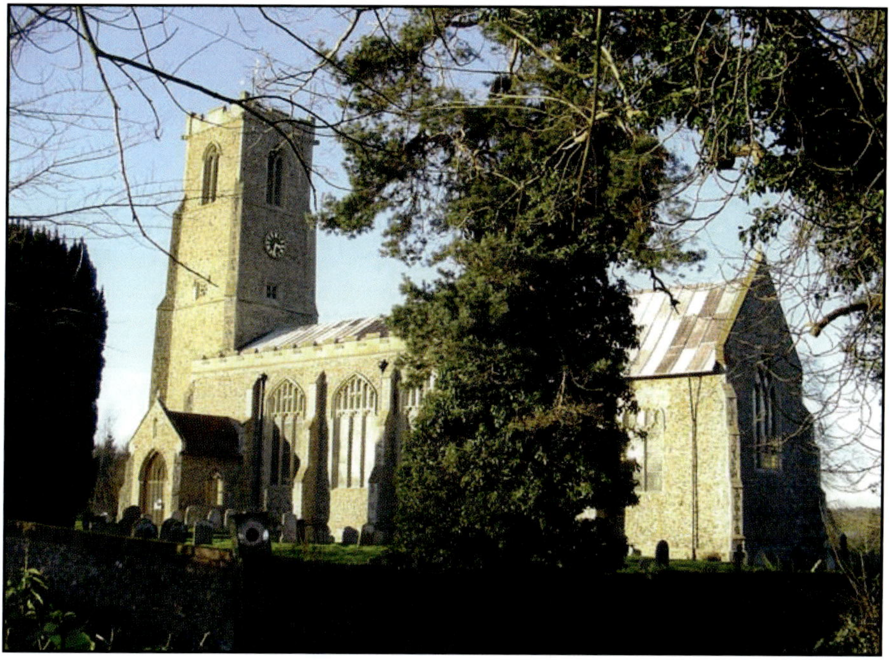

Ranworth is one of the best known churches on 'The Broads' not only because you can climb to the top of the 15th c. tower but because of the beautiful mediaeval screen which is probably the best in England. Another treasure the church has to offer is the Sarum Antiphonary, which was given to the church in the 15th c. when it was rebuilt. The lovely old 13th c. font is the most ancient thing you will see here. The corner piscina is a close second with its trefoiled ogee arch, adjacent is a dropped-sill sedilia. On the north wall of the chancel some pieces of wood are what remains of an Easter Sepulchre, a rare find. There are six misericordes in the choir stalls, and the Laudian-style altar rails are 17th c. Set into the wall is a monument to Thomas Holdiche who died in 1579. Worth a visit and refreshments are available most

RAVENINGHAM	St Andrew	3 miles SE of Loddon.
No of Bells:	3	From the A146 take the
19th c. Deanery:	Brooke	B1136, Hales - Haddiscoe
Hundred:	Clavering	road. Turn south 1 mile east
Union house:	Heckingham	of Hales to Estate entrance.
21st c. Deanery:	Loddon	O.S. grid ref: TM 397964
Benefice:	Raveningham Group	Post Code: NR14 6NS

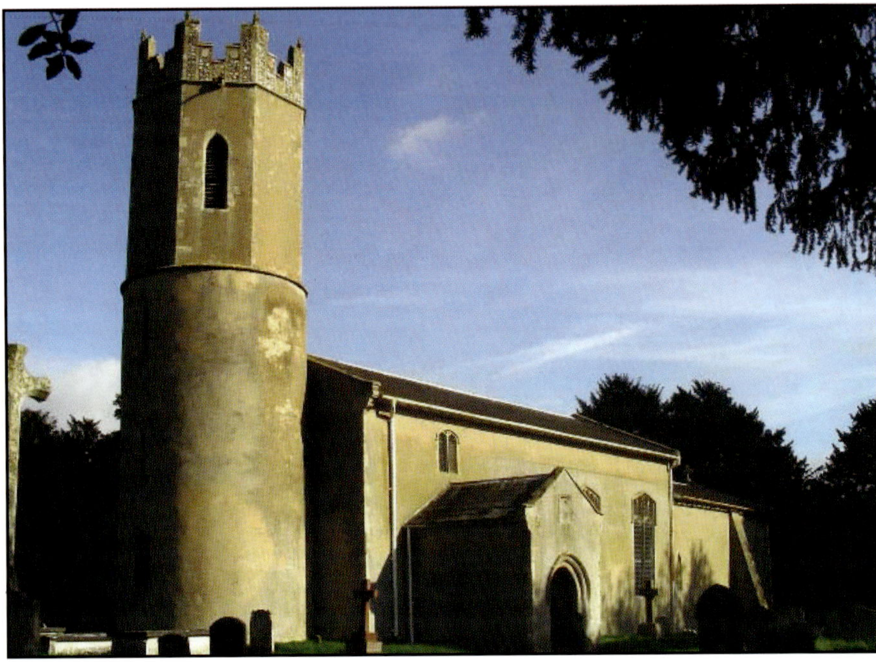

Raveningham church is situated on the Raveningham estate but don't let that put you off visiting. It was built in the 13th c. and has a good Norman pedigree. The round tower has an octagonal belfry stage with double crenulations and pinnacles. There is a Norman door with the original ironwork protected by the porch. The 15th c, font is the traditional type but has atypical designs on the eight facets. Four loins guard the shaft. There is a good brass to John Castle (1593) and his wife Elizabeth nee Plater of Sotterley (1614). A ledger slab recalls the life of Roger Castell (1708): his wife was from the Tallamach *(sic)* family of Helmingham. In the chancel are eight large memorial recesses to Bacon family members. They are quite spectacular, pedimented and crocketted with multifoil cusping in pure white.

REDENHALL St Mary	*****
No of Bells:	8 + sanctus bell
19th c. Deanery:	Redenhall
Hundred:	Earsham
Union house:	Pulham St Mary
21st c. Deanery:	Redenhall
Benefice:	Redenhall

1 m NE of Harleston on the old Harleston to Bungay road. Turn off the A143 at the roundabout, north of Harleston.
O.S. grid ref: TM 263843
Post Code: IP20 9QW

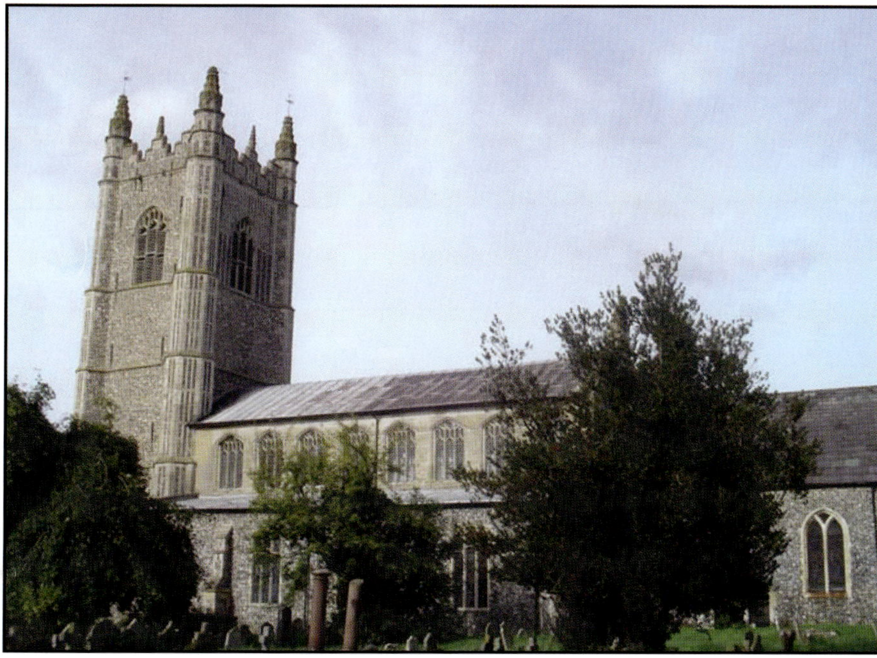

This is a magnificent edifice; the tower can be seen and recognised by its massive pinnacles which extend skywards from octagonal buttresses. Light spills into the nave and both north and south aisles from the 16-window clerestory. There is much to see here. The west doors were presented by the Blacksmiths' Guild. The double-headed eagle on the lectern is uncommon. A hammerbeam roof has tracery in the spandrels. The mid-15th c. Venetian chest is from Gaudy Hall. The parvise over the porch is open; the grand organ dominates the west end. A traditional 15th c. font and an old bier stand in the base of the tower. The Royal Arms of Queen Anne hang on the wall. The panelling around the wall and the sedilia are Victorian as are the many other interesting woodcarvings. Five stars for excellence.

REEDHAM	St John the Baptist
No of Bells:	4
19th c. Deanery:	Blofield
Hundred:	Walsham
Union house:	Acle
21st c. Deanery:	Blofield
Benefice:	Freethorpe

8 miles SW of Great Yarmouth. Turn off the A47, Acle Straight close to the windmill and follow directions to Reedham.
O.S. grid ref: TG 427024
Post Code: NR13 3TZ

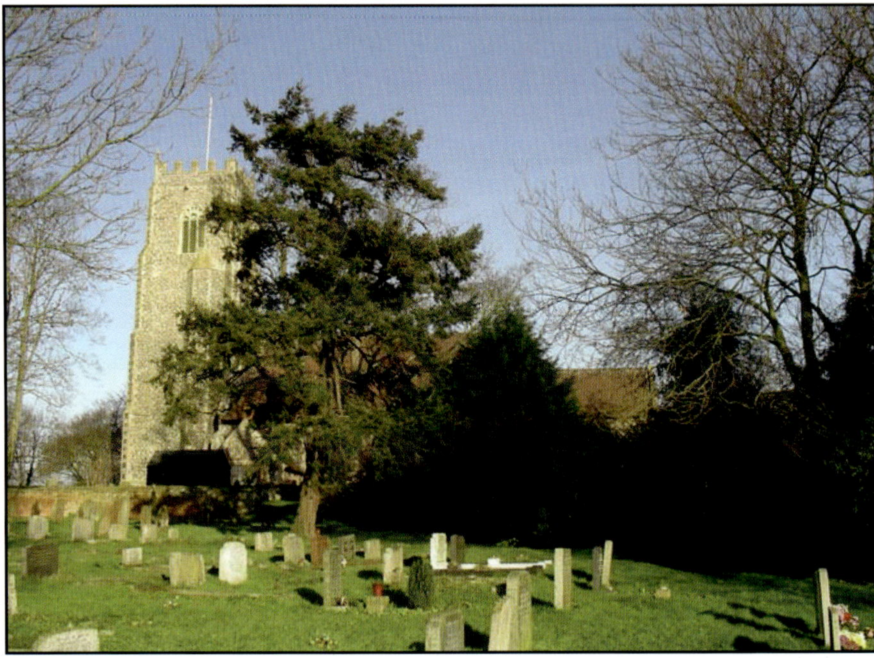

This is a 15th c. tower and church, which used to be thatched until 1981 when it caught fire. Consolidation of the fabric has continued ever since. As the church was completely gutted of anything interesting including the Victorian restorations, it became nothing more than a barn. Unfortunately, it seems to have remained so. It is now bare, hard, and completely lacking in character. However, some people like this kind of whitewash, and varnish image. The only things in the church which are of any great interest are the tomb of Henry Berney (1584), where he and his wife kneel at a prayer desk with their nine children, and the octagonal font, which came from St Michael's Coslany. The modern fittings and painted glass may appeal to some, and I accept that some will like what they see.

REPPS cum Bastwick Sts Peter & Paul.

No of Bells:	3
19th c. Deanery:	Flegg
Hundred:	West Flegg
Union house:	Rollesby
21st c. Deanery:	Great Yarmouth
Benefice:	Flegg Group

10 miles NW by N of Great Yarmouth. From the A149 in Church Road. Or from the B1152 in Sandpit Lane.
O.S. grid ref: TG 421169
Post Code: NR29 5JS

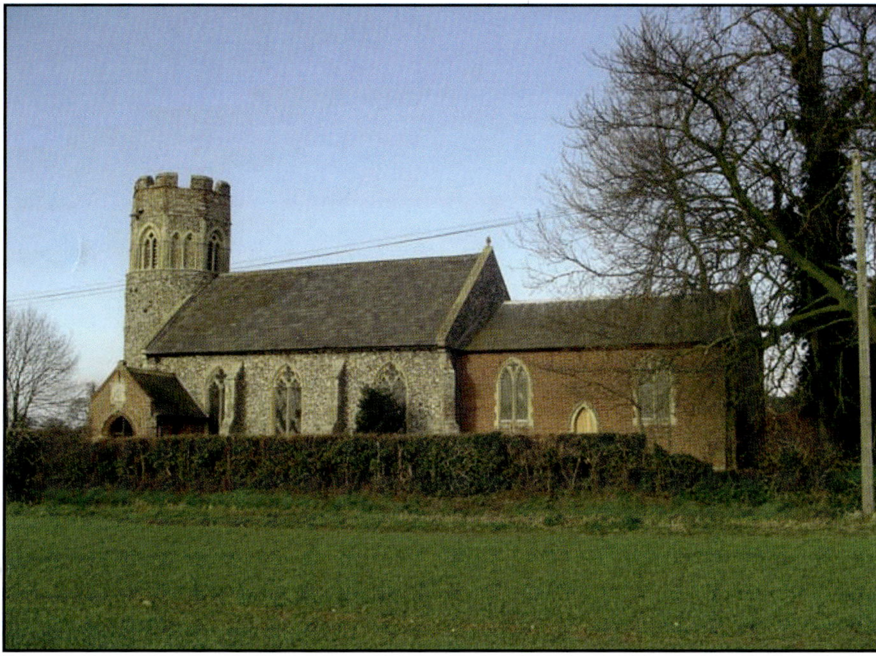

Imagine this church without a chancel, and you would be quite close to a late Saxon church. The tower is late Saxon or early Norman with the octagonal stage added in the 13th c. Just inside the south door is a stoup in a small niche. Of the two roofs, that of the chancel is the more interesting being cambered beam and king post design. That of the nave is simple scissor-braced. Behind a door on the south wall and adjacent to the screen, are the rood loft stairs. The octagonal font is decorated with simple quatrefoils and blank shields; the shaft has half columns and arches between. The new pine pulpit bearing the cross keys of St. Peter stands on a large stone base with steps. The piscina and sedilia have been obliterated from the chancel. A very heavy-looking bier stands by the north door.

RIDLINGTON St Peter
No of Bells: 1
19th c. Deanery: Waxham
Hundred: Tunstead
Union house: Smallburgh
21st c. Deanery: Waxham & Tunstead
Benefice: Coastal

4 miles E of North Walsham. North on the B1159 1 mile before Walcott turn left at the crossroads and continue 1 mile along Happisburgh Rd.
O.S. grid ref: TG 345311
Post Code: NR28 9GA

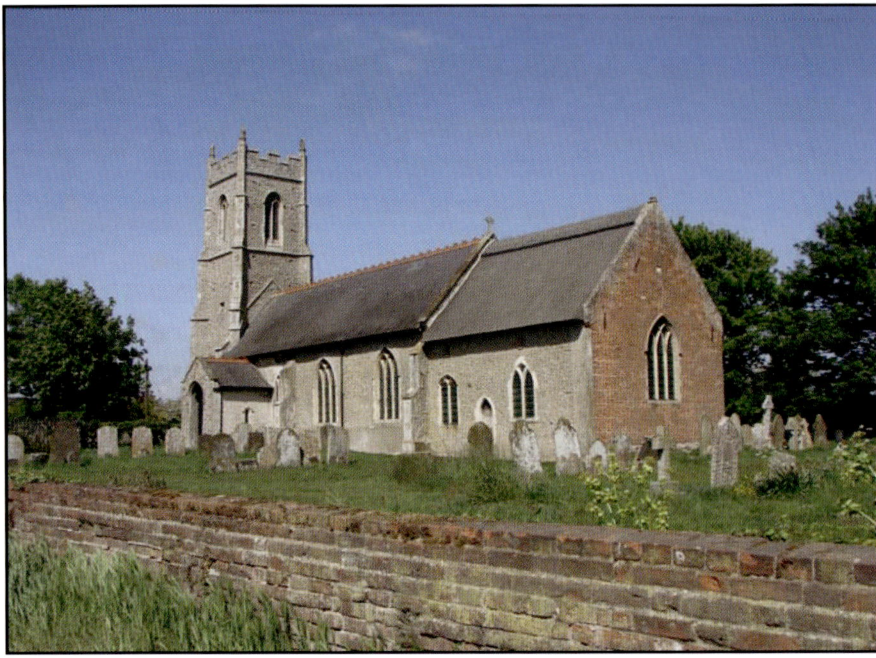

A church has stood here since Norman times, but not this one. The church, as we see it today, is 15th c. and was somewhat over-restored by our Victorian forebears. The tower, with four evangelists as pinnacles above the parapet, was also constructed about the same time. An early, typically Norman octagonal font however bears witness to the origins of the church. Around the bowl are shallow arches so characteristic of the period. All the seating in the nave is modern which somewhat diminishes the character. In the chancel there is a nice cusped piscina and adjacent to it is the dropped-sill sedilia. Unfortunately the screen was removed many years ago leaving the chancel arch looking rather naked. There are no great monuments and nothing of great importance, but it is a lovely church

ROCKLAND ST MARGARET

No of Bells: -

19th c. Deanery: Brooke

Hundred: Henstead

Union house: Swainsthorpe

Consolidated with Rockland St Mary when the parishes united as St Mary

6 miles SE of Norwich off the A146. Leave the A146 near the nursery into Lane opposite and follow for 2 miles into Rockland.

O.S. grid ref: TM 312040

Post Code: NR14 7EY

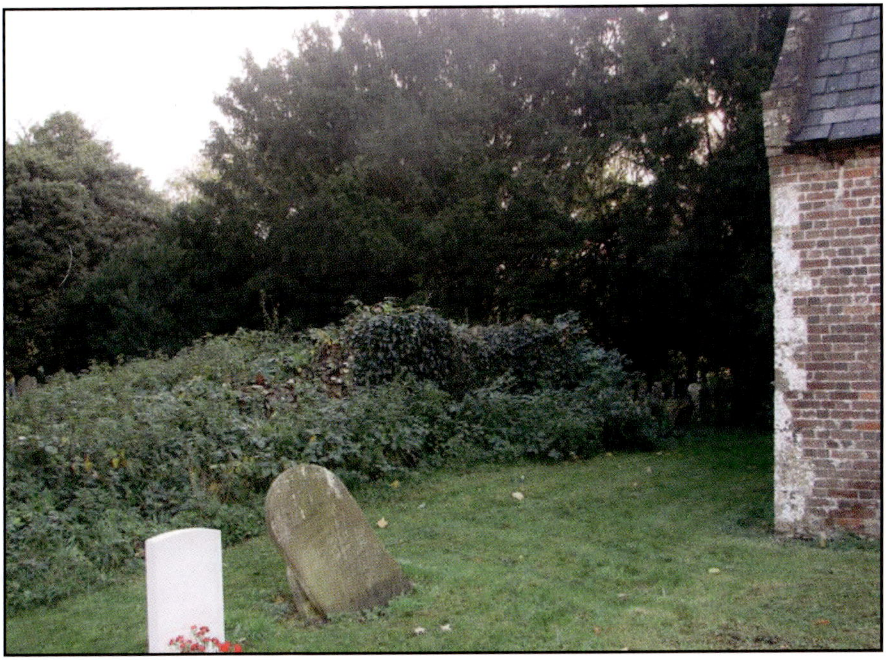

Ruinous, and very little remains of a once prosperous church. Perhaps churches, which share a churchyard are condemned to fail eventually. South Walsham, Kirby Bedon, Antingham; then there is Trimley, Middleton and Creeting in Suffolk to name a few. In fact, I cannot think of any pair of churches where no problems exist, with Reepham and Whitwell, the latter is now a church hall. It seems a recipe for disaster from the start. The clashing of services, where bells are rung in one, during services in the other, are bound to cause problems. Instead of uniting parishes, the church divides them by creating a conflict. St Margaret's was demolished and some materials utilised to repair St Mary's in the early 18th c. Only a low wall remains that once was the west wall of the nave, as it never did have a tower.

ROCKLAND ST MARY St Mary

No of Bells: 3
19th c. Deanery: Brooke
Hundred: Henstead
Union house: Swainsthorpe
21st c. Deanery: Loddon
Benefice: Bramerton

6 miles SE of Norwich off the A146. Leave the A146 near the nursery into Lane opposite and follow for 2 miles into Rockland.
O.S. grid ref: TM 312040
Post Code: NR14 7EY

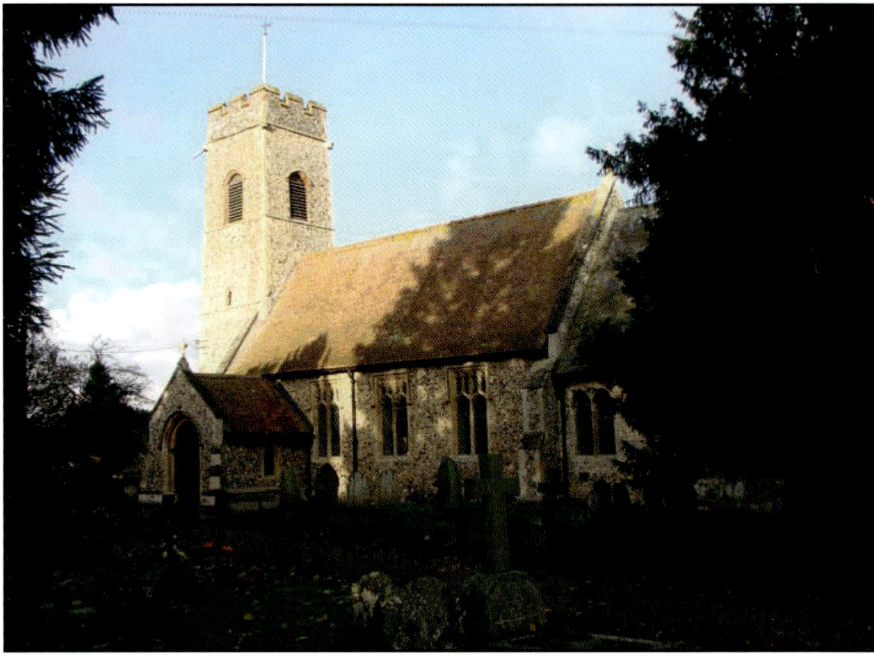

This church once shared a churchyard with St Margaret's *(see previous page)*. The church was originally built in the Early English period (late 13th or early 14th c.) but much restoration has changed its appearance. 16th c. windows have replaced the original ones. Remodelling of the interior included a new Victorian roof. The font is 15th c. with angels holding shields decorating the eight facets of the bowl, and some figures decorate the panelled shaft. The piscina and sedilia were removed during the restorations. What appear to be serpents slither across the west wall of the nave. There are some carvings on the bench ends, but these are of no great age. A ledger slab records the death of Henry Mazey in 1677. The Royal Arms that hang on the wall of the nave are those of Queen Victoria.

ROLLESBY St George
No of Bells: 3
19th c. Deanery: Flegg
Hundred: West Flegg
Union house: Rollesby
21st c. Deanery: Great Yarmouth
Benefice: Ormesby St Margaret

8 miles NW by N of Great Yarmouth. From the A149 in the centre of Rollesby turn south at x-roads to Heath Road T junction.
O.S. grid ref: TG 445157
Post Code: NR29 5HJ

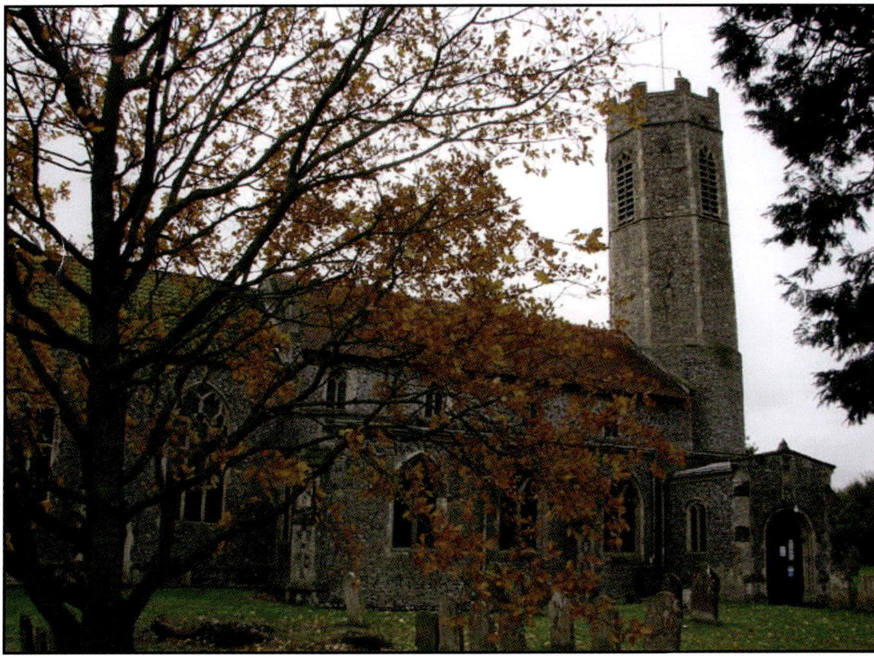

The lower portion of the tower is Norman, the top octagonal two-thirds is 14th c. The south doorway has an unusual multi-cusped arch. While outside, notice the animals on the east gable of the nave. The clerestory windows on the south are tiny quatrefoils, those on the north are more normal. A pseudo-Norman, Victorian font stands on a central shaft and eight slender marble columns. The benches are modern and the pulpit is Victorian. A cusped ogee arch piscina in the chancel is adjacent to the dropped-sill sedilia. Hard against the north wall is a stone carved effigy of a very uncomfortable-looking Rose Claxton (1601) dressed in Elizabethan costume. Another early monument, on the wall nearby, is to Leonard Mapes (1610), at a prayer desk with his wife and children. The windows are very nice.

ROUGHTON St Mary the Virgin

No of Bells:	3
19th c. Deanery:	Repps
Hundred:	North Erpingham
Union house:	West Beckham
21st c. Deanery:	Repps
Benefice:	Roughton

4 miles S of Cromer on the A140. Just after the junction with the B1436 is a lane on the left half-way up a hill. Large car park.

O.S. grid ref: TG 220366
Post Code: NR11 8SZ

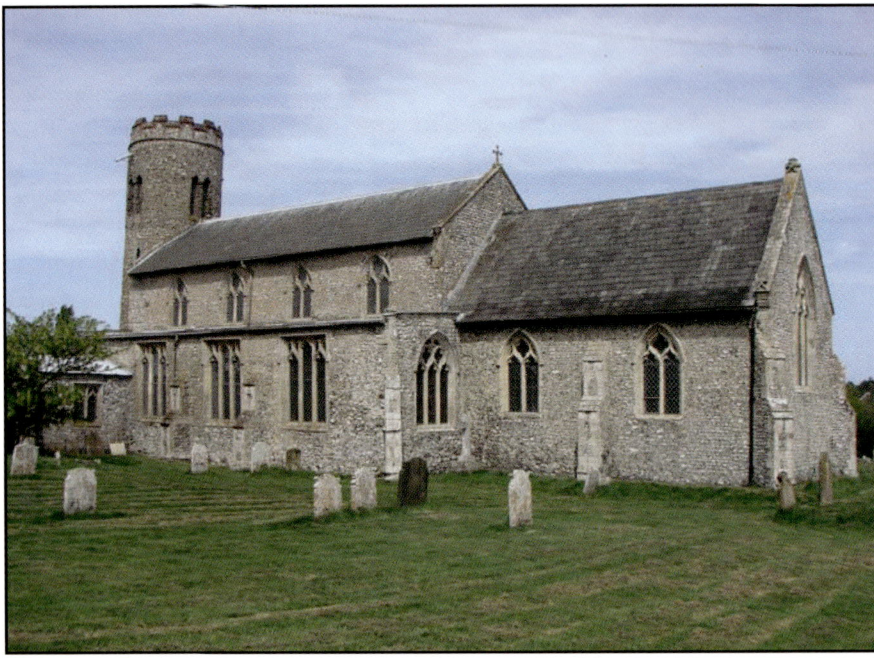

Pronounced Routon, not Ruffton. The round tower dates from before the Conquest. A door high on the east side indicates that it was a defensible refuge in the event of invasion. The church, although originally early English was rebuilt in the 14th c. when the aisles were added. The font is typical of the 14th c. with an octagonal bowl and traceried carving, the shaft is encircled by eight engaged columns. The roofs are Victorian as are the pulpit, altar and lectern. The benches were also replaced at the same time and each one is numbered. The windows of the clerestory have grotesque faces staring down at the congregation. Part of the arch of the piscina remains in the wall adjacent to the dropped-sill sedilia. A second piscina is in what was once a chapel in the south aisle.

RUNHAM	St Peter & St Paul
No of Bells:	3 unusable
19th c. Deanery:	Flegg
Hundred:	East Flegg
Union house:	Rollesby
21st c. Deanery:	Great Yarmouth
Benefice:	Flegg (Sth Trinity Broads)

5 miles WNW of Great Yarmouth. From the A1064 at Filby turn south through Thrigby and follow road to Runham then turn right.
O.S. grid ref: TG 459108
Post Code: NR29 3AH

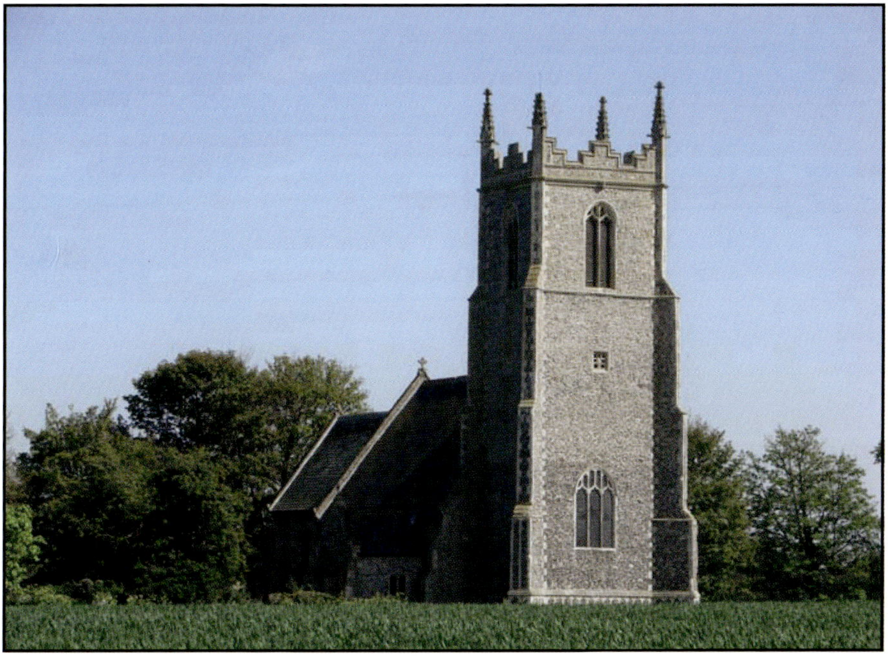

From the outside this is a lovely church with a grand tower for a small parish. Double crenulations and crocketted pinnacles with imps and grotesques thrust skyward and the steep pitch of the roof is elegant. Inside however, is a different story. It is perhaps one of the most run down churches I have seen that is still in regular use. The lime-wash is flaking from the walls. Bird droppings speckle the beams and carpeting. The benches have been ripped out and plastic seats have replaced them. Just inside the door is a stoup. On the opposite wall a small piscina. In the chancel is a plain angle piscina but the sedilia has been completely removed. The octagonal font has a book rest on the west face. The pulpit is well carved and attractive with carved arches and fluted columns. The church is in an advanced state of decay.

RUSHALL St Mary the Virgin
No of Bells: 1, one time 3
19th c. Deanery: Redenhall
Hundred: Earsham
Union house: Pulham St Mary
21st c. Deanery: Redenhall
Benefice: Dickleburgh & the Pulhams

3 m W of Harleston. From Harleston follow the road west from The Thoroughfare near the Swan Hotel, for 3 miles.
O.S. grid ref: TM 197826
Post Code: IP21 4RX

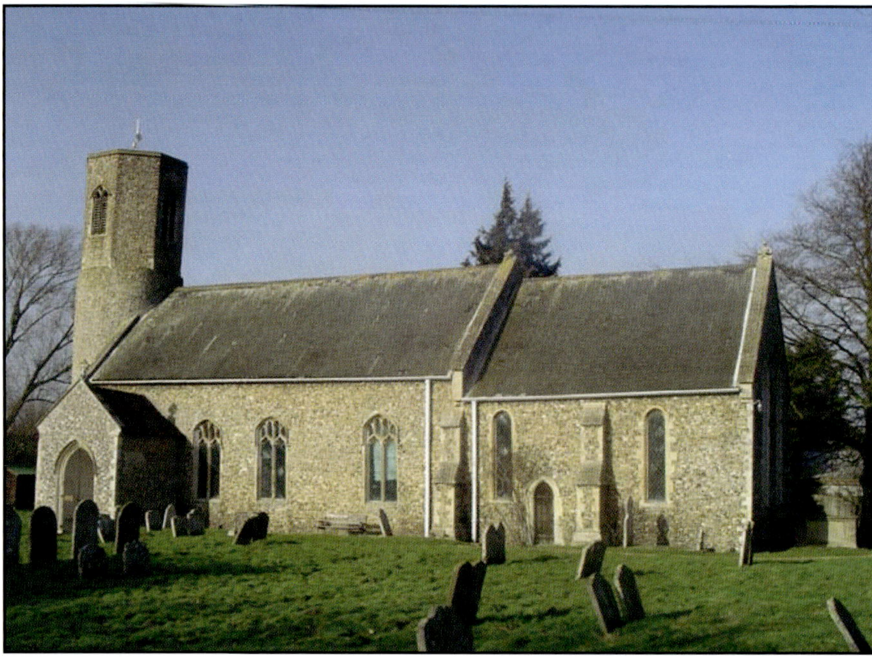

This is basically a Norman church which has been virtually rebuilt. In 1733 it was ruinous and close to being abandoned before being restored by a local benefactor. The lower two-thirds of the tower are original; the unadorned octagonal top was added in the 15th c. when the porch was added. There is a scratch dial on the jamb of the chancel doorway. The simply decorated octagonal font seems to be a slim-line model. Despite this being an ancient church there is very little to see here. There was once a chantry, the arch of which can be seen in the chancel. In the east wall are two lancet windows, revealing that it was built in the Early English period. In the sanctuary is a beautifully carved prayer desk, presented to the church in 1930s. All traces of the piscina and sedilia have been eradicated.

SALHOUSE	All Saints ***
No of Bells:	2
19th c. Deanery:	Taverham
Hundred:	Taverham
Union house:	Horsham St Faith
21st c. Deanery:	Blofield
Benefice:	Rackheath

6 m NE of Norwich ¼ mile north of The High Street, on the top of the hill on the right as you leave the village.
O.S. grid ref: TG 303150
Post Code: NR13 6RR

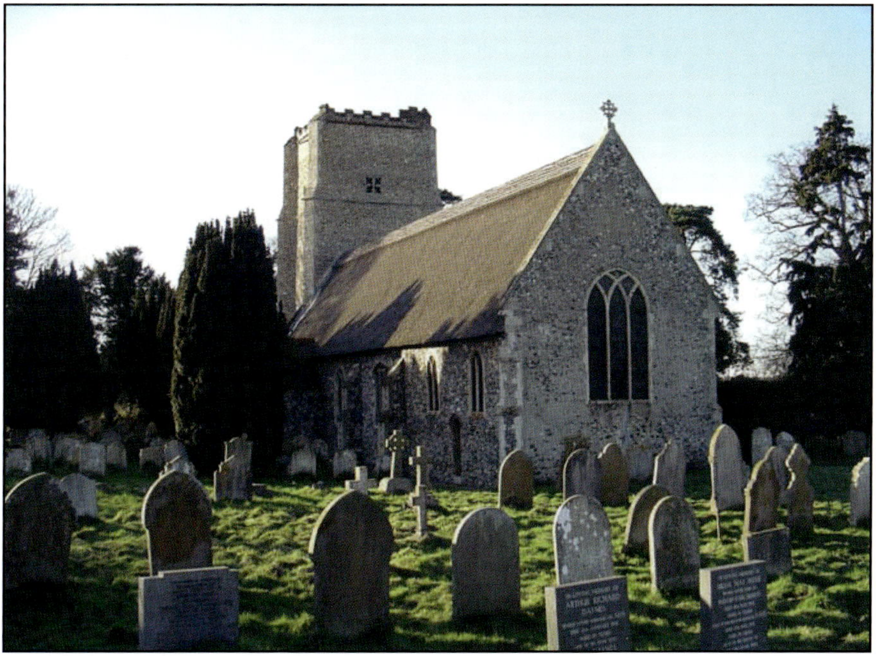

The squat 15th c. tower with its shallow crenulations and thatched barn-like roof distinguish this church from most. It was built in the Early English period. A nice canopied niche above the porch door is vacant. Notice the sound holes of the tower have faces on the drip stones. The old octagonal font is undecorated but may have been at some time in its past life. It is supported on a panelled shaft. There is no chancel arch but the 14th c. arcade has carved capitals, one with heads, the rest foliage, matching the corbels of the wall posts of the scissor-braced and king post roof. The panels in the pulpit were saved from an earlier one. There is a restored hour-glass holder nearby. Behind the font is a half-wheel which was removed some time ago from the belfry. Uncommonly, a Sacring bell hangs in the screen.

SAXLINGHAM NETHERGATE St Mary the Virgin

No of Bells: 8
19th c. Deanery: Brooke
Hundred: Henstead
Union house: Swainsthorpe
21st c. Deanery: Depwade
Benefice: Tas Valley

7 miles S of Norwich. From the A140 turn right at Newton Flotman. Church south of the village.
O.S. grid ref: TM 231971
Post Code: NR15 1TD

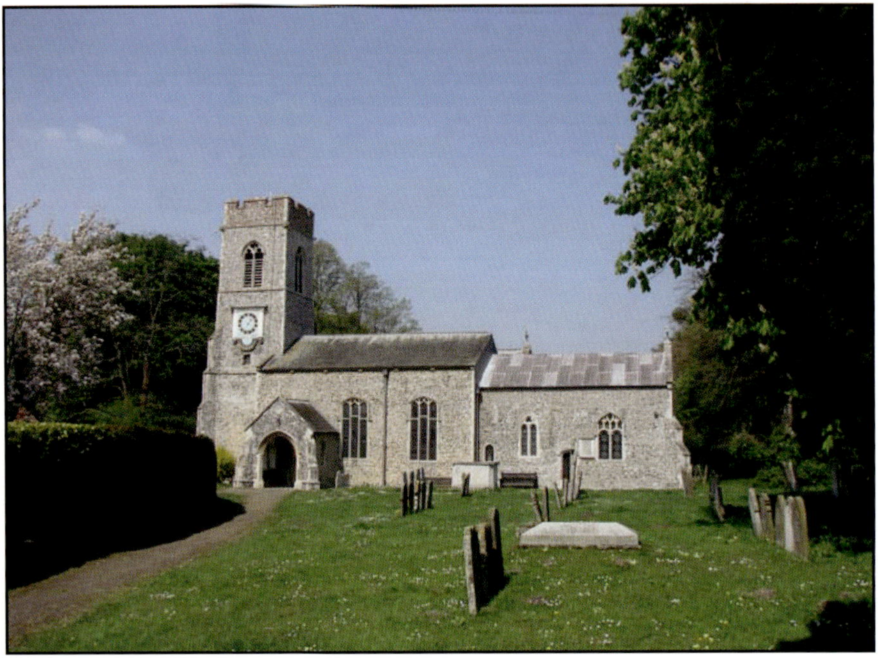

The church was originally built in the 14th c. but has been much altered over time. The later crenulated parapet of the tower is a mixture of brick and knapped flint. Inside the porch is a small niche for a stoup and there is another in the nave. A traditional 15th c. East Anglian font is incorrectly placed against the north wall (as are many others these days). The modern camber-beam and arch-braced roof has nice tracery in the spandrels. The traceried screen is unpainted and is quite pleasing though simple. There is considerable carving on the pulpit with is very attractive. The bench ends, although relatively modern, are adorned with the traditional poppy-heads. A memorial tablet hard against the east wall is to John Baron (1657). Beneath is the simply cusped piscina and dropped-sill sedilia.

SAXLINGHAM THORPE St Mary

No of Bells: -
19th c. Deanery: Brooke
Hundred: Henstead
Union house: Swainsthorpe
21st c. Deanery: -
Benefice: -

7½ miles S of Norwich. From the A140 turn right at Newton Flotman. South of the village, down the lane next to Dairy cottage.
O.S. grid ref: TM 230965
Post Code: NR15 1TE

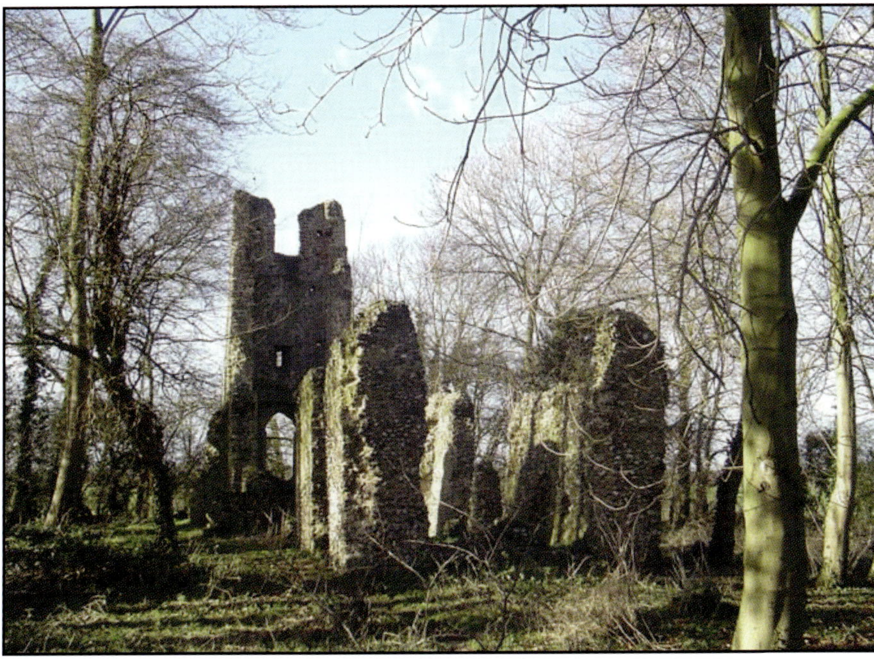

The parish of Saxlingham Thorpe was consolidated with Saxlingham Nethergate in 1740 and the church was already in a ruinous condition. The ruins are set in a small copse at the end of a farm track. You will need your wellies for this one if it's been raining. As can be seen from the picture above, the walls are still standing although some are leaning outwards at a rather precarious angle. The square tower is still at almost its original height. Rather surprisingly, the ruins are clear of ivy, brambles and other creepers and it would seem they are being cared for by someone. One thing is for sure, it was quite a reasonable sized church and the full extent of it can still be seen. Personally, I think this is one of the most picturesque ruins in the county and long may it continue to be with us.

SCO RUSTON St Michael

No of Bells: -
19th c. Deanery: Waxham
Hundred: Tunstead
Union house: Smallburgh
21st c. Deanery: -
Benefice: -

5 miles S of Nth Walsham.
From North Walsham on the B1150, 1 mile south of Scottow opposite a large farmhouse.
O.S. grid ref: TG 284218
Post Code: NR12 8EY

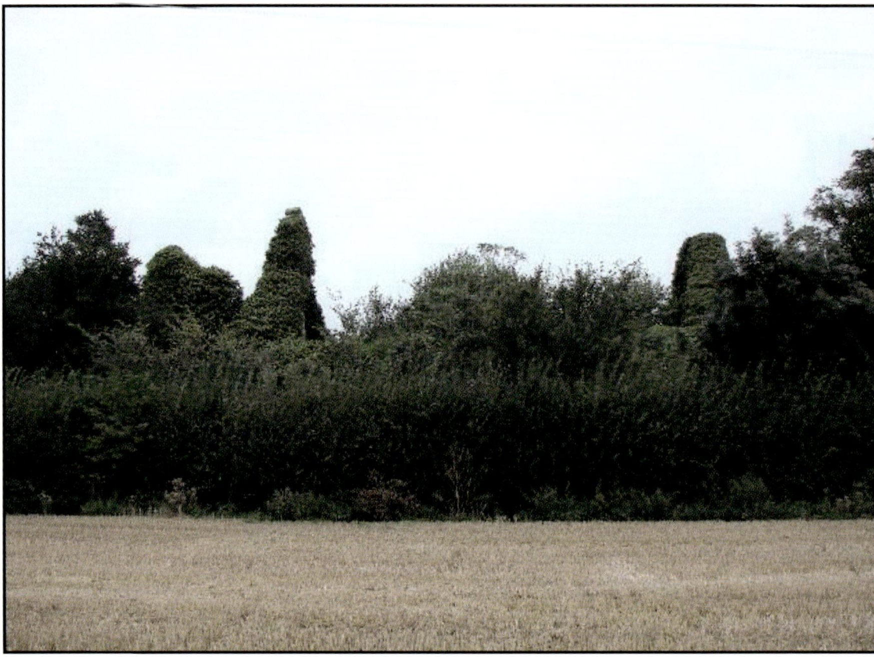

The church was quite small and had a thatched roof. In 1861 the chancel was restored but lack of a congregation forced its eventual closure. The parish was already consolidated with Tunstead. So this is yet another of the ruinous churches Norfolk has to offer. This one is absolutely smothered with ivy, trees, bushes and nettles. It is obviously visited, because the footpath is well trodden. In the picture above, the church is centrally situated. What remains of the fallen west tower is on the left, the peak to its right being the west wall of the nave. The east wall is to the right with tall shrubs in-between. This picture was taken just after harvest, but I feel a better time to visit would be in the winter when the trees have lost their leaves, and the nettles are hibernating.

SCOTTOW All Saints
No of Bells: 6
19th c. Deanery: Ingworth
Hundred: South Erpingham
Union house: Aylsham
21st c. Deanery: Waxham & Tunstead
Benefice: Worstead

4 miles S of Nth Walsham. From Nth Walsham follow the B1150. Before Scottow turn right to Buxton, take 2nd road on the left.
O.S. grid ref: TG 265237
Post Code: NR10 5DF

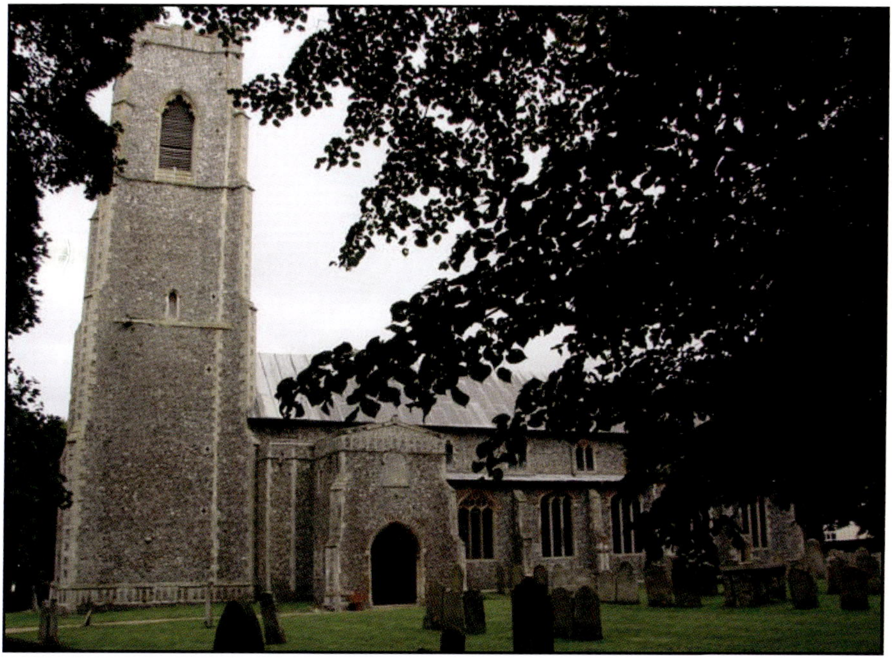

A strange lychgate that wouldn't keep the rain off a thin man. Over the porch doorway is an illegible inscription on a plaque. A green man appears on the groining of the porch which has a small parvise above. A small oven is incorporated at the foot of the parvise staircase. The octagonal font is 13th c. with eight detached marble columns. The cover is attractive having carved sturgeon against a central vase. There are some fine examples of wood carving here, on the lectern and especially on the organ, upon which item I do not often comment. There is also a coffin rest at the west end; notice the faces carved on the legs. In the chancel, a small very old mensa is situated by the 14th c. traceried piscina. There are two sets of Royal Arms, the older is of William and Mary dated 1696, the other of Queen Elizabeth II.

SEA PALLING or PALLING St Margaret

No of Bells:	1	18 miles NE of Norwich.
19th c. Deanery:	Waxham	From Stalham church take
Hundred:	Happing	the road to Ingham and
Union house:	Smallburgh	continue 4 miles to Palling.
21st c. Deanery:	Waxham & Tunstead	O.S. grid ref: TG 429268
Benefice:	Happisburgh	Post Code: NR12 0UR

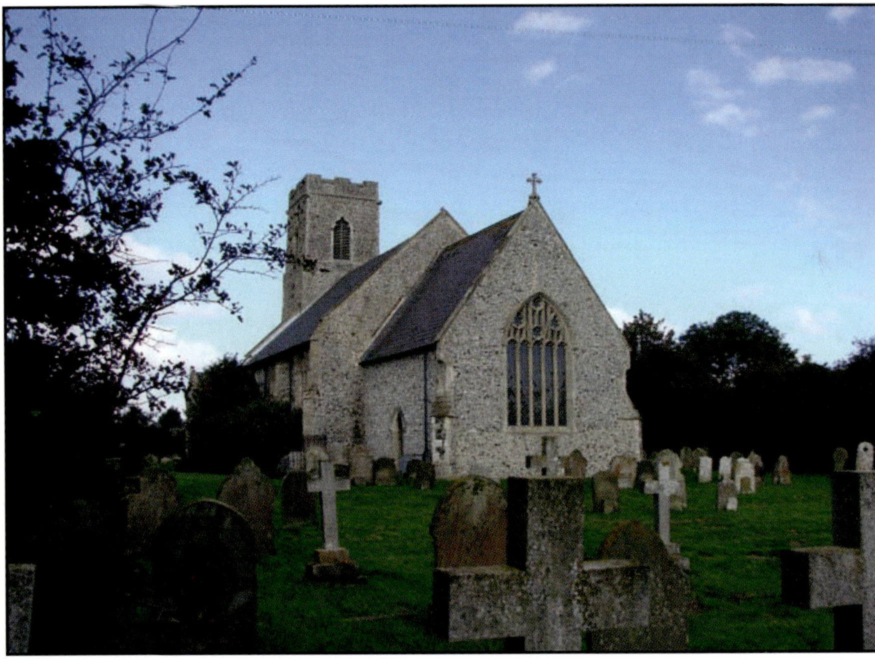

This is a shabby church, but not the worst I have visited. Yet I loved it. It is full of character, it is warm and welcoming. If it were spruced up, I am sure it would lose its charm. It was built in the 14th c. and the original font is still here with its shallow carving of window-like arcading on the octagonal bowl. Before the Commonwealth it was in ruins but was restored in 1674. Since then the Victorians have done their bit and virtually rebuilt it. White, in 1864, described it as thatched, but it is now slated with the pitch of the roof retained. It has one of those horrible stone pulpits which fails to fit in with anything. There are some nice poppy-head bench ends, but on the wall hanging in pride of place are the lists of lives saved by the Palling Lifeboat. It is very impressive and deserves its place of honour.

SEETHING Sts Margaret & Remigius.

No of Bells:	1
19th c. Deanery:	Brooke
Hundred:	Loddon
Union house:	Heckingham
21st c. Deanery:	Depwade
Benefice:	Brooke

9½ miles SE of Norwich. From the A146 turn right at Loddon /Mundham crossroads and continue 3 miles, and past Mundham church on the way.
O.S. grid ref: TM 319979
Post Code: NR15 1DN

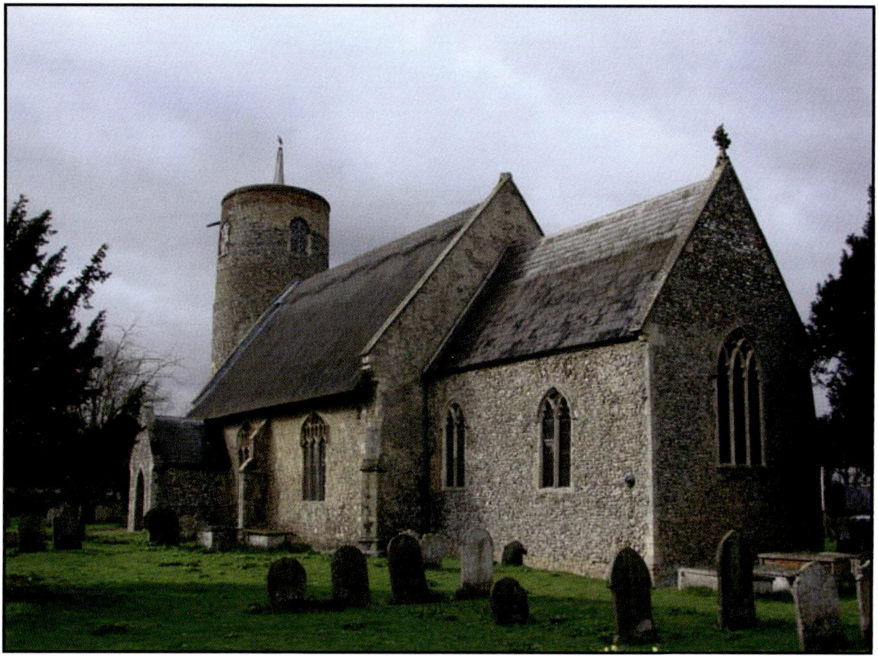

The Norman tower has been added to, and now leans towards the nave at the top. That and the small spirelet, make it quite distinctive. Here you can see one of the celebrated Seven Sacrament fonts, which differs slightly from all the others. It is still in remarkably good condition. The wall paintings are quite special too, St Christopher of course, and 'the three quick and the three dead', one of only a few of this subject. Bench ends have nice poppyhead carvings. Built onto the chancel window sill, and part of the reveal, is the small trefoil piscina. The remainder of the sill is the sedilia. Some of the original colouring is still apparent in the bottom panels of the screen, and the stairs that once led up to the rood loft remain open. The lovely old bier with its detachable top is also on display at the western end of the nave.

SHELTON	Blessed Virgin Mary	6 m N of Harleston, 3 m SE
No of Bells:	1	of Hempnall & 2 m E of
19th c. Deanery:	Depwade	Long Stratton. From Fritton
Hundred:	Depwade	keep heading south to Low
Union house:	Pulham St Mary	Road, Shelton.
21st c. Deanery:	Depwade	O.S. grid ref: TM 220910
Benefice:	Hempnall	Post Code: NR15 2SB

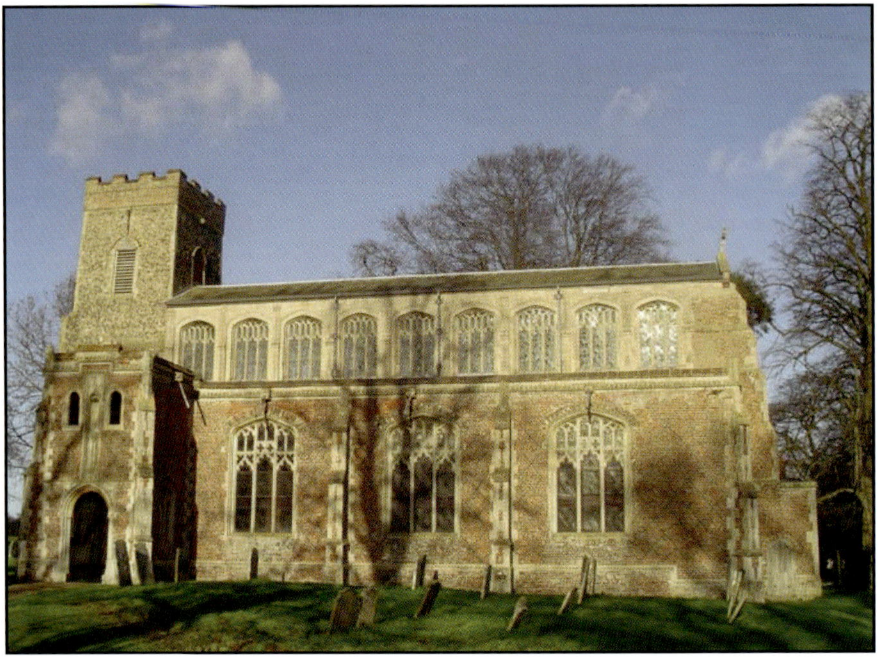

This is a church which is quite different in many ways and is worthy of a visit. Being one of the Hempnall group it is always open. It was built by Sir Ralph Shelton in the 15th c. on the site of a Saxon church, but was not completed until after his death. The tower predates the church by about 100 years. Over the porch are two niches and the Shelton Arms. The parvise was designed, but the floor was never added. The clerestory has nine pairs of windows filling the building with light. The aisles run the complete length of the church. At the east behind the chancel is a small Sacristy or vault, a very rare feature. The 15th c. octagonal font is deeply carved in the typical East Anglian style. Stairs leading to the rood loft are open top and bottom. The tomb monuments are not spectacular but they are interesting.

SHOTESHAM ALL SAINTS All Saints

No of Bells: 5
19th c. Deanery: Brooke
Hundred: Henstead
Union house: Swainsthorpe
21st c. Deanery: Depwade
Benefice: Tas Valley

6 miles S by E of Norwich.
From Poringland church head to Shotesham and turn right at T junction for 200 yds.
O.S. grid ref: TM 246990
Post Code: NR15 1YL

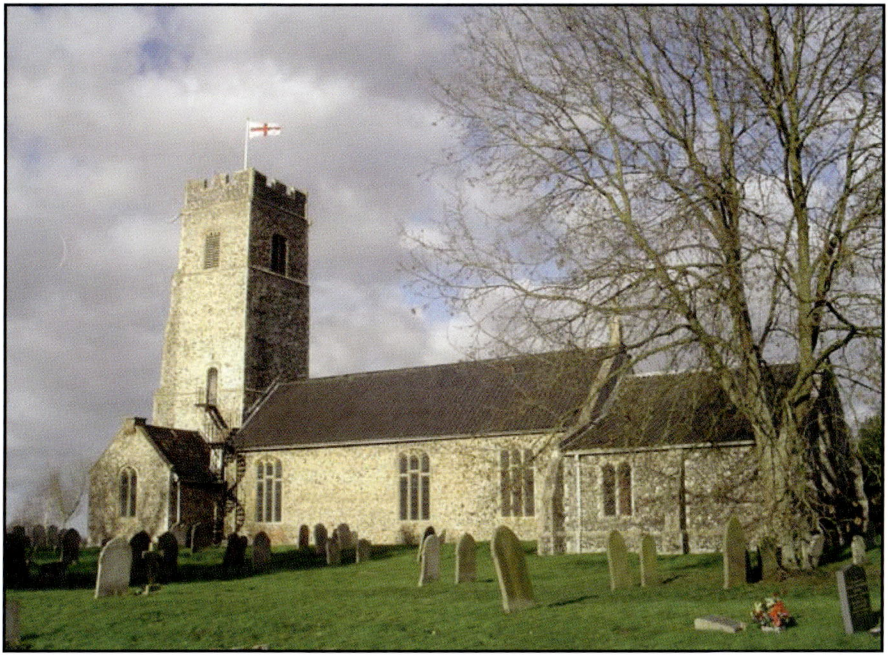

A quite interesting 16th c. church with wall paintings galore, although much faded since being revealed. There were two previous churches on this site, Saxon and Norman. Unusually the method of reaching the belfry is by an external spiral iron staircase. Immediately inside the north door is a Saxon stoup, a relic from a previous church. The lovely 15th c. traditional East Anglian font has the shield of Ely carved around the bowl. Above the elaborately carved stone pulpit is a recess which once held a light designed to cast light onto the rood. Wall memorials include the Bransby family members. Perhaps more interesting is the fact that in the churchyard is buried the mother of Sir Benjamin D'urban after whom Durban in South Africa was named. The Royal Arms are of William IIII.

SHOTESHAM ST MARTIN St Martin

No of Bells:	-	6 miles S of Norwich.
19th c. Deanery:	Brooke	Within 100 yards of
Hundred:	Henstead	Shottisham St Mary (see
Union house:	Swainsthorpe	page 206)
21st c. Deanery:	Depwade	O.S. grid ref: TM 238986
Benefice:	-	Post Code: NR15 1UL

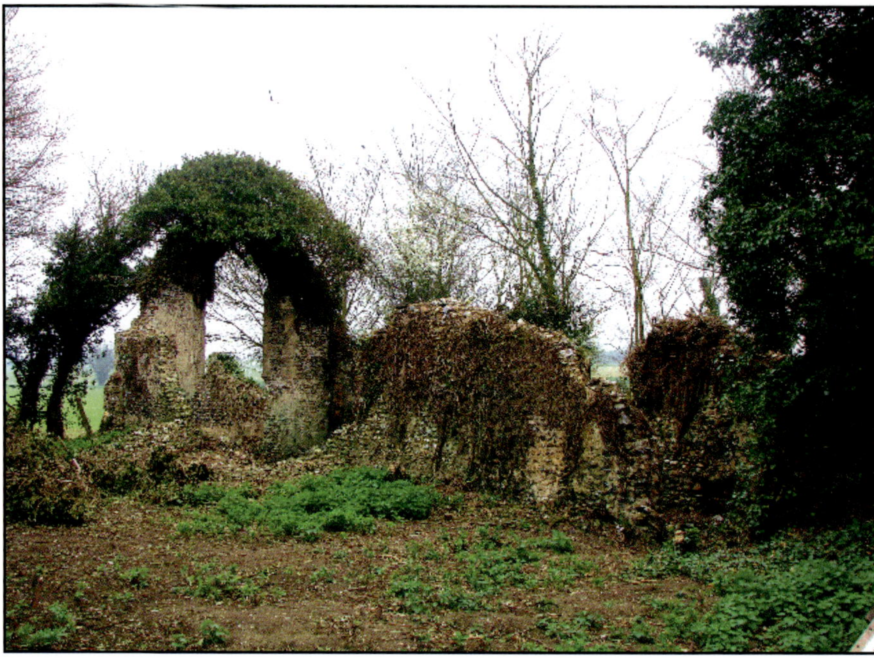

This sad little ruin is just one of two churches that fell into disuse in the four parishes of Shotesham. The other St Botolph, is no more than a pile of stones. Here at least the outline of the church is still seen and the tower is still in a stable condition and a home for more than one family of jackdaws. In the inner wall of the tower, the banner stave locker, now without its door, can be clearly seen. The state of the ruin is very similar to the ruin of Saxlingham Thorpe only two miles away. I would assume that both churches were abandoned about the same time, sometime in the 17th c. We know Saxlingham Thorpe was ruinous in 1740 and that probably didn't happen overnight. At the time of writing the ivy and trees are being cut back hopefully to prevent further damage caused by the overgrowth.

SHOTESHAM ST MARY St Mary

No of Bells:	1
19th c. Deanery:	Brooke
Hundred:	Henstead
Union house:	Swainsthorpe
21st c. Deanery:	Depwade
Benefice:	Tas Valley

6 miles S of Norwich. From Shotesham All Saints head ½ mile towards Saxlingham Nethergate. The church is on the right.

O.S. grid ref: TM 238988
Post Code: NR15 1UL

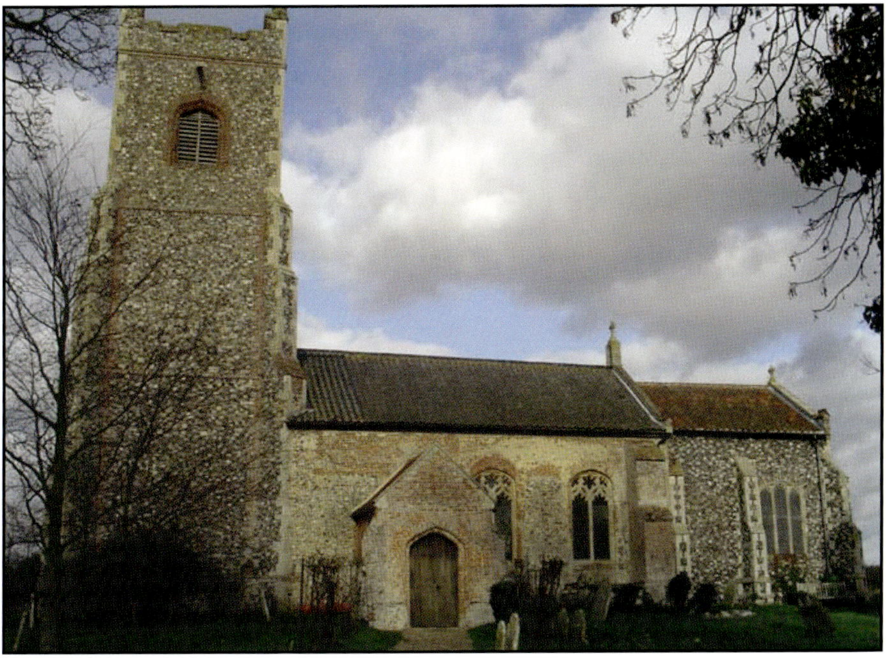

Always locked, even the porch. No keyholder listed. The welcome sign is a travesty of the truth. Above the east end of the nave roof is a sanctus bell turret; it is quite uncommon to find one in this position. The 15th c. font is a traditional East Anglian type with lions around the shaft. The special thing to look for here *(if you can get in)* is the fine brass (hidden beneath a carpet) to Edward and Elizabeth Whyte (1528) a rare survivor. The Royal Arms are of William IIII (sic) which are dated 1833. There is a banner stave locker where the long staves were stored between ceremonies. The church is basically 15th c. but restoration by the Victorians has left its mark. Curiously there is a hole in the porch buttress for which I cannot account as there is not another on the opposing buttress.

SIDESTRAND	St Michael
No of Bells:	1
19th c. Deanery:	Repps
Hundred:	North Erpingham
Union house:	Gimingham
21st c. Deanery:	Repps
Benefice:	Overstrand

3 miles ESE of Cromer on the coast road between Overstrand & Trimingham, close to Sidestrand Hall. Unmissable.

O.S. grid ref:	TG 260398
Post Code:	NR27 0LY

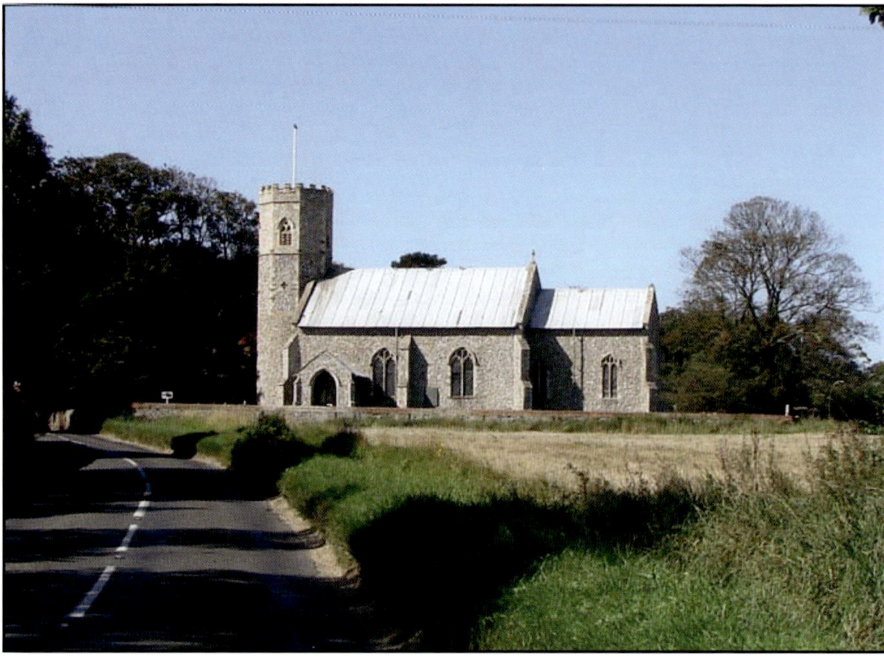

There are two spellings for this small parish; the alternative is Syderstrand. Standing close to the coast road and impossible to miss, this lovely little church has a tall octagonal upper stage to the round tower. The church was completely rebuilt in the late 19th c. to the design of the original, which fell over the cliff in 1916. Inside you will find the plain octagonal font with its modest cover in a baptistery set beneath the tower. Above hangs a rowel decorated with poppies telling us we are in the centre of Poppyland. It was the writer Clement Scott who coined the phrase while lying in the old churchyard surrounded by poppies. There is nothing old here but the history that surrounds this beautiful place. Unfortunately, parking is difficult, but it is worth the short walk back to the church from the car.

SISLAND	St Mary
No of Bells:	1
19th c. Deanery:	Brooke
Hundred:	Loddon
Union house:	Heckingham
21st c. Deanery:	Loddon
Benefice:	Chet Valley

10 miles SE of Norwich on the A146. Turn right at Loddon / Mundham crossroads. Then first right and follow winding road.
O.S. grid ref: TM 344985
Post Code: NR14 6EE

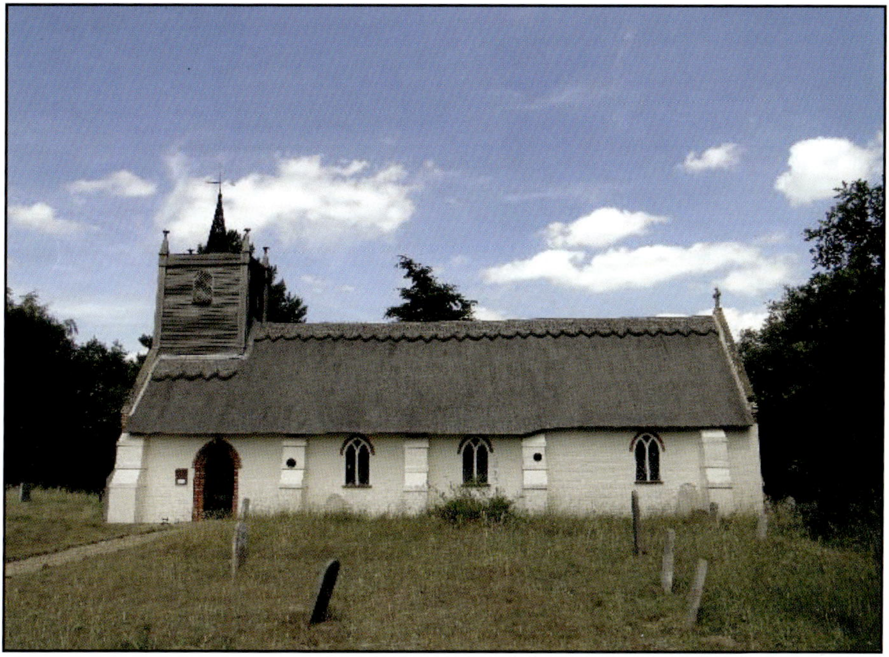

Anciently known as Sizeland. With its whitewashed south and west wall and wooden tower, which replaces the flint structure which fell down centuries ago, the church would have a modern appearance, but for the thatched roof which confounds the eye. A lovely building which almost certainly stands on the site of a Saxon church. The Normans built a church here and the present 1761 building sits almost in its footprint. On the north side are the remains of a 14th c. chantry chapel. Although there is little or nothing pre-1761 except perhaps a typical East Anglian style font, complete with four lions around the base, the church inside obviously is well maintained and well loved. The position of the arches which form the chancel could at one time, possibly, have been the most easterly extent of the original church.

SKEYTON	All Saints	3½ m E of Aylsham. From
No of Bells:	1	the A140 take the road to
19th c. Deanery:	Ingworth	Burgh and Swanton Abbott.
Hundred:	South Erpingham	The church is just over the
Union house:	Aylsham	crossroads after 3 miles.
21st c. Deanery:	Waxham & Tunstead	O.S. grid ref: TG 254274
Benefice:	King's Beck	Post Code: NR10 5AX

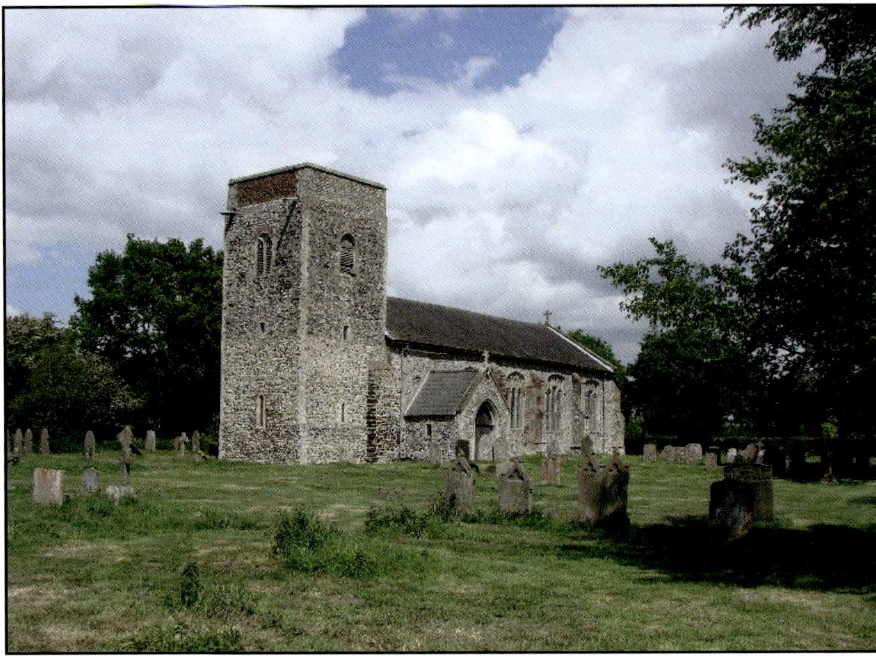

This church may have been built on the foundations of a much earlier one. At the beginning of the 19th c. it was restored in a small way which thankfully has not destroyed the rural charm of the interior. The repair of the tower's parapet however, is a different matter. The font dates from the restoration and although attractive, is out of place. An older one from a redundant church would have been more fitting to the surroundings, especially with the elaborate pinnacled cover, which is twice the height of the font. Most of the furnishings appear to be Victorian as are the cast-iron Royal Arms which hang on the wall. A simple austere trefoil piscina and dropped-sill sedilia in the sanctuary are coeval with the building of the church, only the height of a step defines the chancel from the nave

SLOLEY	St Bartholomew	4 miles S of Nth Walsham
No of Bells:	1	off the B1150. Ignore 1st
19th c. Deanery:	Waxham	road to Sloley. then just
Hundred:	Tunstead	before reaching Scottow
Union house:	Smallburgh	turn left to Smallburgh.
21st c. Deanery:	Waxham & Tunstead	O.S. grid ref: TG 299241
Benefice:	Worstead	Post Code: NR12 8HL

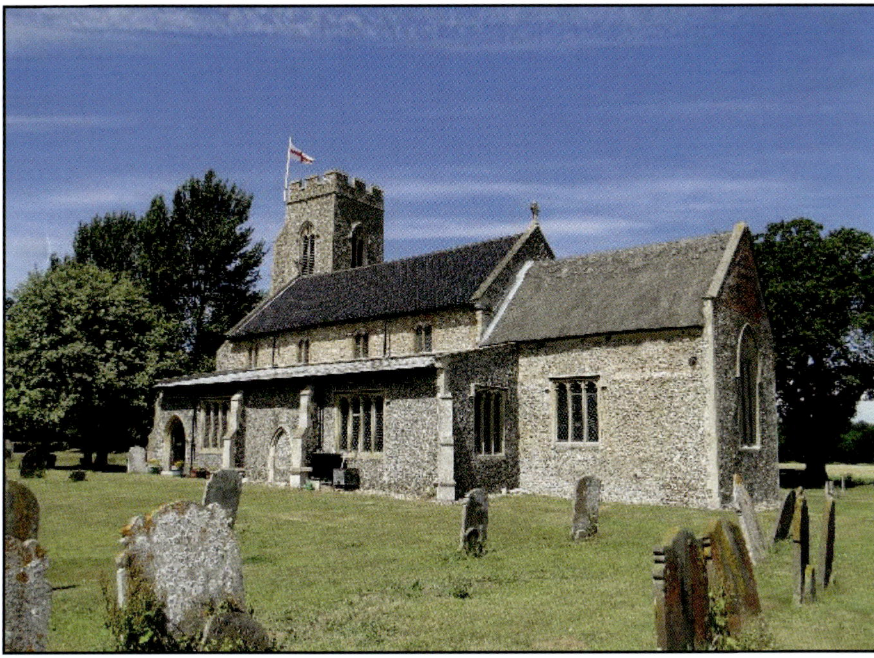

The square 15th c. tower stands north-west of the tiled nave, the chancel is thatched. The nave has a clerestory of eight windows which make the interior very light and pleasant. In the nave itself is the least damaged of all the Seven Sacrament fonts I have seen. Above, the roof is simple arch-braced without a collar and is supported on 15th c. arcades. The chancel weeps to the south by about two feet; the line of the old arch has been intentionally left visible. The north aisle has had a chapel at the east end dedicated to St Erasmus. The south aisle chapel of St James has the tomb of Oliver le Groos beneath an arch. A redundant horse-drawn plough stands on the pammant tiled floor of the nave signifying the bond between the Church and the land upon which so much has depended for so long in a rural area such as this.

SMALLBURGH St Peter

No of Bells:	2
19th c. Deanery:	Waxham
Hundred:	Tunstead
Union house:	Smallburgh
21st c. Deanery:	Waxham & Tunstead
Benefice:	Smallburgh

5 miles SE of North Walsham. Leave North Walsham on the A149 and go through the village. Then turn right into Hall Road.

O.S. grid ref: TG 334239
Post Code: NR12 9ND

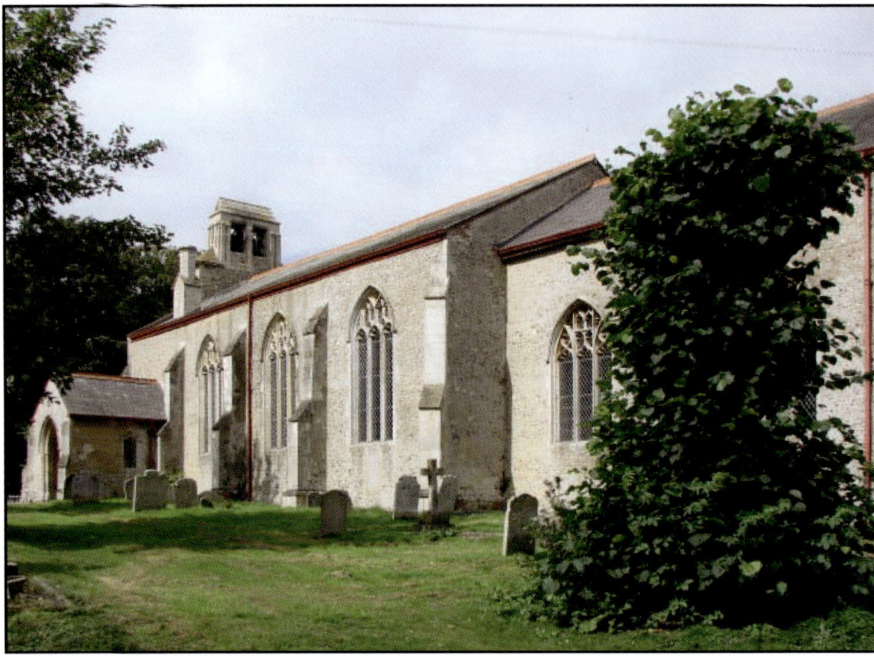

A towerless church with a double bell turret. The tower fell down in 1677 and was never rebuilt. On the west wall of the turret is a shield with the crossed keys of St Peter. Inside the porch is a small stoup. The 15th c. octagonal font is very plain and stands on a central shaft with engaged columns. The nave roof is eye-catching, thoroughly painted in brick-red and white. The two beams nearest the chancel arch have much more detail, like a canopy of honour to a non-existent rood. All the old benches have been torn out and sets of five chairs replace them. The modern pulpit sits on a stone base. Behind it is the old screen, or what remains of it. Either side of the chancel arch are four screen base-panels depicting saints. In the chancel, the piscina has a cusped ogee arch with pierced quatrefoils in the spandrels.

SOUTH BURLINGHAM St Edmund *****

No of Bells:	3	9 miles E by S of Norwich.
19th c. Deanery:	Blofield	Leave the A47 for the south
Hundred:	Blofield	bound B1140. Over the
Union house:	Lingwood	bridge, 1st right then left.
21st c Deanery:	Blofield	O.S. grid ref: TG 372083
Benefice:	Lingwood	Post Code: NR13 4EX

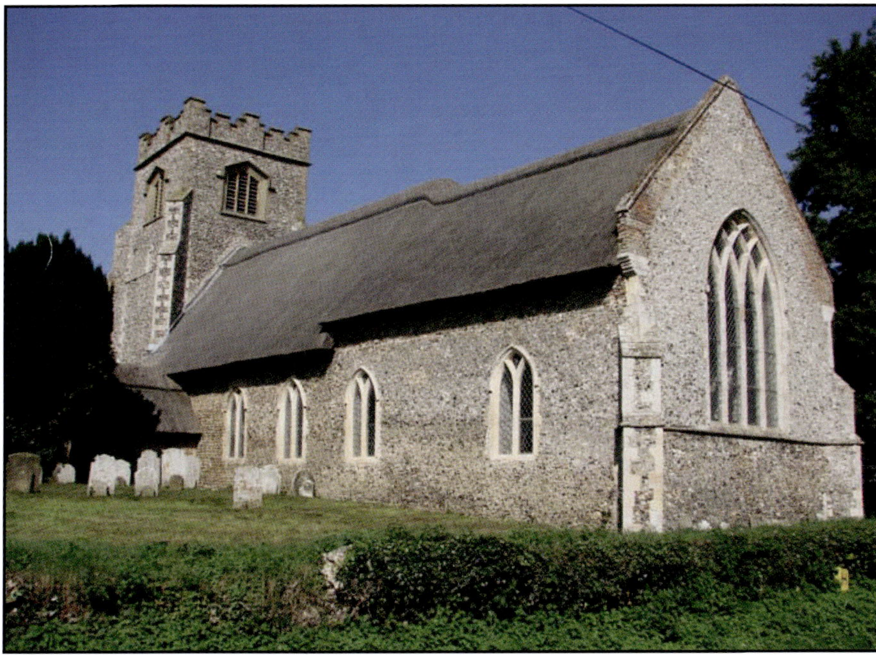

A lovely entirely thatched church and porch which as you will see from the drawing inside the tower, once had a lovely pyramidal cap with dormer windows. Inside the porch there are benches supported by fallen angels. The south doorway is Norman with a 14th c. handle on the door. The north doorway is also Norman, now blocked. Treats await the visitor: the 13th c. font with its curious legs; the beautiful 15th c. sixteen panelled pulpit in its original colours; the saintly figures, animals and grotesques on the bench ends; the lovely traceried screen and the wall paintings. There is more of interest to see in this small church than many of the grander churches in the county. It is as if the Victorians forgot this church existed. The only thing they seem to have done was to put on a new scissor-frame roof.

SOUTH WALSHAM St Lawrence

No of Bells:	1
19th c. Deanery:	Blofield
Hundred:	Walsham
Union house:	Acle
21st c. Deanery:	Blofield
Benefice:	Ranworth Broadside

11 miles ENE of Norwich. From the B1140 west of Acle follow road signs to Sth Walsham or take more direct route from Acle.
O.S. grid ref: TG 366133
Post Code: NR13 6DQ

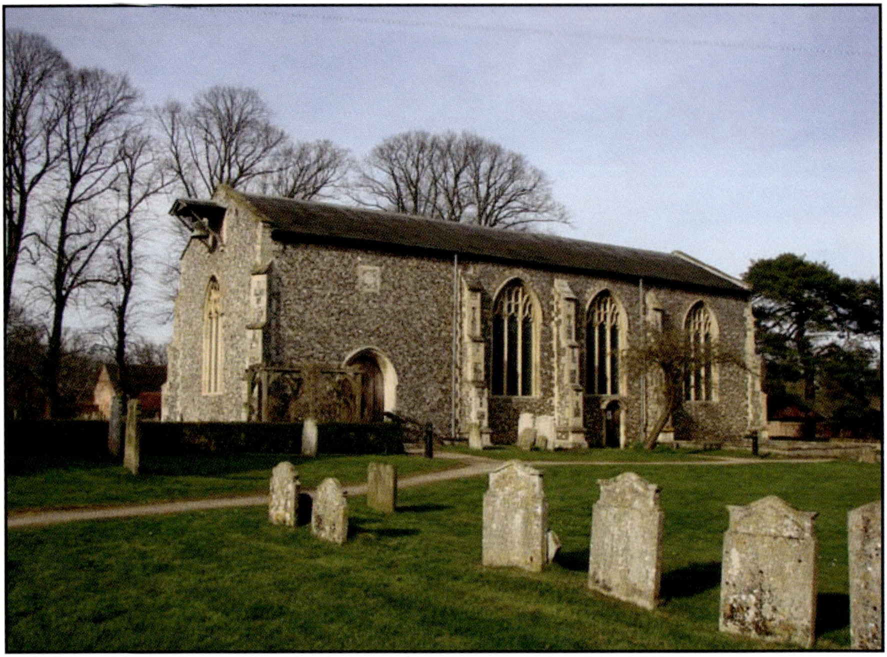

Sharing the same churchyard as St Mary (see overleaf). The church suffered a fire on the 30th June 1827 after having been restored in 1813. The tower remained for some time until a sonic boom caused it to collapse even further and the remains can still be seen surrounded by flowers and shrubs. The church had stood here since the 14th c. and was very large. What remains today is the chancel and a small portion of the nave, the whole nave having stretched between this and the tower. On the west gable hangs a bell, more for Sunday school purposes than any other reason. A modern font sits in the middle of the kitchen. Around the walls are photographs recording the recent history of the building. Today the chancel is modernised and used as a village hall for secular and non-secular purposes.

SOUTH WALSHAM St Mary

No of Bells:	5
19th c. Deanery:	Blofield
Hundred:	Walsham
Union house:	Acle
21st c. Deanery:	Blofield
Benefice:	Ranworth Broadside

11 miles ENE of Norwich. From the B1140 west of Acle follow road signs to Sth Walsham or take more direct route from Acle.

O.S. grid ref: TG 365133
Post Code: NR13 6DQ

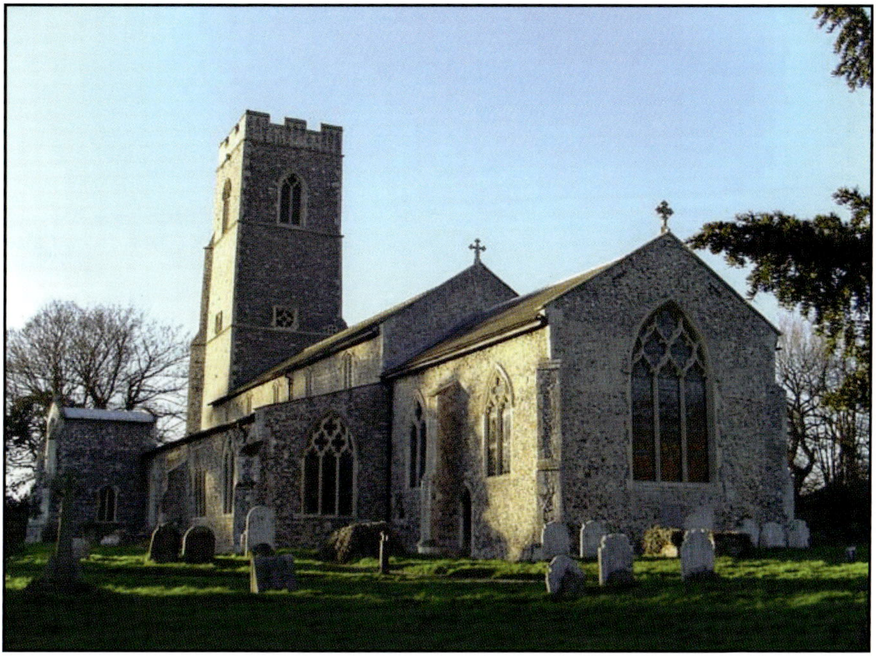

Still standing proud and thankfully complete is St. Mary's church. The nave is earlier than the 15th c. tower and porch which were added later. The porch has a squat parvise which extends above the roof of the south aisle. In the spandrels of the doorway the Annunciation is depicted. The 14th c. octagonal font has quatrefoil and arcaded decoration around the bowl, supported on a shaft with moulded piers. The benches are 15th c. and have nicely carved poppyheads: some have figures on the armrests. In the chancel, the piscina is very plain as is the dropped-sill sedilia. A banner stave locker is set into the wall. The 15th c. screen is traceried and has diapered panels forming the base. The rood loft stairs are still open but no longer lead anywhere. A brass plaque reminds us that James Rownce died in September 1638.

SOUTHREPPS St James
No of Bells: 6
19th c. Deanery: Repps
Hundred: North Erpingham
Union house: Gimingham
21st c. Deanery: Repps
Benefice: Trunch Team Ministry

4 miles SSE of Cromer. From the A149 turn left at B1436 crossroads, take the Northrepps road, church is at the east end of the village.
O.S. grid ref: TG 257368
Post Code: NR11 8NP

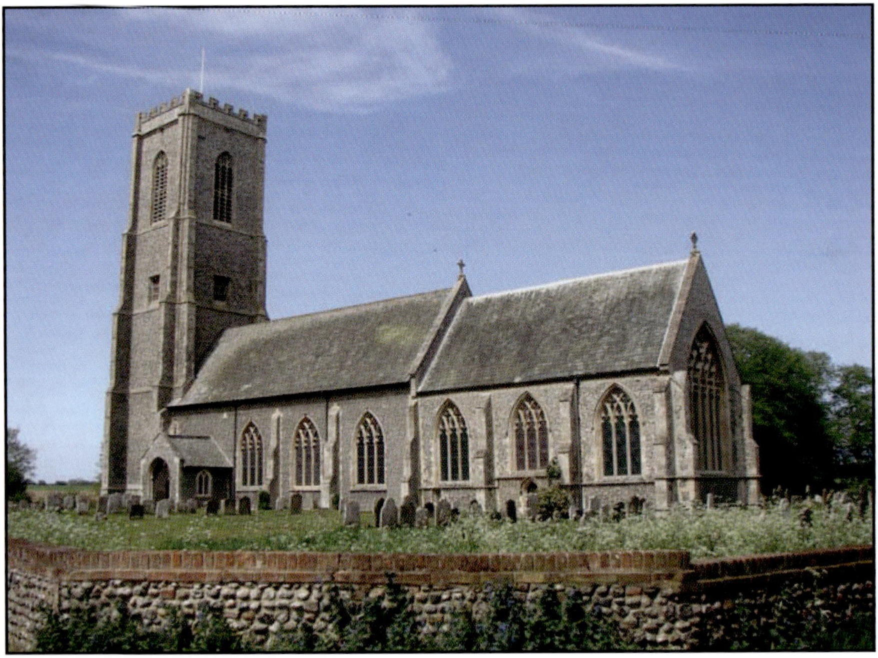

A magnificent church with an elegant 15th c. embattled tower, around the base of which is a string of shields and shells (representing St. James). Beneath the tower is a modern meeting room; above it is the ringing chamber. The octagonal font is decorated with quatrefoils and has an ogee cover. Victorian restoration has been sympathetic but all the furnishings and fittings are modern. On a stone base stands the pulpit with open cinquefoil panels. Part of the old west door is in the west end of the nave with the old parish chest. The upper section of the screen is Victorian but the lower part is original with diapered panels in red and green. In the chancel the later insertion of a window has partially destroyed the cusped and crocketted arches of the piscina and sedilia. The Royal Arms are those of George III.

SOUTHTOWN St Mary
No of Bells: 1
19th c. Deanery: Lothingland
Hundred: Mutford & Lothingland
Union house: Oulton
21st c Deanery: Great Yarmouth
Benefice: Great Yarmouth

6½ m N of Lowestoft
between Gorleston town & Great Yarmouth. At the northern end of Southtown Road, east side.
O.S. grid ref: TG 521071
Post Code: NR31 0JB

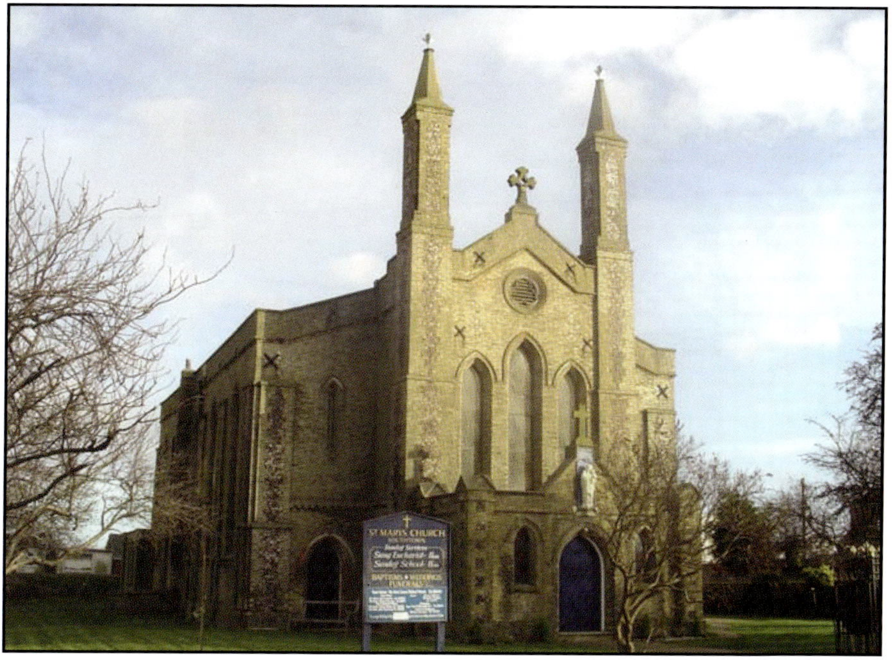

From the outside, there is nothing attractive about this church. It was built by the early Victorians in 1831 in white brick with dressed flint flushwork. There is no tower, but two fine pinnacles point skyward at the west end of the nave. Entrance to the nave is through the west porch; above, on the gable, is a statuette of Madonna and Child. Inside, it is spacious, without internal columnar supports for the roof. The tall windows north and south let the available light flood into this brightly decorated church. The small octagonal font is contemporary with the church and has carved decoration on the facets of the bowl. The pulpit also dates from the same period. There is a piscina and three-seat stepped sedilia, although they went out of use centuries before this church was built. Only open during services.

SOUTHWOOD St Edmund
No of Bells: - was 1
19th c. Deanery: Blofield
Hundred: Blofield
Union house: Lingwood
21st c. Deanery: -
Benefice: -

11 miles ESE of Norwich in Norwich Road, Southwood. look for the sign in the hedge warning 'DANGEROUS STRUCTURE'
O.S. grid ref: TG 391054
Post Code: * NR13 3LR

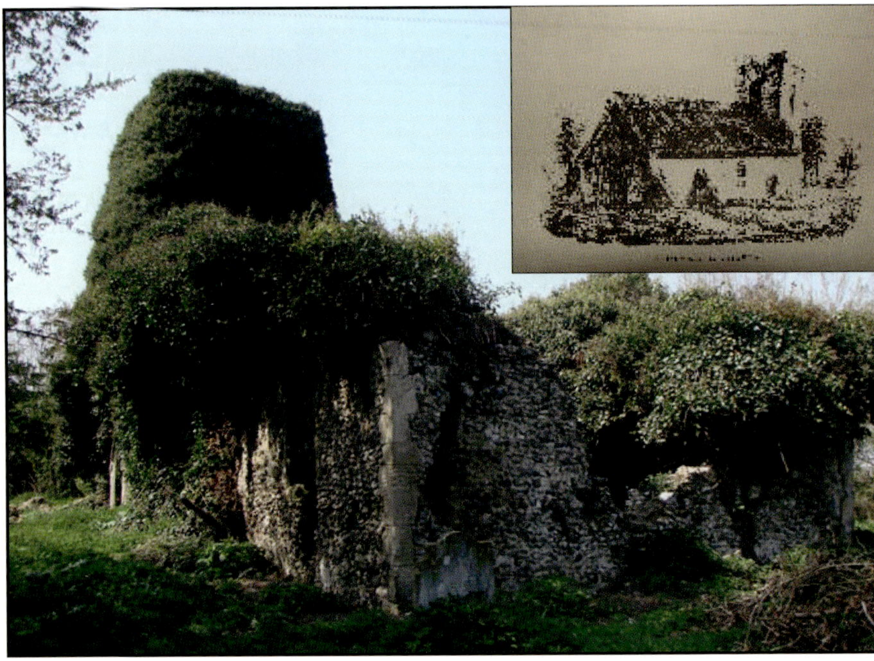

** The postcode is for Hall Cottages, in a parallel road, Norwich Road has no post code.* Southwood and Limpenhoe had been united as joint parishes for some time before this church fell into disuse in the late 1800s. The church was thatched and was modest in every way. I quote from White's Directory 1864: "The church is a plain whitewashed building, with nave, chancel, and square tower containing one bell. There is a triple lancet window at the east end, but the other windows are of the early Decorated period. There is a piscina and an aumbry in the chancel, but the former is plastered over. Here was also a curious piece of tapestry *[now in Limpenhoe]* representing Abraham offering up Isaac. The font is Norman, but disfigured with plaster and whitewash." *(The inset sketch is also in Limpenhoe church).*

SPIXWORTH St Peter
No of Bells: 2
19th c. Deanery: Taverham
Hundred: Taverham
Union house: Horsham St Faith
21st c. Deanery: Norwich North
Benefice: Horsham

3 miles from the centre of Norwich. Leave Norwich on the A140 Aylsham Road and turn right at Horsham St Faith and follow road.
O.S. grid ref: TG 241158
Post Code: NR10 3PS

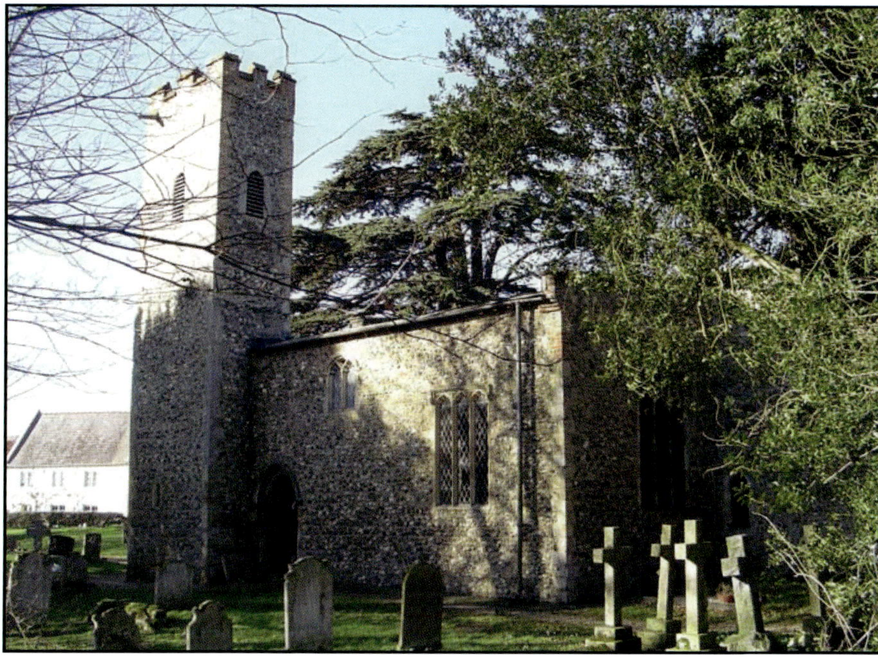

The very slender rectangular tower without buttresses at the extreme southwest corner of the south aisle is most disorientating. Entry is through the west doorway. Inside you will find a 12th c. round Caen stone font which is squared at the base. Being used as a table for leaflets is the old parish chest. Although the rood loft has been removed, the stairs are still open to the top. The screen is Victorian as is the pulpit and most of the fixtures and fittings. In the chancel is the piscina and sedilia with cusped arches below a square label. Against the north wall of the sanctuary are effigies of William and Alice Peck (1634) set into a great pink and black marble memorial with cherubs above. Both lie as in death, dressed in shrouds, whereas most effigies are depicted as merely sleeping and in day dress or armour if a knight.

SPROWSTON Sts Mary & Margaret.

No of Bells:	3
19th c. Deanery:	Taverham
Hundred:	Taverham
Union house:	Horsham St Faith
21st c. Deanery:	Norwich North
Benefice:	Sprowston

2 miles from Norwich city centre. From the A1151 Wroxham Road, turn left before roundabout, then right into Blue Boar Lane.
O.S. grid ref: TG 249126
Post Code: NR7 8AU

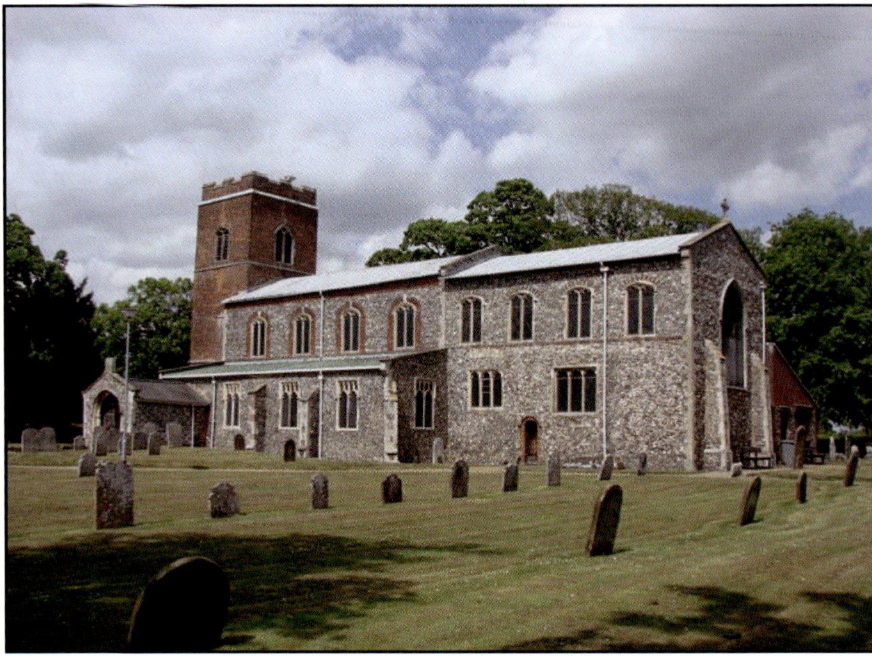

The church is essentially 14th c. but there has been much restoration and very little of the original church remains. The arcades are evidence to this. The 19th c. brick tower (which replaces a Saxon round one) and the brickwork around the clerestory windows are not unattractive. A clerestory in the chancel is uncommon. The font is an 18th c. copy of the 16th c. one in Holy Trinity, Coventry. Behind the Adams memorial tomb are the 15th c. piscina and adjacent sedilia. The walls are bedecked with memorials and there are many tombs, principally of Thomas Adams (1667) and John Corbet (1559). The Christopher Knolles (1610), wall monument is damaged, probably by puritans, but retains its dignity as the parents kneel at a prayer desk with their children.

STALHAM	St Mary	8½ miles SE of North Walsham. From the A149 turn into Stalham town centre. The church is close to the school.
No of Bells:	1	
19th c. Deanery:	Waxham	
Hundred:	Happing	
Union house:	Smallburgh	
21st c. Deanery:	Waxham & Tunstead	O.S. grid ref: TG 373252
Benefice:	Stalham	Post Code: NR12 9DH

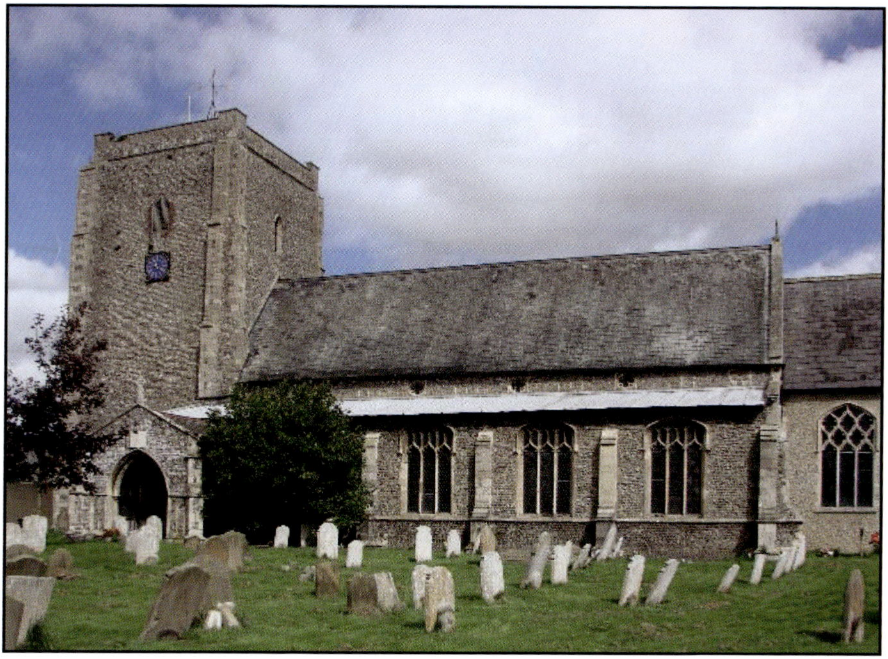

A strange clerestory with only tiny windows, almost identical to those in Rollesby. Above the porch door is a sundial. Just inside the nave is a rarity, although broken: a pillar stoup, not often seen these days. However, the speciality is the spectacular 15th c. octagonal font, carved with the Baptism of Jesus, the Holy Trinity and saints, with eight more around the shaft. It stands on three steps, two of which are decorated. Most of what can be seen is Victorian restoration including the roofs. The painted base of the screen is an exception; one panel depicts St Roch, the only known example. The rood loft stairs lead around the back of a column. Cut into the chancel arch are two squints to allow those conducting services in the aisle chapels to coordinate with the high altar. An interesting church and definitely worth a visit.

STANNINGHALL St Peter

No of Bells: -
19th c. Deanery: as Horstead
Hundred: as Horstead
Union house: as Horstead
21st c. Deanery: -
On private land

Between Frettenham and Horstead. About ½ a mile or so off the B1150 near Stanninghall Farm. Behind farm buildings.
O.S. grid ref: TG 254174
Post Code: NR12 7LX

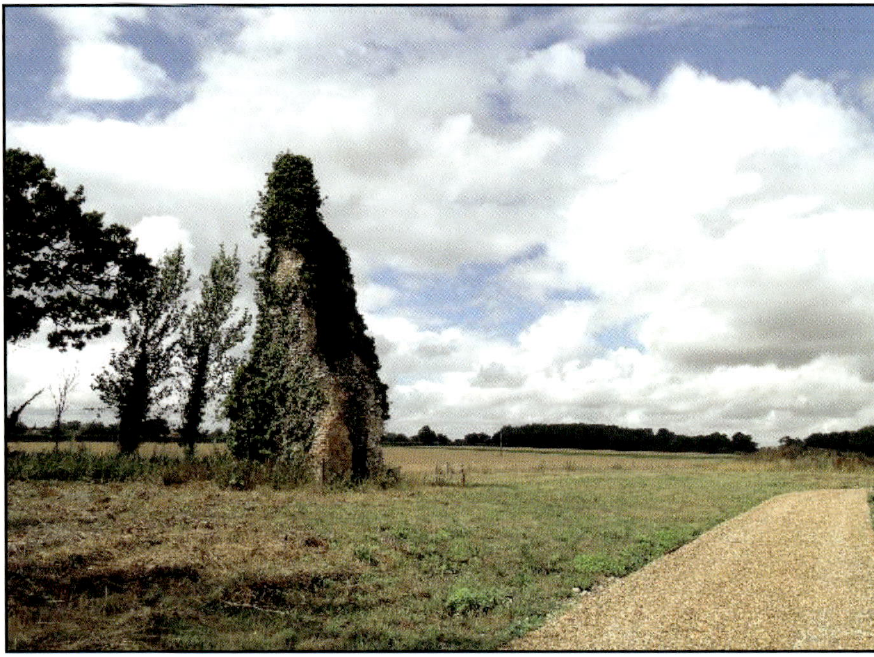

The parish has long been consolidated with Horstead. The church here became ruinous before the reign of Queen Elizabeth. Only the tower remains as a monument to what it once was; what was the chancel is now beneath the gravel track leading to the house. Very little is known about the church. Some walls were still standing until late last century but these have now been demolished as the piles of flint nearby bear witness. It was probably the depopulation of the villages. Many other churches suffered the same fate in Elizabethan times during the unsettled period of struggle between the newly founded Church of England and the Catholics. The ivy-clad ruin we see here today is on private land and it is not advised to seek close examination without first asking permission.

STARSTON St Margaret of Antioch
No of Bells: 6
19th c. Deanery: Redenhall
Hundred: Earsham
Union house: Pulham St Mary
21st c. Deanery: Redenhall
Benefice: Dickleburgh & the Pulhams

2 m N of Harleston in Church Hill, Starston. On the road from Harleston to the Pulhams. Go over the bridge and straight on.
O.S. grid ref: TM 235844
Post Code: IP20 9PF

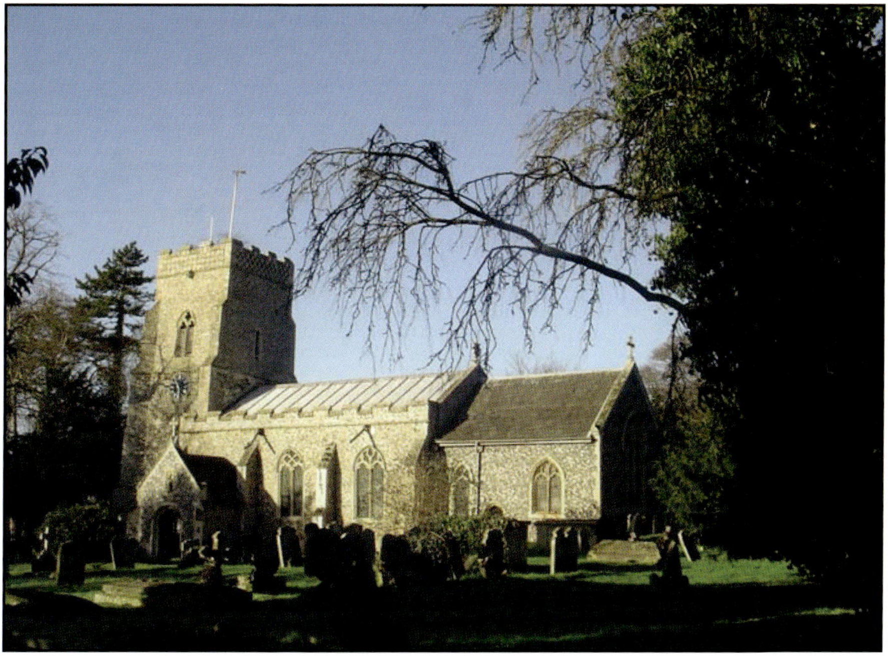

This is a beautiful setting for a lovely churchyard perched on the side of a hill. A chequered parapet atop the squat 14th c. tower, and the gargoyles deserve a second glance. In a niche above the porch door is St. Margaret defeating the dragon. Built on the foundations of a Norman church, a north aisle was added in 1870 when a wall painting of the death of the Virgin Mary was discovered. The nave has a new arch-braced roof; that of the chancel is painted. The wall posts rest on corbels carved with angels. Roses decorate the octagonal font, more are carved on shields with four lions around the base. The reredos is Victorian and matches the panelling in the chancel. A nice wall memorial in the chancel is to Bartholomew Cotton (1636). A good late panelled pulpit. Most of the bench ends have poppyheads.

STOCKTON St Michael & All Angels 3 miles SE of Loddon.

No of Bells:	5	From Beccles head to Norwich. On left, signposted after white house on the right.
19th c. Deanery:	Brooke	
Hundred:	Clavering	
Union house:	Heckingham	
21st c. Deanery:	Loddon	O.S. grid ref: TM 387941
Benefice:	Geldeston	Post Code: NR34 0HJ

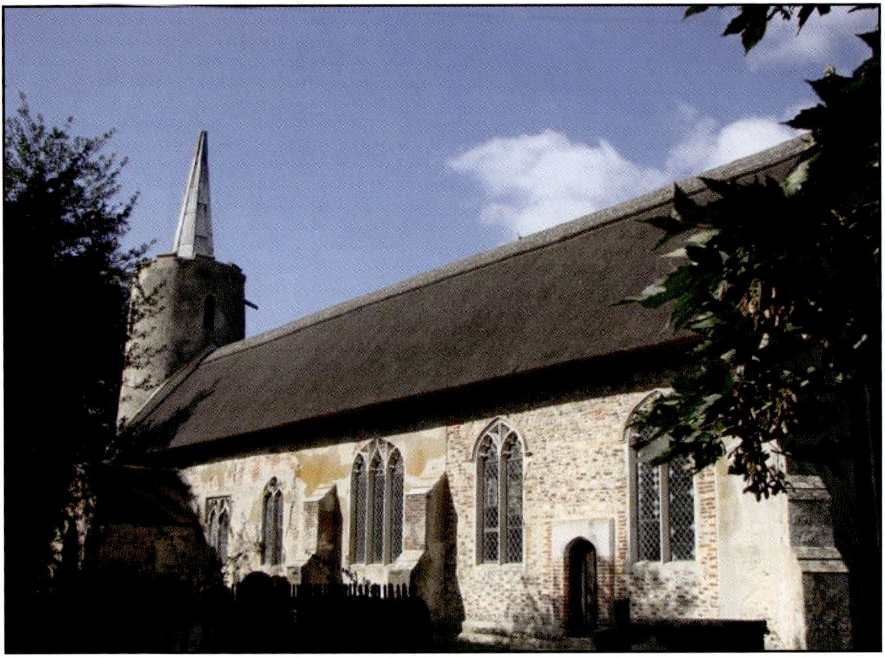

The distinctive leaded spire can be seen from the main road. Beneath it is the crenulated Norman round tower. The roof indicates that no chancel arch is present. Inside the porch is a small niche for a bowl of Holy water. The crudely carved octagonal font is most unusual in having four heads protruding on the alternate corners and a very short shaft. Over the bowl is a crocketted cover, perhaps Jacobean. Above, on the west wall, are the Arms of William IV. The steeply pitched roof is arch-braced with a carved cornice and short unsupported wall posts. Although the benches have a nice variation of poppyheads, they have no great age. Two armrests are in the form of man's best friend. The oak pulpit is very plain. The piscina has been removed and there is no sign of a sedilia.

STOKE HOLY CROSS The Holy Cross

No of Bells: 2
19th c. Deanery: Brooke
Hundred: Henstead
Union house: Swainsthorpe
21st c. Deanery: Loddon
Benefice: Venta

5 miles S of Norwich. Leave Norwich south-bound on A140. Take first turn on the left, past the mill turn right, follow the road.
O.S. grid ref: TG 235007
Post Code: NR14 8AB

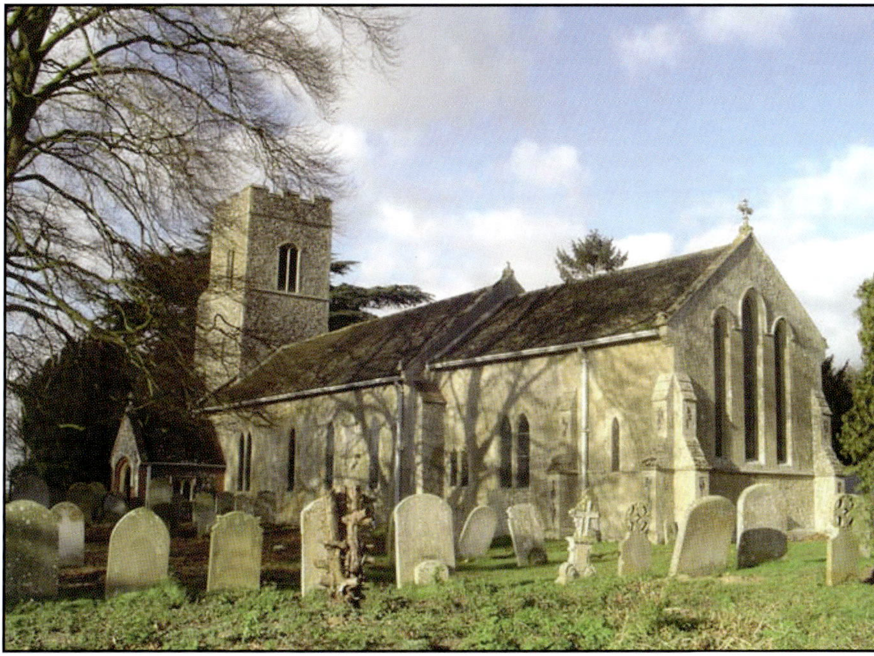

Always kept locked! However the most interesting item, the 15th c. font, stands outside discarded beneath the tower. Everything in the church is Victorian or later. The scissor-frame rafter roof of the nave was part of the restoration. There is a banner stave locker in the wall of the tower and the simple trefoil piscina are all the history you will enjoy here. A single small bench with animal carvings has been saved from the ravages of progress. The other benches have all been removed and individual seating installed. The church seems destined to become just another village hall or children's play group. The pulpit is ornamented with a copper relief depicting the Virgin and Child. Thomas Havers' monument shows not only was he a theologian but a doctor and surgeon with the tools of his trade

STOKESBY cum HERRINGSBY St Andrew

No of Bells:	1	7 miles W of Gt. Yarmouth.
19th c. Deanery:	Flegg	Turn off the A1064 before
Hundred:	East Flegg	Filby and go through
Union house:	Rollesby	Runham for 2½ miles.
21st c. Deanery:	Great Yarmouth	O.S. grid ref: TG 435105
Benefice:	Flegg (Sth. Trinity Broads)	Post Code: NR29 3ET

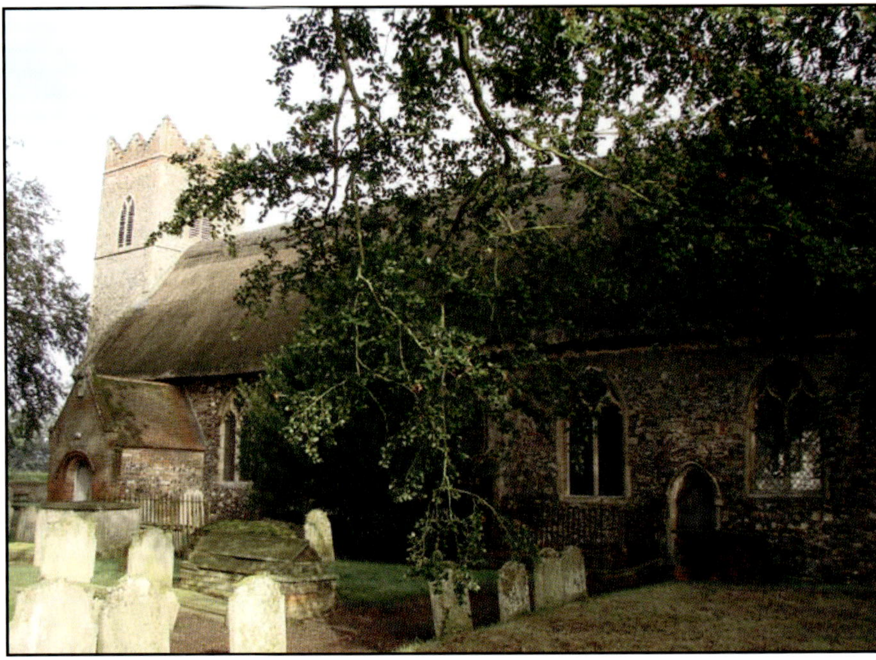

A poor, shabby little church that needs some tlc! The thatched roof is green with moss and is embowered by trees holding in the moisture. The stepped crenulations on the 13th c. tower are brick; like the porch. The door has a fine sanctuary ring handle and other early ironwork. Inside, the walls are plain and dull. The roof is a simple scissor-frame construction. The Victorian pulpit has a tester but no backboard. The screen appears to be of the same design and modern benches take up the front rows. Behind these are six old benches, which are quite glorious, with animals and grotesques that detract from the nondescript surroundings. The carved backs of these have quatrefoil and floral design. E.W and R.W engraved on the ends of two of them are probably the carver's or church warden's initials.

STRUMPSHAW St Mary

No of Bells: 3
19th c. Deanery: Blofield
Hundred: Blofield
Union house: Lingwood
21st c. Deanery: Blofield
Benefice: Lingwood

8 miles E of Norwich. From the A47 turn south just east of Blofield. After railway bridge turn right and continue for 300 yards.
O.S. grid ref: TG 349077
Post Code: NR13 4NT

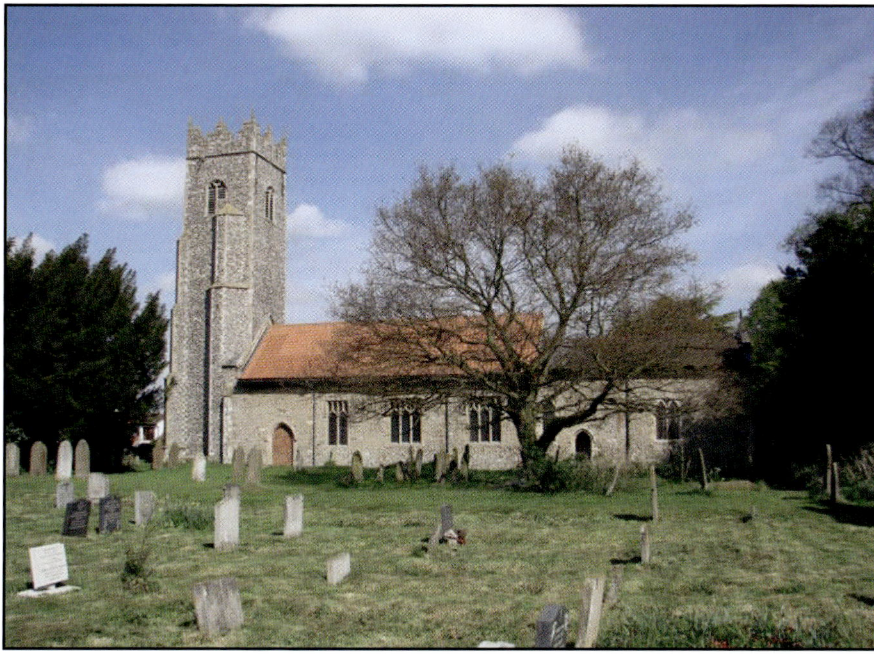

The tall 15th c. tower dominates the church with a turret staircase to the belfry on the south side. The parapet is doubly crenulated and eight pinnacles surmount the merlons. As you enter by the north door, note the mason's mark on the jamb. Just inside there is a banner-stave 'locker' with no door, above hang the Royal Arms of George III. Above that, the ultra-modern roof spans the nave. Set into the south wall is an arch that may once have contained a tomb. The stairs to the rood loft are still open. The 15th c. screen is as it was made, even the colouring is original. Unfortunately, part of it is obscured by the unsightly stone base to the Victorian pulpit. On the south wall of the chancel is a double piscina with a central column supporting the trefoil arches. Adjacent to it are dropped-sill graduated sedilia.

SUFFIELD St Margaret of Antioch

No of Bells:	5, only 1 in use
19th c. Deanery:	Repps
Hundred:	North Erpingham
Union house:	West Beckham
21st c. Deanery:	Waxham & Tunstead
Benefice:	King's Beck

3½ m W of North Walsham. From the A149 turn right near Antinham Hall. Turn left after 1 mile and continue ¾ mile to church.

O.S. grid ref: TG 234313
Post Code: NR11 7EL

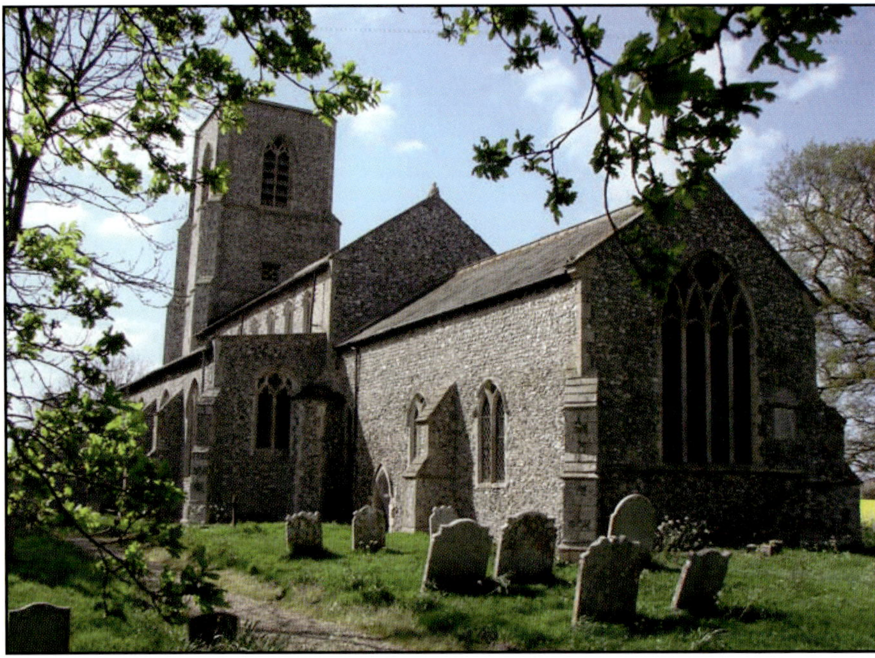

Suffield church is a significant edifice for such a small parish, with a good chequered base course around the 15th c. tower. The rood loft turret is visible externally between the nave and south aisle. Inside and protected by the porch is the 16th c. door with tracery on the upper half. The 15th c. font bowl is quite plain, but beneath, around the corona, are carved angels. Near the north door is a nice stoup set into the wall. The lovely 15th c. arcades are lit by the sixteen two light windows of the clerestory. Only the lower base section of the screen remains depicting eight saints, including the rare saints Longinus, Julian and Sir John Schorne. In the chancel is an early double piscina with a central column and a trefoil design above. There is an elegant tomb to John Hammond (1584).

SURLINGHAM St Mary

No of Bells: 4
19th c. Deanery: Brooke
Hundred: Henstead
Union house: Swainsthorpe
21st c. Deanery: Loddon
Benefice: Bramerton

5 miles E of Norwich. Leave the A146 at the nursery at Framlingham Earl and head for Bramerton and continue following road signs.
O.S. grid ref: TG 305066
Post Code: NR14 7DF

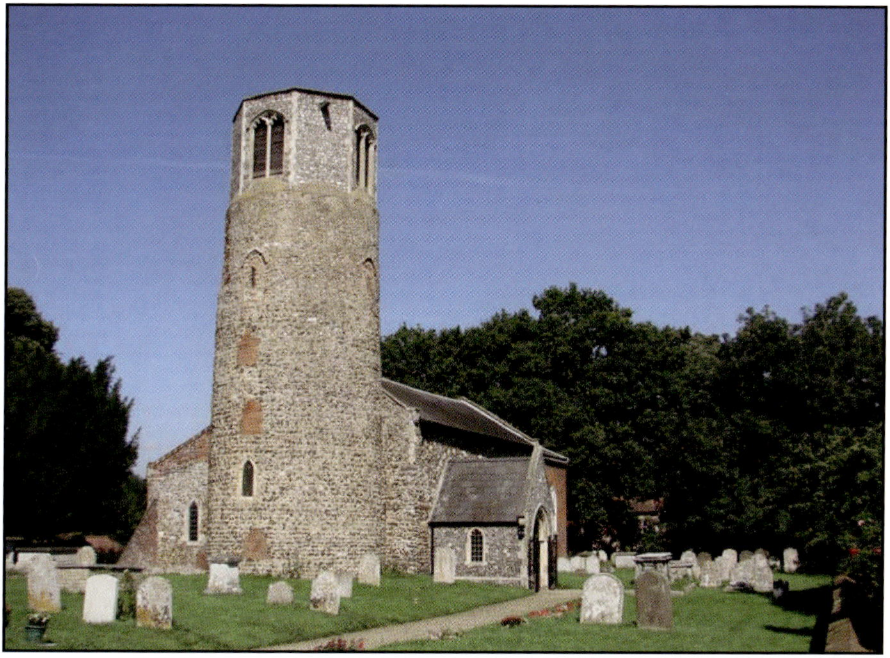

Quite out of the way, but so is Surlingham itself. One of the most peaceful places in Norfolk. The round Norman rubble-built tower has a later octagonal top with a flat roof. Some slit lancet windows in the walls have been blocked. The church was also Norman but was becoming ruinous and was completely rebuilt in the early 19th c. The south side matches the tower; on the north side is a pseudo-Norman door built of brick. They do seem however, to have run out of building materials and have used all sorts for the north aisle and chancel walls. A typical 15th c. East Anglian font has replaced the 12th c. model. The lectern is most unusual with an owl at the base beneath the eagle. A four-wheeled bier stands covered and unused. A small brass effigy in the chancel remembers John Alnwick (1460).

SURLINGHAM St Saviour

No of Bells: -
19th c. Deanery: Brooke
Hundred: Henstead
Union house: Swainsthorpe
21st c. Deanery: -
Benefice: -

5 miles E of Norwich. Follow the direction for Surlingham St Mary and go right. Best to walk the 400 yards or so to the ruin.
O.S. grid ref: TG 308069
Post Code: NR14 7DF

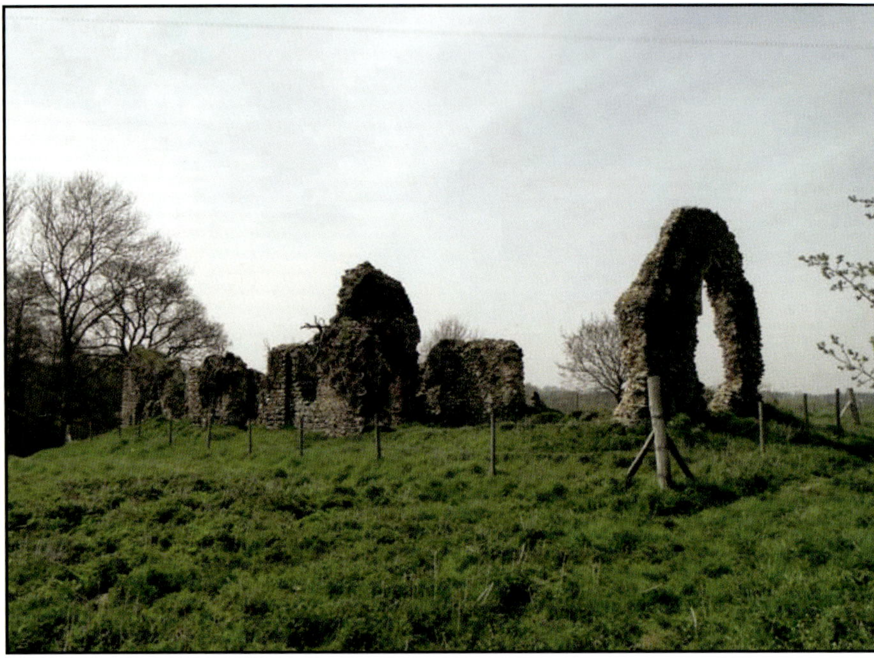

After visiting St Mary's continue walking down towards the marshes. If it's wet, take your wellies. After 500 yards or so, you will come across St Saviour's. The ruins of the tower and chancel arch indicate the small size of the church as it was. It has been in ruins for hundreds of years but is so picturesque and peaceful here and the chosen resting place of Ted Ellis the naturalist who died in 1988. The church ruins overlook Wheat Fen where he used to live with his wife Phyllis. The ruins have been recently cleared of nettles and brambles and it is possible to gain access to the ruin, but not advised. They are in a delicate state and adders have been known to inhabit in the area. It is however, a beautiful place for a picnic, and you couldn't be in nicer company. Ted's, that is, not the adders.

SUTTON St Michael

No of Bells: 3

19th c. Deanery: Waxham

Hundred: Happing

Union house: Smallburgh

21st c. Deanery: Waxham & Tunstead

Benefice: Stalham

10 miles SE of North Walsham just off the A149. Turn into Staithe Road, right into Old Yarmouth Road, 2nd left, 2nd left again.

O.S. grid ref: TG 389241

Post Code: NR12 9SA

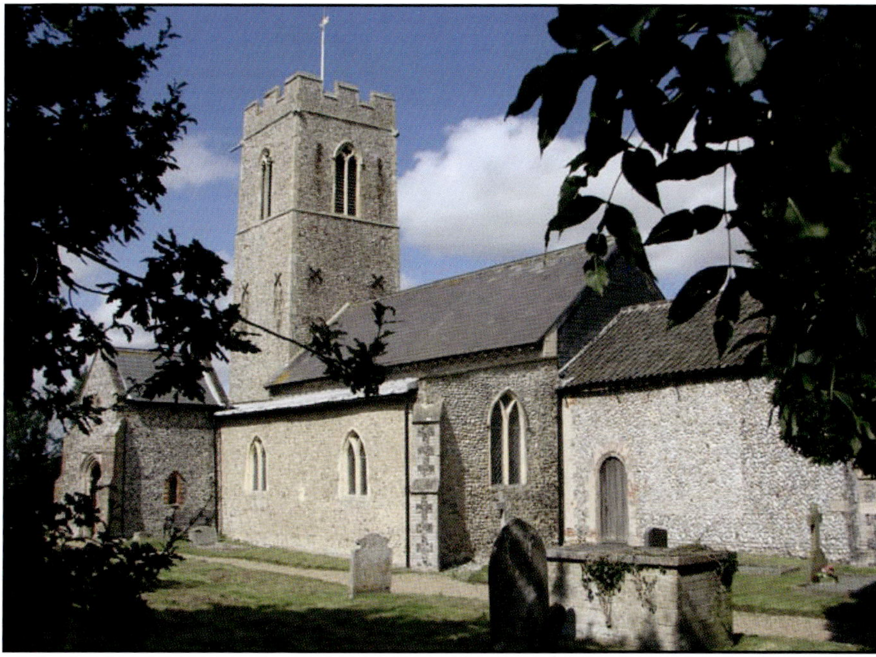

The Tudor porch has a lovely arch over the doorway. Just inside the south door is the access to the parvise which used to be above the porch. On the opposite side is a stoup. The church dates back to the 14th c. but has been very much restored in its lifetime. The chancel was virtually rebuilt in 1849. Although there is no chancel arch, the 14th c. arcade and the variation in the height of the roofs mark the distinction. A handsome 14th c. font has an octagonal bowl with traceried arcading for decoration. The shaft has eight more arcades with columns separating them. Victorian benches have some nice poppy heads, two of them quite early. The pulpit, the date of which evades me, has a carved design around the top. The 14th c. chancel piscina has been removed and the sedilia are divided by the altar rail.

SWAFIELD St Nicholas
No of Bells: 4
19th c. Deanery: Waxham
Hundred: Tunstead
Union house: Smallburgh
21st c. Deanery: Repps
Benefice: Trunch Team Ministry

1 mile N of North Walsham. Leave North Walsham on the B1145 but at Swafield take the Trunch road for about ½ a mile.
O.S. grid ref: TG 287320
Post Code: NR28 0PG

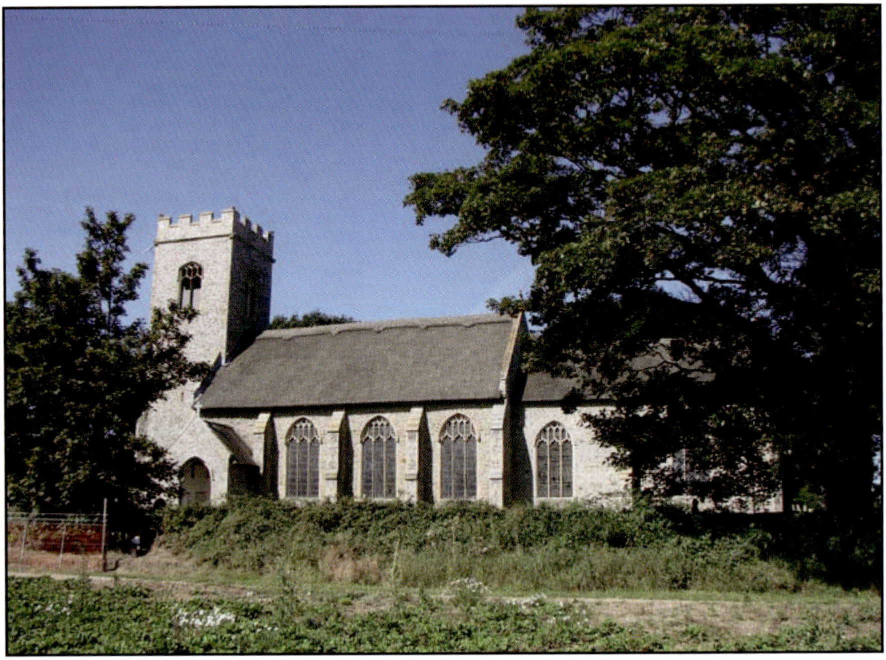

This is a very neat church and nicely proportioned. The Perpendicular windows match each other perfectly and the thatch on the roof is the ideal foil for the grey dressed flint of the walls. Both tower and church are 15th c. with a rebuilt porch that contains a deep stoup. Your eye will be immediately attracted by the re-cut font which has quatrefoil designs around the octagonal bowl. The nave is well lit despite not having a clerestory. Above is the wide span of the timber-lined arch-braced roof. At the apex, various carved bosses can be seen. On the right is the pulpit, and on the left is a beautifully carved lectern in the form of an angel. Behind her the base of the screen has tracery panels with unspoiled paintings of eight saints; Andrew, Peter, Jude, Simon, James the Great, John, Thomas and James the Less.

SWANTON ABBOT St Michael

No of Bells: 1
19th c. Deanery: Ingworth
Hundred: South Erpingham
Union house: Aylsham
21st c. Deanery: Ingworth
Benefice: Waxham & Tunstead

4 miles E of Aylsham. From the A140 at Aylsham go through Burgh & Skeyton. In Swanton Abbott turn left at east end of the village.
O.S. grid ref: TG 266264
Post Code: NR10 5DY

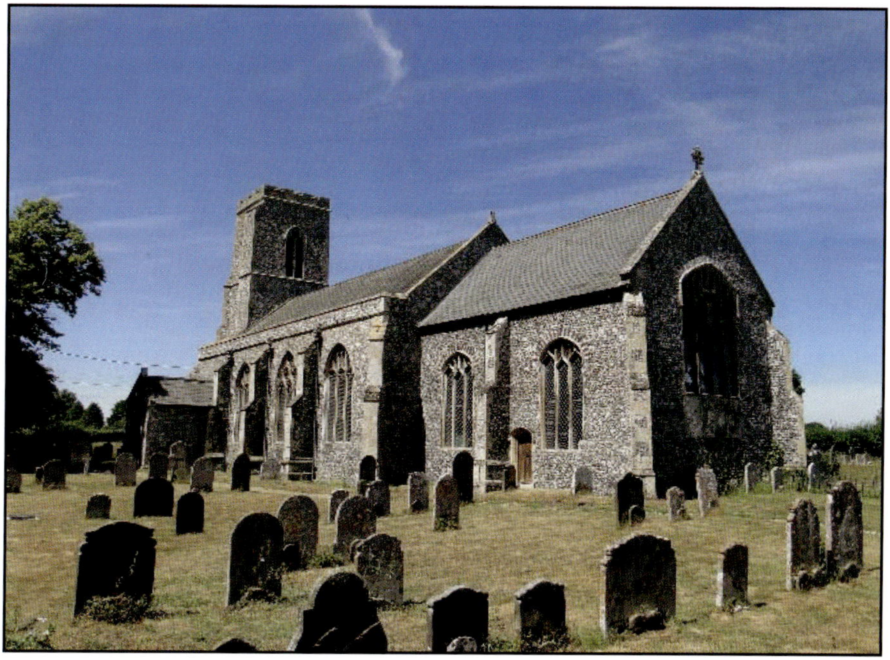

Before entering the church have a look around the outside. There is a scratch dial and next to a window is a memorial stone for Joseph Bear age 3. The 14th c tower has a plain parapet and was built a century after the church, which still has its original door, I believe, complete with knocker. At the west of the nave is the octagonal 14th c. font with quatrefoil design around the bowl and traceried arcades on the shaft. The chancel has been raised to such a height that the piscina is only a few inches away from the present floor level and the old sedilia is actually below it. The reredos, holy table and pulpit are all Victorian but not out of place, with the exception perhaps of the reredos which seems a little over the top in a small church. The screen has been turned around to face the east, and damaged in the process.

THORPE-next-HADDISCOE St Mathias *****

No of Bells:	2	5 miles E of Loddon. From
19th c. Deanery:	Brooke	the A143 at Haddiscoe head
Hundred:	Clavering	NW at the pub and follow
Union house:	Heckingham	the road just over 1 mile.
21st c. Deanery:	Loddon	O.S. grid ref: TM 436981
Benefice:	Raveningham	Post Code: NR14 6PT

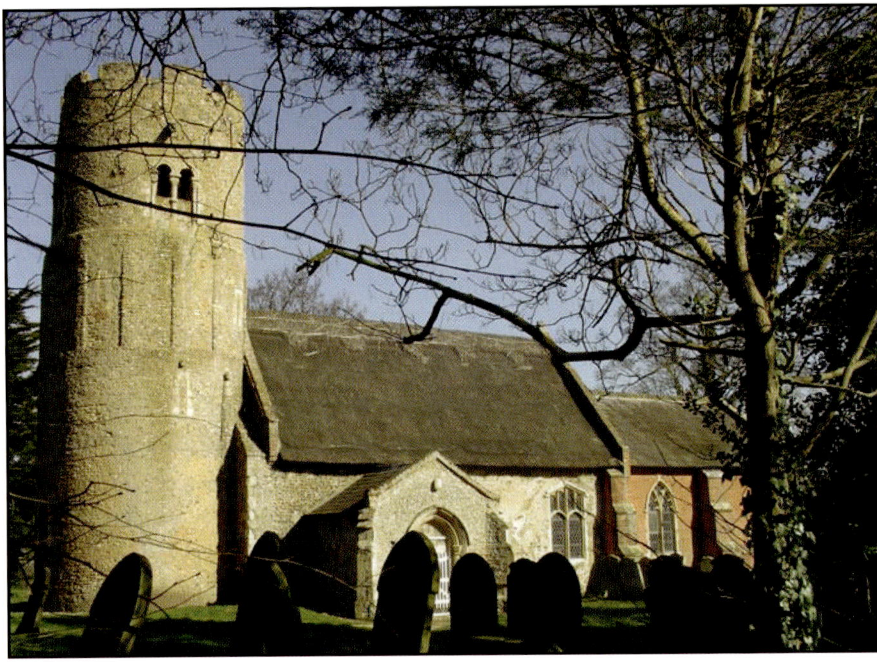

This splendid little church has a Saxon tower base, above that is Norman with typical Norman windows with a knopped central pillar. The thatched nave is of the same period, although both the roofs are later. The porch is later but both the north and south doors are again Norman, the former is now blocked. There are a pair of niches in the west wall which were once lockers. The purbeck square font is from the early 13th c. and is arcaded on all sides. It is supported by a central shaft and columns at each corner, typical of the period. There are no aisles and the restorers have not had detracted from the originality of this superb example of how a Norman church appeared when it was first built; apart that is, from a chancel which was added at a later date and unfortunately built of brick.

THORPE-next-NORWICH St Andrew

No of Bells: 1
19th c. Deanery: Norwich
Hundred: Norwich
Union house: Norwich
21st c. Deanery: Norwich East
Benefice: Thorpe Episcopi

2 miles E of Norwich on the old A1242 road to Great Yarmouth. Immediately before the 'Buck Inn'.
O.S. grid ref: TG 261085
Post Code: NR7 0EW

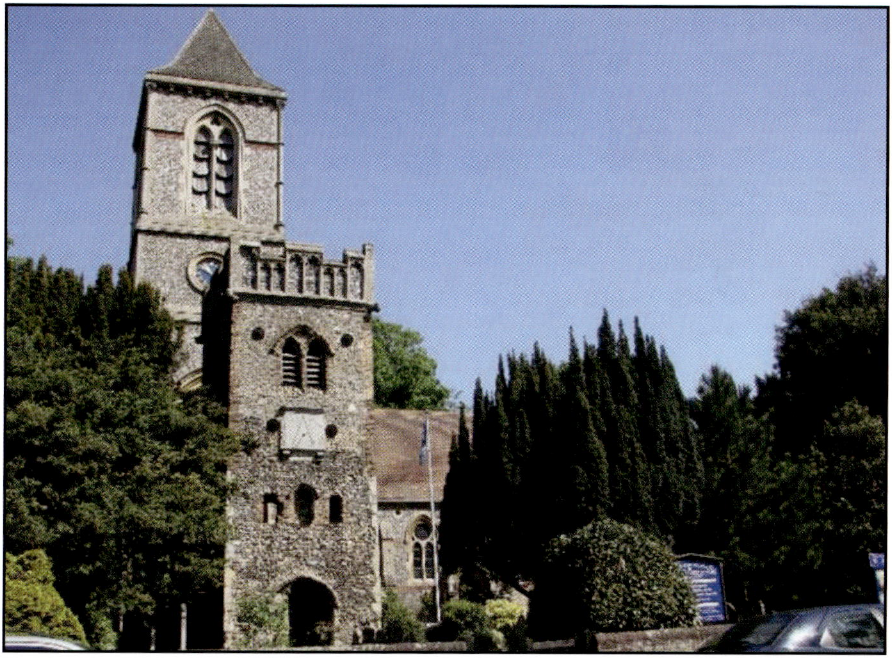

To reach the new church it is necessary to walk beneath the sundial of the tower of the old St Andrew's, which I must say seems to have had much more character than the new one. The detail in the parapet is something you won't see anywhere else. The old thatched church was demolished in the late 19th c. Some of the contents were salvaged, including the lovely Norman font, and the single bell has been re-hung. Entry is by the south tower, which doubles as a porch where monuments adorn the interior walls, rendered unreadable by the height at which they are set. The nave is clean and clinical, and intricate carvings can be seen on the capitals of the grand pillars. An attempt has been made at a sort of rood loft but it is not as impressive as was intended. The fittings and furnishings are of course Victorian.

THORPE MARKET St Margaret
No of Bells: 1
19th c. Deanery: Repps
Hundred: Erpingham
Union house: West Beckham
21st c. Deanery: Repps
Benefice: Trunch Team Ministry

5 miles SSE of Cromer.
From there take the A140, at 2 mls onto the A149 for further 2 mls, then follow the sign to 'GUNTON STATION'.
O.S. grid ref: TG 244354
Post Code: NR11 8UA

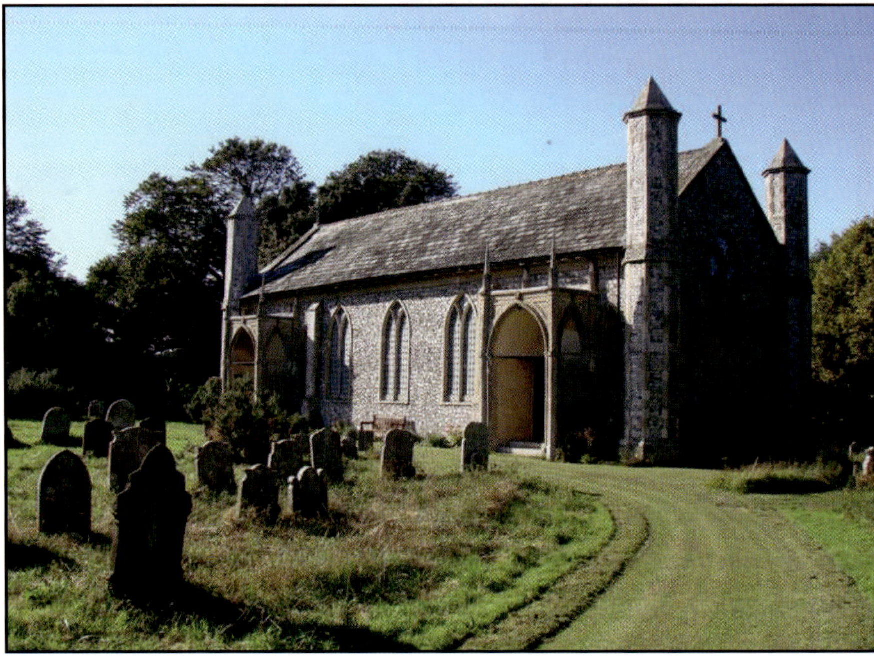

When I first saw this church, I wasn't sure whether I had found the right place. It stands on the site of an earlier church which, like nearby Gunton, was built by the Harbords at Gunton Hall. This church was erected in 1796 by the second Lord Suffield. (The former, by his grandfather.) It has a turret at each corner, two pinnacled porches and a cross on each gable; inside and out it is quite symmetrical. The mediaeval font and many of the memorials were removed from the old building and incorporated in this. The screen, which divides the nave from the chancel, is a simple, yet pleasing design. It reaches to the ceiling and bears the Royal Arms of George III, originally from St Margaret's at Lowestoft. A number of memorials are to the Rant family who were once the landowners here before the Harbords.

THRIGBY St Mary
No of Bells: 1
19th c. Deanery: Flegg
Hundred: East Flegg
Union house: Rollesby
21st c. Deanery: Great Yarmouth
Benefice: Flegg (Sth Trinity Broads)

7 miles NW of Great Yarmouth. On the A1064 head to Filby and follow the signs for the Wildlife Gardens. 50 yards before.
O.S. grid ref: TG 460123
Post Code: NR29 3DR

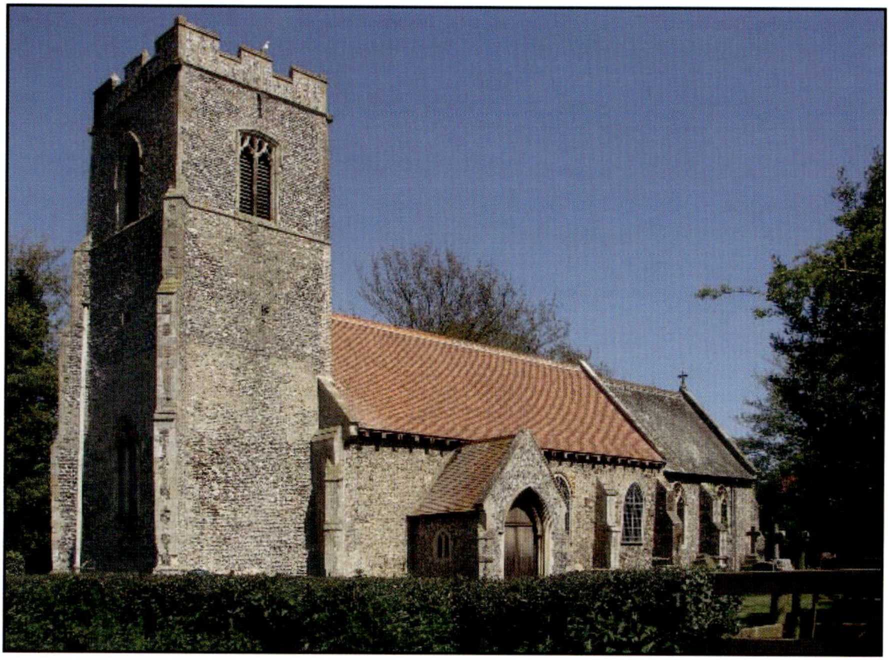

The church and tower are about 14th c. Much restoration and remedial work has lately been carried out and is now probably back in use. Inside the porch is a coeval Early English doorway with engaged columns and male and female heads on the hood-mould ends. The 15th c. octagonal font has quatrefoil design on each facet and panels around the shaft. Victorian benches fill the central aisle. The pierced tracery pulpit is floor-standing and simplicity itself. Opposite is a nicely carved eagle lectern. Consecration crosses have been preserved, one of which is scratched into the plaster. Fancy Victorian metalwork on the altar rail has a foliage design and divides the sedilia, adjacent to which is the simple cusped piscina. The Royal Arms which hang over the north door are of George III.

THURLTON All Saints
No of Bells: 5
19th c. Deanery: Brooke
Hundred: Clavering
Union house: Heckingham
21st c. Deanery: Loddon
Benefice: Raveningham

4 miles E of Loddon. From the Hales Haddiscoe road (B1136) follow road signs. Church is on the east side of the village.
O.S. grid ref: TM 417983
Post Code: NR14 6RN

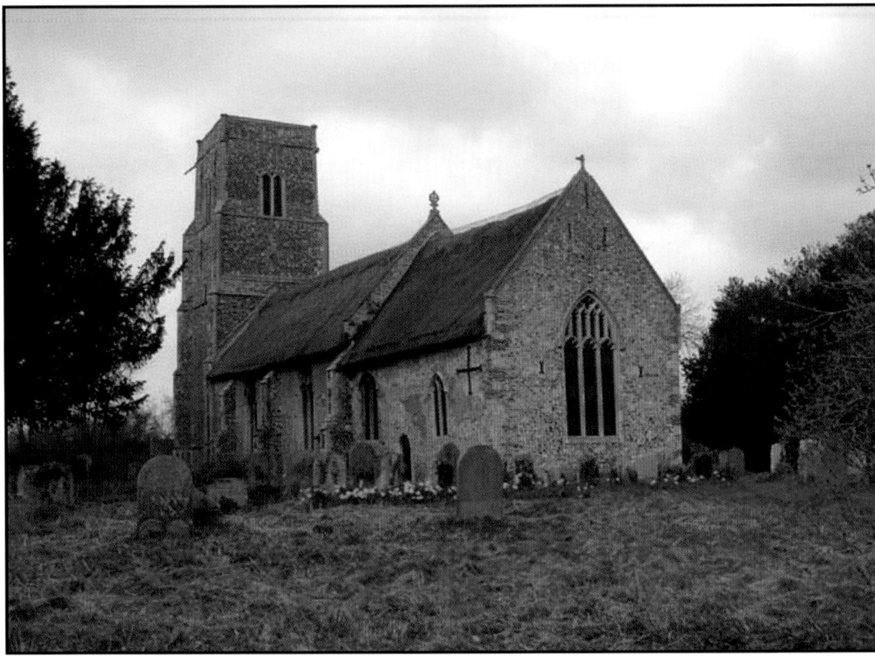

This is another of Norfolk's fine Norman churches. The roof is entirely thatched, the chancel added later and the tower rebuilt in the 15th c. Around its base the tower is decorated with panels and diamond pattern flushwork. The north porch is decorated with brickwork above the doorway, and within is a 15th c. doorway and door. The south doorway however, is Norman with two engaged columns either side and four orders of moulding. The 15th c. octagonal font is typical of the area but relatively plain. On the wall is the customary painting of St Christopher. Both pulpit and reading desk are crisply carved. The lower part of the 15th c. screen has suffered from dampness coming up through the floor, but the upper part is still in good order painted in red, green and gold.

THURNE St Edmund
No of Bells: 1
19th c. Deanery: Flegg
Hundred: West Flegg
Union house: Rollesby
21st c. Deanery: Great Yarmouth
Benefice: Flegg

11 miles NW of Great Yarmouth. Midway between Acle & Potter Heigham. On the B1152 turn west at the x-roads & continue 2 miles.
O.S. grid ref: TG 404156
Post Code: NR29 3BT

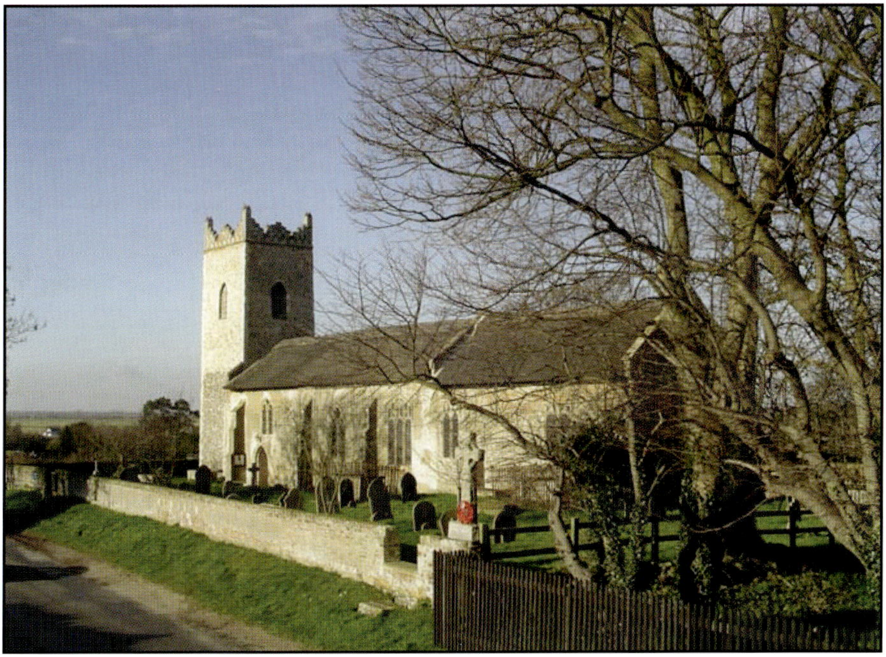

A lovely setting overlooking the marshes and River Thurne. Both nave and chancel roofs are thatched. The tower is crenulated in four stages. There is no porch. The west wall of the tower has a squint. Looking in to it you would see the altar, but looking out, St. Benet's Abbey can be seen in the distance. Coincidence or design? The shallow octagonal font is relatively modern. Benches have been replaced with box-pews. The roof inside reveals the thatch, supported only by plain arch-braces. Between the chancel arch is the old rood beam. A dropped-sill sedilia is adjacent to the trefoiled double piscina which has an octagonal central column. In the opposite wall is an aumbry. A black ledger slab in the sanctuary is to Rev. Caroli *[Charles]* Trimnell (1723) and his father Richard (1721).

THURTON	St Ethelbert
No of Bells:	3
19th c. Deanery:	Brooke
Hundred:	Loddon
Union house:	Heckingham
21st c. Deanery:	Loddon
Benefice:	Thurton

7 miles SE of Norwich. Just off the A146. On the southern side of the valley that is Thurton. Turn west at the bottom of the hill.
O.S. grid ref: TG 327006
Post Code: NR14 6AG

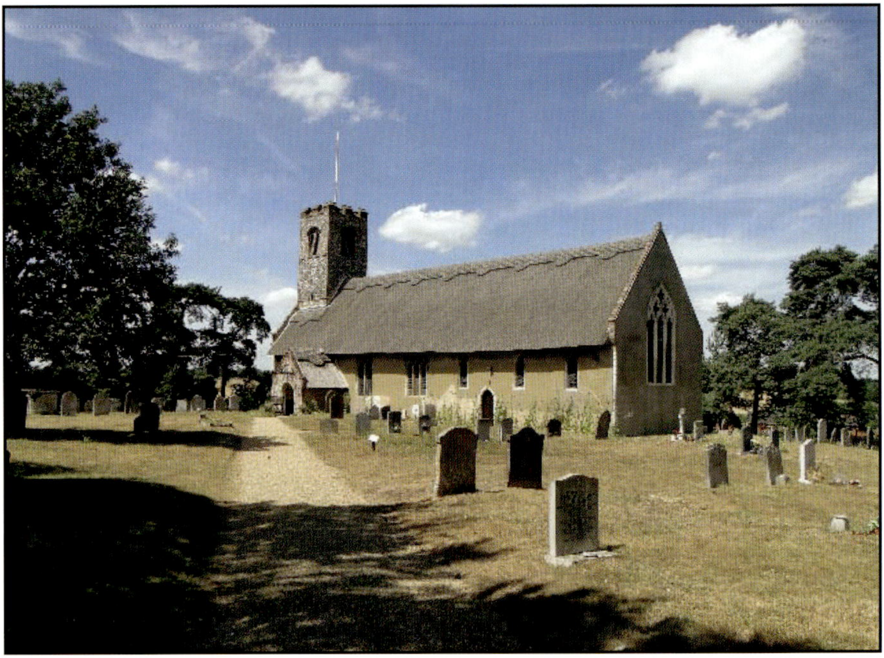

Slightly away from the main habitation, this church is unusual as the tower is incorporated in the nave leaving an unused cavity either side of the tower. The thatched roof runs the whole unbroken length of the nave and chancel. Both north and south doorways are Norman, the former quite plain but the latter has three engaged columns and four orders of decoration. The almost unrecognisable wall painting is of St Christopher. The roof is arch-braced but is plastered over. A rather plain octagonal font with a slender shaft is of no great interest. The old four-wheeled bier is used to display various bits and pieces. At the time of writing, there was a wooden coffin bearer by the nave wall. It would look nice cleaned and oiled, and on display inside the church rather than discarded.

THWAITE	St Mary
No of Bells:	2
19th c. Deanery:	Brooke
Hundred:	Loddon
Union house:	Heckingham
21st c. Deanery:	Depwade
Benefice:	Brooke

12 miles SSE of Norwich. Can be approached from Ditchingham, or Loddon direction by following the signposts. No direct route.

O.S. grid ref: TM 333950

Post Code: NR35 2EF

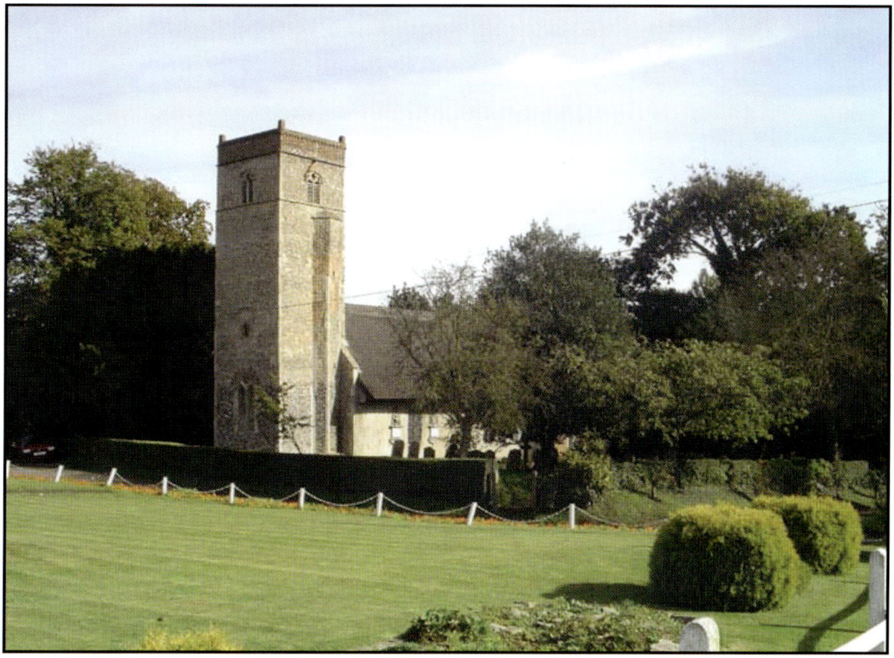

This is a lovely old church in a perfect village setting. The Norman doorway which greets you has two detached columns either side and five orders of decoration. There is no porch. The un-buttressed tower is probably also Norman and has an outside stair turret to the belfry. The chancel is built of brick and was added later. Inside, the thatched nave is simplicity itself. Lime-washed walls and ceiling contrast with the harshness of the blue-painted roof of the chancel. Somehow, it seems impertinent but not offensive. The plain octagonal bowl of the font is supported by eight engaged columns around a central shaft. The very plain pulpit bears the Jacobean date of 1624. There is a black ledger slab in the floor to Catherine London (1664). In the chancel is a simple but unusual corbel piscina.

TOFT MONKS St Margaret
No of Bells: 3
19th c. Deanery: Brooke
Hundred: Clavering
Union house: Heckingham
21st c. Deanery: Loddon
Benefice: Raveningham

5 miles SE of Loddon.
From the A146 just north of Beccles take the A143 Yarmouth road. In Toft Monks, turn left, right, left.
O.S. grid ref: TM 426952
Post Code: NR34 0ES

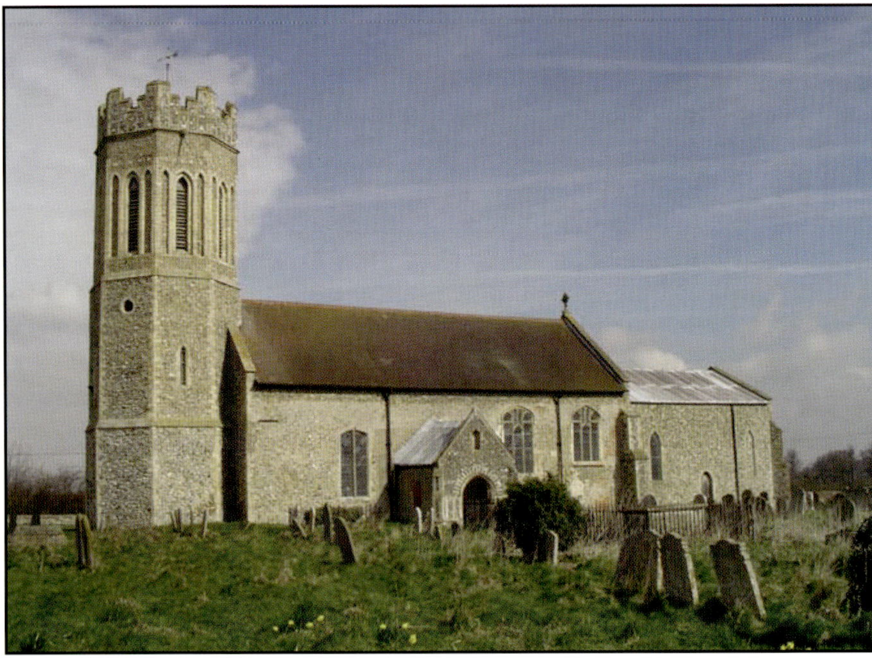

A splendid unusual wholly octagonal 13th c. tower with 15th c. stepped crenulations round the parapet. The belfry stage is triple arcaded on each face and below slit windows. Inside the nave, a doorway into the tower shows it to have been defendable. The nave and chancel are later. The large cambered beam at the west end was used to raise the font cover, which is no longer there. The font itself is an example of an early 15th c. traditional type. The simple arch-braced roof is decorated at the intersections with floral designs. The present cover is relatively modern. A memorial with Arms above is to John Bayspoole (1624). There are two sets of Royal Arms, the earlier, dated 1661, is of Charles II, the other of George II and bears the date 1745. Architecturally, a very interesting tower and church.

TOPCROFT St Margaret

No of Bells:	3, 1 usable
19th c. Deanery:	Brooke
Hundred:	Loddon
Union house:	Heckingham
21st c. Deanery:	Depwade
Benefice:	Hempnall

5 miles NW of Bungay. Best accessed from the B1135 and follow road signs to Topcroft, and Church Road.

O.S. grid ref: TM 265929

Post Code: NR35 1BH

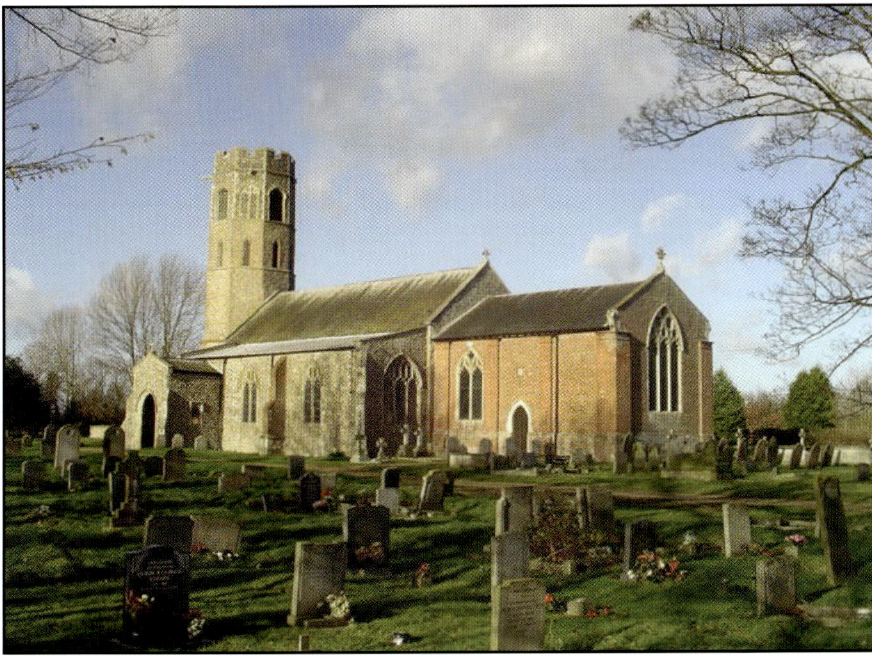

The octagonal embattled top of the tower was added in the 15th c. to the round Norman or possibly Saxon base. The brick-built chancel, rebuilt in 1712, and internally restored in 1876, sticks out like a sore thumb. The south porch has a stoup on the right-hand side and a shelf for a bowl inside; yet another can be found inside the nave. The 15th c. font is of typical East Anglian style with lions round the shaft and in quite good condition. South of the nave is a 14th c. arcade of columns, forming a south aisle. The nave roof is a 'pseudo' hammerbeam with arch-bracing of a type not often seen. Next to the rood loft stairs is the pulpit standing on a single foot. Wall monuments to the Smythe family adorn the walls of the chancel. The wall paintings are from the time the restorations took place.

TRIMINGHAM St John the Baptist's Head

No of Bells: 1
19th c. Deanery: Repps
Hundred: North Erpingham
Union house: Gimingham
21st c. Deanery: Repps
Benefice: Overstrand

6 miles N of North Walsham. The church overlooks the sea between Overstrand and Mundesley.
O.S. grid ref: TG 279388
Post Code: NR11 8EE

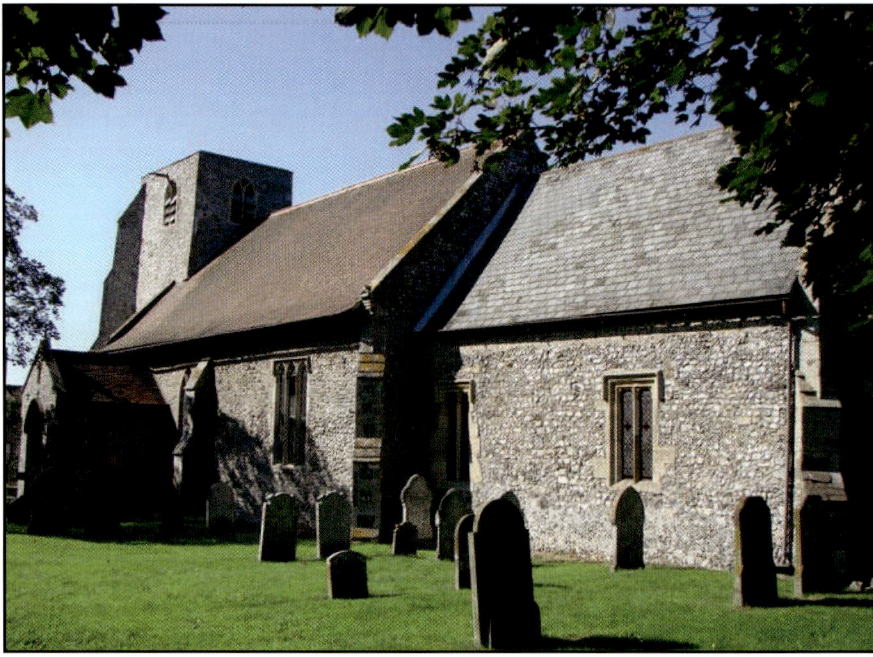

The unique dedication is believed to be due to the fact the church pretended to own the head of John the Baptist to encourage pilgrims to visit. All they had was an alabaster replica. The tower, I think, was never finished and the roofs are modern replacements. The 14th c. font is indifferently decorated and supported on a pillared central shaft. Although the church has undergone restoration, the character has been retained and the feel of the old church is ever present. The screen is the church's best asset. The lower panels bear paintings of Sts Edmund, Clare, Clement, James the Great, Petronilla, Dorothy, Cecilia and Edward. Details are given about them, which is helpful. In the chancel is the original 14th c. piscina, which has seen better days. The adjacent sedilia is in the style of dropped window sill.

TROWSE-with-NEWTON St Andrew

No of Bells:	1
19th c. Deanery:	Brooke
Hundred:	Henstead
Union house:	Swainsthorpe
21st c. Deanery:	Norwich East
Benefice:	Norwich Trowse

1 mile SE of Norwich.
Leave Norwich by County Hall and follow road signs to Trowse, over the railway bridge & 400 yds.
O.S. grid ref: TG 246068
Post Code: NR14 8SX

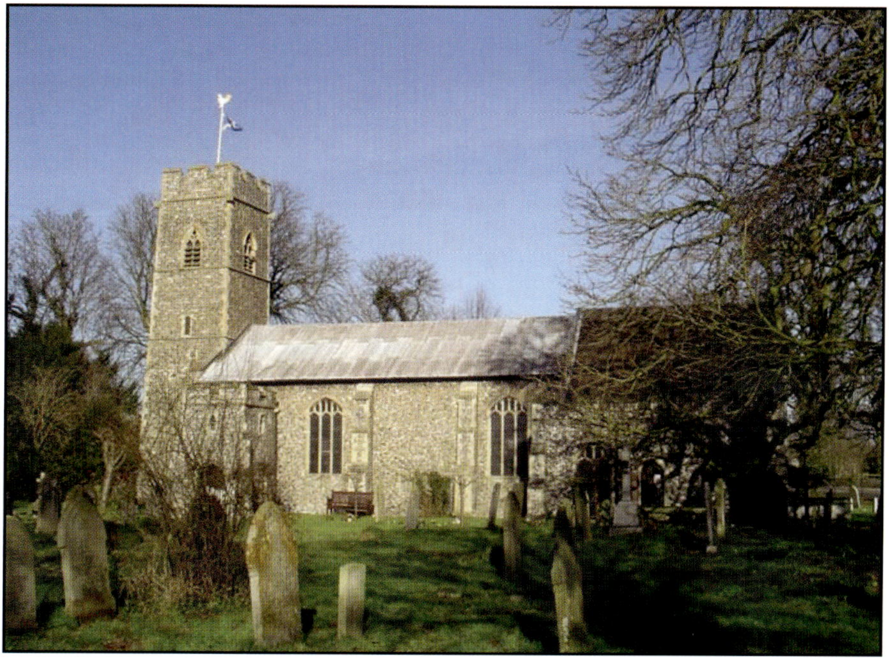

Although the church has a 15th c. appearance, some elements of this church are surprisingly older. The chancel is 13th c. and there is a plaque to Wilelmus de Kirkebei who was prior from 1272 to 1288. Over the 15th c. groined porch is a small parvise. The roofs have been replaced over the years and are relatively modern. The 15th c. octagonal font is in the traditional style with saintly emblems round the bowl. The shaft has lions and seated figures between them. Of all the items of interest in the church I think the 1902 pulpit is the most stunning. Three beautifully carved life-size figures are seated round it playing musical instruments, and in the chancel the reredos bearing a striking resemblance in quality depicts the Last Supper. Almost always locked but well worth the trouble of finding a keyholder.

TRUNCH	St Botolph *****	3 miles N of North Walsham. Leave Nth Walsham by the B1145 and follow to Trunch, passing Swafield church on the way.
No of Bells:	1	
19th c. Deanery:	Repps	
Hundred:	North Erpingham	
Union house:	Gimingham	
21st c. Deanery:	Repps	O.S. grid ref: TG 286349
Benefice:	Trunch Team Ministry	Post Code: NR28 0PT

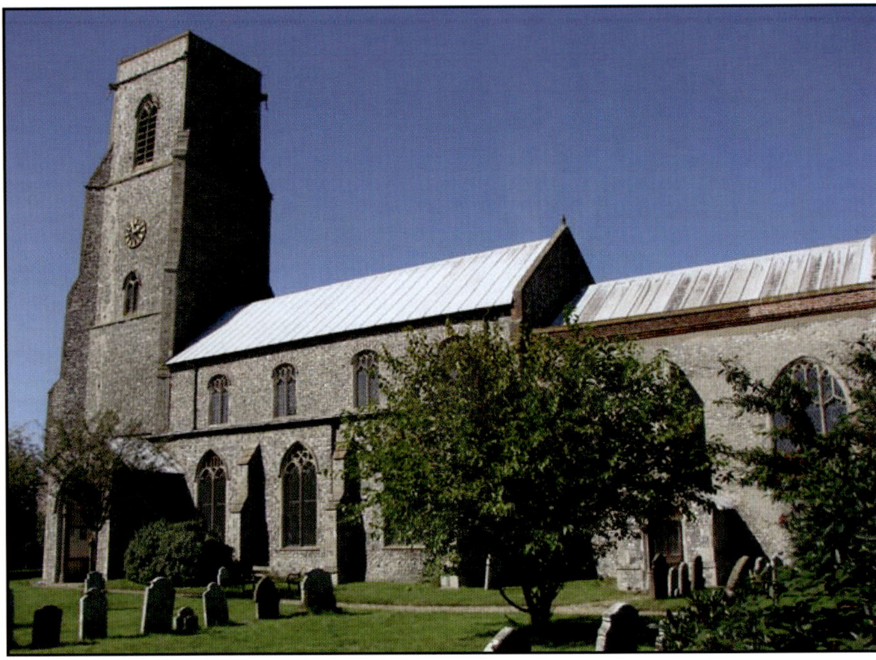

Trunch is a lively and vibrant church and one of the most interesting in Norfolk. The church, clerestory and tower date from the 14th c., the porch was added a century later. Even the chancel door has a porch. The octagonal font has quatrefoil decoration and above it is a quite unique canopy, five feet across and surmounted by a ‘crown’ with six crocketted ogee arches converging in a finial, all still painted in the original colours. Behind it, set into the tower arch, is an arch-braced frame forming the ringing floor for the, now, single bell. The screen has open tracery and twelve saintly panels below. The nave roof is single hammerbeam and the richness of the tracery in the spandrils is outstanding. In the chancel are some old misericordes worth lifting. There is much more to see here but space restricts. Well worth a visit.

TUNSTALL	St Peter & St Paul
No of Bells:	0
19th c. Deanery:	Blofield
Hundred:	Walsham
Union house:	Acle
21st c. Deanery:	Freethorpe
Benefice:	Blofield

8 miles W of Gt. Yarmouth. Turn off the A47 to Halvergate. Continue to T junction and turn right into Tunstall Road for 1 mile. Dead end.
O.S. grid ref: TG 416080
Post Code: NR13 3PS

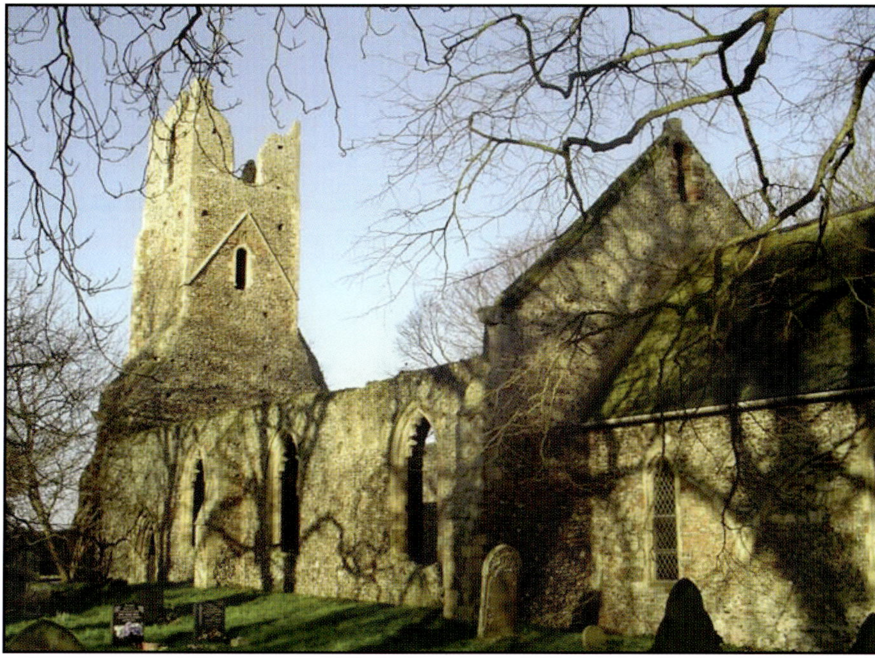

Although the tower and nave are ruinous the occasional service is still held in the chancel, now regarded as a chapel. Many years after the church fell into disuse the chancel was restored by local benefactors Elizabeth Jenkinson and Anne Kelsale in 1705, and was primarily intended as a mortuary chapel. Later however the chapel was extended eastwards and a window inserted. Notice that below the apex of the old roof is a sanctus window. The 19th c. saw a vestry added on the north wall. It is as simple as it can be, but very welcoming.. Architecturally it has little to offer, but the history is all around you, it oozes from the walls. This is probably (and I stand to be corrected) the smallest church in the county and it only has the minimum number of services to retain its status, long may it continue.

TUNSTEAD St Mary
No of Bells: 5
19th c. Deanery: Waxham
Hundred: Tunstead
Union house: Smallburgh
21st c. Deanery: Waxham & Tunstead
Benefice: Tunstead

6 miles S of Nth Walsham. Almost a mile NE of the village! South of the village turn left and left again avoiding railway crossing.
O.S. grid ref: TG 308227
Post Code: NR12 8HU

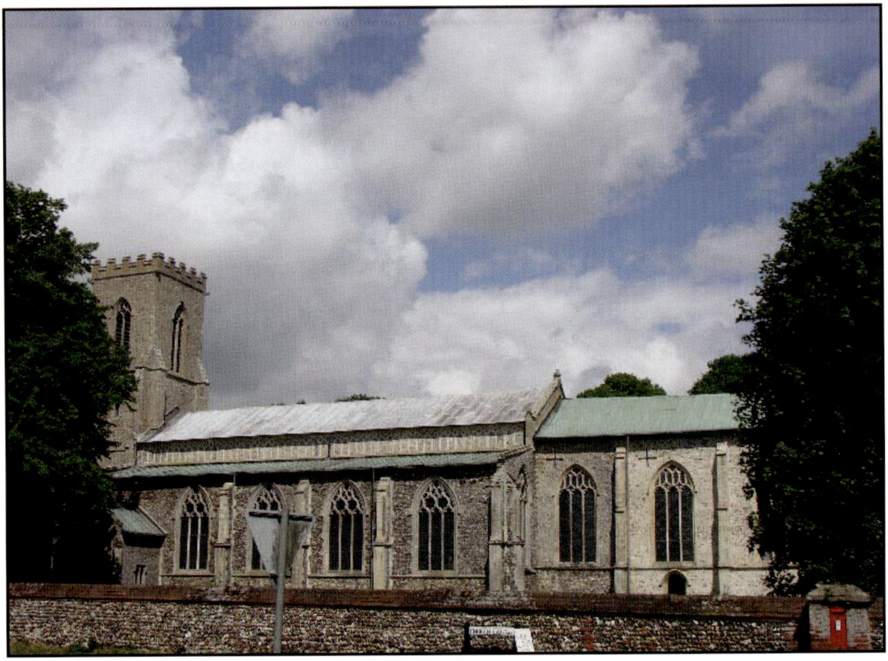

A trefoil trail round the base of the 15th c. tower, and gargoyles below the finely embattled parapet, make this tower quite attractive. Protected by the Victorian porch is a fine door with wrought ironwork radiating from a central boss. Adjacent to one of the splendid columns is an unusual octagonal 'poor-man's box'. Lofty 15th c. arcades lead the eye to the real treasure here; the beautiful 'old style' screen with eighteen saints depicted and named, including the Four Doctors. On the north wall outside is the redundant access turret to the rood loft. Standing on a stone base with steps is the nicely carved pulpit. In the chancel are a matching multi-cusped piscina and three sedile. Behind the altar is a mysterious stone platform with a vaulted chamber below; its purpose is not understood. Perhaps to contain religious relics!

UPTON	St Margaret
No of Bells:	1
19th c. Deanery:	Blofield
Hundred:	Walsham
Union house:	Acle
21st c. Deanery:	Blofield
Benefice:	Ranworth Broadside

9 miles WNW of Great Yarmouth. From Acle take the South Walsham road for 1 mile then right after hotel complex, Church in 400 yds.
O.S. grid ref: TG 393122
Post Code: NR13 6AR

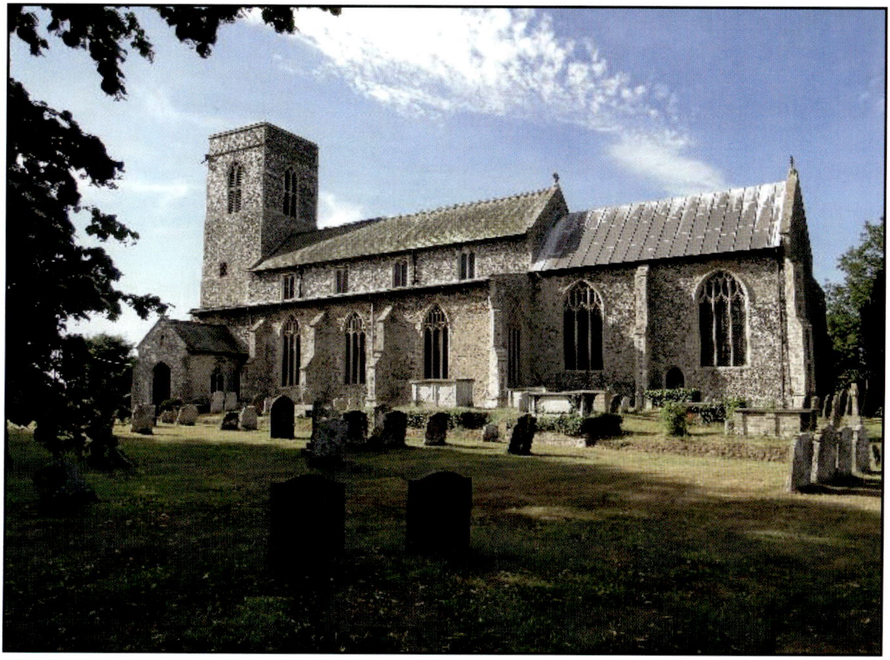

This lovely clerestoried 15th c. church is well worth visiting. The south porch leads into the south aisle rather than the nave. Just inside the door there is a niche with a stoup made from a Norman capital. Nearby is a 'poor man's box' with an iron lid and clasp, probably hewn from the end of an old beam. Against the north wall is an old bier that has seen better days. The 14th c. font probably predates the church. Round the octagonal bowl are angels and emblems of the saints; below are delicately traceried canopies with saints beneath. The whole stands on three steps, the top one carved with quatrefoils and animal figures. The base of the screen depicts the Four Doctors and four saints. Within the dropped window sill of the chancel is the piscina and sedilia. The Royal Arms are of George III.

WALCOTT	All Saints	1½ miles NW of Happisburgh. Follow the road north from there and you will pass the church on the way into Walcott
No of Bells:	1	
19th c. Deanery:	Waxham	
Hundred:	Happing	
Union house:	Smallburgh	
21st c. Deanery:	Waxham & Tunstead	O.S. grid ref: TG 361318
Benefice:	Happisburgh	Post Code: NR12 0PD

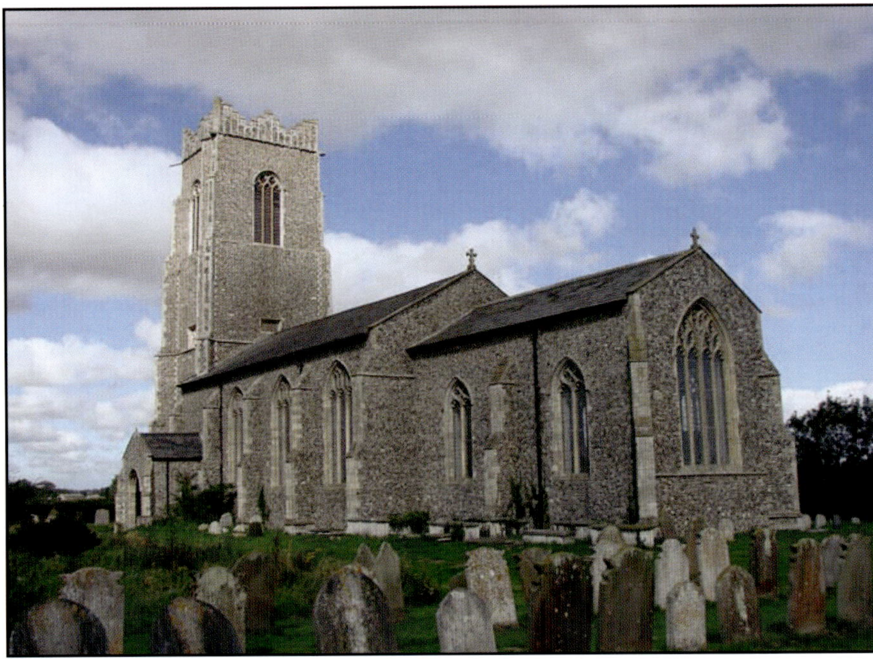

Anciently called Wolcot. The church is ½ mile south of the populated part of the village. A neat looking church with little in the way of shoddy repairs. The parapet has neatly stepped crenulations. The Purbeck octagonal font is 13th c. with double arcades on each facet and still bears some of its original paintwork. The nave and chancel are flooded with light from the large windows. An unusual lectern has the eagle chained to the base and is a memorial to those who fell in the Great War. Another more conventional memorial hangs on the west wall behind the font. Behind the altar rail, the attractive piscina and three-seat sedilia have clustered columns and multi-foil arches. Behind the altar is a beautifully carved reredos, and the parish chest is of a style I have never before encountered.

WAXHAM	St John	5½ miles E of Stalham. Just off the coast road, best accessed from Stalham and then through Sea Palling and take left at right-hand bend .
No of Bells:	None ever installed	
19th c. Deanery:	Waxham	
Hundred:	Happing	
Union house:	Smallburgh	
21st c. Deanery:	Waxham & Tunstead	O.S. grid ref: TG 441263
Benefice:	Happisburgh	Post Code: NR12 0DY

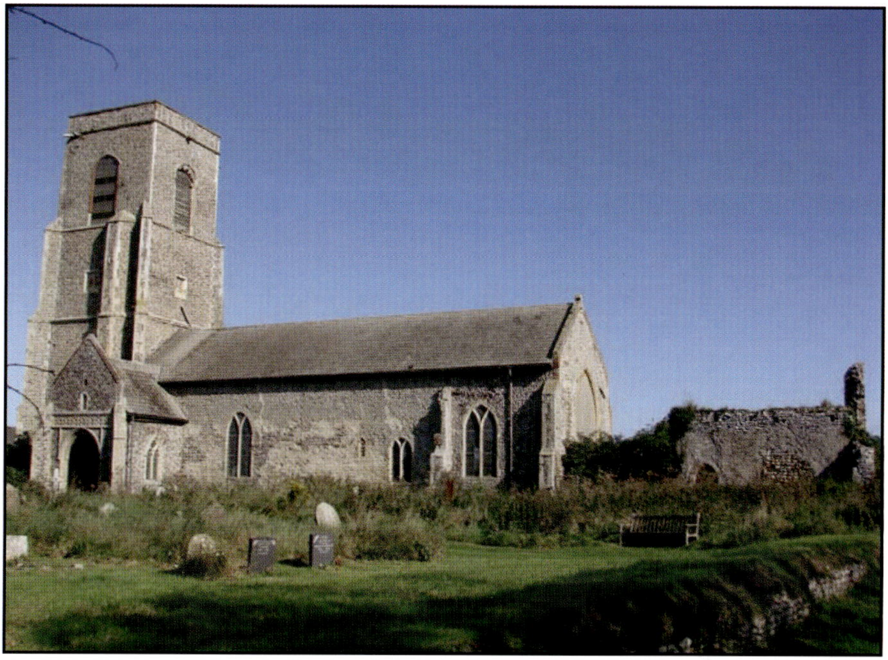

Waxham Parva St Margaret was taken by the sea many centuries ago, Waxham Magna St John remains, the chancel having collapsed centuries ago. Sadly, despite the best efforts of the parishioners, this too may become redundant. The west window of the 15th c. tower has been bricked up. The nave has noticeably few windows on the south and less on the north. The 15th c. porch seems to be in a better condition than the rest of the church. There is nice tracery in the spandrils and above is a band of decorative stonework. The font is from the 14th c. and is decorated with quatrefoils on each of the eight facets. It stands on a double brick plinth. Built into the north wall is a banner stave locker, now minus its door. A significant tomb in the chancel is to Thomas Wodehouse (1571) once lord of the manor.

WEST CAISTER St Edmund the Martyr

No of Bells:	-
19th c. Deanery:	Flegg
Hundred:	Flegg
Union house:	Rollesby
21st c Deanery:	-
Benefice:	-

1 mile WSW of Caister Holy Trinity church. Take the dual carriageway from Yarmouth and follow signs to West Caister. For O.S. ref. & postcode see page 253.

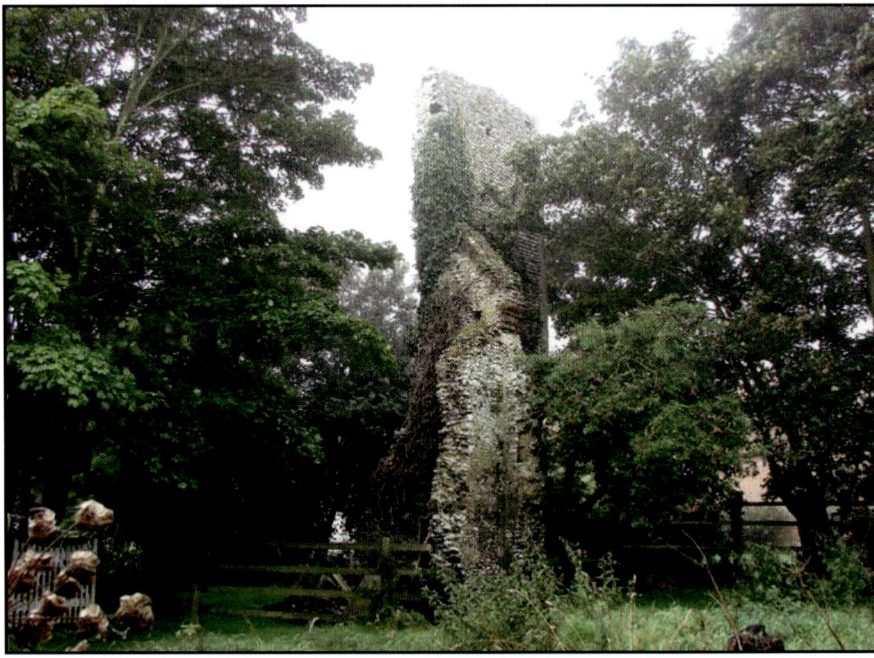

This lovely ruin is in someone's back garden. What I wouldn't give for one like it. In 1608 the two Caister parishes of St Edmund and Holy Trinity were consolidated and the church of St Edmund was left to decay. Gradually over the years piles of rubble have been carted away and when the rest of the tower finally hits the ground, as it surely will, that too will probably be removed. A few years ago it was protected from the worst of the weather by a thick coat of ivy and that perhaps is why we can still see something of the mediaeval church that once stood here. Now, with the protection removed, the frost and rain will erode these last vestiges of what was once a focal point and place of worship for the Early Edwardian population of the parish, including the Fastolffs who once lived in nearby Caister Castle.

WEST CAISTER St Edmund the Martyr

No of Bells: 0
19th c. Deanery: Flegg
Hundred: Flegg
Union house: Rollesby
21st c Deanery: Great Yarmouth
Benefice: Caister

1 mile WSW of Caister Holy Trinity church. From A1064 / A149 roundabout left after motor museum.
O.S. grid ref: TG 508117
Post Code: NR30 5SY

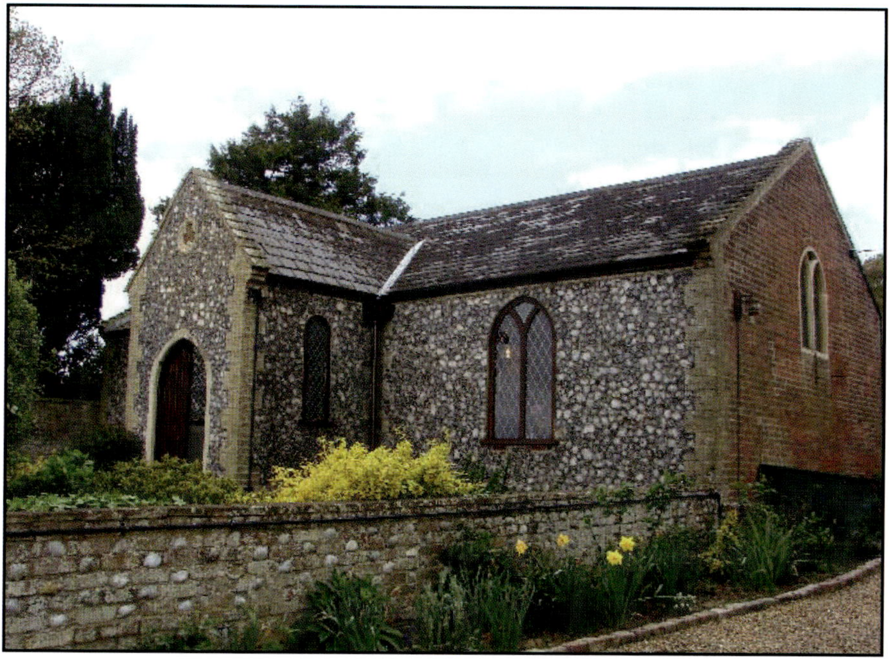

In the mid-1850s this church was built probably as a need was felt locally to have a church nearer home. After the demise of St Edmund's *(previous page)* in the 17th c. the villagers worshiped at Caister Holy Trinity *(page 36)* some distance away. Or perhaps Caister was too High Church for them. But, whatever the reason this little church has a good congregation. The square font is simplicity itself; round basin and shaft on a square base without any form of decoration. The bare emulsioned walls express the desire of the people to keep the services simple, without elaboration, pomp or ceremony other than traditional rituals of worship. On the Altar rail are two wolf heads carved into the woodwork, the only reference I found to St Edmund. It could easily be mistaken for a Village Hall.

WEST SOMERTON St Mary

No of Bells:	1 - (13th c.)
19th c. Deanery:	Flegg
Hundred:	West Flegg
Union house:	Rollesby
21st c. Deanery:	Great Yarmouth
Benefice:	Flegg (Coastal)

9 m NNW of Great Yarmouth, & 1 mile west of Winterton on the road towards Martham. Turn left just after The Street.

O.S. grid ref: TG 475195
Post Code: NR29 4DR

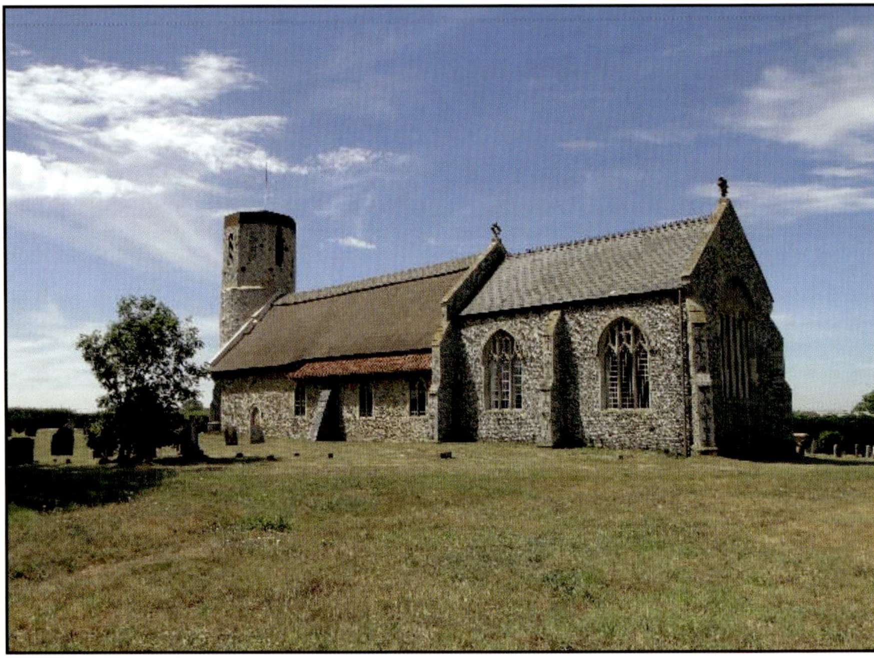

It's quite certain that a church has stood here since long before the Norman invasion. Some 11th c. walls are incorporated into the 14th c. nave. The tower is Norman with a 14th c. octagonal upper section. The wall art which once adorned the nave was painted in the 14th c. and the chancel was added in the 15th. The screen dates from that period, as does the lovely concave panelled and delicately traceried pulpit. The plain octagonal font is early 15th c. In the chancel is a dropped-sill sedilia but no trace of the piscina remains. On the walls are memorials to members of the Rising family, but perhaps what most people come here to see is the grave of the 'Norfolk Giant', Robert Hales, who grew to a height of 7 feet 8 inches and weighed 32 stones. In his lifetime he was presented to Queen Victoria.

WESTWICK	St Botolph	3 m S of North Walsham.
No of Bells:	1	Take the B1150 through
19th c. Deanery:	Waxham	Westwick village. Left after
Hundred:	Tunstead	parkland and then 1st left
Union house:	Smallburgh	again after 300 yds.
21st c. Deanery:	Waxham & Tunstead	O.S. grid ref: TG 285259
Benefice:	Worstead	Post Code: NR10 5BW

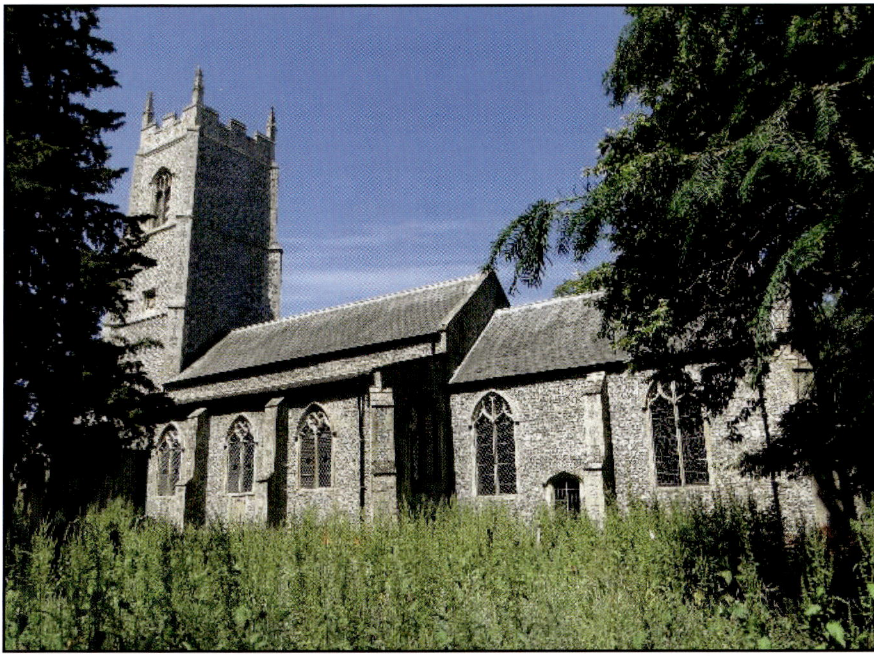

The church, on the Westwick House Estate is quite remote from the village. There is no keyholder listed so I couldn't gain entry. There must be something very valuable inside to risk a broken window costing thousands to replace. Atop the embattled parapet of the tower are four crocketted pinnacles and around the base is a course of shields and emblems. Through a window I could see the carved octagonal font with lions around the base, but the screen which I was informed was restored during the Victorian era and has the images of twelve saints, I could not. Most of the fittings and furnishings are Victorian as are the Victorian Royal Arms which hang over the tower doorway. This is a nice church, but without visitors it might as well not be there and is no more than a shed to keep stuff in. Poor show!

WHEATACRE All Saints

No of Bells: 1
19th c. Deanery: Brooke
Hundred: Clavering
Union house: Heckingham
21st c. Deanery: Loddon
Benefice: Raveningham

7 m SE of Loddon hidden behind trees in Church Road which is the Haddiscoe - Burgh St Peter Road.
O.S. grid ref: TM 460939
Post Code: NR34 0AU

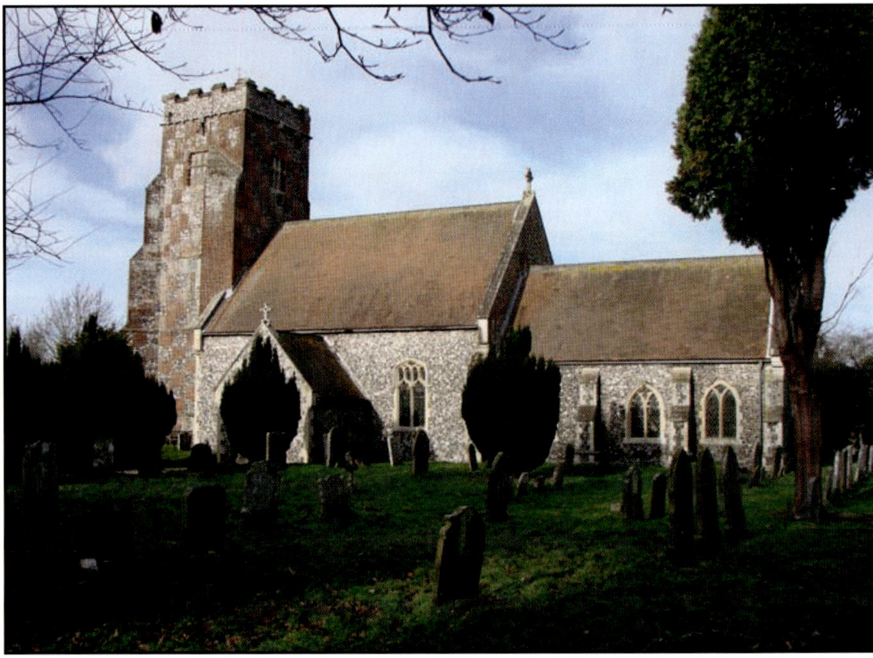

The 16th c. west tower has chequering in flint and brick, giving it a quite unique appearance. The chancel is the earliest part of the present building, once flanked by two chapels, the south having been demolished centuries ago, but the blocked arches remain. The 14th c. doorway beneath the porch has the head of a king and queen as hood-mould terminals. Inside the nave is a typical East Anglian font which was painted many years ago and is happily peeling. The five feet tall font cover is more interesting, with some lovely examples of the woodcarver's art, although this, like the rood screen, has no great age. Set into the window reveal of the south chancel window is a small piscina, the like of which I have not yet encountered. The names Gooch, Gwavas and Chester are mentioned on black ledger slabs.

WHITLINGHAM St Andrew

No of Bells: -
19th c. Deanery: Brooke
Hundred: Henstead
Union house: Swainsthorpe
21st c. Deanery: -
Benefice: -

3 m E of Norwich City centre. at the far end of Whitlingham Lane. On the right, in woodland and now almost inaccessible.
O.S. grid ref: TG 274078
Post Code: NR14 8TZ

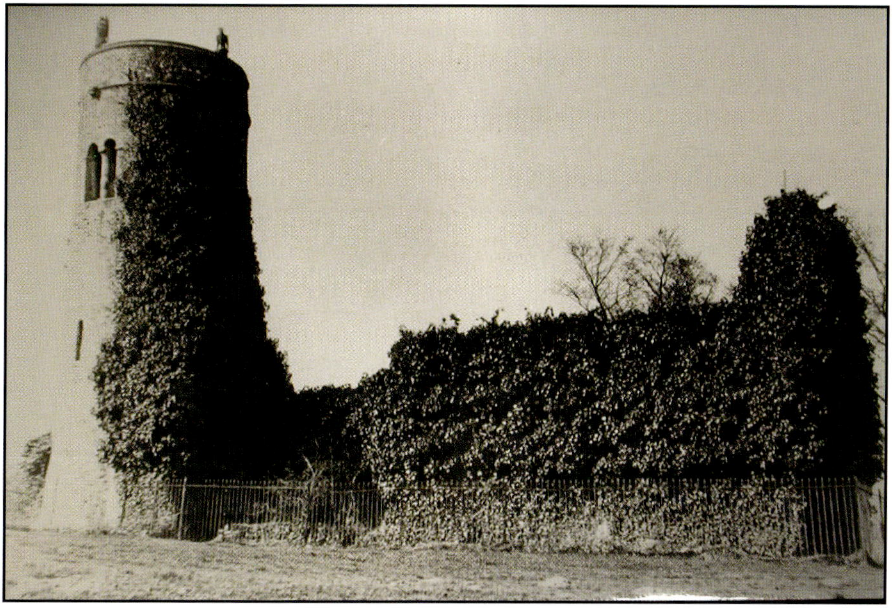

With acknowledgements to the unknown photographer

At the far end of Whitlingham Lane, which is 100 yards south of Trowse bridge, are the remains of a once lovely church. It was already falling down in 1630 and for almost 300 years remained as you see it above. In 1940 the tower eventually collapsed, and even more recently the ivy and tree roots have taken their toll. The structure is now no more than a few walls and heaps of rubble, some lying at the bottom of the hill on the north side. During Victorian times the ruin was enhanced and to some extent consolidated into a picturesque ruin. As can be seen from the above 19th c. photograph the grass was kept neat and tidy and it was on the route of a popular walk and was probably a picnic area. On the top of the tower *[seen above]* are two remaining saintly figures of which there were once four.

WICKHAMPTON St Andrew *****

No of Bells: 1
19th c. Deanery: Blofield
Hundred: Walsham
Union house: Acle
21st c. Deanery: Blofield
Benefice: Freethorpe

8 m W of Great Yarmouth in Church Road. Turn south of the A47 towards Halvergate, turn right then first left to Wickhampton.
O.S. grid ref: TG 427054
Post Code: NR13 3PB

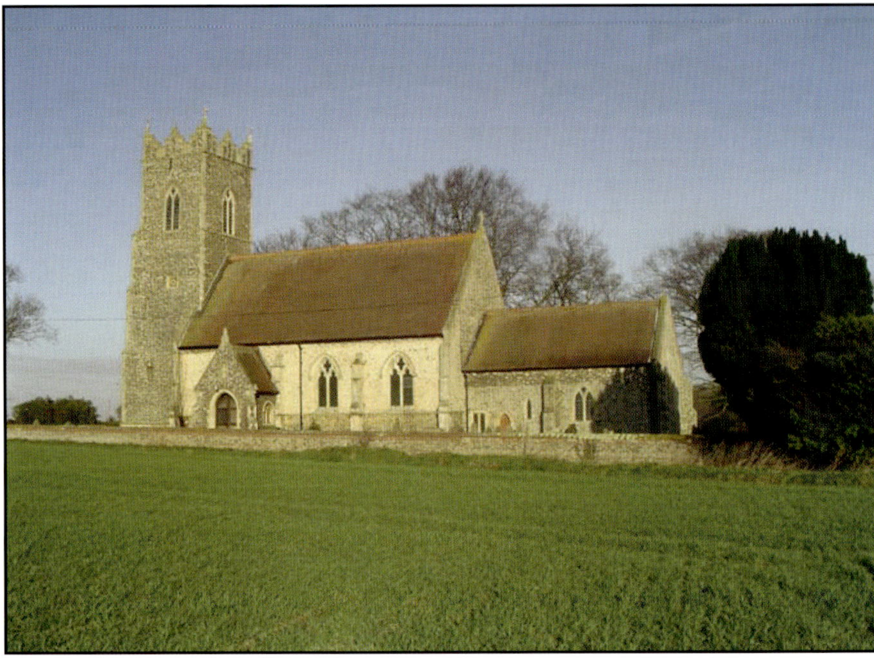

This lovely church is open daily and you are made to feel welcome with kettle and tea for you to help yourself. What a difference from nearby Halvergate. The church is 14th c. and the chancel a century older. The splendid 15th c. tower can be seen a good way off in this flat landscape. On the north wall is a painting of the three quick and the three dead; probably the best example you will find in Norfolk. Adjacent is St Christopher. The Seven Acts of Mercy are also depicted in fine detail and is explained in a framed copy of the paintings. There are two 13th c. effigies in canopied tombs: they are of Sir William Gerbrygge and his wife. The Royal Arms of George II dated 1737 are above the south door. The 'Norman' font is a replica. A Jacobean pulpit, and an old chest are on display near the door.

WINTERTON Holy Trinity & All Saints

No of Bells:	5	8 m N x W of Great Yarmouth. The church tower is unmistakable as you approach the village.
19th c. Deanery:	Flegg	
Hundred:	West Flegg	
Union house:	Rollesby	
21st c. Deanery:	Great Yarmouth	O.S. grid ref: TG 490194
Benefice:	Flegg (Coastal)	Post Code: NR29 4AP

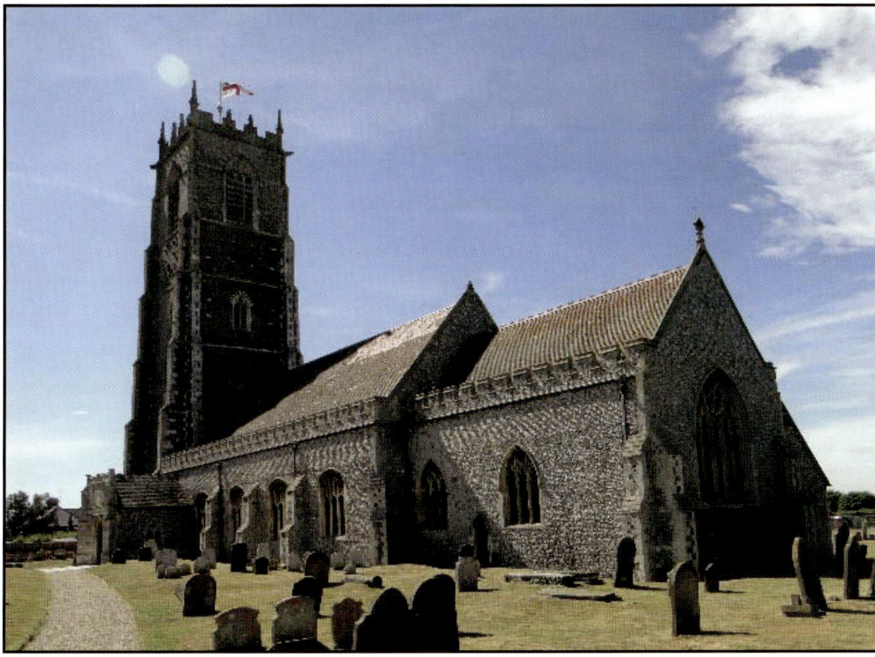

The 130-foot tower is what makes this church so special. At the top are gargoyles, crocketted pinnacles and figures sitting on the merlons, among them a wodewose. The nave and chancel walls are embattled for their entire length. The effect is very pleasing. The porch has four empty niches and two stools on the buttresses but alas no figures. A simply decorated font has an elaborate modern 'conical' cover. A very ornate modern roof to the nave spanning 34 feet has arch-bracing and king posts. High on the wall over the chancel arch are the rare Royal Arms of Charles I. The traceried screen is Victorian as are most of the fixtures and fittings. The piscina has a multi-cusped arch. Marble wall plaques have been removed temporarily from the wall for safety; one of them is to Engle and Elizabeth Knights.

WITTON St Margaret (by Nth Walsham)

No of Bells: 1
19th c. Deanery: Waxham
Hundred: Tunstead
Union house: Smallburgh
21st c. Deanery: Waxham & Tunstead
Benefice: Coastal

3 m E of North Walsham. Leave on the Bacton Road, right at the crossroads, then left and left again.
O.S. grid ref: TG 331315
Post Code: NR28 9TR

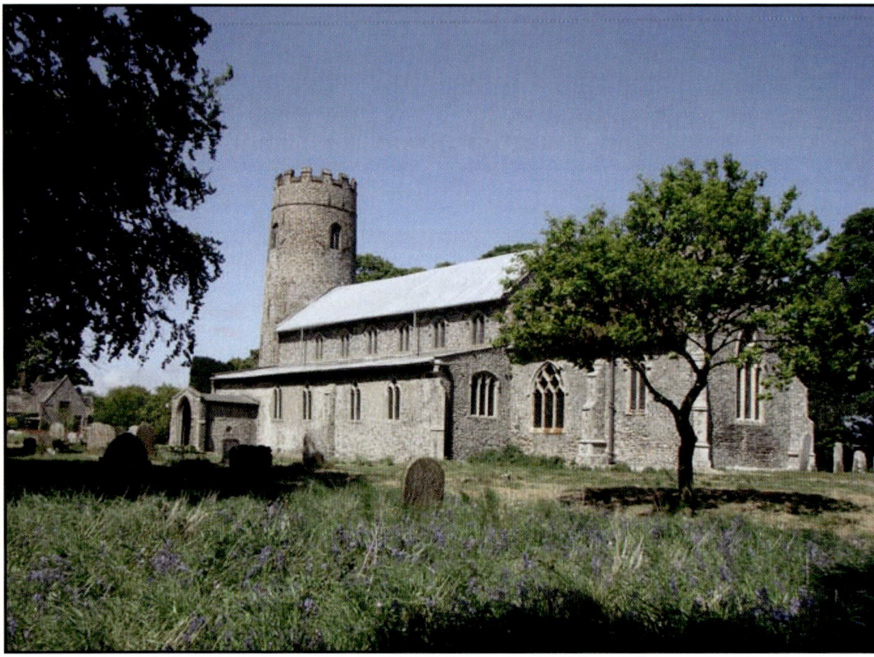

[The post code will direct you north of the church] This is a lovely round-tower church with a clerestory and arcade supporting it. The lower part of the tower is pre-Conquest, the upper portion and parapet (of different materials) are comparatively recent. The north and west end of the nave are late Saxon, evident by the small round splayed windows. The 13th c. chancel was added later. The 15th c. font is octagonal with quatrefoil design on the bowl and a traceried shaft. A watercolour painting of the mediaeval wall paintings, now covered over, hangs on the north wall of the nave. A monument to Elizabeth Norris (1769) has a free-standing statuette and a pile of books; most unusual! A two-seat graduated sedilia has arches decorated with dog and tooth mouldings standing on columns.

WITTON St Margaret (by Norwich)
No of Bells: 1
19th c. Deanery: Blofield
Hundred: Blofield
Union house: Lingwood
21st c. Deanery: Blofield
Benefice: Great Plumstead

5½ m E of Norwich. Turn north off the A47 by the masts, into Church Road. Take 1st right then left at junction. Then 150 yards.
O.S. grid ref: TG 314098
Post Code: NR13 5DN

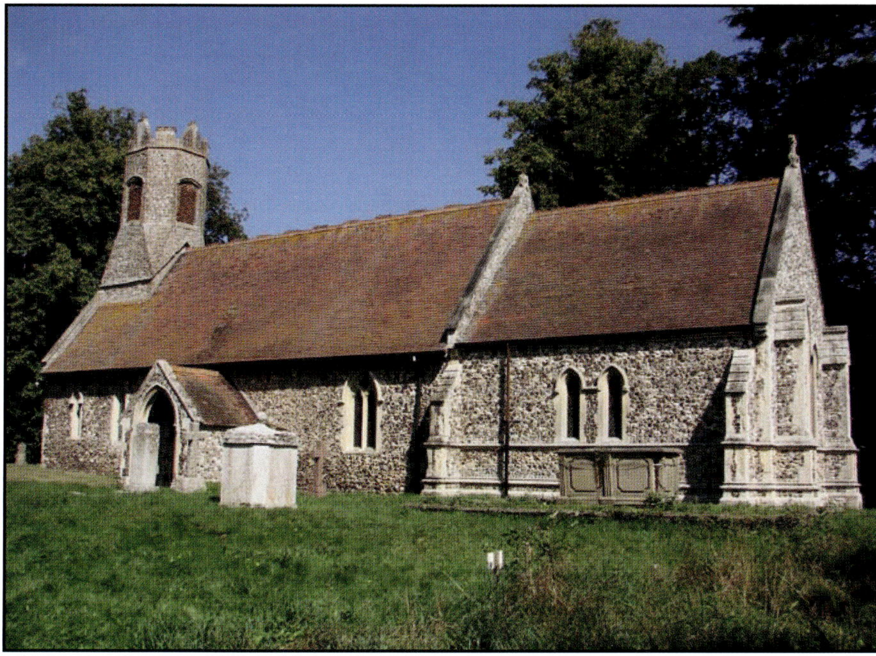

The strange 'pepper-pot' tower is the most striking thing about this church, which regrettably it is usually locked. Somewhat over restored by enthusiastic Victorian benefactors, everything of interest has been carted away in a tumbrel and dumped. Even Cautley wrote *'S. porch, nave, and chancel. There is nothing of interest.'* Mortlock ignored it all together. A sad state of affairs for such a nice rural church in such a lovely peaceful setting. I did find however a very obliging key-holder not too far away. Inside the nave is an octagonal font with simple arcading around the bowl resting on eight columns round a central shaft. The reveals of the windows are decorated, and yet more painting within the trefoil piscina, but I cannot even guess at the subject or date. All fixtures, fittings and roofs are Victorian.

WOODBASTWICK St Fabian and St Sebastian

No of Bells:	2	8 m NE of Norwich. Either from the B1140 via Salhouse, or by turning left 1 mile south of Wroxham.
19th c. Deanery:	Blofield	
Hundred:	Walsham	
Union house:	Acle	
21st c. Deanery:	Blofield	O.S. grid ref: TG 332153
Benefice:	Ranworth	Post Code: NR13 6HJ

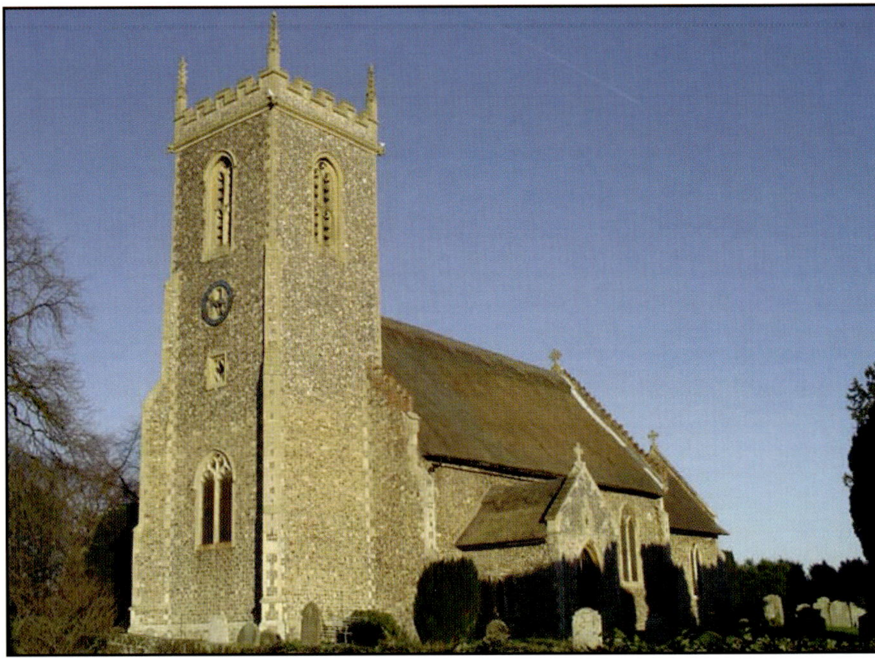

The church has a unique dedication to these two saints. A statuette of St Fabian is over the porch door. The unusual goblet-style font is only one of the many Victorian artefacts to be found here. The late 19th c. saw the church virtually stripped and the interior restructured. A few old poppy-head bench ends can still be found but most are relatively modern, as is the pulpit and reading desk. The roofs are supported on cambered tie-beams with crown posts bearing small bosses at the intersections. Two nice cusped piscinæ in the aisles are obscured by radiators. In the chancel is an angled piscina opening into the sedile. The wall is strewn with memorials to the Cator family. One in particular is to Elizabeth Bowes-Lyon, who was bridesmaid and later sister-in-law to Queen Elizabeth the Queen Mother.

WOODTON All Saints

No of Bells:	6
19th c. Deanery:	Brooke
Hundred:	Loddon
Union house:	Heckingham
21st c. Deanery:	Depwade
Benefice:	Hempnall

6 m NW of Bungay, turn into Church Road off the B1332 or at 5 miles take the B1135 (to Hempnall) and north. West of the village.
O.S. grid ref: TM 285945
Post Code: NR35 2NB

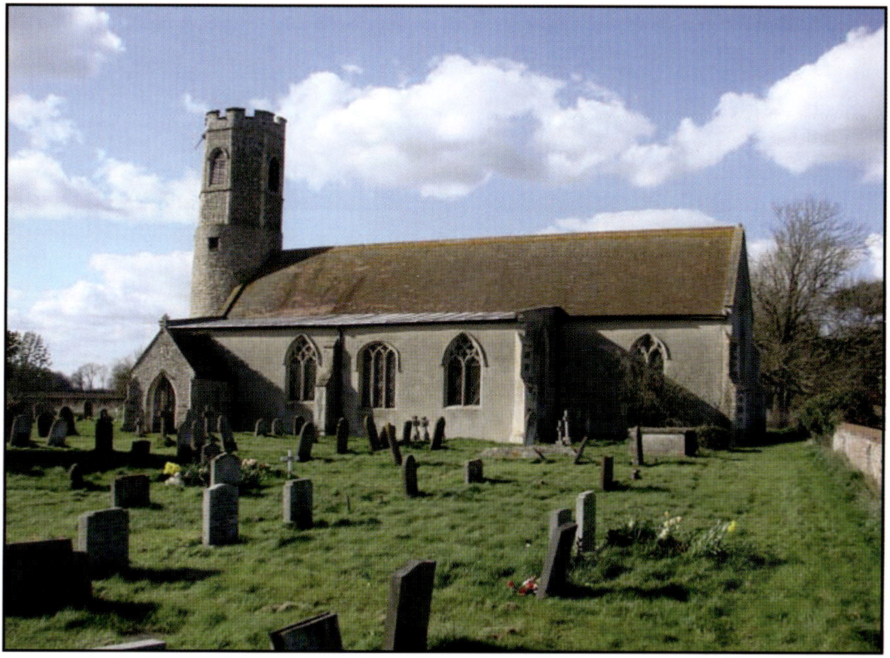

In a similar style to Topcroft this church too, has a Norman round tower and an embattled octagonal top. In the north wall is an arch which may be an intramural burial. The south aisle has an arch-braced roof, the remaining roofs are more modern. At the west end is the square Norman font with shallow arcading, supported by a central shaft and a column at each corner. The benches and most other fittings are Victorian. Unusually the piscina is corbelled with a surround, the adjoining sedilia is a simple dropped-sill bench. Badly placed at the extreme east of the north wall is a memorial to Ann Suckling (1653). Her ancestry is written below her portraiture. Other members of the Suckling, Bone and Yelloly families are buried and have memorials here.

WORSTEAD	St Mary *****	3 m S of North Walsham.
No of Bells:	6	On the A149 at 1½ miles
19th c. Deanery:	Waxham	turn south towards
Hundred:	Tunstead	Worstead. Unmissable in
Union house:	Smallburgh	the centre of the village.
21st c. Deanery:	Waxham & Tunstead	O.S. grid ref: TG 302261
Benefice:	Worstead	Post Code: NR28 9RW

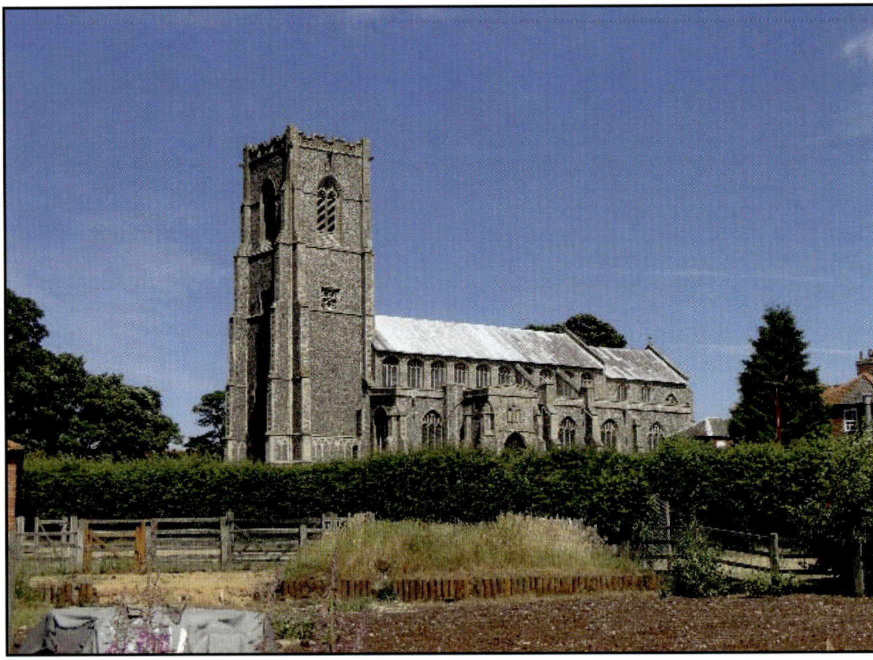

Records exist of the church being built in 1379 and was completed in twenty years. The vestry was added 50 years later as was the south porch which has a parvise. The clerestory has two flying buttresses over the aisles taking the outward thrust of the hammerbeam roof. The 15th c. font has its original tall crocketted cover. Unusually there is a screen beneath the ringing gallery in the beautiful tower arch dated 1550. The rood screen is almost eighteen feet high and is dated 1511. The panels below have been skilfully repainted and depict various saints, apostles and 'the man of sorrows'. There are aisle screens just as interesting although not so detailed. I loved the old bier with rails for a canopy. A wheelie bin stands in the south aisle and looks somewhat out of place. Apart from that, well worth a visit.

WROXHAM	St Mary the Virgin
No of Bells:	6
19th c. Deanery:	Taverham
Hundred:	Taverham
Union house:	Horsham St Faith
21st c. Deanery:	Waxham & Tunstead
Benefice:	Wroxham

6½ m N of Norwich. From Norwich turn left off the A1151. Once in Wroxham, over the railway bridge and into St Mary's Close.
O.S. grid ref: TG 296175
Post Code: NR12 8SG

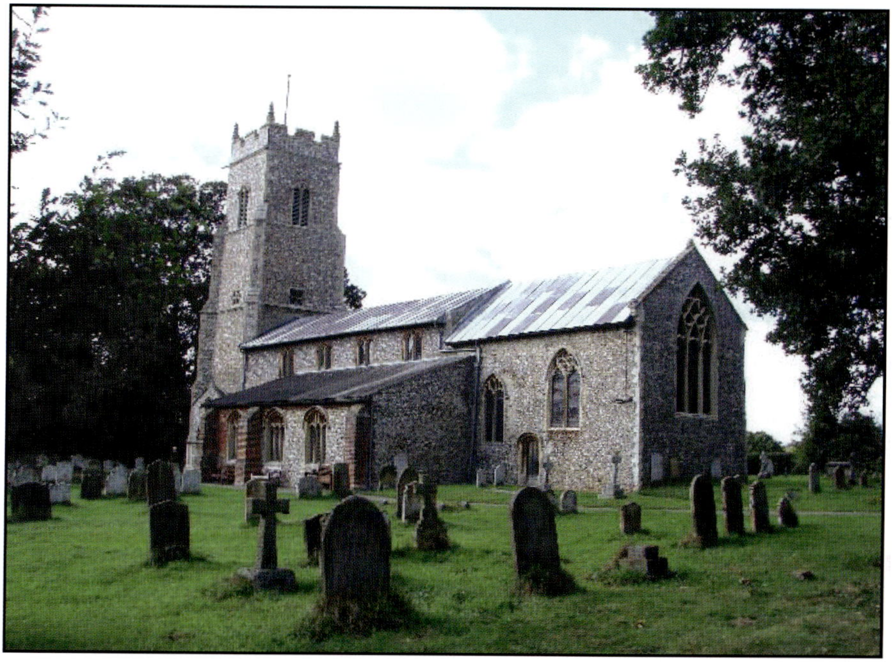

The tower was built in the 15th c. but judging by the beautiful Norman south doorway the church is more than two centuries earlier, at least in part. The blackened doorway has curious faces on all of the six engaged and knopped columns, and has seven orders of decoration. Just inside the door on the right is a niche for a stoup, on the left is the stairway to the tower. Most of what is to be seen inside the church is Victorian including the simple arch-braced roofs of the nave and chancel. On the walls of the latter are a number of plaques and monuments. It is a simple church with modern fixtures and fittings and very little to excite the imagination; but it is a pleasant church and usually open and welcoming to visitors. The south doorway alone makes this church worth a detour to the south side.

YELVERTON with Alpington St Mary the Virgin

No of Bells:	3	5½ m SE of Norwich. Turn
19th c. Deanery:	Brooke	right off the A146 just past
Hundred:	Henstead	'The Gull' PH and follow
Union house:	Heckingham	1½ miles to destination.
21st c. Deanery:	Loddon	O.S. grid ref: TG 293022
Benefice:	Thurton	Post Code: NR14 7PB

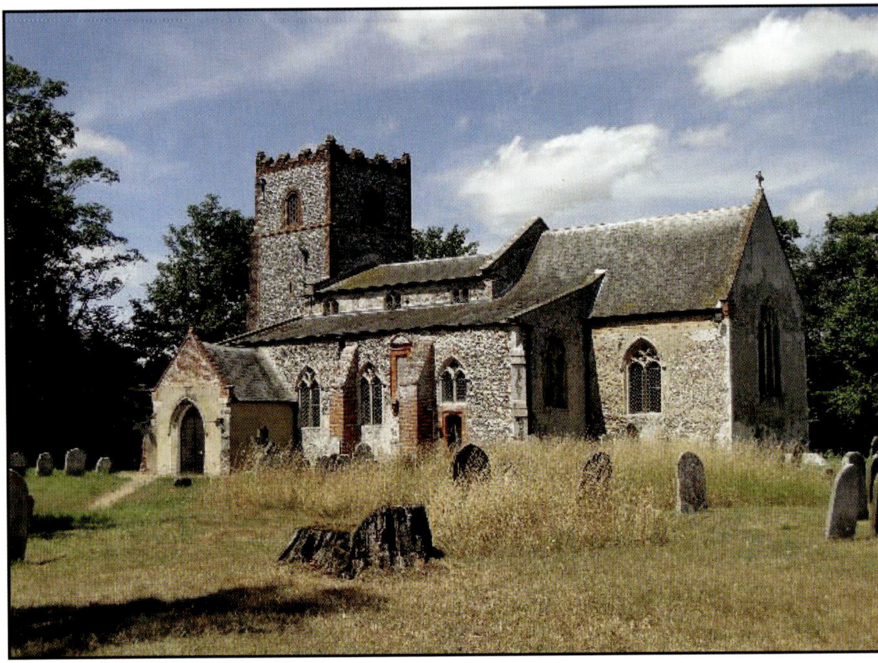

The short flint-and-brick tower has a brick embattled parapet. The church is a modest affair dating from the early 14th c. with a 15th c. arcade. The south aisle was once a Lady chapel. The font seems to be a replica of a Norman font. In the chancel is a simple piscina with cusped arch and adjacent is a dropped-sill sedilia. The roofs are modern, that in the nave is arch-braced with tie beams. The rood screen is lovely with fine tracery, but only the bottom part is of significant age. The lower panels are painted, still in their original colours, with angels holding scrolls. A sacring bell has been mounted in the upper exit to the rood stairs. A memorial in the south wall is to Elizabeth Hood (1705). Inside on the chancel wall is a touching memorial to Humphrey and Anne Rant (1661).

Ruined or Lost Churches not Featured in the text

It should be noted that this list is not comprehensive and other sources may reveal other, more obscure churches. I have attempted to list all the churches in the area covered by this guide. For other churches the guide pertaining to the area should be consulted. I have included all the information available to me at the time of going to press, but I accept that more details may be available in other sources. For more information on many of the churches below I recommend 'The Ruined and Disused Churches of Norfolk' by Neil Batcock, for the Norfolk Museums Service 1991. ISBN 0905594037.

Alpington /Apton, St Martin. Pre-Conquest. Village depopulated and close proximity to other churches. Demoted to chapel in the 14th c. Abandoned late 16th c. No visual remains. Exact location uncertain. TG 29 00.

Ashby, St Mary. Built c.1100. Reasons for depopulation unclear. Much confusion seems to exist between this and Oby church. Remains existed in living memory. No visual remains. TG 425152.

Barton Turf, unknown dedication. Pre-Conquest. Two churches in close proximity of each other, abandoned before 13th c. Precise whereabouts unknown. No visual remains. TG 35 23.

Bedingham, St Mary. Unknown age. Two churches in the same churchyard. Village unable to support both. Abandoned 16th c. No visual remains. TM 285934.

Beeston, St Andrew. Pre-Conquest. Gradual depopulation and decline of village. Less than 10 householders in 1428. Abandoned in the 16th c. No visual remains. TG 25 14. Just north of Norwich.

Blo Norton, St Margaret. u/k construction date. Decay and the close proximity of St Andrew. Abandoned in 1394. Stood in the same churchyard as St Andrew. No visible remains. TM 012796.

Bracondale, St Nicholas. Pre-Conquest. Closed by the Dissolution after 1428. Exact whereabouts uncertain No visual remains. TG 23 07.

Burgh, St Peter. St Peter. Probably pre-Conquest. Scatter of rubble in field west of the present church of St Mary. TM 493937.

Carleton Rode. Two churches recorded in Domesday.

Carrow, St James. Unknown age. Still in use in 1520. Abandoned by mid-16th c. Little known. No visual remains. TG 24 07.

Eccles, St Mary. 11th - 12th c. Coastal erosion and encroachment of the sea in 1604. 1000 acres of land including the village washed away in a storm. Rubble visible at extreme low tide. TL 754988

East Beckham, St Helen. Unknown age. Consolidated with West Beckham. Abandoned circa 1700. Rubble wall at TG 155398.

Great Yarmouth, St Benedict. Pre-Conquest. Abandoned. c. 1100. De Losinga's new church favoured. No records of its whereabouts probably within the old walls). No visual remains. TG 53 07.

Heigham, St Philip. u/k construction date. Further details unknown

Heigham, St Bartholomew. 15th c. just outside the walls of the city. Bombed in WWII. The tower remains at TG 217098

Hempnall, St Andrew . Pre-Conquest. Two churches mentioned in Domesday. Abandoned before 16th c. No visual remains. TM 213950

Herringsby, St Ethelbert. u/k construction date. Abandoned after village deserted in mid 16th c. Demolished in 1610. No visual remains. TG 446103

Holverstone, St Mary. u/k construction date. Consolidated with Rockland St Mary & Burgh Apton.

Horning, unknown dedication and construction date. Not consolidated. An Abbey church, demolished at the same time as the Abbey.

Hunstanton, St Andrew. Norman. Precise date and proximity unknown.

Keswick, St Clement. Probably pre-Conquest. Coastal erosion sometime just after 1382. No visual remains. TG 351333

Langhale, St Christopher. Pre-Conquest. Parish deserted c. early 17th c. Parish consolidated with Kirstead in 1421. No visual remains. TM 295966

Little Hautbois, St Mary. Probably pre-Conquest. Population dispersed. 16th c. No visual remains. TG 251217

Little Rackheath, Holy Trinity. U/k construction date. Village deserted, church abandoned 15th c. No visual remains. TG 28 13

Little Waxham, St Margaret . U/k construction date. Abandoned. Last reference was in 1383. Village deserted No visual remains. TG 445265

Mannington, St Mary. TG 142319.

Markshall, unknown dedication. Details unknown. TG 23 04 Consolidated with Caistor St Edmund,date unknown .

Martham, 2 churches mentioned in Domesday; nothing more known.

North Walsham, A Saxon church, Further details unknown.

Norwich, All Saints. Near Fyebridge demolished about 1550. Consolidated with St Paul's.

Norwich, All Saints. Timberhill / Ber Street area. Demolished circa 1532. Present church built in the site.

Norwich, Holy Trinity. Rebuilt as St John Maddermarket in the 15th century.

Norwich, St Bartholomew. Consolidated with St John Sepulchre in 1549.

Norwich, St Botolph. Consolidated with St Saviour's in 1548.

Norwich, St Catherine. Originally dedicated to St Winwaloe. Consolidated with St Stephen. The area was depopulated by the plague in 1349 and the church was converted to a chapel.

Norwich, St Christopher. situated somewhere east of St Andrew's Hill. Burned down in the reign of Henry III. Consolidated with St Andrew and St Michael at Plea sometime after 1216.

Norwich, St Clement, Cunesford. Exact site unknown. Consolidated with St Julian's in 1482. The Saxon church was de-consecrated in 1551 and was still ruinous in 1774.

Norwich, St Clement, Fyebridge / Colgate. Age unknown. The Saxon church was demolished to build the present church.

Norwich, St Crouch or Crowche. Invention of the Holy Cross. Somewhere near St Andrew's. Consolidated with St Andrew and St John Maddermarket in 1551. Ruins were cleared in 1745 and the Public House known as 'The Hole in the Wall' was built on the site.

Norwich, St Cuthbert. Totally demolished about 1530-35. Consolidated with St Mary the Less in 1492.

Norwich, St Edmund. A Norman church. Exact site unknown.

Norwich, St Edward. Consolidated with St Julian in 13th c. Served as St Hildebrond's hospital until the Dissolution.

Norwich, St George, Colgate. Situated in Muspole Street. Present church built on the same site.

Norwich, St George, Tombland. Present church built on the same site.

Norwich, St Helen. Built in 1249 and demolished a short time after being given to the Hospital in 1270. The present St Helen's was built soon after. TG 238090.

Norwich, St Peter, Southgate. Some remains at O.S. ref: TG 235077.

Oby, Dedication unknown. U/k construction date. Village depopulated in the late 16th c. Some fragments utilised in the building of a barn. No other visual remains. TG 415144.

Ormesby, St Andrew. Unknown age. Population unable to support four churches in one village. Late 16th c. No visual remains. TG 493150.

Ormesby, St Peter. Unknown age. Population unable to support four churches in one village. Late 16th c No visual remains. TG 491146

Overstrand, St Martin u/k construction date. Coastal erosion. In the late 14th c. No visual remains. TG 24 41.

Oxwick, Existence of a church believed, but unconfirmed.

Poringland Parva, St Michael. Saxon. Consolidated with Poringland Magna *(now just 'Poringland').*

Raveningham, Two churches mentioned in Domesday.

Overstrand, St Martin. Unknown age. Coastal erosion. Late 14th c. No visual remains. TG 24 41.

Scratby, All Saints. Pre-Conquest. Parish consolidated with Ormesby, church demolished in 1548. Coastal erosion decreased the size of the parish. Close proximity of four churches in nearby Ormesby. No visual remains. TG 507154.

Seething, Two churches mentioned in Domesday. *(One may have been nearby Mundham.)* No visual remains. TM 31 98.

Shipden , *(Near Cromer)*. Unknown dedication. Possibly a Saxon church. Cliff erosion circa 1400. No visual remains. TG 220425.

Shotesham, St Botolph. 14th c. One of four churches in the parish which could not afford the upkeep. Abandoned early 16th c. A low wall remains. TM 239993.

Southtown, *(Gt Yarmouth)*. St Nicholas. Possibly Pre-Conquest. Recorded in 1254 and 1379. Abandoned, united with Gorleston in 1511. Tower stood as a landmark into the 16th c. No visual remains. TG 52 06

Stoke Holy Cross, Holy Cross. Possibly pre-Conquest. Two churches recorded in Domesday. Abandoned possibly as early as 12th c. Whereabouts unknown; possibly near Blackford Hall present church built on the same site. No visual remains. TG 252017.

Thorpe, *(Near Norwich)*. Pre-12th c. Destroyed in 16th c. Probably to build St Andrew's 'Old Church', (TG 2670900. No visual remains.

Thorpe Market, Two churches mentioned in Domesday.

Thurketeliart , Unknown dedication. Pre-Conquest Unknown history. Only reference recorded in Domesday. Parish abandoned circa 12th c. Positive site of village remains uncertain. Somewhere near Aldeby. TM 44 93.

Topcroft, St Giles. Unknown age. Abandoned in the early 16th c. Exact whereabouts unidentified. TM 26 92.

West Poringland, St Michael. Unknown age.
Village deserted and the church abandoned before 1540. No visual remains. TG 2622010

Winston, St Andrew Probably Saxon. Abandoned when the village was deserted circa 1440. No visual remains. TM 400931.

Worstead, St Andrew. Pre-Conquest. Abandoned in the 16th c. due to the close proximity of a second church in the village No visual remains. TG 303259.

Wheatacre, Two churches mentioned in Domesday. (One may have been Burgh St Peter).

Wyndle, St Andrew. Almost certainly Saxon. Abandoned when the village was deserted circa 1440. No visual remains. TM 426932.

Index of Names appearing in the text

Name	**Parish**
Chester, family	Wheatacre
Churchman, Thomas	Norwich St Giles
Clabburn, William	Norwich All Saints
Claxton, Rose	Rollesby
Clippesby, John	Clippesby
Clowes, family	Caister Holy Trinity
Coleman, family	Kirby Bedon
Cooke, Dame Mary	Broome
Corbet, John	Sprowston
Cotton, Bartholomew	Starston
Dalling, family	Earsham
Dashwood, family	Rackheath
Dawson, Rev. Jonathan	Martham
de Ingham, Sir Oliver	Ingham
Deneaw, Peter	Blofield
Dunwich, William de	Bixley
Durban, mother of Sir Benjamin	Shotesham All Saints
Ellis, Ted	Surlingham St Saviour
Fastolff, family	West Caister
Freston, William & Margaretta	Needham
Garney, family	Hedenham
Garney, family	Morningthorpe
Gerbrygge, Sir William & wife	Wickhampton
Gilman, Will	North Burlingham
Gleane, Thomas	Hardwick
Gooch, family	Wheatacre
Goudy, Henry	Claxton
Grimer, Robert	Mundham
Grindley,family	Halvergate
Gwavas, family	Wheatacre
Haggard, Sir Rider	Ditchingham
Hales, Robert (Suffolk giant)	West Somerton
Hammond, John	Suffield
Harbord, family	Thorpe Market
Harbord, family	Gunton
Harbourne, William	Mundham
Harcourt, Boys	Brumstead
Harcourt, Elizabeth	Brumstead
Harcourt, Elizabeth, Snr	Brumstead

Name	**Parish**
Havers, Thomas	Stoke Holy Cross
Hayward, William	Norwich St Clement Colegate
Herne, Sir John & Mary	Arminghall
Holdiche, Thomas	Ranworth
Home, Lady Caroline	Ormesby St Margaret
Hood, Elizabeth	Yelverton
Ingram, Nicholas	Norwich St Peter, Hungate
Ives, John	Belton
Johnson, William	Norwich St Etheldreda
Kedington (nee) Margaretta	Needham
Kerrison, family	Kirstead
Kirkebei, Wilelmus de	Trowse with Newton
Knights, Engle & Elizabeth	Winterton
Knipe, family	Kirby Bedon
Knolls, Christopher	Sprowston
Knyvet, family	Rackheath
Laws, Herbert	Burgh Castle
Layton, Jonathan & Charles (bros)	Cantley
le Bois, Sir Roger & wife	Ingham
le Groos, Oliver	Sloley
London, Catherine	Thwaite
Lucas, family	Filby
Mapes, Leonard & family	Rollesby
Mazey, Henry	Rockland St Mary
Mileham de Burgh, Robert	North Burlingham
Morse, John & Sarah	Norwich All Saints
Muskett, family	Clippesby
Newbury, William & Anne	Buckenham St Nicholas
Norris, Elizabeth	Witton next North Walsham
Pallyng, Thomas	Clippesby
Paston, family	Mautby
Paston, family	Paston
Paston, John	Norwich St Peter, Hungate
Paston, Lady Katherine	Paston
Paston, Sir Edward	Blofield
Paston, Sir William	North Walsham
Peck, William & Alice	Spixworth
Penrice, Thomas	Little Plumstead

Name	Parish
Pettus, Augustus & Abigail	Norwich St Simon & St Jude
Pettus, Sir John	Norwich St Simon & St Jude
Pettus, Sir Thomas	Rackheath
Petus, Sir Thomas	Norwich St Simon & St Jude
Petwode, Margaret	Norwich St Clement Colegate
Pit, George	Arminghall
Plater, Elizabeth, nee	Raveningham
Preston, family	Beeston St Lawrence
Randall, family	Kirby Bedon
Rant, family	Thorpe Market
Rant, Humphrey & Anne	Yelverton
Revans, Jeremiah	Norwich St Martin at Oak
Reve, Lydia	Blofield
Rising, family	West Somerton
Rosebury, Susan, Countess of	Bixley
Rownce, James	South Walsham
Shirley, wife of Rev. James	Frettenham
Smythe, family	Topcroft
Sotherton, Thomas	Norwich St John, Maddermarket
Spendlove, family	Hedenham
Springfield, 2nd Lieutenant	Alburgh
Springfield, Captain	Alburgh
Stracey, family	Rackheath
Suckling, Ann	Woodton
Suckling, John & wife	Norwich St Andrew
Suffield, Cewcelia Annetta	Gunton
Tallamach, family	Raveningham
Trimnell, Rev. Caroli, (Charles)	Thurne
Trimnell, Richard	Thurne
Vesey, William	Bradwell
Waiet, Earl Ralph	Norwich St Peter Mancroft
Walpole, family	Freethorpe
Ward, family	Kirby Bedon
Ward, family	Bixley
Wells, Rose	Cantley
Whyte, Edward & Elizabeth	Shotesham St Mary
Wodehouse, Thomas	Waxham
Yelloly, family	Woodton

Notes on Royal Arms and Achievements

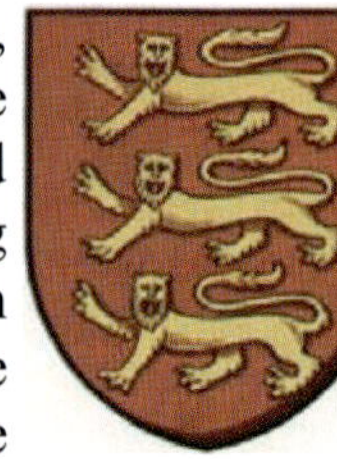

Royal Arms are sometimes exclusive to one monarch, although not personal to the sovereign, and designed by The College of Arms. The use of Arms is said to have started with Henry II, but we know only of them first being displayed by Richard I. A simple red (Gules) shield with three gold (Or) lions passant guardant. i.e. walking while facing the viewer (right). These have remained on the monarch's Arms to this day. However, it was not until the reign of Henry VIII that Royal Arms were displayed in churches.

It took seventeen years, beginning in 1517, for Martin Luther and John Calvin, and eventually Parliament to bring about the Reformation and the founding of an independent Church. The resulting legislation proclaimed Henry VIII supreme head of the English Church and the position was used by him to completely break away from Rome. Edward VI continued to support his father's aspirations, as did Elizabeth, and Protestantism finally became fully established as the 'Church of England' under Elizabeth's rule.

The Royal Arms were then displayed as a sign of loyalty to the Crown and obedience to the Sovereign as Head of the Church of England. Following the Restoration in 1660 the display of the Royal Arms in churches became a legal requirement. The law has never been repealed, although today many churches no longer have Royal Arms on display.

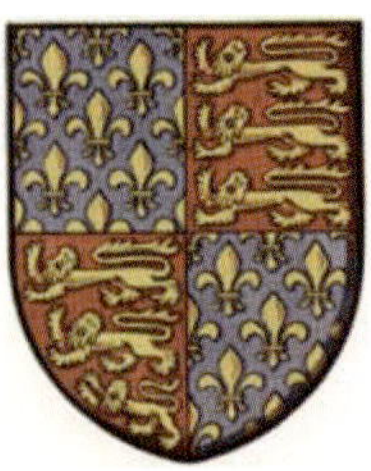

By the reign of Henry VIII the Arms had changed The fleurs-de-lys were added when Edward III laid claim to the throne of France. The red dragon of Wales and the harp of Ireland were also later incorporated. By the time Elizabeth ascended the throne the Arms had undergone many changes and her full achievement can be seen on page 279. There are a number of pitfalls in reading the Arms. E R can refer to Edward or Elizabeth, both are similar, although only a few of Edward still survive, and none in Norfolk. Edward VI (1537-1553) and Elizabeth (1558-1603) were both Tudor and some confusion has even arisen among experts. The most elaborate example of Elizabeth's Royal Arms in Norfolk are at Tivetshall St Margaret (page 278). Bearing in mind the destruction of all to do with the Monarchy during the Commonwealth (1649-1660) it is really not surprising so few exist. Other good examples can be seen at Preston and Rushbrooke, both in Suffolk.

Church wardens were not always willing to spend money on new Arms every time there was a change of Monarch. At Blo Norton the Arms that hang on the wall are attributed to William and Mary, but the motto below is unique to James I. Careful examination of the 'W' and 'M' will show them to have been painted over the 'J' and 'R'.

Often one will find that the Stuart Arms of Charles bearing 'C R' have been altered to 'G R'. Most of the Charles's Arms have floriated letters and those of the first Hanoverian King, George I, usually do not.

Queen Anne used the Stuart Arms in two different forms, primarily the Stuart Arms, but after 1707 and the Act of Union with Scotland the Arms changed with the lion of Scotland included on the first and fourth quarters, the second quarter bore the three fleurs-de-lys of France, and the harp of Ireland the third.

Hanoverian Arms remained the same from 1714 to 1800, after which time the fleurs-de-lys of France were finally removed.

Although I have used the term 'Arms', the term in modern use, the true identity is 'Achievement'. The Achievement has the lion and unicorn as supporters, helm, crown, garter and all the other heraldic devices which surround the Arms themselves.

During the Commonwealth, as already mentioned, many of the Arms were destroyed; however, a few remain. The Commonwealth had its own Arms which can be seen at North Walsham and illustrated on page 285.

Hanoverian Arms can normally be distinguished by the white Saxon horse included in the fourth quarter. Between 1800 (when the fleurs-de-lys were finally omitted) and 1816, it also featured on the escutcheon of pretence, in the centre surmounted by a coronet and /or bonnet which denotes to which monarch they belong. *(A bonnet is the velvet cap set into the top of the coronet).*

It is hoped these pages will help with recognition and where to find those illustrated. Remember, however, that almost each one is different from the other. They were painted, carved or cast as required by local artists and craftsmen, some of whom were better than others, and were not mass produced. There are many different interpretations and in some cases the escutcheon is circular or oval. Many are wholly improper and do not comply with the rules of Heraldry.

Occasionally after modifications have been made by churchwardens the original motto has been left unaltered, giving us a good clue to the original date of the Achievement. Close examination may reveal some surprises.

Listed below are the mottos which the various monarchs used during their reign.

One good example of the incorrect motto can be found at Blo Norton where the motto is of James I. The Achievement is quite correctly

Stuart but is 85 years earlier, and not the Arms of William and Mary. *(see overleaf)* The initials 'J R' have been altered to 'W r et r M' for William and Mary, see page 280.

Monarch	**Motto**	***(English translation)***
Henry VIII	DIEU ET MON DROIT	*(God and my right)*
James I [early]	BEATI PACIFICI	*(Blessed are the peacemakers)*
James I. [late] after the union with Scotland]	EXURGAT DEUS DISSIPENTUR INIMICI	*(Let God arise and His enemies be scattered)*
JAMES II	QUI LEO DE JUDA EST UT FLOS DE JESSE LEONES PROTEGIT ET FLORES MAGNE JACOBE TUOS. (Dated 1687)	*(He who is the Lion of Judah the fine flower of Jesse's line, Guards great James, thy lions and thy fairest flowers)* [The only known example was at Fressingfield in Suffolk and was subsequently destroyed during Victorian restorations].
Elizabeth I & Anne	SEMPER EADEM	*(Always the same)*
William & Mary	JE MAIN TIEN DRAY	*(I will maintain the right)*
Hanoverian	DIEU ET MON DROIT	*(God and my right)*

Below are the Royal Arms of the monarchs named beneath each. The Stuart Arms applied to all Stuart monarchs from James I to Queen Anne. They did however differ as illustrated above when William and Mary (daughter of James II) were joint rulers, the Arms were impaled (equally divided) with her Arms on the dexter (right) side and his on the left (sinister). After she died in 1694, William discontinued the impaled shield and the Nassau shield was placed centrally. When Anne succeeded to the throne in 1702 she reverted to the Stuart shield until 1707 when the Act of Union with Scotland came into being, the Scottish lion being impaled on the 1st and 4th quarters. The Hanoverian succession saw the Arms change again, with the fourth quarter displaying the shield of Hanover and an escutcheon of pretence placed over it. In 1801 the fleurs-de-lys were removed and the Hanoverian Arms placed centrally on a small shield, later removed when Victoria succeeded in 1837. Since then they have remained unchanged.

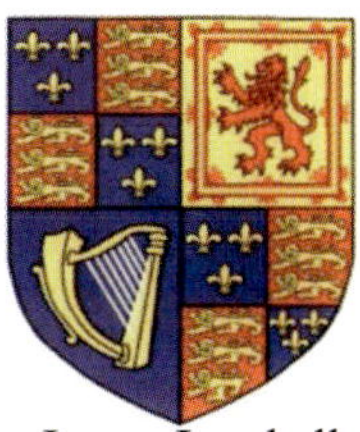

James I and all Stuart Monarchs

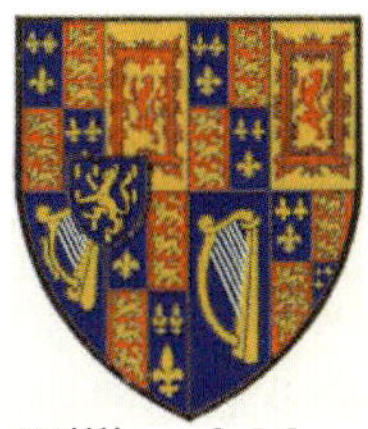

William & Mary

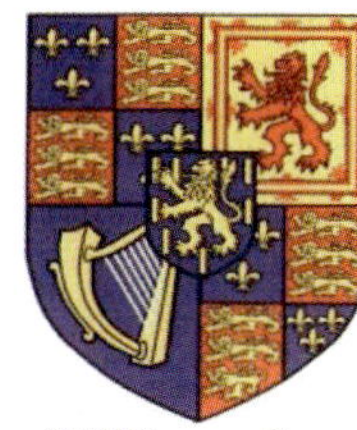

William after Mary's death

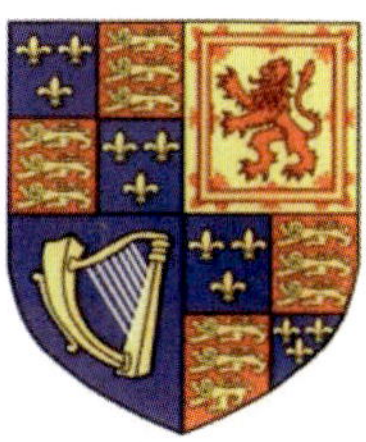

Anne before 1707

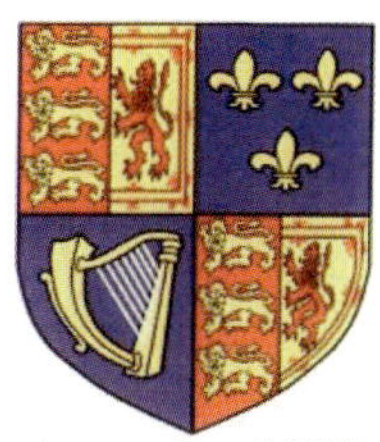

Anne after 1707

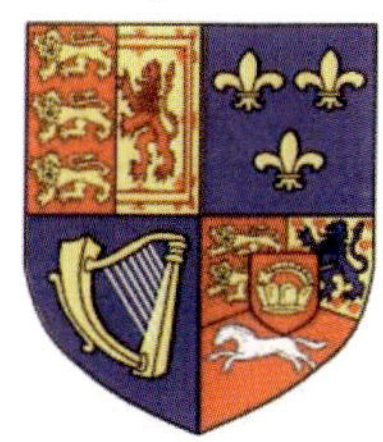

Georges I, II & III before 1800

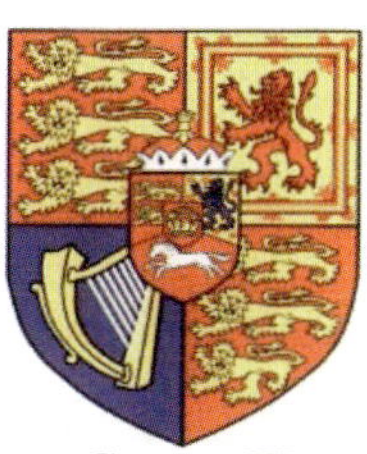

George III 1800 - 1816

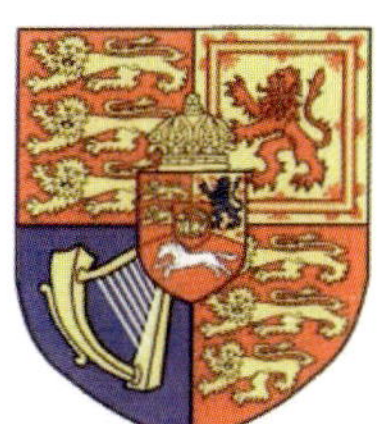

George III after 1816

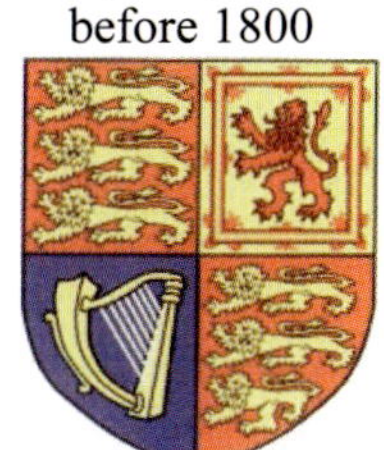

Victoria & all thereafter

The Royal Arms are not always displayed in a shield-shaped form. Depending on the artist they are occasionally circular or oval The Achievements which surround the Arms differ considerably in many cases and the interpretation is often inaccurate and even comical.

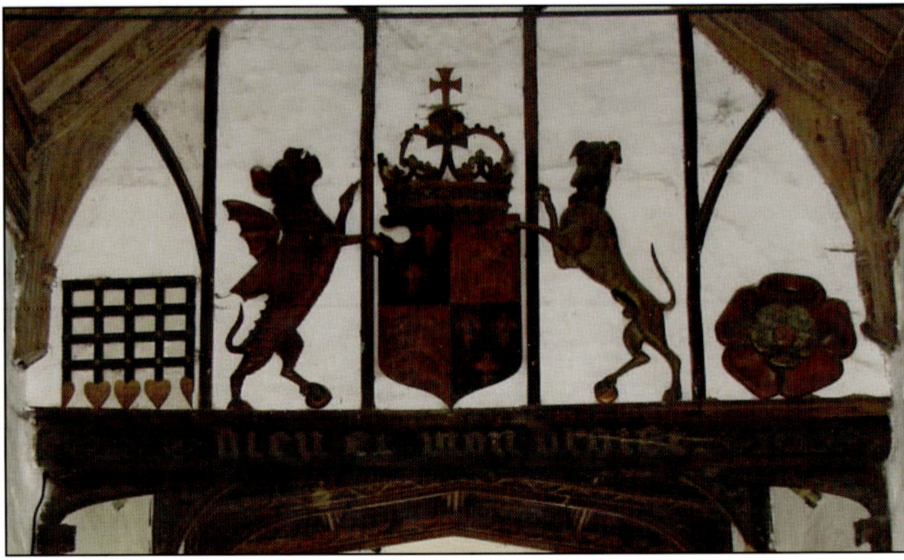

These Royal Arms are of Henry VIII, with a dragon and greyhound as supporters. These were later replaced by a lion and dragon. They can be seen at Rushbrooke in Suffolk and because they are unique I have included them here. They are above the western-most beam of the nave.

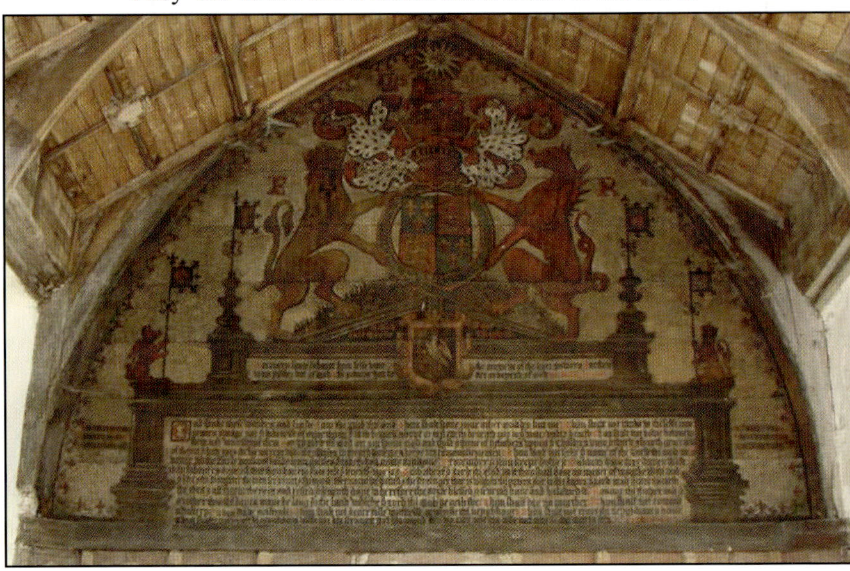

The Royal Arms of Queen Elizabeth at Tivetshall St Margaret. Cautley describes these as probably the finest in the country. They are painted on the tympanum of the chancel arch.

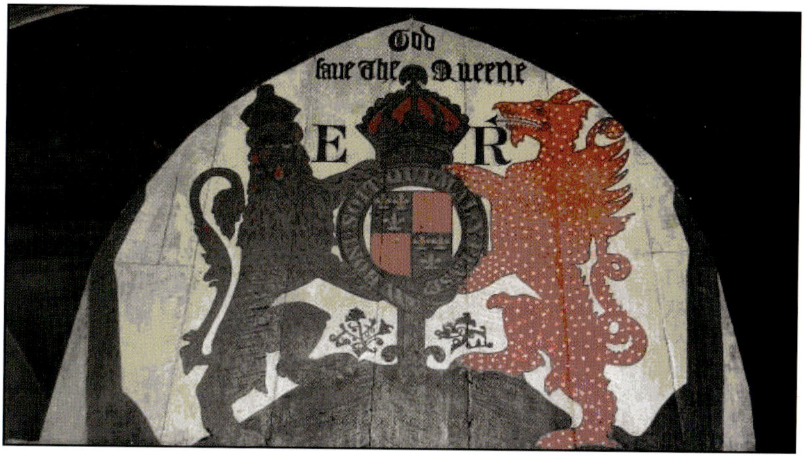

Elizabeth I at Preston, Suffolk.
Regarded as the finest of its type in the county.
Note that a dragon precedes the unicorn.

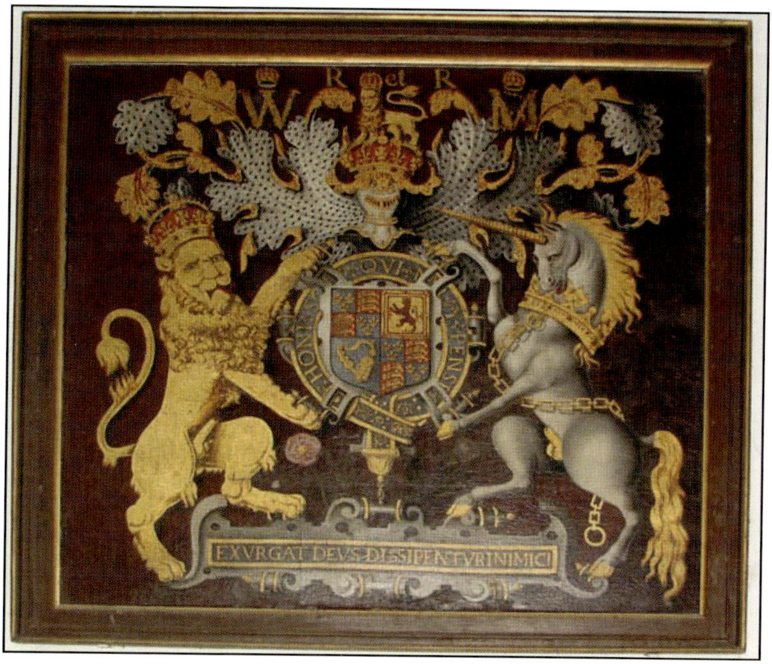

The Arms of James I with his motto, which have been updated to William and Mary. Blo Norton.
On close examination the J and R can still be discerned painted over beneath the W and M.

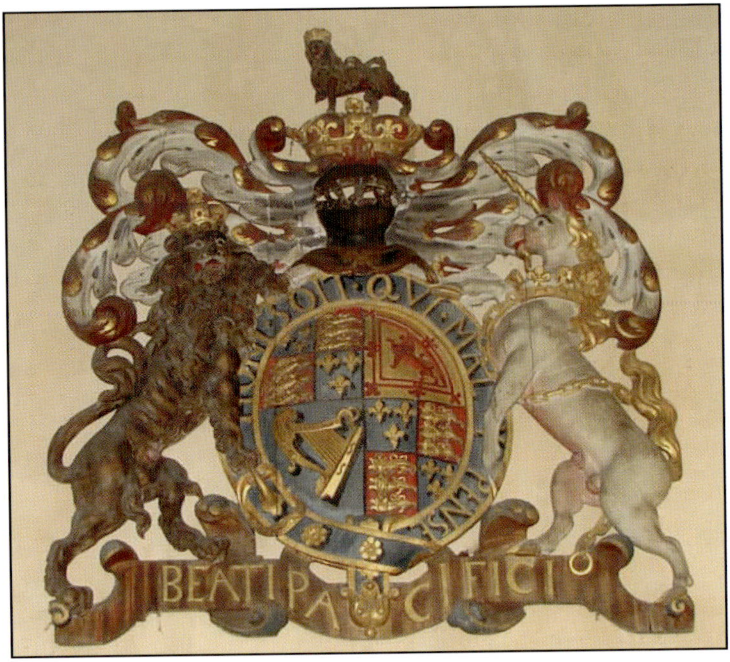

Carved wood Arms of James I, as indicated by his early motto of peacemaker between England and Scotland. Kimberley.

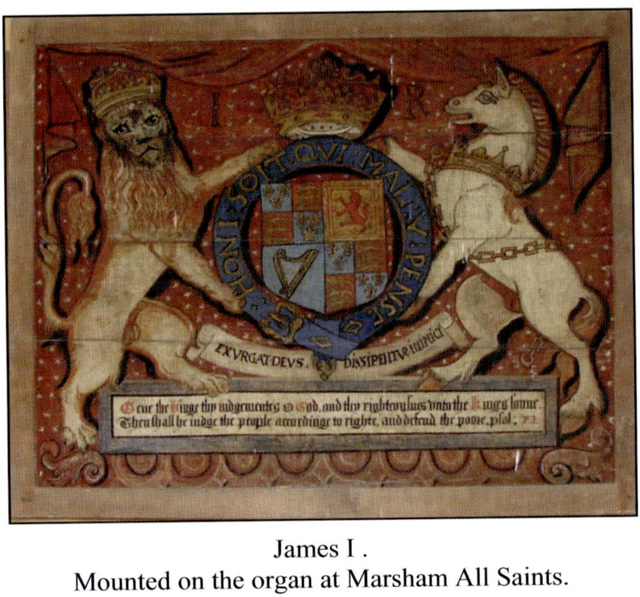

James I .
Mounted on the organ at Marsham All Saints.

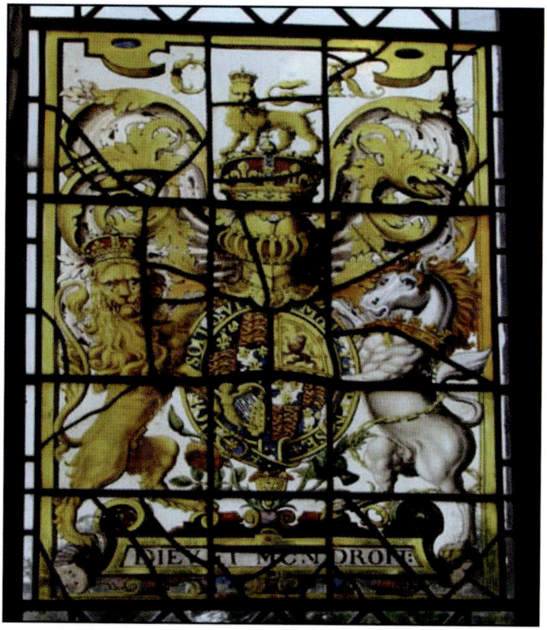

The Royal Arms in stained glass at Barningham Winter inscribed C R.

Almost certainly Charles I as it was donated to the church in all probability after being removed from the window at the Hall during the Civil War

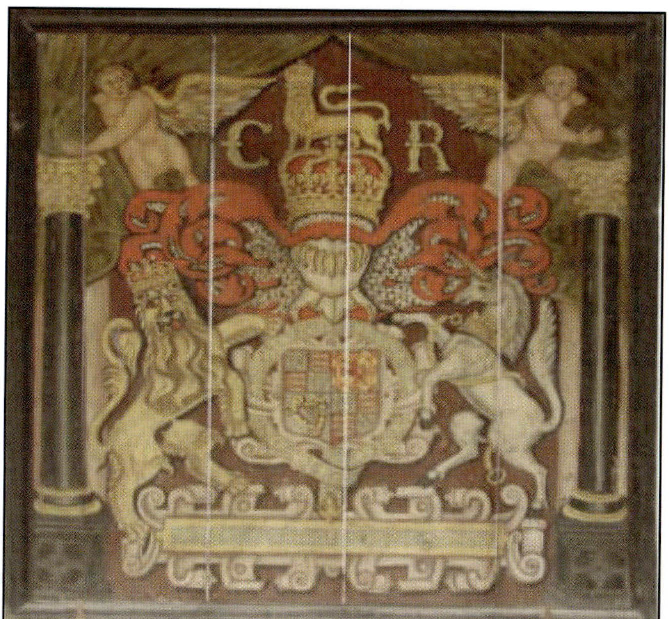

Charles I (note the floriated C R)
Wilby All Saints.

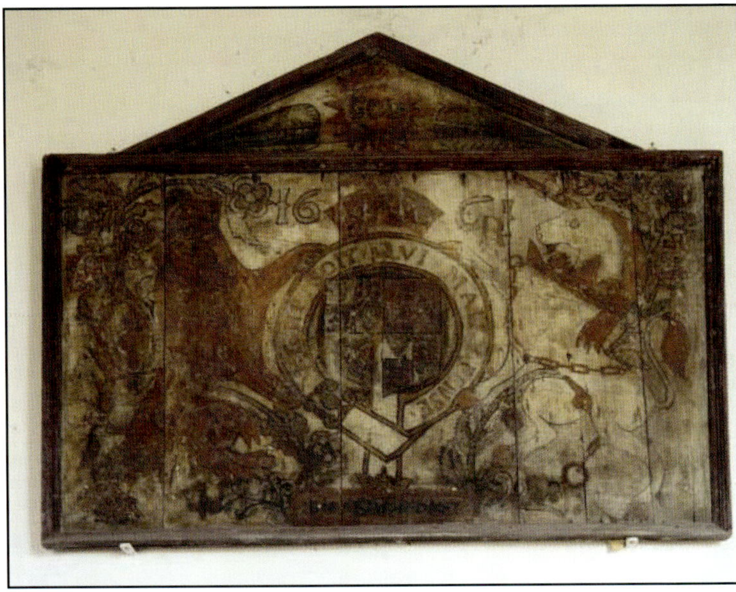

Charles II, dated 1661
Toft Monks St Margaret

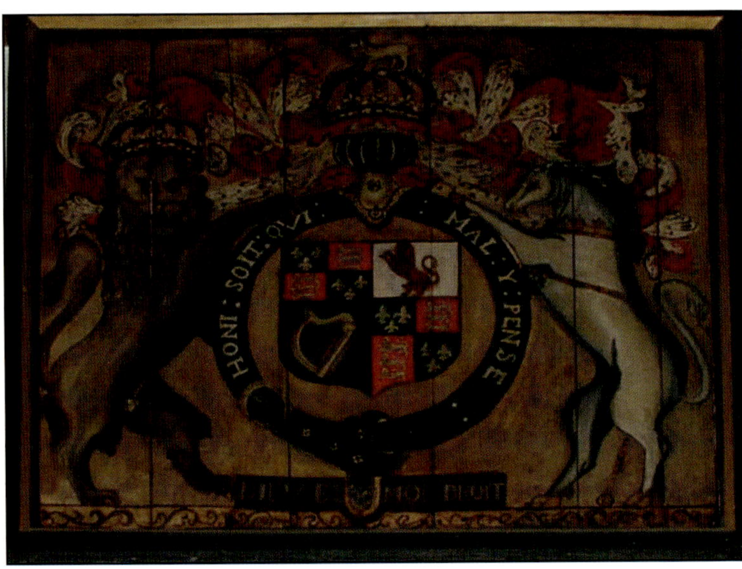

Stuart, unattributed, probably Charles II , on wood
Hoveton St John

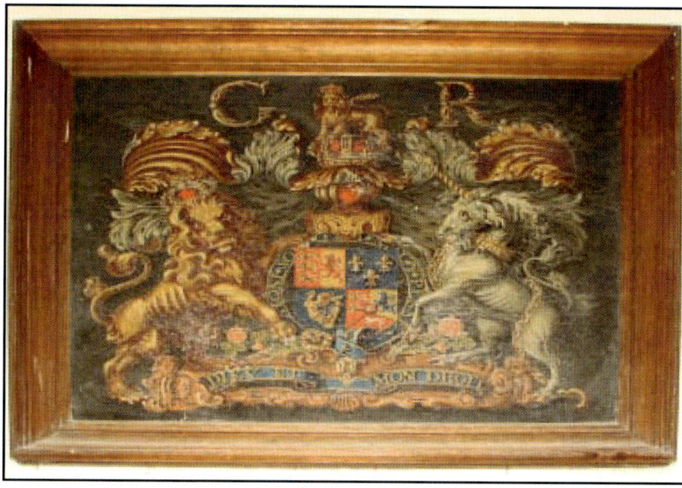

Inscribed as George I but these are Stuart Arms not Hanoverian, probably of Charles I.
[Note the floriated lettering with the C changed to a G]
Spixworth St Peter.

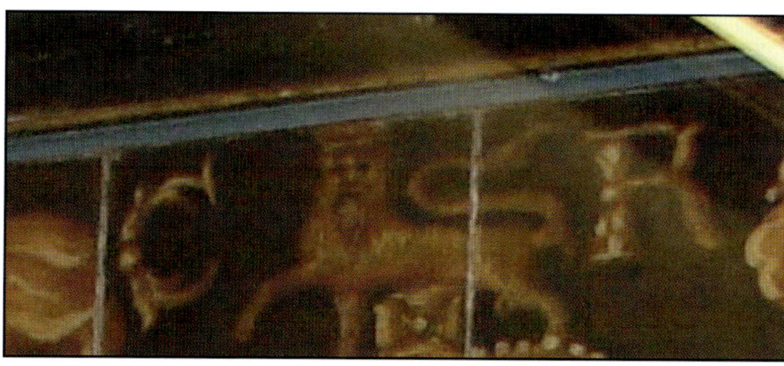

Genuine Charles I at Gorleston with the floriated lettering.
[behind glass]

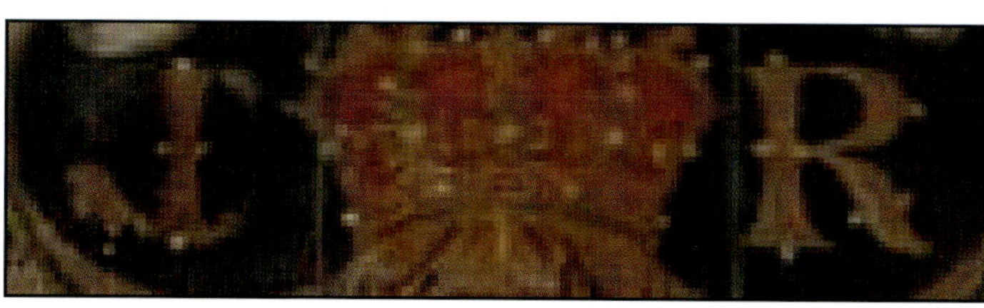

Charles I 'C R' modified to 'J R' at Great Snoring
(see full Arms on page 287)

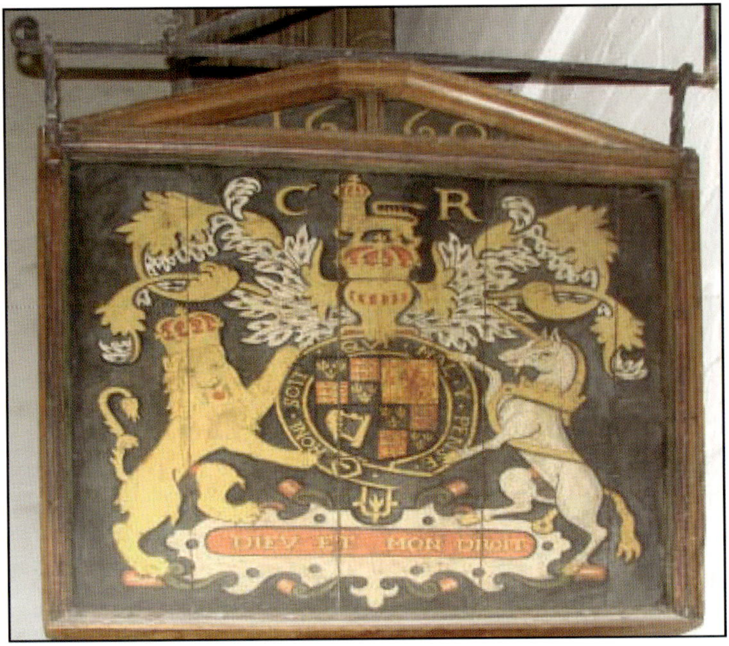

Double sided, Charles II, the reverse, that of the Commonwealth can be seen below. North Walsham.

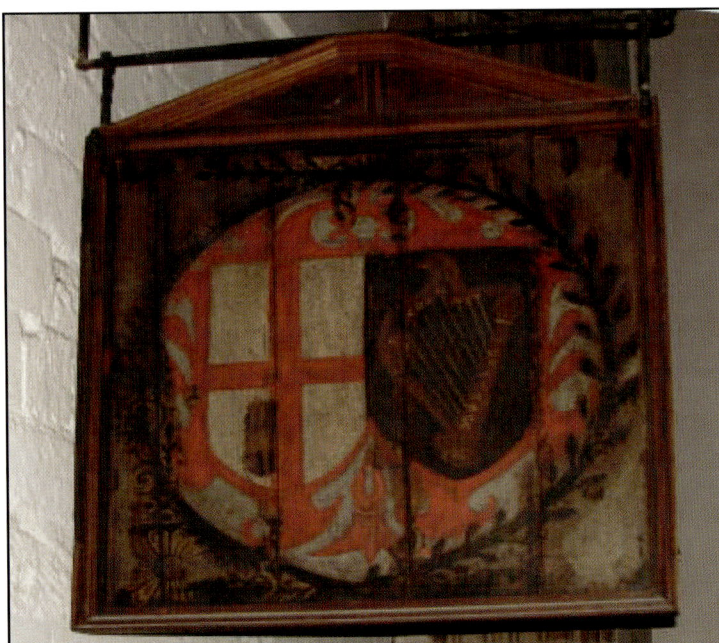

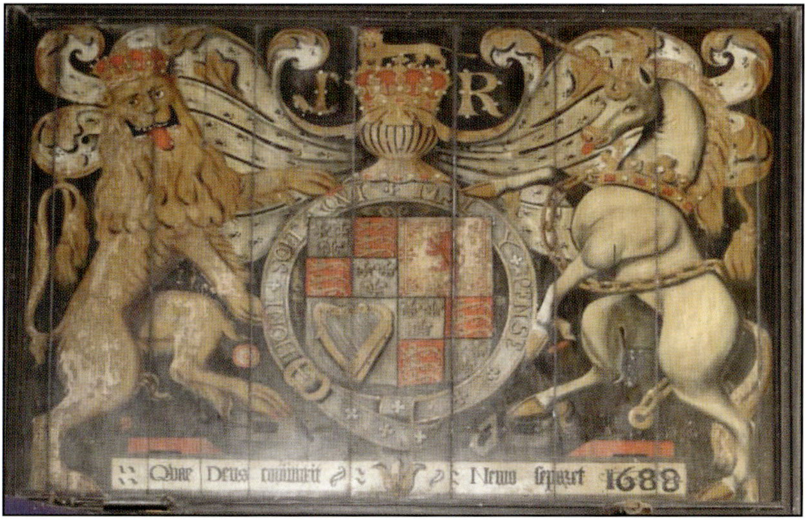

The Royal Arms of James II at Great Snoring. Close examination of the 'J' shows that it is a modified 'C' and that these are the over-painted Arms of Charles I. The date (1688) would suggest they are trying to keep up with those at Little Snoring [below] which are genuine.

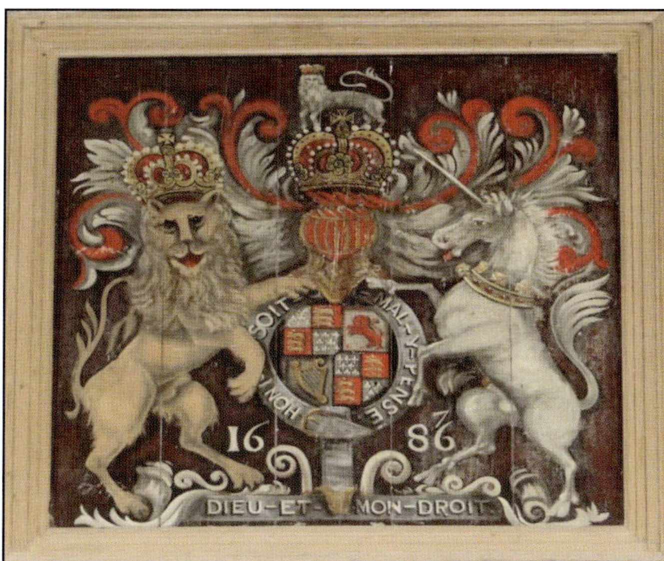

The rare Arms of James II at Little Snoring. They are dated 1686/7 which indicates January 1st to March 25th 1687 by our modern calendar.

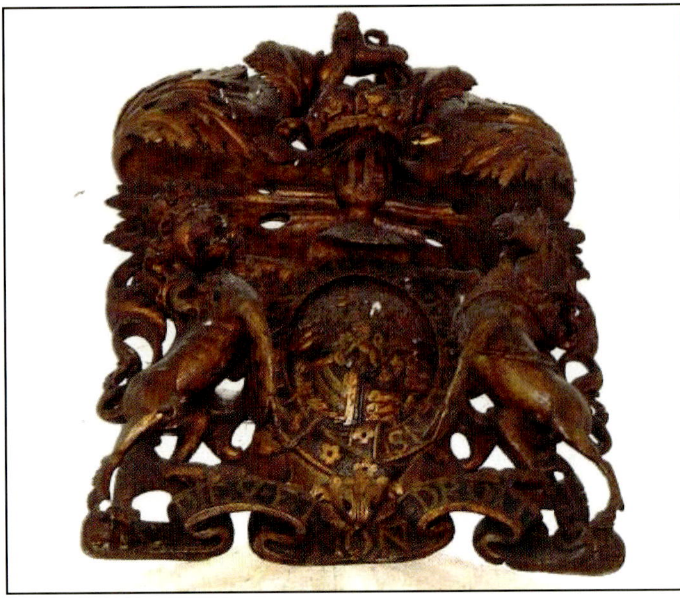

These William and Mary Arms are carved in wood, painted and gilded. They can be seen at Wyverstone St George.

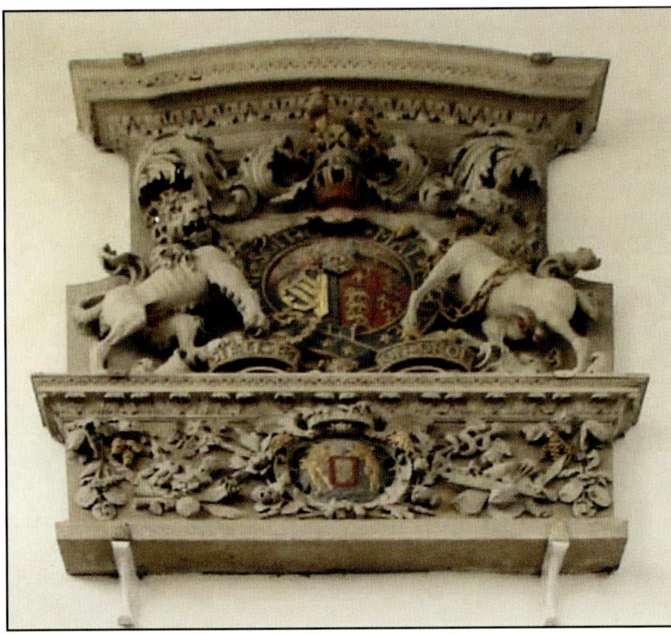

Arms of William III At Shelton St Mary carved in relief with additional panel below.

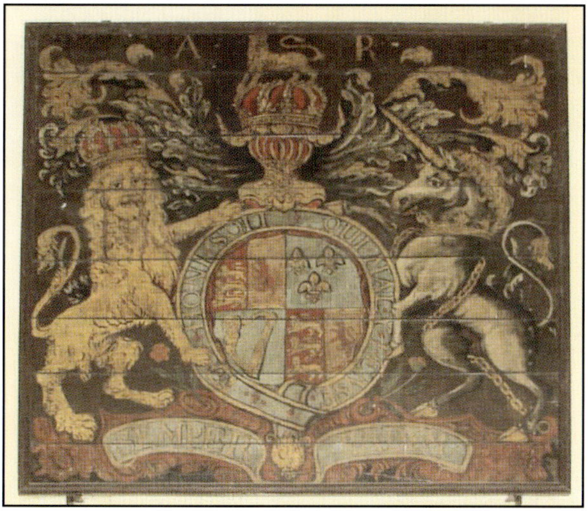

Arms of Queen Anne painted on horizontal wooden boards.
Bunwell

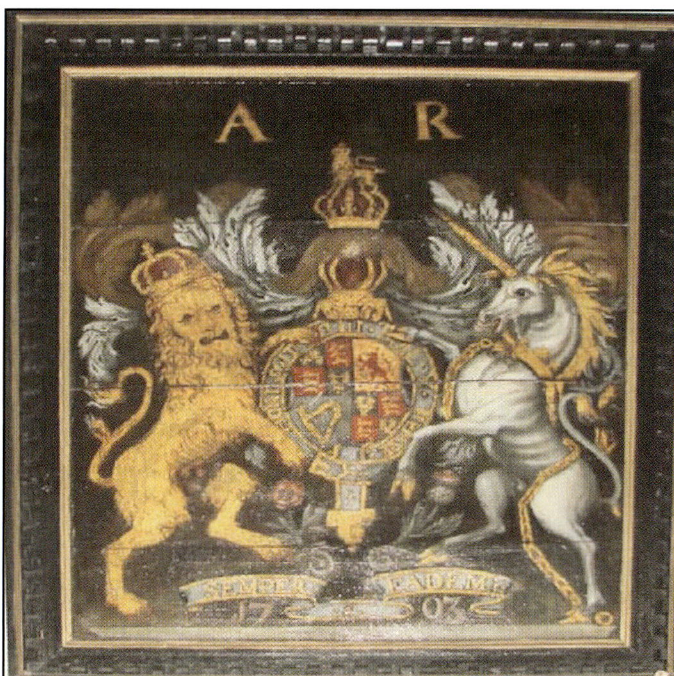

Arms of Queen Anne, Fersfield

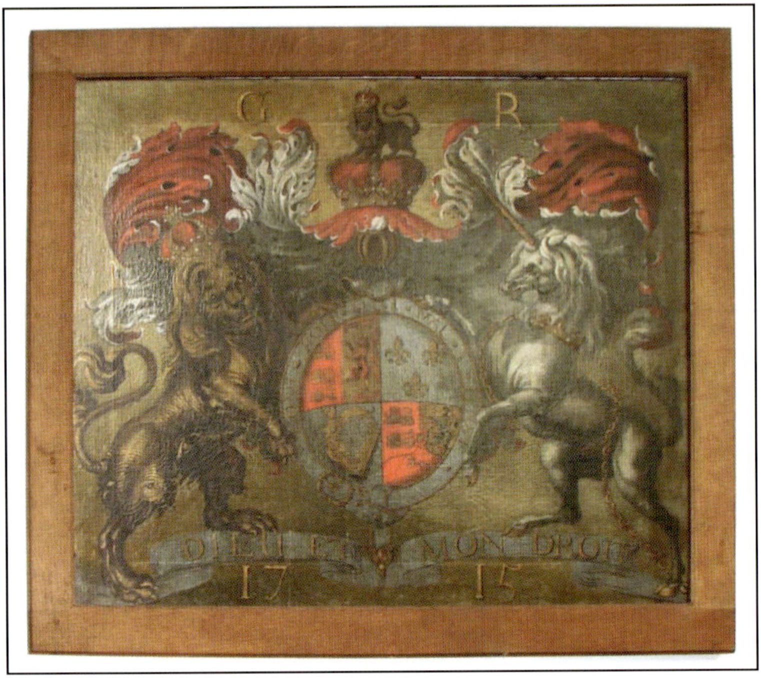

George I 1715. Gunton, St Andrew

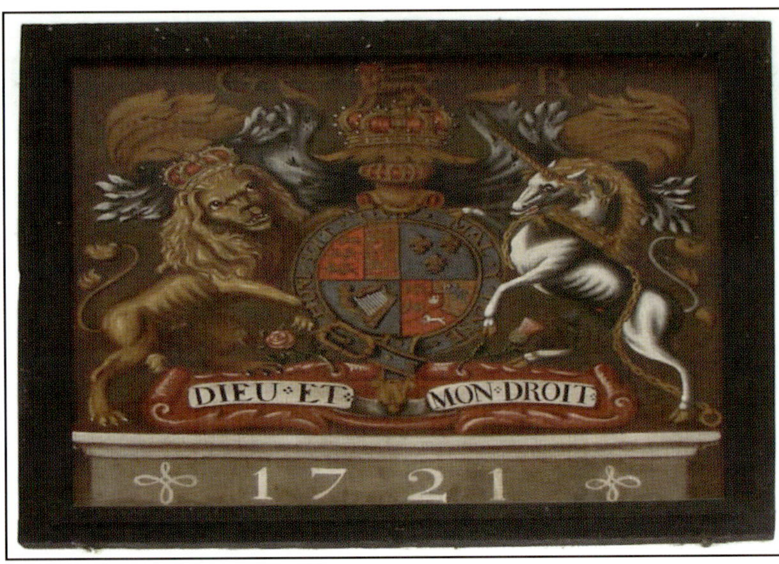

George I dated 1721
Ellingham St Mary

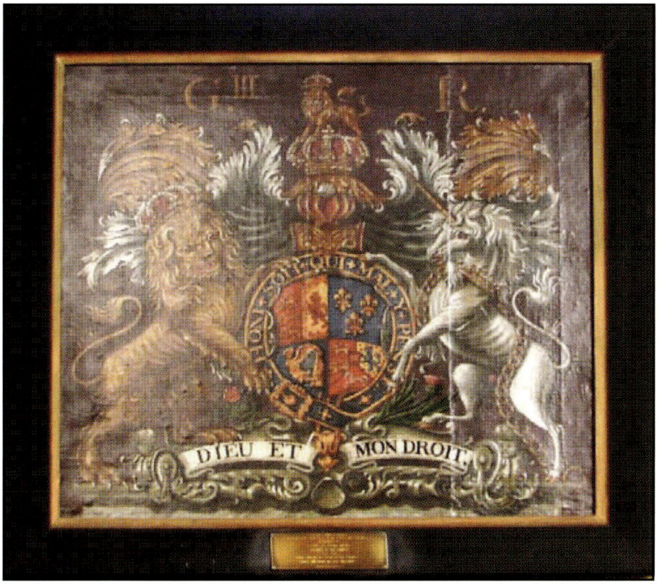

George III on vertical wooden boards
Southrepps St James

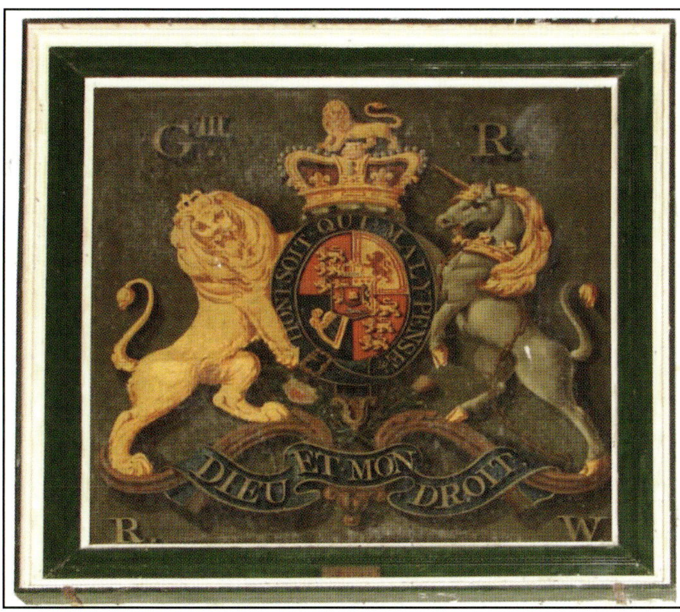

George III on canvas
Denton St Mary

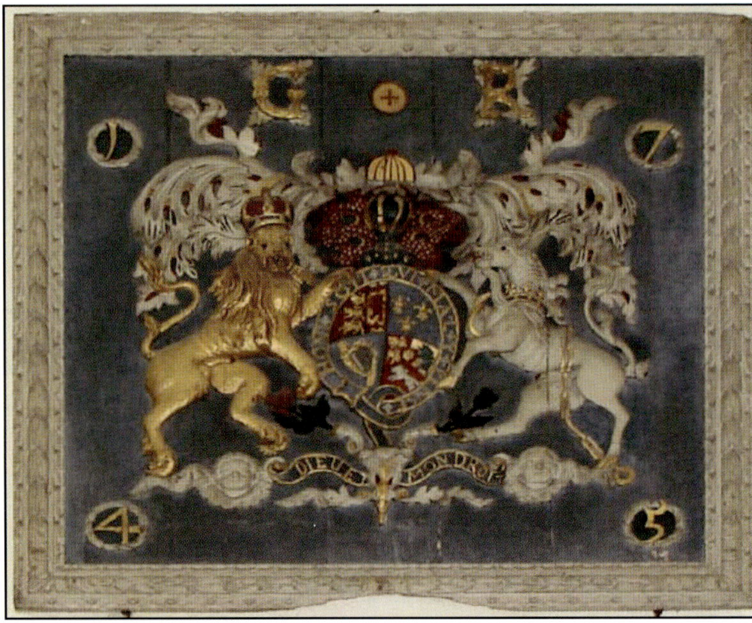

George II dated 1745 at Reepham St Mary
Considerable artistic licence.

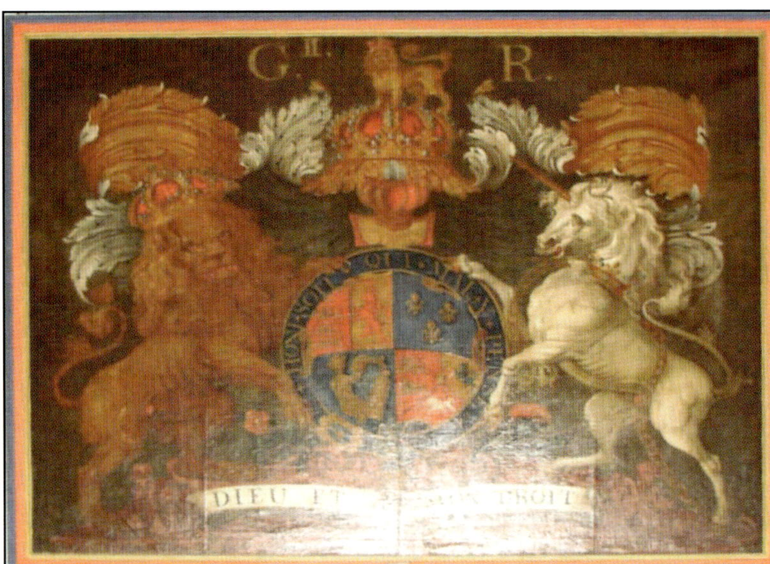

Very large Arms of George II, at Wymondham St Mary

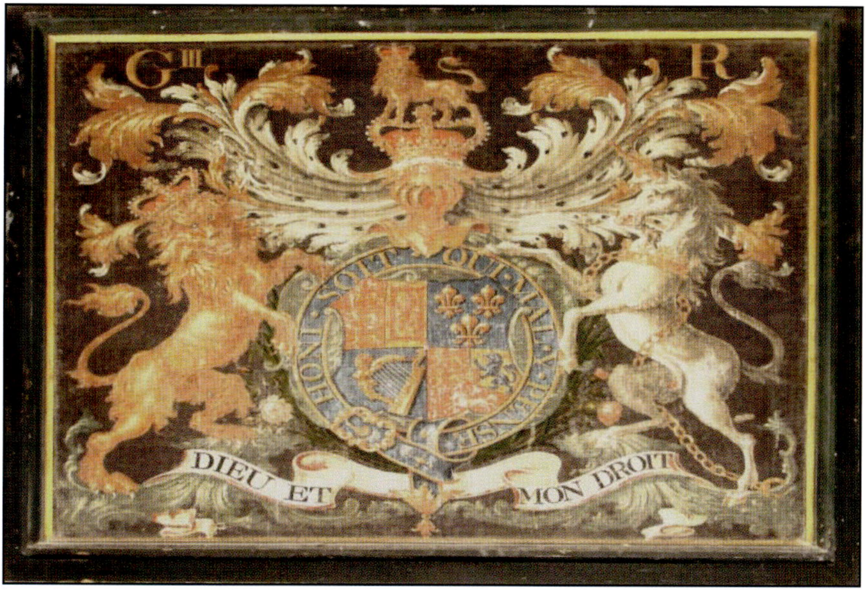

George I Arms re-attributed to George III
Strumpshaw St Peter

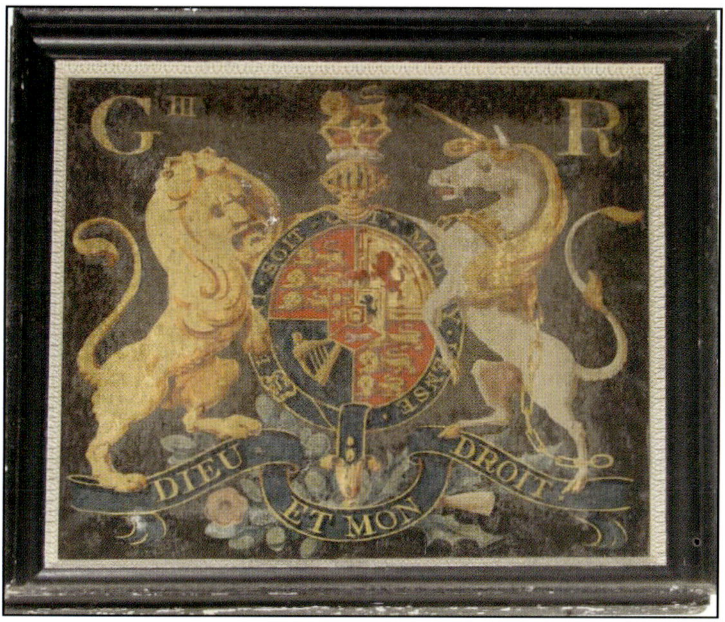

George II Arms re-attributed to George III
Morningthorpe

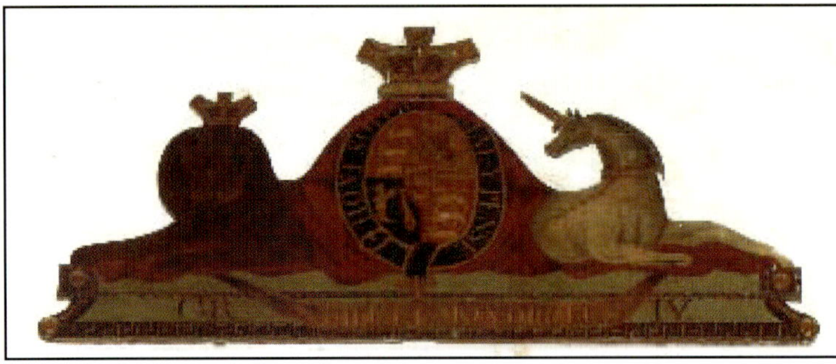

George IV Hanoverian painted on fretted wood.
Newer style with lion and unicorn couchant *(lying down)*
Lingwood St Peter

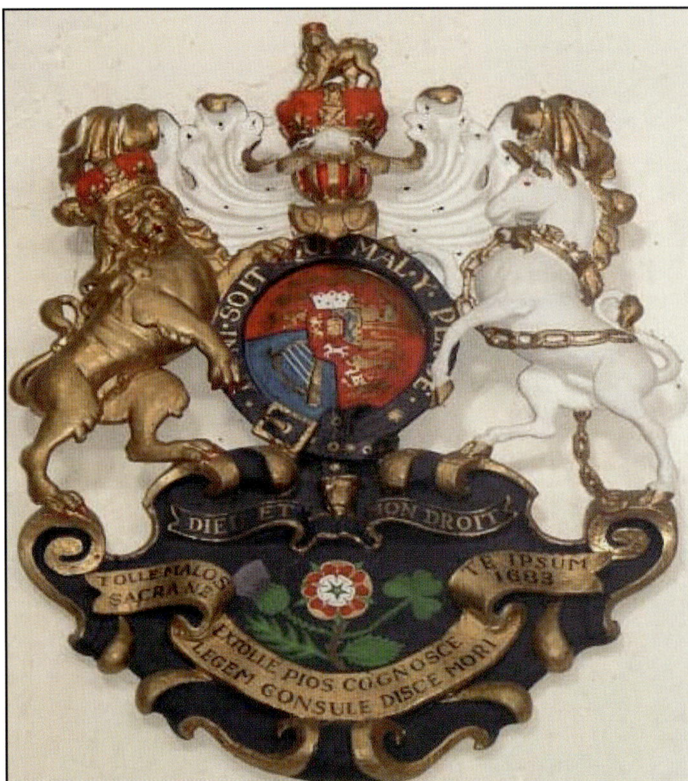

Arms of George II at Ashill. The unique banner tells us to 'Cast out the impious, extol righteousness and the law, and be prepared to die'; probably the choice of the benefactor

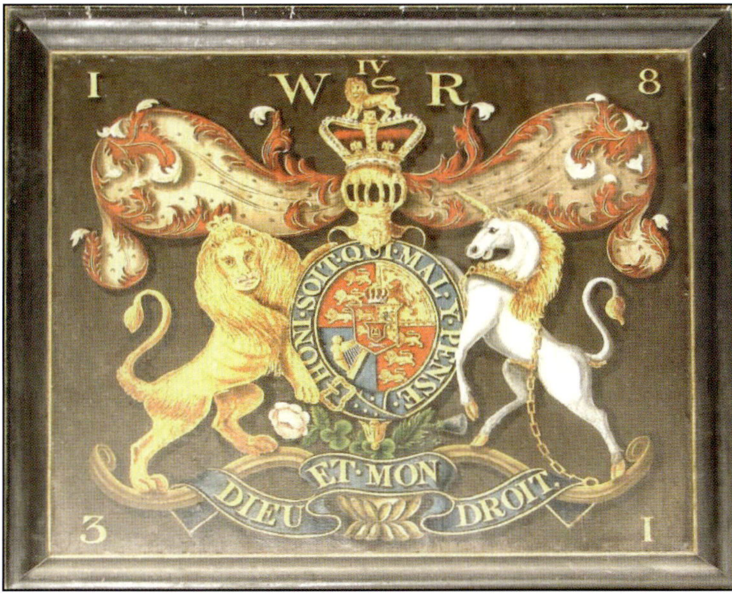

William IV, 1831.

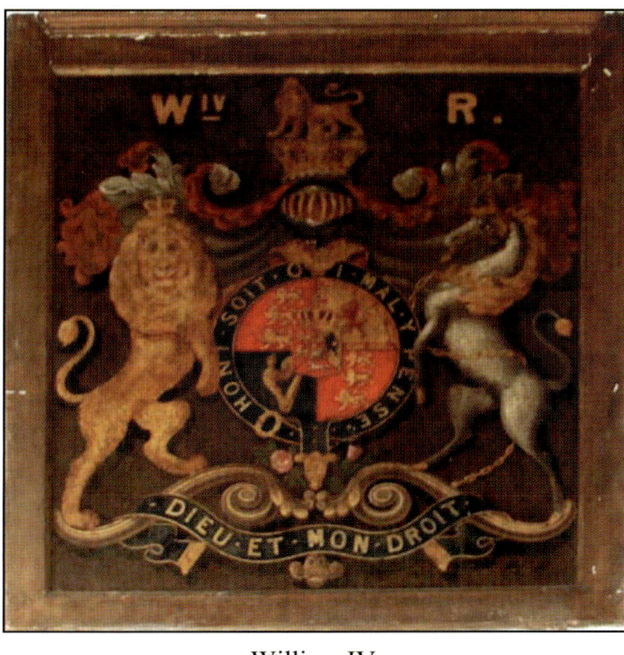

William IV
Stockton St Michael

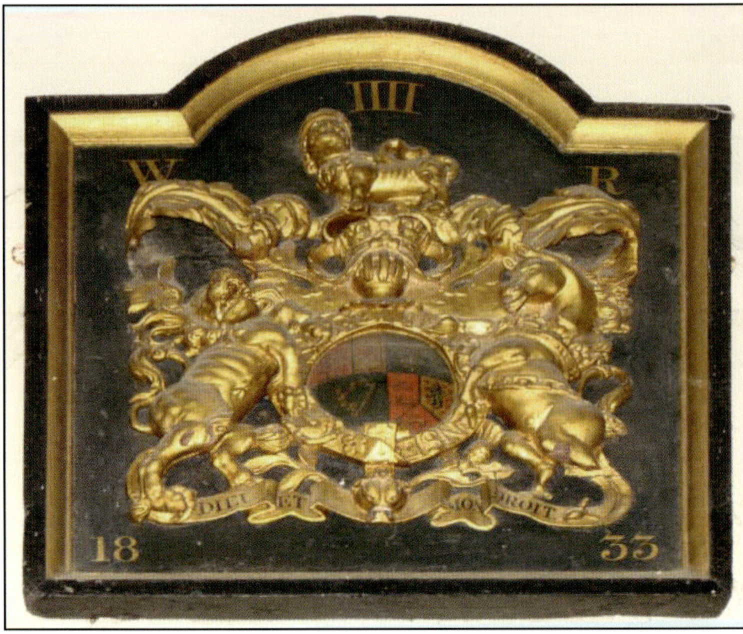

William IIII dated 1833.
Shotesham All Saints.

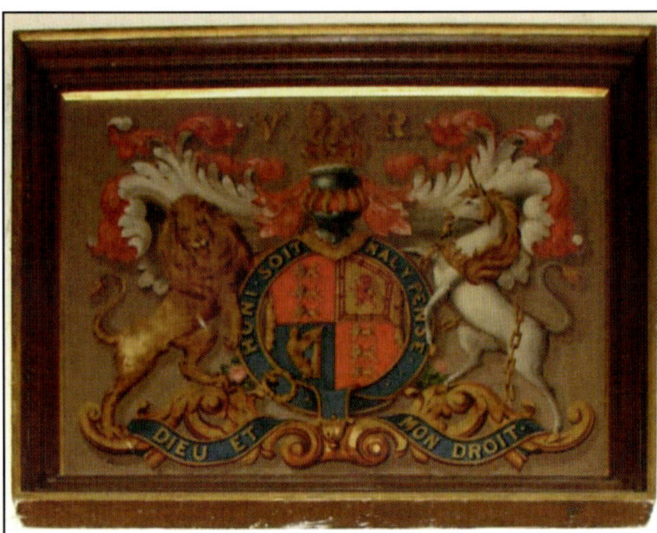

Queen Victoria on canvas.
Hempnall St Margaret

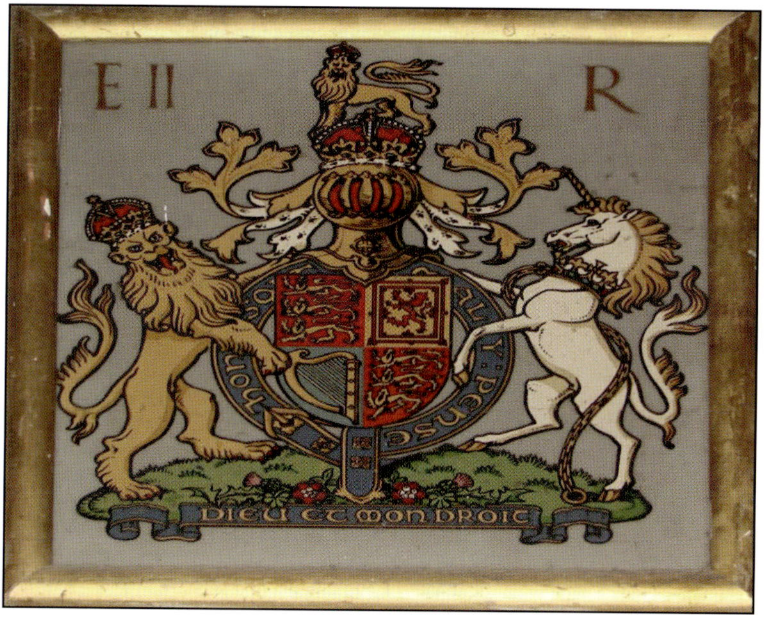

Queen Elizabeth II
Brundall St Laurence

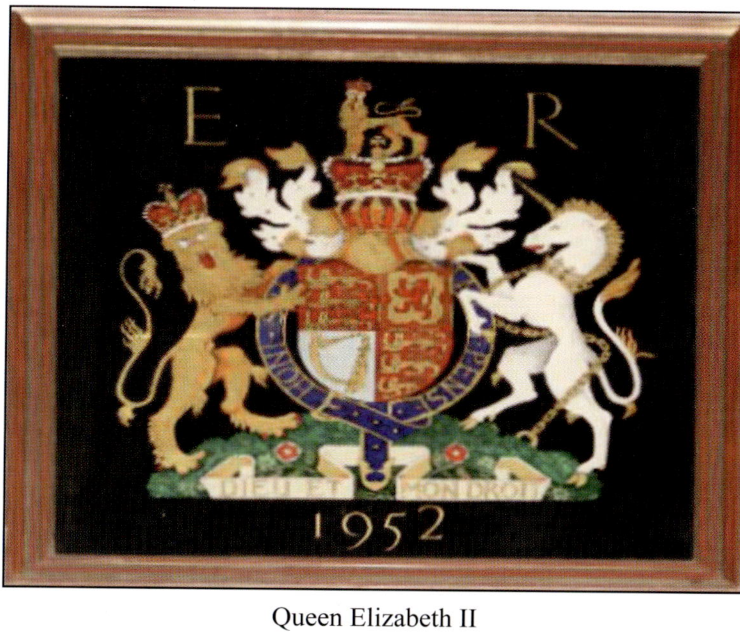

Queen Elizabeth II
Ormesby St Michael

Some Irregularities

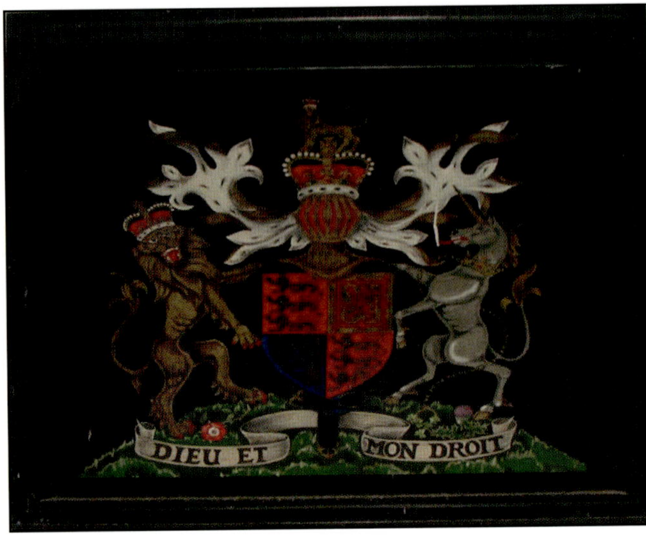

Hanoverian, unattributed, on unusual black background
Kirby Cane All Saints

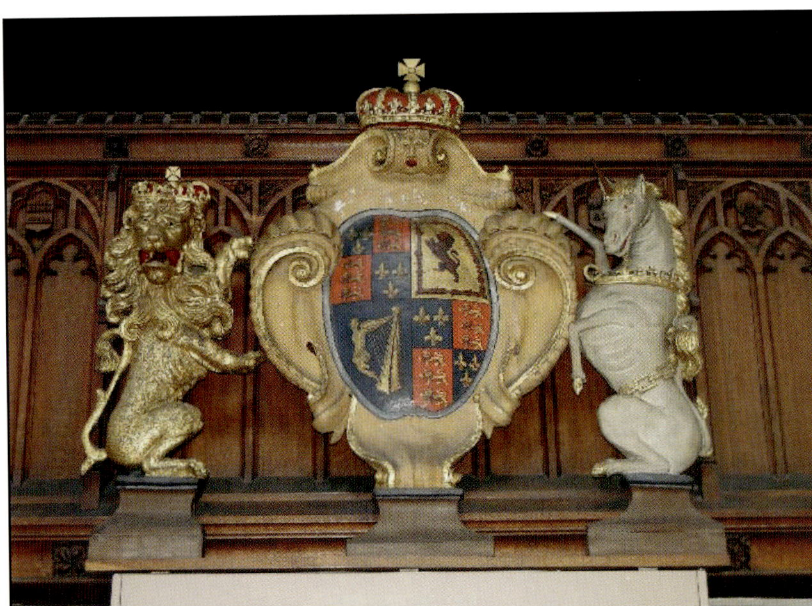

These huge and beautiful Arms can be found at Upwell St. Peter.
The supporters are sejant instead of rampant.

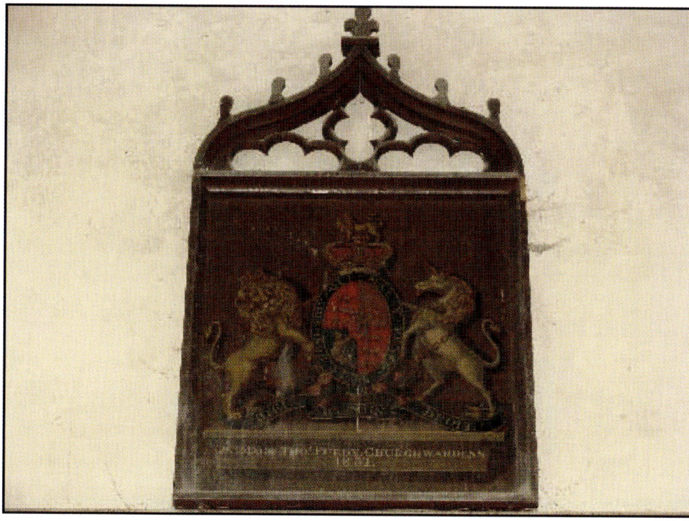

Unattributed but dated 1831 with the names of the church wardens at the time of William IV, the escutcheon however is that of George III.
Paston St Margaret

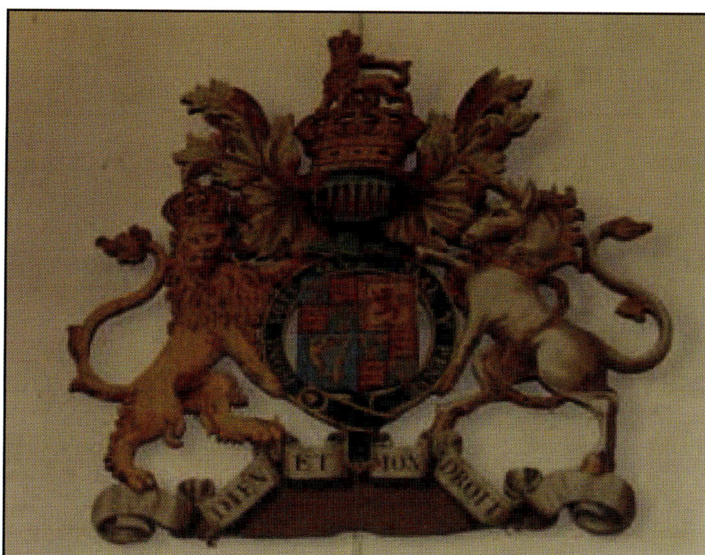

Unattributed Stuart Arms, cast and painted.
Raveningham St Andrew

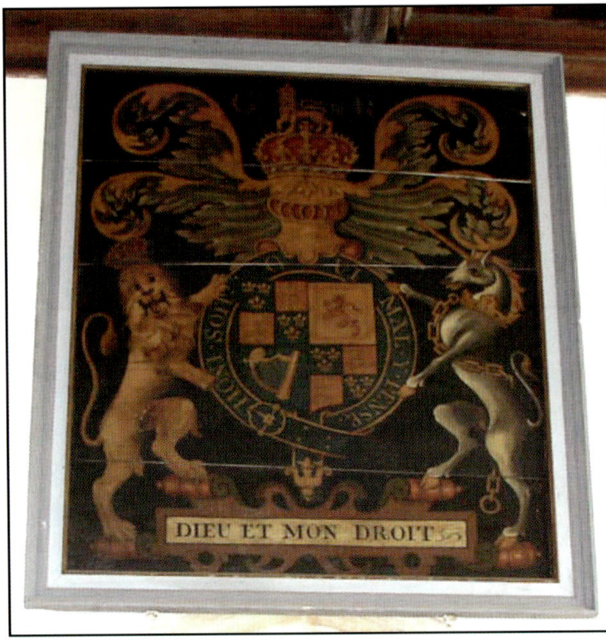

Inscribed as George III, but the Arms are of James I.
Northrepps, St Mary

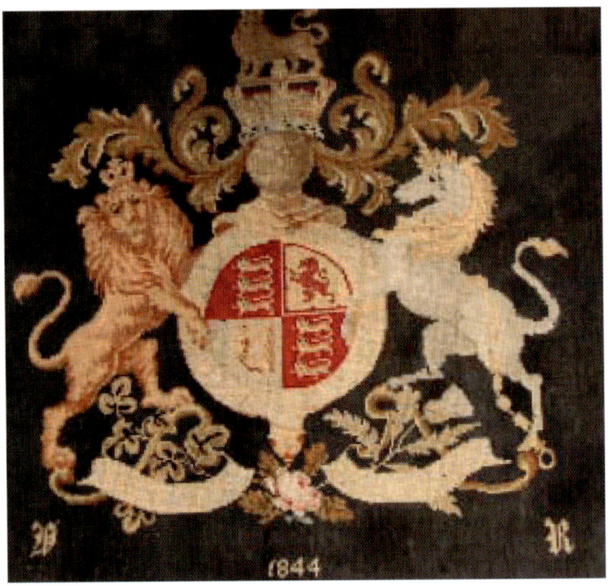

Embroidered Royal Arms of Queen Victoria
dated 1844 at Wolferton

GLOSSARY of Terms, Architectural & Ecclesiastical

Achievement The correct name for Armorial Bearings which include the shield (the coat of Arms) supporters, lion and unicorn, the helm, crown, garter and banner etc. (see Coat of Arms)

Annunciation Referring to the Archangel Gabriel giving Mary the news to was to conceive the son of God.

Antiphonary A book containing a collection of biblical songs.

Apse A semi-circular domed projection at the east end of the church, usually forming a chancel. Also called an 'apsis'.

Apsidal Being or having an apse.

Arcade A series of arches usually one or both sides of the nave where an aisle is present. These can also be blank, blind or closed where an aisle has been or for decorative purposes.

Arch-braced A braced wooden arch which carries the weight of the roof. Large spans are sometimes accompanied by tie-beams if there is a risk of the walls spreading out with the weight of the roof.

Aumbry A small cupboard usually set into the wall of the sanctuary in which are stored the Holy oil and other accoutrements used at baptisms and confirmations etc. If the contents are present an eternal flame or lamp is usually burning close by.

Banner Stave Lockers A tall narrow cupboard commonly near or beneath the tower in which mediaeval guild banner staves were stored.

Barrel roof A roof boarded with planks giving it the appearance of the inside of a barrel

Base course Usually seen around the base of a tower or porch, less commonly elsewhere to give a decorative effect. Usually flushwork.

Battering/ Battered The leaning outwards of an inner wall as it rises to the top while the external face remains vertical.

Bier A stand or four wheeled trolley on which a corpse or nowadays a coffin is placed, to be carried or wheeled to the church, or the grave. These can even be horse drawn but are not the same as a hearse.

Billet moulding Also known as log decoration due to resemblance to a line or series of small logs in one, or more commonly, two rows.

Black Death Refers to the period of the plague between 1348 and 1349 which in less than two years reduced the population of East Anglia by one third.

Box Pew Pews with sides of three feet or more which became popular in the 17th c. in which the elite could be separated from the rabble; occasionally fitted out with cushions and curtains.

Brasses Memorial portraits which were popular for those that could afford them from the 14th until the 17th century.

BVM Blessed Virgin Mary.

Canopy of honour An ornamental roof-like projection above (usually) the rood or rood screen. Occasionally over an altar.

Capital/cap The top of a pier or column, upon which the arch rests.

Carillon A set of bells sounded either from a keyboard or mechanically.

Carstone Otherwise known as gingerbread stone due to its similarity to a ginger biscuit. It is in fact a soft brown sandstone sometimes found scattered in fields or quarried from Snettisham.

Chamfer A surface made by smoothing off the angle between two stone faces.

Chevron Zigzag moulding (Norman, twelfth century).

Cinquefoil Five-lobed.

Clerestory The part of the nave wall above the side aisles with windows to allow more light into the nave. i.e. 'clear storey' the storey of clear glass.

Clunch Hard chalk material.

Coat of Arms The name given to the Heraldic shield. Originally worn as a vest over armour to identify the wearer. Often commonly, often erroneously used as a term for the Achievement.

Cob Un-burnt clay mixed with straw.

Coeval Being of the same date; contemporary with.

Collar A timber beam connecting rafters or wall-posts.

Conventual Being part of or pertaining to a convent.

Corbel A piece of carved stone or wood projecting from a wall; usually to support part of a roof. Almost always carved or decorated.

Cornice Decorative projection along top of wall.

Course Horizontal layer of stones or bricks in a wall, sometimes decorative.

Credence Shelf A shelf or table upon which is placed the bread & wine used in the Eucharist in the belief that if it is poisoned it will some-how manifest itself.

Crenel A gap in battlemented parapet.

Crenellated Embattled, having battlements.

Cresset A reservoir for an oil or fat lamp.

Crocket Carved decoration on the sloping side of a spire or pinnacle usually thorn shaped and pointing skyward.

Cupola A small domed turret on a roof or top of a tower, usually with a door.

Cusped /cusping A carved pointed figure created by the intersection of three or more arcs or foils, giving a foliate appearance.

Decalogue board A board bearing the Ten Commandments. Traditionally flanked by Moses and Aaron..

Decorated Architectural style around 13th – 14th century. 1280 - 1377.

Diapered Decorated in a diamond pattern. Usually referred to screens or flint-work.

Doctors Four Doctors recognised by the Western Church for their doctrine. They are St. Ambrose, St. Augustine, St. Jerome and St. Gregory.

Dog-tooth 12th - 13th c. ornamentation consisting of four leaflike projections radiating from a raised centre. (from dog-tooth violet)

Donative A benefice that can be bestowed by its founder or patron without reference to the diocesan authorities. (adj. consulting such a benefice).

Dormer Window placed vertically in sloping roof.

Dressing Carved stonework around openings.

Drystone Un-mortared masonry.

Early English Period 1175 - 1280.

Embattled Battlemented, with battlements. Also Crenellated

Engaged (column) Refers to being attached to the jamb along its length. Not free-standing. (opposite of detached).

English Renaissance Period 1625 - 1700.

Escutcheon Shield or shield-shaped emblem bearing a coat of arms.

Fillet A narrow flat band.

Finial Decorative carving at the apex of an arch, pinnacle spire or end of a roof.

Fleche A slender spire, especially on a church above an intersection of the nave and transept.

Fleuron A carved flower.

Flushwork Patterns made in the masonry using flint or stone, neither sunken nor raised.

Fluting Concave mouldings in parallel.

Flying buttress Buttress which is not attached to the wall it supports at the lower portion, to allow passage through, or to save weight, or look more elegant.

Foils Lobes used to embellish the head of an arch or a circular opening. Trefoil, 3; quatrefoil, 4; cinquefoil, 5; octofoil, 8 etc..

Foliated Carved with or representing leaves.

Footings Bottom part of wall.

Freestone High-quality sandstone or limestone.

Fresco Painting on wet plaster wall.

Gable/ Gablette A wall covering end of a roof-ridge / Smaller version

Galilee A small chapel or porch at the west end of some mediaeval churches. For use when the church is closed.

Gallery A platform raised above the congregation for musicians or as an additional seating area for members of the congregation. Usually at the west end.

Gargoyle A carved stone usually with a spout to throw rainwater well clear of the foundations. Not to be confused with grotesques.

Georgian Period 1700 - 1825.

Gnomon That part of a sundial which casts the shadow.

Gothic Architectural period 12th - 16th century.

Green man Harking back to folklore, a green man is usually depicted with a foliate face mask, representing fertility. Seen on screens and columns.

Grisaille A glass monochrome picture in shades of grey.

Groined A roof with sharp edges at intersection of cross-vaults.

Grotesques Outlandish, distorted or bizarre characterisations of people or animals, not necessarily ugly as in gargoyles.

Half-shaft Roll-moulding on either side of opening.

Hammer-beam Beam jutting out horizontally at right angles at the top of a wall to support other beams and arch-braces

Hanoverian Pertaining to the reign of the House of Hanover, 1714 - 1837

Hatchments Lozenge shaped frames bearing the coat of arms or Achievement of a deceased person, made for the funeral and displayed outside the home of the deceased for one year and later retained in the church as a memorial. Derivation of Achievement

Headstock The wooden beam which carries the weight of a bell.

Heartshrine A small niche, similar in appearance to a piscina, into which an embalmed heart was placed.

Herringbone Brick or stone laid diagonally.

Hood or Hoodmould A moulding over an arch, window or door to deflect dripping water or just decorative.

Hour glass A large egg timer by which the preacher could time his sermons.

Impost Wall bracket to support arch.

Intramural Within the wall. Early practice of burial for VIPs.

Ionic Order of Greek architecture characterized by a column with scroll-shapes on either side of the capital.

Jacobean Period 1603 - 1625. Reign of the Kings James.

Jamb Side of an arch, door or window against which the door or window. closes.

Joist Timber stretched from wall-to-wall to support floor boards.

King post A vertical roof support set between a horizontal cross beam and rafter to offer additional support for the ridge. see also Queen post.

Knop A decorative knob or boss.

Knopped Having knobs or bosses usually as decoration.

Label A square moulding over a door, window or object, a dripstone.

Lancet (window) A long, narrow window with pointed head. (1190 - 1280 in date).

Laudian Pertaining to Archbishop William Laud (1573 - 1645).

Linen-fold Decorative wood, or occasionally stone, carving developed in the Tudor period giving the appearance of folded linen.

Lintel Horizontal stone or beam bridging opening.

Long and short work A Saxon technique of having one quoin stone lengthways and the next width-ways and so on as the corner progressed upwards.

Loop narrow opening in a wall

Louvre / louver (Bell) Louver – to allow the sound of bells to escape through the tower wall.

Low side window A low window in the west of the chancel from or through which a bell could be sounded and/or the Ter Sanctus observed by those outside.

Lucarne A small slit or opening to allow light into spires and towers.
Mass dial see Scratch dial.
Mensa A stone slab forming the top of an altar. Usually has five consecration crosses around the edge.
Merlon The solid part of embattled parapet.
Misericord Projection under a choir stall or seat, serving (when the seat is turned up) to support a person standing, usually carved, sometimes with grotesques.
Moulding A form of masonry or wood decoration.
Mullion Vertical division of window.
Mural A wall or a painting on a wall.
Nailhead Pyramidal moulding.
Nave The body of the church, the central aisle.
Needle A tie beam which passes through a wall, with an eye in the end [like a sewing needle] and through which is passed a cross-member to prevent it withdrawing or the wall/s spreading.
Newel The centre-post of circular staircase.
Niche A recess usually arched, made in a wall to contain a statue or other object.
Nookshaft A shaft set in the angle of a jamb or pier.
Norman Period 1066 – 1190 Romanesque.
Ogee-headed Arch moulding showing in section a double continuous curve, convex below passing into concave above, back to front S.
Open joint A wide, un-mortared space between faces of stones.
Order Relating to the carved sections of an arch or doorway.
Oriel A projecting window in wall; originally a form of porch, often of wood.
Pamment Earthenware floor tile usually 1 foot square.
Parapet A low wall on outer side of main wall.
Parclose screen A screen to delineate a private chapel or to enclose part of the nave for whatever reason.
Parvice A balcony in front of a church or enclosed courtyard.
Pateræ A circular ornament, resembling a dish, often worked in relief on friezes.
Peculiar A church or parish under the jurisdiction of a diocese other than that in which it lies.
Pediment A low-pitched gable over porticos, doors, windows, etc.
Perpendicular English architectural period, circa. 1377 - 1547.
Pier A support for arch, usually square as opposed to pillar or column which is round.
Pilaster A shallow pier used to buttress a wall.
Pinnacle An ornament crowning a spire, tower etc. or small spire on top of a building.
Piscina A basin, usually set in or against a wall, with a drain running directly

into the ground (to prevent sacrilegious use of Holy water) for washing vessels after the sacrament.

Pitch The slope of a roof.

Pitching Rough cobbling.

Plinth Projecting base of wall.

Pointing Mortar or cement in joints between brickwork.

Poppyheads Ornamental carving at the end of church benches and / or pews. *[There are endless variations, very few looking like poppy heads]*

Priest's door Or chancel door. A private entrance for the priest to prevent him having to enter the nave, which was for the laity.

Principal A main truss or rafter that supports a roof.

Purlin A horizontal timber in a roof supporting rafters.

Quartering/s Combination of different coats of arms on one shield. pl. the Coats of Arms so displayed.

Quatrefoil Four-lobed.

Queen posts Similar purpose as a king post but always in pairs width-wise.

Quoin Dressed corner stone at the outside angle of a building.

Rampant In heraldry, mainly applied to the supporters either side of the crest; standing erect upon hind legs with head in profile.

Reliquary A coffer or shrine or place for keeping or displaying religious relics.

Reredos The decorative screen behind the altar.

Respond/s Half-piers found in the jambs of arches.

Retable A frame enclosing carved or painted panels placed at the back of an altar (similar to a reredos).

Reveal The thickness of the wall from the inside edge, to the window or door.

Rib Rraised moulding dividing vault.

Romanesque Prevailing architectural style, eighth to twelfth century, with rounded arches.

Roofridge Summit line of roof.

Rowell A circular frame with candles placed around the circumference and raised by means of a pulley, to illuminate the rood or canopy of honour.

Royal Arms The shield shaped heraldic device usually displayed in The Achievement, issued to the Monarch by the College of Heraldry. Common term for The Achievement.

Rubble Un-worked stone/s not laid in courses.

Rustication Worked ashlar stone, with faces left deliberately rough.

Sacring bell A bell which is rung during the Sacrament to inform those outside the church.

Sacristy A room in a church to house the sacred vessels and vestments, similar in use to a vestry, and occasionally used as such.

Saltire A diagonal; equal-limbed diagonal cross. St Andrew's style cross.

Sanctuary The part of a church nearest to the altar, usually behind the altar rail.

Sarum Old Salisbury. see also Antiphonary

Saxon Pre 1066.
Sciapus A legendary Scandinavian figure with enormous feet.
Scratch dial A crude sundial with central hole (into which is inserted a gnomon) with rays usually scratched on a buttress or quoin-stone of a church to indicate the time of the next service, also mass-dial.
Sedilia [pl.] seats for clergy during parts of long mediaeval masses (usually in or on the south wall of the sanctuary, often a dropped window sill.) [singular: 'sedile']
Sejant Referring to the supporters usually on heraldic arms; in a sitting posture.
Septaria A semi-hard brownish clay-like stone with calcite bonding.
Serpent 18th c. deep-toned wind instrument, shaped as a double S.
Seven Sacraments (The) Baptism, Holy Communion, Confirmation, Holy Orders, Reconciliation, Matrimony & Anointing of the sick.
Seven Sacraments Font An 15th c. font, the Seven Sacraments displayed around the octagonal bowl
Shaft A narrow column. i.e. supporting the font.
Shingle A wooden tile, usually of cedar.
Soffit The underside of arch, opening or eaves.
Sounding board see Tester.
Spandrel The space (roughly triangular in shape each side) between an arch and its square hood-mould. Also found in roofs in the space between the beam and arch-brace and/or rafter.
Splay A chamfered, or sloping face. Window reveal, wider on the inner wall than at the window.
Squint Observation hole in wall or room.
Stool A level base or foot, usually wedge shaped on which a figure would stand in a niche.
Stoup A carved bowl for holding holy water to purify oneself before, or as, entering the church.
Stringcourse Continuous horizontal mouldings on a wall-face.
Stuart Pertaining to the reign of House of Stuart, 1603 - 1714.
Sundial Means of indicating the time by the shadow cast by a gnomon, usually on the south porch gable or the tower.
Tester A suspended canopy over a pulpit also 'sounding board'.
Tie beam A large horizontal beam at the base of a roof (or top of a wall) to prevent the walls spreading outwards with the weight of the roof. Occasionally piercing the wall and pinned-through outside. (see Needle)
Tracery Intersecting rib-work in upper part of window or decoratively carved in wood.
Transept Either of the arms of a cross-shaped church at right angles to the main body or nave of the church. Usually North or South.
Transom Horizontal division of a window.

Trefoil Three-lobed.
Tudor Period 1547 - 1600.
Turret A small tower, round or polygonal, tapered or straight.
Tympanic Pertaining to the tympanum.
Tympanum The stonework filling the space between the horizontal lintel of a doorway and the arch above it. Pl. tympana.
Victorian Pertaining to the reign of Queen Victoria, 1837 - 1901.
Volute A decorative spiral scroll in stonework found on some Ionic capitals.
Voussoir A wedge-shaped stone forming part of an arch, not the keystone.
Wag(g)on roof see Barrel roof.
Wainscote A panel on the lower portion of a wall, in a different material from that of the upper part, usually wood.

Wall-stair Staircase built into thickness of wall. as rood-stairs or stairs to the parvise or tower.
Weathering The sloping surface to throw off rainwater on buttresses and battlements etc.
Weep This term applies to the chancel being misaligned with the nave, fabled to represent the head of Jesus inclined to the right when on the cross. More realistically due to using the shadow of the sun from the tower in laying out the foundations or in reconstruction, ensuring that
Wodewose or Woodwose. Wild man with beard carrying a club. Usually found on the base of a font accompanied by lions, occasionally as a pinnacle. (occasionally erroneously referred to as a Woodhouse)

Pages for your Notes

Extent of East Norfolk as covered in this volume coloured green (265 parishes)

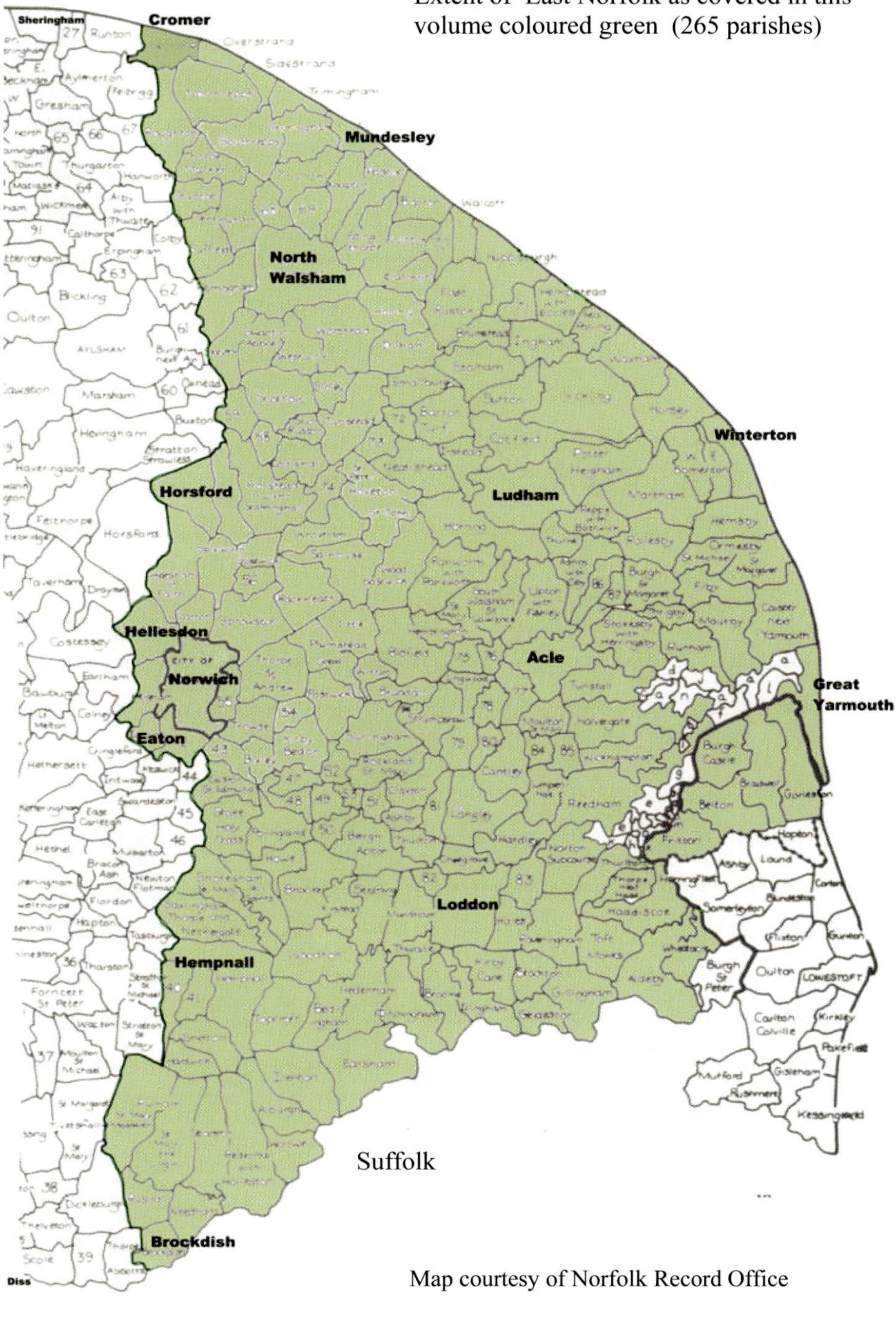

Map courtesy of Norfolk Record Office